PROBLEM-SOLVING STRATEGIES

FOR

WRITING

IN

COLLEGE AND COMMUNITY

PROBLEM-SOLVING STRATEGIES
FOR
WRITING
IN
COLLEGE AND COMMUNITY

Linda Flower
CARNEGIE MELLON UNIVERSITY

HARCOURT BRACE COLLEGE PUBLISHERS

Fort Worth · Philadelphia · San Diego · New York · Orlando · Austin · San Antonio
Toronto · Montreal · London · Sydney · Tokyo

Publisher	*Earl McPeek*
Executive Editor	*Michael A. Rosenberg*
Acquisitions Editor	*John Meyers*
Product Manager	*Ilse Wolfe West*
Project Editor	*Denise Netardus*
Art Director	*Candice Clifford*
Production Manager	*Linda McMillan*

Cover Image by Dennis Farris

ISBN: 0-15-505496-1

Library of Congress Catalog Card Number: 97-75031

Address for Editorial Correspondence: Harcourt Brace College Publishers, 301 Commerce Street, Suite 3700, Fort Worth, TX 76102.

Address for Orders: Harcourt Brace & Company, 6277 Sea Harbor Drive, Orlando, FL 32887-6777. 1-800-782-4479.

Web site address: http://www.hbcollege.com

Harcourt Brace & Company will provide supplements or supplement packages to those adopters qualified under our adoption policy. Please contact your sales representative to learn how you qualify. If as an adopter or potential user you receive supplements you do not need, please return them to your sales representative or send them to: Attn: Returns Department, Troy Warehouse, 465 South Lincoln Drive, Troy, MO 63379.

Printed in the United States of America

7 8 9 0 1 2 3 4 5 6   067   9 8 7 6 5 4 3 2 1

Preface

Writing a book with multiple editions is like taking a journey to an unknown but continually beckoning destination. Each new edition marks a milestone in your own life and thinking and an expanding sense of what is central to the nature of writing and what is most important to learn and teach.

This new edition of *Problem-Solving Strategies for Writing in College and Community,* marks a watershed in the evolution and extension of a rhetorical approach to writing. This expansion of a prior work is not just the addition of another site for writing, but is a widening of the vista. It supports a growing recognition of the connections between colleges and the communities in which they exist, between individuals and the societies they make. It also recognizes that the strategies for writing, learned in classrooms, can be translated into strategies for not only participating in the larger world, but also making a contribution to it. For me, this journey began with the publication of the initial *Problem-Solving Strategies for Writing* in 1981 and the exciting new burst of research in composition that was letting us see writing afresh, as a rhetorical thinking process. And in the classroom, it let my students and me launch an exploration into this wonderfully challenging intellectual process and into how we as writers could develop a self-aware stance and strategic control of our options. Since then this book and my own thinking have been expanded by important new ideas about composition, about the role of discourse communities, and about the larger social context that shapes writing, even as we use writing to shape ourselves and others. But perhaps the most significant step in this journey for me, which is the basis of this new edition, is the opportunity to look at rhetoric in action in the larger community that links academic and civic discourse, where problem solving and writing come into the service of the goals that move and unite us.

Let me say briefly what this book is about and the bond I see between college and community writing, and between classroom and community- or service-based learning.

PRINCIPLES AND STRATEGIES

This book is written for people with realistic reasons for writing: students writing academic papers, professionals producing reports, and citizens creating the public discourse of democracy. Grounded in the tradition of rhetoric, it describes a goal-directed process of inquiry and persuasion that is motivated by personal and social purposes.

It is also written for people who want to know why, who want to understand the principles behind the process. Grounded in the research tradition of cognitive rhetoric, it describes writing as a thinking process that we can come to better understand. It is organized around a set of goals and strategies for reading a rhetorical situation, planning discourse, generating and organizing ideas, and designing and revising prose for readers. This focus on the process is not because writing follows a simple or linear progression—in fact just the opposite is true—but because writers engaged in a literate act need to be aware of a repertoire of strategies and options for reaching their goals at different points in the process. This book is about being a flexible writer, thinker, and problem solver, who not only knows multiple approaches to writing, but also has that level of conscious awareness of his or her own strategies, assumptions, and thinking that opens up the door to critical awareness and conscious choice.

 PROBLEM SOLVING AND INQUIRY

Problem solving is a powerful metaphor of thinking about writing: it foregrounds the importance of one's goals, the possibility of strategic choice, and responsibility for one's actions. It places writing squarely in the personal, social, and rhetorical situations that pose problems for and motivate writers. And unlike metaphors of talent or imitation or simple acculturation, it calls for flexible learning. It can take advantage of modern composition research, not to prescribe normative processes or textual patterns, but to share with students an expanding picture of the contexts for writing, the goals they entail, and the repertoire of strategies writers experienced in that context bring to it.

Problem solving, as I have always seen it, is both a social and cognitive process—a social and rhetorical act as well as a personal art. It is important to distinguish between a narrow image of problem solving—focused only on reaching solutions—and a rhetorical image which gives equal weight to problem posing. In the earlier versions of this book, that commitment to critical thinking was found in the extended scenarios of students wrestling with understanding, naming problems, and, more formally, defining problems—and realizing that you construct the problem by naming it.

In this new version of the book, the problem posing that drives problem solving comes to the foreground in two ways: in the powerful and thought-provoking accounts of community problems that fill the second section and in the focus there on intercultural inquiry as a way to understand and act. Inquiry, as we shall see in the writing of students and others, compels us to go beyond understanding, empathy, or critique alone, to a problem-solving stance based on both provisional, revisable understanding and commitment.

COLLEGE AND COMMUNITY

This book also reflects a growing recognition across the country of the connections between colleges and the communities in which they exist. For some this is motivated by the ideals of participatory democracy and its responsibilities, for others by a desire for connectedness and social justice. And for others it is the recognition that plunging students into compelling social contexts with real readers gives a new logic to writing instruction and a new relationship between student and teacher. It is this recognition that has led teachers to transform "community service" into the emerging practice of "service learning."

We cannot overlook the problems of this new educational agenda. If community outreach is going to exist in college and university programs as more than an experience of service, it has to prove its power to contribute to intellectual growth, to teach sophisticated skills, and to motivate rigorous inquiry. It is one of my goals for this book to help students see the intimate connection between their participation in the community and the ideas and strategies explored in the first section of this book and in the context of academic discourse. The opportunity to play new roles in the real world works in two ways: it shows why writing is worth learning and how strategies learned in the classroom can translate into strategies for participating in and contributing to the larger world.

Equally important, this book is designed to expand the arena for learning by showing how writing and problem solving are a road into intercultural inquiry and collaborative social action. Writing in and for communities, especially communities in need, offers a powerfully motivating real world context for learning to write. But more than that, it shows how writing—the attempt to understand for one's self and to persuade others—can support a more generative, collaborative way to stand in a democratic and intercultural society.

My own involvement with the Community Literacy Center here in Pittsburgh over the past eight years has given me a compelling vision of the possibilities. It has shown how writing, education, and research can work hand-in-hand building a new sense of community. But the necessary limits of my own experience, and my admiration for the growing network of teachers across the country teaching community-based inquiry, set me on my own inquiry into some impressive—and highly distinctive—programs and teachers from Massachusetts to California, Florida to Washington. This book reflects the kinds of writing these teachers find most important.

More importantly, the examples of writing from these diverse programs, which are a corner stone of this section, show the breadth of imagination behind community-based courses and the impressive writing and learning that they help students attain.

ORGANIZATION OF THE BOOK

The book is organized in two parts. The first part centers on a basic set of goals and strategies for writing, illustrated in the context of academic discourse. The second part frames a new context for writing, but regularly refers the reader back to the parts of section one that explain relevant strategies.

Part I   Strategies for Writing: Problem Solving in Academic Discourse

Chapter 1 gives a cognitive and social view of writing by bringing the reader into the rhetorical situation of a real writer. It maps the territory of college and community discourse, introduces writing as a meaning-making process, and introduces key concepts.

Chapter 2 looks at familiar theories and models of the writing process, and helps students analyze their own strategies for writing.

Chapter 3 anchors the discussion to come with a case study of a real student, Joan, and the task of doing personal writing for a rhetorical situation.

Chapter 4 shows how writers construct their own internal representations of meaning and how writing can change what we know.

Chapters 5 through 7 and 9 through 12 present strategies for the major tasks and goals writers must handle, from planning and generating ideas, to organizing ideas, to understanding readers and designing with them in mind, to evaluating and editing prose.

In addition, Chapter 5 introduces the practice of collaborative planning, in which a writer and a partner go beyond initial plans "to say" something toward developing more sophisticated plans "to do" something in writing. It shows students how to use this practice to make thinking visible as a basis for reflection.

Chapters 6 and 7 compare alternative strategies for invention and introduce issue trees as another visual technique for organizing ideas.

Chapter 8 returns to the art of discovering problems, in a more formal way than Chapter 1, and leads students through the stages of problem analysis from an awareness of a problematic situation to a problem definition to a thesis.

Chapters 9 and 10 help students recognize writer-based prose and create a more reader-based text.

Chapters 11 and 12 combine practical editing techniques with strategies for testing the text from a reader's point of view.

Chapter 13 introduces the research paper through two case studies on *doing* research and developing arguments when writing research papers, consulting reports, and proposals.

Part II Community Writing: Problem Solving in Civic Discourse

This part of the book invites students to see themselves and their writing in the new context of working with and for their community. This part focuses on three kinds of community writing:

1. Writing that supports observation and reflection.
2. Writing that helps community organizations do their job.
3. Writing that supports inquiry and dialogue.

These chapters build on and refer back to the Part One strategies for planning, organizing, and revising, for reading rhetorical situations, for recognizing textual conventions, and for collaborating with others.

Chapter 14 uses a series of thought-provoking readings to pose a new problem: When you move out of the classroom into the community, what is your role? And how do you move from reflection to reflective action?

Chapter 15 takes a strategic approach to reflection, helping students use observation and written conversation to discover new dimensions to situations and their own experience.

Chapter 16 deals with the interpersonal and organizational demands of building a working relationship with a community group. The heart of the chapter is learning how to learn: how to mine a new genre or discourse for features that meet your own rhetorical purposes.

Chapter 17 introduces the challenging process of inquiry into open questions, surrounded by generative rival hypotheses and alternative interpretations. It supports students in the process of intercultural dialogue and in writing papers that reflect multiple voices and diverse perspectives.

Chapter 18 expands this dialogic process into live community problem-solving dialogues, public videos, and reports.

ACKNOWLEDGMENTS

More than any other book I have written, this one reflects the collaboration and inspiration of many people, starting with my family of friends and colleagues created by Pittsburgh's Community Literacy

Center: Wayne Campbell Peck, Joyce Baskins, Lorraine Higgins, Elenore Long, Donald Tucker, Jennifer Flach, Joseph Dominic, and all the college mentors and urban teenagers it has been my privilege to know. My own understanding and this book also reflect the wisdom and effective practice of many teachers around the country, including Linda Adler-Kassner, Nora Bacon, Virginia Chappell, Brian Conniff, Pamela Dean, Wade and Susann Dorman, Ruth Fisher, Marjorie Ford, Amy Goodburn, Anne Gere, Eli Goldblatt, Dixie Goswami, Shirley Heath, Anne Herrington, Bruce Herzberg, Bruce Horner, Laura Julier, Ilona M. McGuiness, Joy Ritchie, Jan Shoemaker, Ira Shor, Joyce Speiller-Morris, Patricia Stock, Betty Youngkin, with special thanks to Tom Deans and Deborah Minter.

It would have been hard to imagine a more supportively critical and generative group of readers for this manuscript. Their own commitments to the goals of community writing must have given them that extra measure of energy and imagination. I want to thank Linda Adler-Kassner, University of Minnesota; Rebecca Bell-Metereau, Southwest Texas State University; Tom Deans, University of Massachusetts/Amherst; Bruce Horner, Drake University; Deborah Minter, University of Nebraska, Lincoln; and Ann Watters, Stanford University.

At Harcourt Brace, Acquisitions Editor John Meyers has been the editorial energy behind this new direction, Leslie Taggart has been an outstandingly thoughtful and substantive developmental editor, and Katie Frushour, assistant editor, was a driving force in our search for imaginative programs. At Carnegie Mellon, Kathy Meinzer kept everything under her careful hand and eagle eye.

Finally, I must always thank my best and constant collaborator, Tim Flower.

Contents

PART II

COMMUNITY WRITING
Problem Solving in Civic Discourse

PART I

STRATEGIES FOR WRITING
Problem Solving in Academic Discourse

chapter one

A Portrait of Writers in Action

This is a book about how to write: how to say what you mean and how to relate to your reader. It is also about writing in the real world and handling the problems people face when they need to write academic papers, persuasive reports, concise memos, and essays that can open a reader's eyes. In writing this book, I have imagined you, the reader, as a person who writes to make something happen, whether your audience is a professor, an employer, a peer, or a community reader. I have assumed that, whatever your goals are, you are interested in discovering better ways to achieve them.

Your goal as a writer might often be as basic as making your words say what you really mean. Or it might be as complicated as persuading another person to change his or her mind. In either case, your success will depend in part on the skills and writing strategies you bring to the task. So in this book we will focus on three kinds of strategies:

1. The strategies you have for *understanding your rhetorical situation,* that is, for being aware of the people and expectations that surround any occasion for writing. To have insight into a rhetorical situation you need to know why you are writing, who is going to read it, and what they will be looking for. What is your relationship with the reader; what are your shared goals? What is your role: Are you an authority, a learner, or a critic? What kind of writing does this context call for: personal reflection, crisp professional prose, or an academic investigation? Knowing how to "read the context" lets you uncover some of the goals, expectations, and constraints that surround the social act of writing. Even more important, it sets you up to find your own path among these multiple forces, even when they come in conflict with one another. These strategies also can put you in touch with the supportive network of collaboration and conversation that surrounds good writing.

2. The strategies you have for *adapting your writing to the needs of a reader.* Good writing is writing that achieves your purpose in a dialogue with some real reader. It goes beyond merely being "correct" to meeting the needs of readers. Some readers come to a text with immediate, practical concerns—the hiking club needs directions, the

planning committee needs information—and only you can give it to them. But others, who are merely interested in your topic or in what you might say, will not feel motivated to continue reading or to "dig out" ideas if the text does not speak to them or the discussion does not seem thoughtfully crafted. Readers become impatient if a text is hard to follow, if its ideas are not fully explained, or if its point is hard to remember. Writers make this dialogue work by trying to imagine readers' needs and responses, and by making the prose itself easy to read, the point of the discussion easy to see, and the reasoning of the arguments easy to follow. Good writers do not simply express themselves; they plan their writing around a goal they share with the reader and design it to be understood and remembered.

3. The strategies you have for *the act of composing itself,* that is, for guiding your writing process, dealing with difficulties, and monitoring and reflecting on your own thinking. These composing strategies include techniques for getting started, for generating ideas, for organizing them, and for reviewing what you have written. They include informal collaborative strategies for listening and talking over ideas with other people. Everyone has composing strategies, even if they aren't aware of what they are. The set of strategies you use has a large impact on how fluent and efficient you are—on how much time and effort it takes to create a satisfying page of text. Even more important, your strategies will determine how well you explore and use your own knowledge as you write. Some writers have a large repertoire of powerful writing strategies on which to draw; other people appear always to be at the mercy of their inspiration.

In brief, the goal of this book is to help you gain more awareness and control of your own composing process—to become more reflective and productive as a writer and more effective with your readers.

❧ WHY TAKE A PROBLEM-SOLVING APPROACH TO WRITING?

How do people become good writers? How do they become attuned to the social context of their work? How do they develop the ability to compose, to collaborate, to adapt to readers? The popular mythology of writing gives us two answers. First, it tells us that the ability to write is simply a question of talent. Some people are just born with "a way with words"; others aren't, and that's that. Secondly, the myth says that the process of writing depends on inspiration. If a writer is lucky or talented—or waits long enough—inspiration will come, paragraphs will flow, and the paper will write itself.

Like all myths, this one is right about some things. There are real differences among writers, and inspiration, if you can get it, is a fine composing method. However, there are two problems with this myth. One is that it leads capable people to give up too soon. It assumes that people can't really *learn how* to write except for learning rather mechanical skills such as correct use of grammar and punctuation. So, the myth says, if you weren't born with talent or don't feel inspired, there's nothing much you can do. Secondly, in addition to being discouraging, this myth is just plain wrong about what actually happens when people write.

If we looked at composing as a thinking process, we would find that it has much in common with the problem-solving processes people use every day when they are planning a trip, taking an exam, making a decision, or trying to make a diplomatic request. The general research on problem solving in the past twenty years has discovered a great deal about the special strategies that successful artists, scientists, inventors, and business managers use to go about solving problems in their work. These experts in their fields are characterized by two things: a great deal of knowledge about their topics and a large repertory of powerful strategies for attacking their problems. Good writers share these qualities. They are people who have developed better ways to entertain the problem of writing.

Research on composing has also exploded the myth that good writing is a lonely creative act that depends solely on the private insights of an individual writer. It is true that the writer is ultimately responsible for what he or she chooses to say, but the process of creating insight and understanding is a highly social one. Whether we are writing a personal reflection, a research paper, or an editorial, the very act of writing puts us in a dialogue with others who have talked and written about these issues before. We are part of a conversation that has extended over history and shaped the ideas with which we think; insights are a creative use of what has gone before.

Good writers are highly aware of their place in this dialogue; they see their writing as a social, rhetorical, and collaborative action. Moreover, they enter into this social process in a strategic way by talking over work in progress, having a friend read a draft, or choosing to write with other people when it would improve the work. Informal collaboration is a normal part of their composing process. They bring the expectations of people from their pasts into their current thinking, imagining the voices of former teachers, supervisors, friends and other writers as they compose. But at the same time that they solicit ideas, advice and criticism, they are conscious of the social influences they may want to criticize, resist or reject. A problem-solving approach to writing helps you become a reflective participant in this social conversation.

In this book we will look at some of the research on what effective writers do, in part because it has uncovered some very effective strategies that anyone can use. But more than that, it will let you see the principle behind the practice and give you some insight into the logic of the strategies you are learning. In the long run, this sort of knowledge about why things work is the best knowledge, because it lets you continue to teach yourself.

The special strength of a problem-solving approach is really a frame of mind or an attitude—one that may be quite different from other ways you have approached writing. As a problem solver your first concern is not with the finished product—with fitting into a format or convention, with following the rules of grammar, or even with producing a polished style. Instead, your attention is squarely focused on your own goals as a writer, on what you want to do and say. The formal features of a finished text *do* matter, but they matter because they can help you achieve your goals as a writer. Problem solving is a goal-directed frame of mind.

Moreover, concentrating on goals and figuring out how to reach them seems to let people marshal quite surprising skills and knowledge they didn't know they had. It is easy and, in fact, quite normal to feel a little uncertain and helpless when you are facing a new piece of writing. And speaking from experience, I can also say that it is quite normal to write first drafts that even your typewriter doesn't want to read. However, a problem solver takes a very practical, "let's see what we can do" attitude toward these stumbling blocks. This attitude not only gets the process going, it lets you use more of the real powers you do have. A problem-solving approach assumes that if you know what you want to do, you can usually find a way to do it.

A second reason to approach writing as a problem solver takes us back to the fact that expert and novice writers often use different strategies. A problem-solving approach assumes that there is often a "better" way and that writers can substantially expand their repertory of strategies. There is no guarantee that any given strategy will do the job—some problems are hard. But an awareness of your own decisions and a knowledge of alternatives gives you the incalculable power of conscious choice.

In my own work as a teacher and a researcher, I need to write a good deal. If I can't show what I've learned, my research will not be of much use to anyone. And like many students, I have to write to the demands of schedules, eagle-eyed editors, and the readers in my field. So when I sit down to write, it feels good to know that there are strategies and principles behind this process—that it's not just a game of chance I play with my muse. However, I didn't begin to actively enjoy writing—to feel secretly excited about the time I spend thinking at the computer—until I stopped seeing my writing as a polished, finished product. With that "finished product" perspective, the only way to succeed was to sound as elegant and authoritative as the published writers I was reading. And somehow I never did. The pleasure came when I began concentrating on what I wanted to accomplish and trying to figure out how to do it. For me, problem solving turns composing into a goal-directed journey—writing my way to where I want to be.

In this chapter we will examine snapshots of writers from three different perspectives which let us see how writers, as thinkers and problem solvers, are shaped by their social and rhetorical contexts. At the same time, we will see how they become shapers of those contexts as they take action, make decisions, and make meaning. Our first snapshot of *writers as problem solvers* is of two real students coming to grips with academic writing. It shows how writing works as a goal-directed, collaborative thinking process that helps people understand issues and problems. Our second snapshot of *writers in context* goes back to the roots of rhetoric in ancient Greece to show how writers and speakers stand within a circle of peers and, in our more modern view, within different discourse communities. This will lead us to our third snapshot of *writers making meaning*—a composite picture that places cognition in context and individual writers within a community. This portrait will show how both writers and readers interpret, negotiate, and construct meaning. Together, these three pictures will give us a set of important concepts for talking about what writers do and for exploring real rhetorical situations.

SNAPSHOT 1: WRITERS AS PROBLEM SOLVERS

Carter and Jeannie are real students. They are in a writing course in the second semester of their freshman year and are facing a problem many writers face—making the transition from the writing they did in high school to the academic writing expected in college. Because they recorded their "collaborative planning" sessions on audiotape as a regular part of their course work, we are able to listen in on an actual planning discussion in the dorm as these two writers talk over their individual papers due on Monday. The assignment was to write about a "discourse problem" of their own choosing:

> Use your reading from Peter Farb's book *Word Play* [a chapter on how different cultures and communities use language to create insiders and outsiders] to analyze a "real problem" other students might face and want to read about.

TRYING TO UNDERSTAND PROBLEMS

By the time we enter the discussion, Carter has already defined a problem he thinks other freshmen face as well, which is the difficulty students have "switching writing styles for different writing assignments" and "switching assignments from class to class." In response to Jennie's questions, Carter begins to describe his own experience as a writer who found that the strategies he had developed in high school were no longer working in college. Moreover, strategies that worked for one college course didn't always work in others. As you read this slightly edited excerpt from Carter's planning session tape, look closely at the image of academic writing he is building. Does his image and his sense of the problem fit your experience?

30 CARTER: And my audience, they're probably gonna expect a lot of examples. I'm gonna have to use a lot of examples to prove to them that different writing styles exist, and I want my audience to be able to relate their own experiences to this and maybe see how it affects them.

31 JENNIE: So what kind of examples are you gonna use? Can you give me an example?

32 CARTER: Um, okay, I'll give you a real big example. Switching from high school writing to college writing.

33 JENNIE: Uh-huh.

34 CARTER: In high school . . . you could get away with, you know, BS in a lot of papers. And you'd get good grades, just 'cause it sounded intelligent, even though it really didn't say much. In college, they don't go for that stuff. You gotta really, you know, go write, and you can't BS your paper, because they'll know right away that you're doing that.

Here Carter goes off on a short tangent, but Jennie is an active supporter and pulls him back by restating the plan as she has heard it and asking for something that would make this idea "more real."

37 JENNIE: So some of your main points are gonna be that from high school to college—in high school, you can get away with saying things that aren't really relevant. In college, you can't. But how are you gonna explain that? Are you gonna give a specific example in your life? With like: In high school I did this, in college I can't do that. I think it would become more real.

38 CARTER: Yeah. Okay. I can do this. In high school, in my senior year, we had to write a thesis paper. And we had an entire semester to do it. And just like me, I waited until the last three weeks of the semester to do it. And I didn't have all the research done that I should have, but I started working on it real hard. And I had a lot of pages. It ended up being 15 pages long.

39 JENNIE: Wow!

40 CARTER: Well, that's what she expected—she said 10–15 pages. And it was really long and drawn out, and it didn't really say much of anything, but it sounded like it did. You know what I mean?

41 JENNIE: Yeah. That's a good example. I really like that.

42 CARTER: I got an A on it.

43 JENNIE: Oh! Congratulations!

44 CARTER: It really didn't say anything, so I was so happy, and I got an A in English, and that made my day, and then I graduated, and I was even happier. But, for college . . .

45 JENNIE: Yeah. That's a good example.

46 CARTER: I'm not done yet.

47 JENNIE: *(Laughs)* Sorry, Carter.

48 CARTER: *(Laughs)* Okay. And comparing that to the first semester of college, I took a class on cultural history which is probably the most boring class I've ever taken in my life . . . we had to write a five-page paper on African nationalism, which I had no idea, and I waited like the night before it was due to start that . . .

51 JENNIE: You have a bad habit of doing that.

52 CARTER: I know. . . . So I wrote five or six pages on nothing, but I included the words "African nationalism" in there once in a while. I thought, why this is just like high school, I can get away with doing this. I got the paper back, and it was a C−, or a C, or something like that. It said "no content." And I was introduced to the world of college writing.

The Problem of Entering New "Worlds"

Much like this chapter, Carter is trying to create a portrait of writers thinking and acting on a problem. He has identified a rhetorical situation that all of us have had to face—the need to enter a new community with new expectations and to learn new ways of writing. And for most of us, learning to do academic writing is an important part of entering the "world of college." In Carter's portrait, writers are problem solvers, trying to read the situation, understand what is expected, make decisions (and guesses), and use feedback to keep learning. Carter does not see writing well as a question of some generic "talent," but as the ability to switch among different "worlds" or communities, to use the "styles" and provide the substance those communities expect. However, as Carter and Jennie show, there is more to academic writing than knowing its conventions.

Finding Versus Solving Problems in Academic Writing

Like many academic writers, Carter and Jennie are using their papers to understand or analyze a problem. As *problem-solvers,* they are not looking for a quick fix or an easy solution to Carter's problem of entering academic discourse. Unlike a "Dear Abby" or a how-to column that provides answers, and unlike a personal narrative that would simply tell his story, Carter's paper is an academic problem analysis; he is trying to define and explore a problem, to help readers see the problem as he sees it. Like most academic writing, the really important and hard part about this analysis is finding and defining the issue or problem he wants to talk about. It is Carter—not the assignment or the outside reading—who defines "switching writing styles" as an issue that matters for freshmen. And it is Carter who has to define just what it means to "switch styles." As a reader, you may or may not already agree that this version of the problem gets to the heart of the matter, or that it is a significant conflict in your attempt to enter academic discourse. So if Carter hopes to convince you that his image of the situation matters, he will have to use examples and reasonable arguments to support his analysis of the problem.

This process is the stock in trade of most academic writers, from college freshmen to professors. People in the academic discourse community use writing to discover, define, and analyze problems—and to convince other members of that community that their image is a good one.

Finding Versus Solving Problems in Community Writing

In the larger community, people also use writing to analyze public and neighborhood questions and to grapple with broad civic and social issues. Community writing—as we are defining it here—is the writing done by professionals and volunteers in public and nonprofit institutions and by everyday people in grassroots communities. For them, community writing and action often go hand in hand, because a written text lets them define a situation as a *problem* in order to motivate people to actions that are wise, timely, and just.

For example, the **Thought Provokers** that follow compare introductory paragraphs from two very different documents. One is a

---

Thought Provoker on
What Is the Problem?

A Proposal for Community/University Collaboration

The Problem: The Troubled Connection
Between Learning and Work

What is the problem? Would everybody see the problem this way?

The transition in our region's economy has precipitated a life crisis in poverty neighborhoods. As youth seek a road to work that leads to self-respect and self-sufficiency, the guidance and identity offered by an earlier, industry-based culture of work no longer apply.

As more and more children grow up in *low-employment* ghettos created by our region's economy, we need a visionary effort to prepare this generation for the demands of a new economy. We can not locate this problem in "the youth" themselves nor in the need for sustaining jobs alone—as critical as that is—but in the need for a culture of learning, connected to the culture of high-performance work. It is a culture that demands flexible learners—problem solvers who can write, speak, and use technology.

From CMU Center for University Outreach. (1997). *Constructing Roads to Learning/Roads to Work.* Pittsburgh, PA.

formal proposal trying to convince a foundation that they should fund a community outreach program in which college students, like Carter and Jenny, would help inner city teenagers develop writing and computing skills. The second document came out of a community/ university collaboration. It is trying to do an unusual thing—to convince health care professionals that this grassroots text, written by people in the neighborhood, has valuable information to consider. It is turning the tables, telling professionals that this is *their* problem, too. In both texts, the writers motivate readers to listen to them by showing that they can help the reader understand and respond to a genuine problem.

If you look closely at most of the *significant* writing people do in personal, professional, academic, and community settings, you will notice that it is often a way to talk about problematic issues and to understand as well as help solve problems—whether the text is a personal journal, a business report, college essay, research article, a community action report, or a proposal. To be a problem solver is first and most importantly to be a problem finder and problem poser.

Thought Provoker on
Whose Problem Is It?

Getting to Know You: A Dialogue for Community Health

The Importance of Dialogue in Health Care

What is the problem? Would everybody see the problem this way?

More than ever, community residents must work in genuine partnership with health care providers to create health in their lives and in their communities. And yet, residents who are served by urban clinics and their physicians and nurses who work in them often have very different backgrounds. Cultural, educational, and economic differences between caregivers and patients can create barriers to communication and interfere with effective treatment. Patients who misunderstand diagnoses or have personal or cultural reasons **not** to comply with treatment may waste precious resources and may walk away feeling frustrated and misunderstood. Physicians may, in turn label patients as uncooperative and be disappointed by the lack or results in their prevention and treatment programs.

From Lorraine Higgins and Theresa Chalich (Eds.). (1996). *Getting to Know You.* Pittsburgh, PA: The Community Literacy Center and The Rainbow Health Center.

THINKING ABOUT GOALS

But writing itself is also a problem-solving process. That is, writing is a process in which people are constantly setting goals, trying various strategies to reach their goals, and evaluating where they are now. Problem solving is a thinking process by which people reach goals. Let us look at Carter's transcript again, not just to see his argument, but to learn how a writer like Carter is going through this thinking process. In Latin, the word *cognito* means "I think." Looking closely at the *cognition* or *cognitive process* of writers as they plan reveals not only what writers are doing, but what they are thinking and what they are telling themselves about how to write.

As problem-solvers, these writers are trying to "read" this new situation, use their past experience to make sense out of it, and set goals for what to accomplish in this paper. For instance, two of Carter's key goals are "to prove" that these different styles exist and get his readers "to relate" their own experience to his analysis. Jennie adds the important subgoal of trying to make this idea "become more real." These are intelligent and ambitious goals. Unlike the high school self he described, Carter is not depending on a BS strategy to fill a page. He has tackled a genuine, difficult problem many writers face; he is looking hard for evidence to support his claim, and he is showing a sophisticated concern for how readers might respond. Therefore much of his planning is spent figuring out how he can reach those goals. Would it work for example, to use examples and a personal experience narrative, to give detail, or to create a dramatic contrast between a high school and college experience? Carter isn't just telling his story; he is using that story to reach his goals—to make a point and analyze a problem he thinks other freshmen face.

Because Jennie and Carter are real students, they show us the realistic mix of good thinking, effective problem-solving and uncertainty and difficulty that are a normal part of learning something new. Can you predict how some of their experiments and decisions will turn out? For instance,

- Compare the assignment with the parts of the rhetorical situation Carter and Jennie talk about: what do they think are the interesting, relevant, or important parts? Might their teacher (whom we will hear from later) have any different reading of the goals for this assignment?
- As problem-solvers, Carter and Jennie also have a repertoire of "standard" goals and strategies they call on frequently. Carter talks about trying to "sound intelligent," about planning to prove a point with examples, and about ignoring organization when he is not writing for his English class. Do you think he needs to question any of his assumptions or "standard" strategies?

When you are entering a new discourse or facing a new kind of writing, which is more important: learning what goals you need to set, learning new strategies for meeting those goals, or knowing when to use what you already know? One thing is certain, although you will probably learn some new strategies from this book, you will also find that becoming *aware* of the strategies you already use lets you take more control of your own process. It expands your options, lets you switch strategies, and helps you get going when you become stuck.

COLLABORATING

In this portrait of the writer as a problem solver, you are an individual trying to communicate your understanding of a problem, and you are a strategic thinker aware of your own goals and strategies. But does this mean that either writing or problem solving is a solitary, intensely private act? Our mythology assumes that creativity comes from isolating yourself from other minds and spinning ideas out of some private inner recess. And it is true that when Carter hands in his paper, he and he alone will be responsible for what he says. However, if we look closely at what experienced, effective writers do and at their thinking processes, we see a very social process that depends both on shared ideas and relationships between people. As this transcript suggests, collaboration with other people can play an important role in writing, even when the collaborator is not a co-author, does not write a sentence and (in some cases) is not even there!

For instance, although Carter's freshman history course is now long over, the voice of its instructor is still in his ears, and, in Carter's interpretation, that voice is not only saying "no content," it is saying "change your strategies for writing." Likewise, Carter's relationship with his current writing instructor and her advice from a previous conversation comes to life in the here and now of his planning and plays a role in what he chooses to do. In this sense, then, Carter is not alone as he is thinking, but is able to call up the ideas, advice, attitudes, and even voices of other people, including his own past self.

And then there are also the unseen, even unbidden collaborators that we hear but may not notice—the voices in the back of a writer's mind that say "be cool, BS, and don't act serious about school," or "your ideas don't really count; just show you know the material," or "you know you never could write; might as well give up now." Maybe we want to reserve the term "collaboration" for face-to-face work toward a common goal and simply call these experiences internal monologues and dialogues. Nevertheless, the point is clear. As we think and plan, we are drawing on past experiences, past conversations, and past responses to ourselves and our work. And the goals we set and the parts of the rhetorical situation we pay attention to (and the parts we ignore) are shaped by our relationships with other people: teachers, parents, and peers. Some of those voices will be sensible, supportive, and liberating. But some will be voices you need to question or challenge. And some, like the criticisms of past papers that can paralyze a writer, are voices you need to put aside or replace with a live collaborator who cares about what you can do now.

Jennie is one of those collaborators—a direct and committed face-to-face supporter. But how does she actually influence this writing process? In this session, Jennie does not contribute any "new" ideas. However, it is her comments in turn 37 that prompt the "welcome to college writing" story, which becomes the main supporting example in Carter's paper. And later, in turn 53 (while Carter is basking in the success of his example) it is Jennie who goes back to review his other main points. What role do collaborators like Jennie play? As you read the following excerpt, look for the ways Jennie influences Carter's thinking and look for the signs of how other voices and other people's attitudes and values enter into his writing process.

53 JENNIE: Great, Carter. . . . Okay, so that's an example for one of your points. What about an example for how writing varies? Well, I think you already kinda told me that, how writing varies from Technology and People to Introduction to Writing [two freshman courses Carter was taking]. Just, you would say, one needs more content than the other—I mean more facts and details and not as much style.

56 CARTER: Yeah. Well, I can give a specific example for that. For a problem analysis paper in Introduction to Writing, my first draft wasn't very well organized, and well, you know, we handed the papers in and got them back, and [the professor] commented on them. . . . She said my paper wasn't very well organized, and she gave me ideas of how I could structure it better. . . . You know, make it more smoothly flowing . . . And so I wrote it like that . . . real paragraph form, everything was ordered, and everything like that. Good spelling. Good grammar. Good punctuation.

59 JENNIE: Oh, that was nice.

60 CARTER: That was very nice of her. I got a B on the paper, so I was real happy.

63 JENNIE: Yeah. So that's necessary in an English paper.

64 CARTER: Yeah. But in Technology and People, we have papers due almost every Friday. . . . They'll give us a problem, and they'll ask us to give a possible solution of the problem, you know, in a report form sort of. And my papers for Tech and People, usually they'll have maybe a paragraph, and then maybe a problem, like an equation worked out, or something like that. They won't really be structured . . . so it's really different.

As even this brief excerpt shows, writing and thinking involve a variety of relationships with other people. Imagining readers and their expectations helps you set goals, and the response of readers helps you learn. At the same time, working collaboratively can let you realize even more of your own potential when a supportive listener helps you to develop ideas or prompts you to try new strategies or solve new problems.

SNAPSHOT 2: WRITERS IN CONTEXT

Our first portrait of writers as problem solvers looked at people entering a new rhetorical situation and trying to scope out what was expected, what was possible, and what was worth doing. As a writer and reader of this book, you may be at a transition point, too, where you need to read a new rhetorical situation and its expectations. This second portrait will suggest ways to look at that context and your role in it.

STANDING IN A CIRCLE OF PEERS

In ancient Greece, where the practice of rhetoric developed, the rhetor stood within a circle of peers using the art of rhetoric to analyze issues and to persuade. The very term "rhetor" means "I speak." In the law courts of Athens, citizens argued their own cases before their peers, and in public forums, they debated not only philosophical questions about social values but heated political issues about democracy, war, and the unification of Greece. They debated decisions about admitting foreigners, free trade and free speech that would affect the growth of Athens as a commercial and cultural center. And at festivals like the Olympic games, rhetorical performances ran side by side with athletic events as celebration and formal competition among the speakers. Although Plato, Aristotle, and the sophists developed competing schools of rhetoric and differed on how it should be taught, the study of rhetoric was at the center of Greek education for philosopher-kings, for political and commercial leaders, and for the voting members of the society. Given this context, it is no wonder that the art of rhetoric developed as the *art of persuasion*—a body of knowledge and strategies that let ordinary citizens stand up within a circle of peers to raise issues, investigate problems, and build convincing arguments about issues of the day. The study of logic and persuasion begun in Athens is still a cornerstone of Western education.

This image of a rhetor building arguments, speaking out within a circle of peers, is a useful starting point for examining your own rhetorical situation. It helps us visualize a writer (rhetor) who is both an individual with a case to make and a member of a community which has a reason to listen. It locates the act of writing or speaking within a specific context, such as a legal court, a public forum, or a speech at the Olympic games. And it reminds us that ancient Greek writers moving from one context to another had to know the distinctive conventions of argument and style that were expected, even required, in these different situations.

WRITING WITHIN A DISCOURSE COMMUNITY

On the other hand, to understand other parts of your rhetorical situation, you will probably need to go beyond this image from ancient Greece. For instance, the circle of peers who could vote and speak in fifth-century Athens was a limited circle; it excluded women, foreigners, and slaves. The community to whom you will write in your college and working life will include people who are not like you, whether you find yourself in a multicultural college classroom, a multinational corporation, or talking as a layperson in the midst of a group of experts. How do you talk effectively across the boundaries of knowledge, values, and cultural background? As a writer you already operate in not just one community, but in a number of different *discourse communities,* such as the communities formed around academic fields like physics, economics, and English or around civic affairs or civil rights. The *discourse,* or conversation, of a community is simply the way its members talk with each other—the special words they use, the typical ways they argue and the assumptions and commonplaces on which they all agree. For example, the academic community talks about "analysis," "synthesis," and "interpretation," and its members tend to assume that an argument built on analysis and evidence is stronger than one built on personal testimony.

To enter a community, you must learn to talk as if you belong. When you are in an economics class, you are expected to think, talk, and write like an economist—to enter that community as if you were a regular member, to use its specialized language, and to carry out its discourse practices. For example, a common practice in writing and talking about economics, which you may be expected to use, is the practice of organizing your ideas (about the rise in automotive costs, for example) into a predictive model, then using that model to analyze or lay out the trends that actually occurred. To other economists this practice—translating the assertions you want to make about trends into a predictive model—is seen as an effective way to make an argument. However, an hour later you may walk into an English class where you are entering a different community with its own discourse practices, which could range from writing personal-experience essays to analyzing problems and building arguments. And later that night, you could find yourself in the discourse community of baseball fans, where membership depends not only on knowing where your team is in the standings, but on being able to talk the lingo of RBIs, season averages, ERAs and know the appropriate putdown for the opposing team. In all of these situations, readers (and listeners) bring strong expectations about what's important, how to argue, and the roles each of you is supposed to play in the discourse.

Entering the Conversation

It helps to think of entering a new discourse community as similar to the process of trying to enter a conversation. Kenneth Burke, a famous, modern academic writer, describes discourse itself as an on-going conversation.

> Imagine that you enter a parlor. You come late. When you arrive, others have long preceded you, and they are engaged in a heated discussion, too heated for them to pause and tell you exactly what it is about. In fact, the discussion had already begun long before any of them got there, so that no one present is qualified to retrace for you all the steps that have gone on before. You listen for a while, until you decide that you have caught the tenor of the argument; then you put in your oar. Someone answers; you answer him; another comes to your defense; another aligns himself against you, to either the embarrassment or gratification of your opponent, depending upon the quality of your ally's assistance. However, the discussion is interminable. The hour grows late; you must depart. And you do depart, with the discussion still vigorously in progress.
>
> *Source:* Kenneth Burke. (1973). *The Philosophy of Literary Form: Studies in Symbolic Action* (3rd ed., pp. 110–11). Berkeley: University of California Press.

Put yourself in the position of the newcomer. What does it take to enter the conversation within a discipline or within a college class (not to dominate it, just join in)? Notice how the strategies that help you learn a new kind of discourse are similar to the ways people enter any new social group.

1. Listen carefully to the conversation already going on. What are the issues, what are the problems people care about, what are the questions they see as important?
2. Respond to those issues. Let people see how the new idea or comment you have to add fits in the picture—even if you disagree with the picture.
3. Look for and use the conventions—the language, the organization, the kinds of evidence—that people in that discourse community expect and value. Try to understand the community in which you are writing and speak to readers in a language you and they can share.

 ## SNAPSHOT 3: WRITERS MAKING MEANING

Our third portrait is about both cognition, or thinking, and about context; it pictures writers and readers as thinkers, problem-solvers, meaning makers who are located within a social and rhetorical circle that influences them both. But the focus here is on the fact that writers are in the business of *making* meaning (which as we will see is not limited to making *text*). Figure 1–1 helps visualize how some of the obvious features of the writing process (readers, writers, texts) are connected to other features we often overlook or don't talk about. Because each of these features can have a large impact on writing, I am asking you to read this figure as a snapshot taken with a wide angle lens that tries to bring more of the action and actors

FIGURE 1–1
Meaning Making in a Social and Rhetorical Context

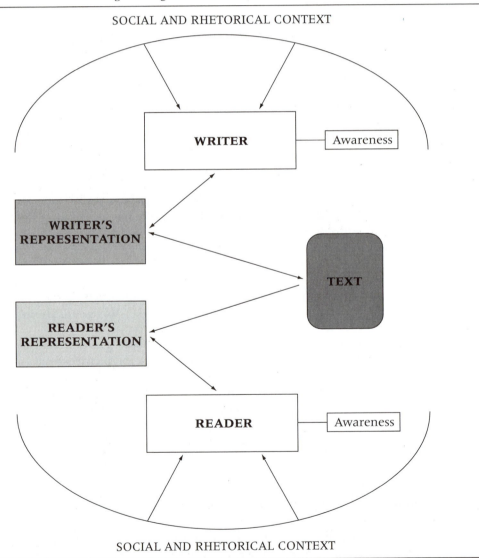

into focus. We will then use these ideas to discover some things about Carter and his readers.

The Social and Rhetorical Context

The larger outer circle indicates some of the forces that exert an influence on writers, readers, and the meanings they construct. Sometimes these forces, which make up the immediate rhetorical context, are direct and obvious: the assignment, the classroom or work situation, the readers. Other influences are apparent once you think about them, such as the writer's own goals, the knowledge he or she has (or doesn't have), and the very language a writer uses to think about a topic. For instance, our society has begun to replace words like "he" (as a generic pronoun) and "chairman" with "he or she" and "chair" because the former words worked in subtle but pervasive ways to exclude women from our image of a situation. Some other forces that arise from our cultural and social backgrounds may be harder to see, but can have great force. They are the assumptions at work the minute we notice whether the speaker is an insider or outsider in the discussion, a man or a woman, black or white. Writers are acting on such assumptions when they use overly formal or inflated language to signal status or expertise, or any language, for that matter, that signals who they are.

These social and cultural influences often involve issues of authority and power. For example, many writers graduate from high school believing that they should not use "I" or speak in the first person, or that they do not have the authority to argue for a position but should always find an authority to quote or at least back them up. If you ever held this theory, you might ask yourself, did it grow out of a *social assumption* about the status of students' ideas? Or did it grow out of the practice of writing research papers—a particular *discourse practice* common in high school that discourages the use of first person? Either way, your writing was influenced by a social force or a convention. Discourse communities and their practices not only exert a strong influence on the language, ideas, and rhetorical moves of writers, they also affect what readers expect (and see) in a text. For example, a news story in the *New York Times* is expected to be impersonal and objective in both its language and perspective. But when that story is published as part of the writer's memoirs or autobiography, readers expect a first-person, personal account that reveals attitudes, feelings, and insight.

Negotiating the Rhetorical Situation

But wait, you may be saying, I have read investigative reporting that was full of insight and argument, and personal journals that were full of detailed, factual observations. Many students do use "I" and take a stand even when they are doing research papers. And you are right, these cultural, social, and linguistic forces are like the conventions of a community and even like the multiple goals of writers themselves. They will influence, but they won't determine what a writer does. Writers and readers actively *construct* their meanings in response to and in the face of forces like these. For instance, many academic writers now make a point of using "I" (as in "I have argued that . . .") in the face of this convention. They do so to acknowledge that they are offering a position, not pronouncing a general "truth."

Although much of our response to social forces and conventions can be unconscious, at times people actively *negotiate* their rhetorical situation in two senses of the word. In one sense, writers are juggling the power relations among these different forces, like a union negotiator, resisting some expectations, accommodating others. For instance, you may take a conventional stance or join the consensus of your class on some points, but choose to stand out on others. In another sense, writers negotiate meaning when they try to make their text respond to the rhetorical situation by finding the best path through it. Just as you might "negotiate" a challenging stretch of road with curves, holes, and straightaways, or run the rapids of a river in a canoe, writers create a response that tries to take as many of their goals, expectations, and opportunities into account as possible while avoiding the potholes and rocks. The meaning they create is a response to their rhetorical situation and has negotiated a particular path through it.

When you look at Figure 1–1, read the connecting lines as saying that information and influence are indeed flowing from the situation to the writer and the reader. However, the influence that context has finally does depend on what writers and readers make of it as they construct a meaning.

For example, in designing her assignment ("Use your reading from Farb's book. . . ."), Carter's instructor's intended to present students with some specific challenges, which were mentioned in the evaluation criteria given with the assignment:

1. Did you apply your reading to a real discourse problem or an issue which you define in the paper?
2. Did you use the material from [the assigned reading] for a purpose of your own, and did you make your own purpose as a writer apparent to readers?
3. Did you use your purpose and/or your sense of a problem to organize the rest of the paper? Is each paragraph relevant to your purpose and to the logical development of your analysis?
4. Did your paper meet college-level standards for correctness and style?

However, Carter never thinks about how to use the readings in his planning session and never mentions Farb in his paper. How do you predict the instructor will respond to the way Carter negotiates the forces or voices this set of criteria represents?

Personal Representations of Meaning

You have probably already spotted the most unconventional feature of this portrait. In it, writers do not simply create a text that "expresses" what they know and readers do not simply "see" the writer's meaning. (You can see one of these older, simplified models of writing as sending and receiving messages in Chapter 9.) Instead, when you, as a writer, plan to write, you are creating a large, complex mental *representation* in your own mind. I use the word representation rather than simpler terms such as image or picture because it helps us remember that this mental network of knowledge includes associations, tangents, things you can't say, memories, key words, images you can't put in words, feelings and so on. When you present a meaning in text—in logically organized, standard written English, for example—you are building a new, different *representation* of meaning in the special medium of written language.

Readers, of course, cannot see directly into the complicated personal meaning in your mind. Although readers sometimes care about what the author "thought" or "felt" and often try to imagine the writer's intentions or personal meaning, these are always inferences that *they* create. What readers must do is to build their own personal representation of the meaning of a text, or of what this dialogue with a writer is saying. This new representation is influenced, of course, by their backgrounds and contexts. In short, both readers and writers are building complex, personal representations of meaning. Moreover, your text and your personal mental "image" are separate representations of meaning, even though both of them are being built as you are planning and writing your text.

Let us use a thought experiment here to see how these ways of representing meaning can differ. Consider the concept of "problem solving." What does it mean to you? Spend sixty seconds to jot down different ways you *represent* this idea to yourself here in the margin.

Looking at your notes, did you think of finding "solutions" and doing math, or did you think of exploring "problems?" Did you visualize a writer thinking through a difficult paragraph or walking around a room trying to imagine a reader's response? Does your image involve "strategies" or heuristics like brainstorming or talking to someone else? Maybe your image includes things you have read on the strategies of successful problem solvers, or ways to break through mental blocks? If someone tried to piece together a map of what the concept of problem solving means to you, would your personal, mental representation include experiences of facing and managing problems yourself as a teenager or a child? Does your idea map associate being a problem solver with yourself or only with other people? What attitudes and feelings about being a problem solver are part of your personal representation? In school, problem solving is often associated with getting a right answer. But in facing personal problems, such as dealing with parents or choosing a college, or professional problems, such as budgeting tight resources, problem solving means figuring out the best decision under the circumstances. And that means living with the uncertainty of your choice. Did your representation have these different categories of school, personal, and professional problems? If so, did it also separate school from personal and professional problems in the way my representation does?

If you could stand back and survey your information, experiences, and attitudes, you could start to map your personal, mental representation of the meaning of that concept. Now suppose you were asked to write "an introduction to problem solving for college writers." You would be constructing a similar, though much more limited, representation of meaning in the act of producing your text. And then there would be a third representation—the text you actually write for others to read.

We can best illustrate this difference with one other example. Consider some of the ways you think about yourself: the images you have, the words you use to describe yourself in your own thoughts, the relevant experiences that come to mind. Then think of the way you chose (or hoped) to represent yourself when you wrote your college application essay—a very selective image constructed for the purpose of that text. You may have even constructed different images for different readers. And then think of the text itself—a representation that exists not in the images, words, memories and multiple associations that tumble through your mind, but in specific well-chosen words, placed in a stable organization, presented in standard, written English and the conventions of a formal essay. The point Figure 1–1 makes, then, is a very simple one. People do not simply "know" facts, they "represent" meaning to themselves. Although all the forces in that outer circle influence meaning, people construct their own. And when they write or read a text, they construct a personal representation of meaning—in the language of thought—that is related to, but still different from, their written text.

Carter's transcript gives us a glimpse of some of the rich memories, stories, surprises, writing stratgies, images of a good paper, teachers' comments, associations, and attitudes that are part of his representation of what it means to have "difficulty switching writing styles." Of course, that means Carter is going to have to make some important choices when he begins to build his written representation of this *web* of meaning in a two to three page text. That's why his goals are such an important part of this representation too. In addition to the claims he wants to make and the story he wants to tell, Carter has ideas about how he wants this paper to affect a reader:

> I'm gonna have to use a lot of examples to prove—to prove it to them that different writing styles exist, and I want my audience to be able to relate their own experiences to this, and maybe, and see how it affects them.

Other people, including teachers past and present and his collaborator play an important role in this drama of constructing goals and meaning. For instance, Jennie asks him to make a more detailed "how-to" plan in order to be even "more real."

> But how are you gonna explain that? Are you gonna give a specific example in your life? With like . . . In high school I did this, in college I can't do that. Like I think it would become more real.

But sometimes we really need someone to challenge our private representation of reality or of how to do something. Remember the specific goals Carter said he used for writing his papers in Technology and People (turn 64)? "And my papers for Tech and People . . . Usually, they'll have maybe a paragraph. And then maybe a problem, like an equation worked out, or something like that. They won't really be structured. I mean, I'll just have like one, problem one, and then all that, you know, so it's really different." Carter seems pretty confident that his representation is a good one. But what if Carter's collaborative partner had been Matt, a senior who read Carter's text for us and seemed to have a very different sense of what that course required?

Sometimes it is very hard to imagine these different representations, especially when they are tied to social or cultural differences. Yet this is precisely what many students who join a community

---

How might Carter reply to Matt? Which representation does the teacher probably hold?

Thought Provoker on
Conflicting Representations of Readers' Expectations

I don't think this person has a very good grasp on the style that you need when you write papers for Technology and People. He said it was in columns, no distinct paragraphs, don't worry much about grammar or spelling, except for the technical terms. Sorry, but that's not going to write an effective paper. . . . I mean you could get by if you had a poor TA, but if you want to stand out . . . you're still going to have to concentrate on organization, grammar, spelling and writing style.

> ### Thought Provoker on
> ### Trying to Grasp Different Representations
>
> I try to notice—and to gauge—the different reactions when differ-
> ent people speak. . . . I've been trying to furiously take notes about
> my perceptions about what's going on while the group sessions are
> happening. Part of that is that I want to know about concepts of
> power that are going on in that room. . . . And I think that there
> are a lot of reasons as to why we don't know about the writers' con-
> ceptions of power. All of us . . . student mentors, save one, are
> white, and I suspect that most of us are from the middle-class. We
> just don't know how to operate outside that.
>
> From Elenore Long. (1994). *The Rhetoric of Literate Social Action: Mentors
> Negotiating Intercultural Images of Literacy.* Dissertation. Pittsburgh, PA:
> Carnegie Mellon University.

outreach or service learning project are there to learn. The next
Thought Provoker is from the journal entry of Keith, a college mentor
working with a group of inner city teenagers. Notice how he is using
writing to help him think about how different people in this group
represent the idea of "power."

Sometimes writing is the best way to share a part of our own private representations and assumptions and get a little "reality check"
from other people.

The Text

For writers and readers, the text is the centerpiece of this whole
transaction; it is also the problem. On the one hand, the text is not
just a carbon copy of the representation in the writer's mind. Sometimes it reveals more than writers intend to say; often it fails to represent all that writers would like to communicate. Readers do not
have access to the complex sound-and-light show going on in the
writer's mind. They read the text. Moreover, they do not simply "decode" the text to "get" the meaning, they too construct their own internal representations, which are influenced by their goals in reading
and all the other social, cultural, linguistic, and conventional forces
that affect writing. Texts do their work in the midst of two powerful,
creative, and constructive processes: writing and reading.

On the other hand, for all the uncertainty of communicating,
text is a very powerful way to represent your meaning. It allows
people to create and then reflect on carefully crafted statements,
organized in ways that serve a reader's needs or that make a new
understanding possible. This way of looking at texts, then, predicts

that communicating calls for much more than merely expressing your thoughts on paper. Learning how to construct texts and anticipate how readers also construct meaning gives you a strong place to stand within the circle of discourse.

Awareness

Finally, you may have noticed a small feature on this map labeled Awareness, which both the Writer and the Reader possess. In this image of the rhetorical situation, large and powerful forces of society, culture, and experience are at work to shape meaning, even as writers and readers negotiate and construct their own representations in their minds and in texts. Much of this shaping process is swift and unconscious, and there are good reasons for that. If we had to think about everything we did, we would not have the attention left to do it. However, there are times when we want to stop and question our own assumptions, look closely at the conventions of a discourse community, or recognize our own strategies. Sometimes, but only sometimes, people rise to this increased awareness of their own thinking process and/or of the forces that shape meaning. Because such awareness doesn't just happen, and because it is one of the best ways to learn about writing, this book tries to create some opportunities for reflection that let you make that small area of Awareness a larger part of your composing process.

WELCOME TO ACADEMIC DISCOURSE: CARTER AND HIS READERS

Our three snapshots of writers in action focused on the writer. But now we must turn to another creative force—the fascinating, perplexing, and sometimes frustrating wild card in this whole process—the reader. As Figure 1–1 suggests, the reader is not simply the passive recipient of your meaning (via text) but is just as constructive and creative as you, the writer, are, interpreting your text and imagining your possible meaning as part of constructing his or her own meaning. You can never "control" this constructive process. But you can get better at anticipating and shaping it. That is why we will conclude this chapter by looking at Carter and his readers, letting you test your ability to predict their response to this text. At the same time, notice how Carter actually carried out the goals he described to Jennie.

Three readers read Carter's text, thinking out loud with a tape recorder running. One was the Instructor, who looked back at this and other papers sometime after the course was over. Since she held most of her comments until the end of the paper, they are printed there. The other two readers give us a blow-by-blow account of their responses as they read the text for the first time, revealing their moments of confusion, interest, impatience, and appreciation. One of these readers was a Senior, who took this class himself four years before. He offers us the perspective of an experienced insider. The third reader, whom we will call the Outsider, was a professional person who had no connection with the discourse community of this class, but who had a general interest in the topic and in writing. You, as the fourth reader, may be able to stand in for the target audience of college writers facing a new discourse community. Think aloud *as you read,* commenting on what strikes you and/or how you interpret the text now. To compare your response with the other readers, be sure to comment at the points which are marked with a large •.

Carter Xxxxxx

Introduction to Writing

> "Difficulty in Switching Writing Styles for
> Different Writing Assignments"
> Discourse Problem

Throughout our educational careers we are asked to write many different types of papers. These papers range from a 25 page thesis paper to a short one page paper on Macintosh development for Tecnology and People. It is obvious that these two papers would require different writing styles. • The thesis paper, for instance, would require extensive research, a lot of time, and "hundreds" of rough drafts, while the Technology and People assignment would require an hour of reading, an hour of writing, and one if any rough drafts. This is a simple example, but this type of thing occurs very often, and sometimes can cause problems. •

These problems include such things as deciding which type of writing style to use for differnt assignments, trying to figure out what each class wants out of a paper, and keeping these writing styles straight. Another problem that could go along very easily with these, and would be very relevent to college freshmen like myself, would be switching from high school writing to college writing. •

I found that the hardest transition that I had to make between high school and college, other than the work load, was learning how to write "college style." In high school I wrote just about the same way for every paper, lots of B.S., one or two drafts, and not a whole lot of content. In spite of writing like this I still got by with good grades. I thought I could get by writing like this in college. I couldn't have been more wrong. ·

The last big paper I wrote in high school was my senior thesis paper. We were given an entire semester for the paper, but as usual I waited until the "last minute." My paper was 15 pages long, lacked content, but I still got an "A." My first big writing assignment in college was for a class called Introduction to Culture and History. It was on the "exciting" subject of African Nationalism. We had two weeks to read up on the subject and do the paper, but I put it off until the last night and had absolutely no grasp of what African Nationalism was. I tried the same approach as I did for the thesis paper. My paper was 6 pages long with no content. When I got the paper back it had a "C–" on top along with the comment "A lot of B.S., but no content!" I learned the hard way that when your in college you have to learn how to write "college style." ·

While I was learning how to write "college style," I soon learned that writing "college style" entailed more than just spending more time, and filling the paper with more content. Unlike high school, different classes wanted different things out of writing assignments. For example, writing assignments for the class Tecnology and People expect a lot of tecnical terms, solutions to problems, and don't really pay that much attention to grammar and spelling, while writing assignments for Stratgies for Writing expect perfect grammar and spelling, and concentrate more on writing style and organization. This can be confusing, trying to figure out how each class expects you to write for their own particular assignments. ·

Another problem that goes along with this is once you know what the class wants out of a paper, trying to figure out what type of writing style to use for each particular assignment. After about two weeks or so I finally figured out what Tecnology and People wanted out of a paper. The next two assignments we had, a report, and a problem solution, I wrote with two totally different writing styles while still trying to give the class what it wanted out of a paper. The first paper, the report, I wrote similarly to how I write a Stratagies for Writing paper. I kept it in paragraph form, used good grammar, good spelling, and tried to make it look somewhat professional looking. For the problem solution paper, my main concern was just getting the problem right. The paper was in columns and had no distinct paragraphs. I didn't worry too much about grammar or spelling except for the technical terms that the grader would be specifically looking for. So, in addition to knowing what a class wants out of its writing assignments, one must also know what writing style would be best suited for each particular assignment. ·

These different writing styles for different classes and assignments can cause problems if we let ourselves get confused over which style to use. The best way to overcome this, for me at least, is to sit down before starting to write a paper and ask some key questions like "What class is the paper for?", "What does this class tend to look for in its writing assignments?", "What type of writing style does this particular assignment lend itself to?", and "In lieu of these things, what would be the best writing style to use for this paper?" If we ask ourselves these and other key questions before we start writing a paper it will become easier and easier to do well in each class, while staying away from the dreaded "C– more content needed." ·

Here is how three other readers were responding to this text. Notice the differences in what each reader is attending to at any given point and what each is adding to the picture. How does the representation each of them is building—their image of the "meaning" of this text—differ from yours?

Carter Xxxxxx

Introduction to Writing

"Difficulty in Switching Writing Styles for
Different Writing Assignments"
Discourse Problem

Throughout our educational careers we are asked to write many different types of papers. These papers range from a 25 page thesis paper to a short one page paper on Macintosh development for Tecnology and People. It is obvious that these two papers would require different writing styles.

> OUTSIDER: Humm. I see "different" in the title, in the first sentence and now here, but it doesn't tell me anything. Different length? Is this going to be about "style?"
>
> SENIOR: Well, at the moment, it's kinda boring. By the way, "technology" is misspelled. One thing that I was taught in my writing class was that you wanted to avoid giving blanket statements like "it is obvious that", "it is important that." It's a lot more effective . . . um . . . just to

write why it is that way. You could probably go right to the part about the thesis paper.

The thesis paper, for instance, would require extensive research, a lot of time, and "hundreds" of rough drafts, while the Technology and People assignment would require an hour of reading, an hour of writing, and one if any rough drafts. This is a simple example, but this type of thing occurs very often, and sometimes can cause problems.

OUTSIDER: I'm not sure what it's "an example" of. "This type of thing?" "These problems?" I got pointers here and I can't tell what they are pointing to.

SENIOR: That's true about the time. But the last sentence . . . is confusing. At this point, I have no idea why it can cause problems. Actually, I think it's fine to have different writing styles and to be a flexible writer. It's just part of the . . . um . . . what's the word . . . comes with the job. Comes with the territory. The only way I can see that causing problems is if you only know one style and you have to adapt. There's no way you can write a one-page paper the same way that you do a thesis.

Well, that was the introductory paragraph, and it's going to explain the problem of having to adapt. The audience [the writer has in mind] doesn't seem to be very educated or he's expecting that they've never encountered anything like this before because . . . "This is a simple example. . . ." Sounds kinda condescending.

These problems include such things as deciding which type of writing style to use for differnt assignments,

SENIOR: Different is misspelled. It says "differnt."

trying to figure out what each class wants out of a paper, and keeping these writing styles straight. Another problem that could go along very easily with these, and would be very relevent to college freshmen like myself, would be switching from high school writing to college writing.

SENIOR: Okay. I have a hard time seeing how that's a problem. I think that switching from high school writing to college writing is fine. It is the obvious thing, again. It's more . . . in cases like these, it's more appropriate to figure out why this is a problem and explain that. . . . The problem I see is that they're used to high-school writing, and they're going to start—and they're going to keep writing as if they were in high school, even though they're in college. That could be made clear.

OUTSIDER: We're in the land of miscellaneous. Not much beyond the obvious: long papers different from short, high school from college. But this seems more promising. I like the beginning of the third paragraph. A promising personal example and now we finally got to style, so I'm happier.

I found that the hardest transition that I had to make between high school and college, other than the work load, was learning how to write "college style." In high school I wrote just about the same way for every paper, lots of B.S., one or two drafts, and not a whole lot of content. In spite of writing like this I still got by with good grades. I thought I could get by writing like this in college. I couldn't have been more wrong.

> SENIOR: It's switching gears. Now that I realize that it's not going to be outlining problems in . . . in using different writing styles, that it's going to be a more personal paper, I'm a little bit more willing to forgive the sort of stuck-up, arrogant tone that I detected in the first paragraph. . . . It's not trying to explain anything to other people as far as writing problems go. It's going to be about this person's transition process between high school and college writing.

> OUTSIDER: Nice twist and clincher in the final sentence. Little sense of drama. Great big improvement. If I were talking to this person, I'd suggest they junk the first two paragraphs. . . . The writer hasn't mentioned a contrast here, but I recognize it, so I'm curious how the second half of the comparison comes out.

The last big paper I wrote in high school was my senior thesis paper. We were given an entire semester for the paper, but as usual I waited until the "last minute." My paper was 15 pages long, lacked content, but I still got an "A." My first big writing assignment in college was for a class called Introduction to Culture and History. It was on the "exciting" subject of African Nationalism.

> SENIOR: Hey, I thought that African Nationalism was an exciting subject.

> OUTSIDER: Nice use of quotation marks.

We had two weeks to read up on the subject and do the paper, but I put it off until the last night and had absolutely no grasp of what African Nationalism was. I tried the same approach as I did for the thesis paper. My paper was 6 pages long with no content. When I got the paper back it had a "C–" on top along with the comment "A lot of B.S., but no content!" I learned the hard way that when your in college you have to learn to write "college style."

> OUTSIDER: Good quote: "A lot of B.S., but no content." I like that. Another real good, almost journalistic punchline ending to the paragraph. And we continue with the idea of college style, so now we're getting more consistent and sticking with the idea of style.

> SENIOR: The previous paragraph set this up by saying that he couldn't have been more wrong. This paragraph supports it very well and is a good follow-up. What stands out for me is how much better the paper has become now that it's more obviously objective and specific.

While I was learning how to write "college style," I soon learned that writing "college style" entailed more than just spending more time, and filling the paper with more content. Unlike high school, different classes wanted different things out of writing assignments. For example, writing assignments for the class Tecnology and People expect a lot of tecnical terms, solutions to problems,

> SENIOR: Misspelled technical. Misspelled technology.
>
> OUTSIDER: Here we go to that lame word "different" again, so I'm not interested. And I still don't know what this Technology and People is. Oh well. And an unexpectedly striking part where the writer says he or she didn't pay that much attention to grammar and spelling. We've had plenty of evidence of that!

and don't really pay that much attention to grammar and spelling, while writing assignments for Stratgies for Writing expect perfect grammar and spelling, and concentrate more on writing style and organization. This can be confusing, trying to figure out how each class expects you to write for their own particular assignments.

> SENIOR: Well, unfortunately, we're going back to generalizations, which I don't like.
>
> OUTSIDER: I'm not sure where we are at the end. I can't say we've progressed at the end of this paragraph.

Another problem that goes along with this is once you know what the class wants out of a paper, trying to figure out what type of writing style to use for each particular assignment. After about two weeks or so I finally figured out what Tecnology and People wanted out of a paper. The next two assignments we had, a report, and a problem solution, I wrote with two totally different writing styles while still trying to give the class what it wanted out of a paper. The first paper, the report, I wrote similarly to how I write a Stratagies for Writing paper. I kept it in paragraph form, used good grammar, good spelling.

> OUTSIDER: (Laughs)

and tried to make it look somewhat professional looking. For the problem solution paper, my main concern was just getting the problem right. The paper was in columns and had no distinct paragraphs. I didn't worry too much about grammar or spelling except for the technical terms that the grader would be specifically looking for. So, in addition to knowing what a class wants out of its writing assignments, one must also know what writing style would be best suited for each particular assignment.

OUTSIDER: I guess we're just getting a string of examples. The student apparently figured out what the class wanted, but we don't know what the writer discovered. So there's something that's interesting here— what was discovered. . . . I'm real interested when the author says here, "I wrote with two totally different writing styles." This to me is a really striking thing. I wish at this point the person had accepted the challenge of this by trying to make this the thesis. He's apparently capable of writing in "two totally different writing styles!" This is a neat trick. Okay, so I'm looking forward to the explanation of how it was done.

SENIOR: I'm not exactly sure how it's going. . . . I'm disappointed. It picked up when he was using the description from the history class. But now I'm getting the feeling that it's just going to tie itself up into a confusing, generalized statement at the end. We haven't seen how this person changed their writing style, except for that one specific mention of the writing class. . . . I would be more interested in seeing if this helped the person to write in their history class, because it was the most effective example I've seen so far.

   I'm not sure in what way the paper is going to go, especially because it's obvious by the blank space that this is the last page, I'm not sure what the overall point is going to be.

OUTSIDER: *(Rereads the previous paragraph)* I don't know if this is exceptional or typical, or what the alternative is to "writing paragraphs" *(Laughs)*. . . . So apparently this person's idea of professional is doing it by some image of traditional correctness: spelling, grammar, punctuation, usage. *(Turns pages)* Okay, we don't know what the result is. I'm curious about that. Apparently this was tailored on an assumption that a writing class looks for correctness, so I'm a little disappointed there; it just seems conventional. An idea of style as correctness. Okay, now the second paper—getting the content right. Columns. Technical terms. Well, we get a kind of amorphous definition of "style." Apparently this switch means paying attention to style or paying no attention to style? I think . . . or minding your p's and q's for your English teacher and paying attention to the subject for another course?

These different writing styles for different classes and assignments can cause problems if we let ourselves get confused over which style to use.

OUTSIDER: We go back to this cop-out use of the term "different" style for "different" classes. Seems the writer really had his or her big chance there in the middle of the last paragraph. This to me is the center of this essay and the germ of a better or much more interesting one.

The best way to overcome this, for me at least, is to sit down before starting to write a paper and ask some key questions like "What class is the paper for?", "What does this class tend to look for in its writing assignments?", "What type of writing style does this particular assignment lend itself to?", and "In lieu of these things, what would be the best writing style to use for this paper?" If we ask ourselves these and other key questions before we start writing a paper it will become easier and easier to do well in each class, while staying away from the dreaded "C– more content needed."

> OUTSIDER: Well, the writer seems to have kind of a check list, so this is more interesting than I expected. And the writer closes with kind of a tip. There's one of those clever paragraph endings that have been useful for this student in high school. But the key to the paper is the penultimate paragraph, which is quite interesting.

The Outsider and the Senior show us two interested but demanding readers in the act of interpreting a text, revealing their own expectations, and moment-by-moment responses. The Instructor, as you might predict, shows us a reading shaped by a somewhat different set of goals. Her tone, as she made these two summative comments, was strongly positive.

> INSTRUCTOR: He's doing reasonably well in setting up that he is talking about different writing styles and supporting it by first giving the dichotomy of high school and college and then giving the dichotomy of different college classes. Those are strong organizational points that I would praise him for. He doesn't give the kinds of real specific details I would like to see him giving. And I would like to see some text references to the [assigned reading] or other appropriate text to support this.
>
> Here where he's talking about paragraph form, good grammar, good spelling, I would like him to talk more about what he means about worrying about paragraphs, worrying about grammar. The irony, of course, is that in this course spelling and grammar were not big focuses, but clearly in his mind they were big focuses, which is kind of interesting. In my mind this unit emphasized analyzing problems.

In addition to reading this text, I had asked the Instructor to comment on what she was looking for as an evaluator of these papers and what might of accounted for the grade (a C–), which seemed rather low given her positive reading of the paper's organization and support. As you may have noticed, Carter and Jennie never discussed criteria no. 2 in the assignment printed above, which was to use the assigned reading for the course. Although we know Carter had read the assigned chapter—it had, in fact, stimulated his thinking about writing styles—it did not appear to be a part of the meaning he represented to himself in planning or in the text. However, the instructor's expectations for this text were clearly shaped by all the criteria, including no. 2. When I asked her to comment on the major features that would determine the grade, she said:

> I had asked them to use [the assigned reading] very specifically and then to develop it with things from their own observations and own experiences.

At the end of the paper she remarks:

> I would tend to give more credit to overall organization. The support here is fairly sophisticated. The problem is, he didn't do the assignment; he doesn't relate it to the reading. That's enough to make a big difference to the grade. Like writing a great answer to the wrong question.

Her evaluation of another paper in the class offers a revealing contrast and an insight into the Instructor as a reader. Unlike Carter's, this paper relied very heavily on the source test. Here her comment was:

> There needs to be a point to all the things she is saying. I would be unhappy with this. Why are you using all these examples from the reading, what purpose do they serve, what point are you trying to get your reader to understand?

Like the other readers, the Instructor brought a number of expectations to these texts. Some expectations, like the use of sources, came from the goals she herself set for the assignment. But parts of her response show us that she was also reading like an average reader—trying to construct a meaningful, coherent statement connected in various ways to her own knowledge of the topic. Each of these readers appears to have constructed a somewhat different reading or representation of the meaning of this paper, picking different features as interesting and making different predictions about what could or should come next.

However, there are also some expectations and desires all three of these readers seem to share. They are looking for a purpose and a point which stands at the center of the piece. And they will keep trying to follow that point all the way through, expecting to tie each new paragraph to it. When they can't make the link, or when they get a "pointer" they can't interpret, they assume the writer has failed them. Although they are all constructing somewhat different patterns of meaning from this text, the structure of the text itself plays a very important role by prompting these readers to set up certain strong expectations. Perhaps it is not surprising, but these readers aren't at all willing to read pat or "obvious" statements. They expect the writer to tell them something interesting (even though they seem interested in many different possibilities). And they seem willing, even eager to learn. But at the same time, they all expect "interesting" ideas to be explained, supported by evidence, or developed with examples. It seems that having high expectations goes hand in hand with taking Carter seriously and enjoying his text.

In the chapters that follow, we will be looking at strategies that help you plan and generate your own sense of purpose and point, and to create a text that helps readers construct a coherent meaning in line with those purposes. We will look at ways to generate ideas, planning both alone and collaboratively, to organize a text with built-in cues to readers, and finally to evaluate your writing in terms of both the conventions of a given discourse, such as academic writing, and in terms of how particular readers might respond.

PROJECTS AND ASSIGNMENTS

1   One of the most common reasons for writing in academic and professional situations is to study a problem. Write a brief paper that lets you explore a problem or examine an issue that is relevant to you and other members of your discourse community. You may, like Carter, address the discourse community of college freshmen, or you may choose to speak to other readers. Like Carter, don't assume that you need to "solve" a problem, but use your writing to "find" a problem and describe the conflicts that are creating a problem for someone. Here is a checklist that will help you define a meaningful problem.

Checklist: Finding a Problem to Write About. Write a paper on a topic or problem of your own choice, using the following checklist to help you with the important process of problem *finding.*

☐ a. *What are the problems, issues, questions, and experiences I have been thinking about lately?* Don't wait for inspiration; begin with an active search of your own knowledge and experience. Some writers start with what is called a *felt difficult;* they look for ideas that trouble them, or for conflicts in their own mind or in their everyday experience. They look for the issues or controversies that keep coming up in course-related reading or in lectures and class discussions. Some writers keep a journal of interesting observations, experiences they have puzzled over, or mini-inspirations that might be interesting to develop. A good way to begin a search is to spend 10 minutes jotting down a list of "topics I have been thinking about lately" or "topics on which I am a (relative) expert." The underlying principle is to listen to what is going on in your own mind and to actively review your own knowledge. Then ask these potential problems to pass a test or two.

☐ b. *Is this problem worth analyzing—for me as the writer? Will writing this paper let me explore a question or conflict I see or think through an experience or issue I want to understand?* When writers ignore the goal of writing for themselves, they often start with enormous issues such as nuclear disarmament—problems on which they have limited inside information and an uncertain reason to write. They have a topic, but not a problem. Or they choose narrow practical problems they have already solved, such as, how can I budget my money over the next month? Practical problems can present an interesting puzzle, but who needs to resort to pondering, deep thinking, and/or writing to understand and solve them? Look for a problem that makes the time you put into writing personally worthwhile.

☐ c. *Do I have more than just one "good idea?"* Unless you plan to do research, don't be seduced by a single "good idea." Do you have enough information or experience to explore the problem—as you have defined it? If not, could you define the issue to fit what you really do know about?

☐ d. *Is my contribution to the conversation going to be meaningful to a real reader?* Remember, a "meaningful" contribution can be based on many things—on your personal experience, on having thought about a problem, or on having done some research. When writers ignore this test, they often write a clever, witty, "well-formed" essay, one that has a story line, or a gimmick, or which dutifully cranks out an introduction, three paragraphs, and a conclusion—but which simply fails to say anything interesting or significant that someone else might want to hear. This strategy also leads to papers on "significant topics" (more nuclear disarmament)—but in two pages what can you say on such topics that anyone would really want to read?

When writers forget the second half of this test (having a real reader in mind) they often sound as if they were writing to some imaginary reader/teacher who had a strange and perverse desire to read pompous, decorative essays built on grand generalizations and a staggering vocabulary. Forgetting that there is a real reader out there—a normally impatient and sensible person—can lead writers to produce a "well-crafted" but empty essay that no real reader would ever finish. The simple question, "Would I choose to read this to the end?" is a good test. If you wouldn't finish it, what are you assuming about the person who would?

2 Explore your own rhetorical situation. Choose a paper from another course or other piece of writing you have done recently (an application, a letter). Tell the story of that piece of writing, using the expanded circle in Figure 1–1 to describe your rhetorical situation. What social forces and conventions do you see working in the text; what influences can you infer? How did your own personal representation of meaning go beyond what you said in the text: what were your goals, your personal associations, your questions and problems? Describe yourself as a problem solver, thinking your way through this situation. Are you more aware of anything about this text or your writing strategies now than you were at the time? And then try to piece together what you know about how your reader(s) interpreted your text and why they saw it the way they did. In the end, reflect on the most interesting thing this story uncovered about you or your context.

3 Find an example of two people writing on the same topic, as in movie reviews, book reviews, or essays on a controversial subject. Discuss how two writers, looking at the same information, created different meanings and why.

4 You are a Rhetoric Detective. You have been assigned to compare the rhetorical situations of two different papers (such as the ones you examined in Projects 1 and 2). Were you part of different discourse communities as you wrote each one?

In writing your detective report, start with an overview of the case and your definition of the problem that you want to solve. In order to support your conclusion, draw on both your own intuition and the answers you get to the following *Discourse Community Checklist:*

☐ a. What was the writer's motive or purpose(s) in each document? (Why write?)

☐ b. What could the reader have expected to get by reading on? (Why read?)

☐ c. What discourse conventions did the writer use? (Why write it this way?) Does the text have any distinctive features that might reveal the conventions used in a given discourse community? These conventions can appear as global features, such as the sort of topic or organizing idea that appear to be suitable, or the kind of evidence and argument the writer uses, or the format and organization, or the voice and personal stance the writer takes, down to more local features of vocabulary, sentence style, and even punctuation.

☐ d. What was the context for each piece? (When, where, and why was it written; where was it sent, submitted, or published?)

5 Here is a more complicated Rhetoric Detection case. Take a controversial issue or problem (such as IQ testing, the effects of marijuana, or government loans to students) written up in a weekly news magazine. Then use the *New York Times Index* to locate a related news story in the *Times*. Finally, you can use the *Readers' Guide to Periodical Literature* or the *Social Sciences Index* to dig up your third piece of evidence—a more in-depth journal article on the same problem.

Were these three articles written to different discourse communities or not? What can you figure out about the expectations and conventions of the community(ies) you investigated? (Use the *Discourse Community Checklist* in Project 4 above to help you build your case and be sure to give a full citation of your sources—and any other informants—in the report.)

6 The Rhetoric Detective tests Carter's theory of what English teachers expect. In his paper, Carter offers us his theory of what was expected in his freshman composition course. Let us compare the representation he creates in his text (as we, of course, interpret it as readers) with some other possible representations we could build by reading these comments ourselves.

☐ a. Carter and the Instructor: How well does Carter's image of his writing class (and of what this instructor would expect) predict what she actually noticed as a reader? Where do they match; where do they differ? Once you have compared his interpretation of the "writing style required in his freshman course" with what the Instructor actually pays attention to, consider this question: Which force do you think had more influence on the representation he built, his reading of the current situation or his prior knowledge and assumptions about English?

☐ b. Carter's Text and Carter's Own process: In his text Carter offers us an image of the things writers in his Composition class must concentrate on. Now look back at the transcript of his planning session with Jennie. What does he, in fact, concentrate on in his own planning? How well does the representation of English class created in his text account for his own process?

7 A journal entry. As you work on your current assignment, take a close look at your process by jotting down notes as you are working and then developing your observations more fully in a journal. Pay special attention to how you carry out the separate activities of planning and getting ideas, drafting a text, and revising. Ask yourself, what was the most interesting feature of my own process?

IF YOU WOULD LIKE TO READ MORE

If you would like to read more about discourse communities and their expanded circles of influence, as well as the transitions people must make from home to high school to college, see:

Bartholomae, David. Inventing the university. In *When a Writer Can't Write: Studies in Writer's Block and Other Composing Problems,* edited by Mike Rose, 134–65. New York: Guilford Press, 1985. / Here is a revealing description of the expectations university faculty bring when they read and evaluate freshmen placement essays.

Flower, Linda. *The Construction of Negotiated Meaning: A Social Cognitive Theory of Writing.* Carbondale: Southern Illinois University Press, 1994. / This book uses the stories of Carter, Jennie their freshman classmates and a group of advanced writers to show the logic of learners as they negotiate the social and cognitive process of taking literate action.

Flower, Linda, Victoria Stein, John Ackerman, Margaret Kantz, Kathleen McCormick, and Wayne Peck. *Reading-to-Write: Exploring a Cognitive and Social Process.* New York: Oxford University Press, 1990. / This close look at a group of college freshmen—as they are writing in the dorm or reflecting on their own decisions—reveals some striking differences in the ways these writers represented a standard college assignment to themselves.

Heath, Shirley B. *Ways with Words: Language, Life, and Work in Communities.* Cambridge, England: Cambridge University Press, 1983. / This ethnographic account shows the ways children grow up using language in three neighboring social and economic communities.

Rose, Mike. *Lives on the Boundary: The Struggles and Achievements of America's Underprepared.* New York: Free Press, 1989. / Rose's own story as both a university teacher and an underprepared student himself shows what it can mean to enter an intimidating but liberating new discourse community.

chapter two

Understanding Your Own Writing Process

For some reason, many common expressions about writing make it sound like a pretty clean-cut, no-nonsense business. All you really have to do, they suggest, is "find a topic, decide what you want to say," and then, depending on which cliché you prefer, you "write it up, write it down, express yourself, say what you mean, put it in words, and/or polish your prose." Yet all of these common descriptions, which make writing seem fairly straightforward, fail to account for the sudden bursts of insight writing can bring, just as they fail to explain why sometimes the words don't come—even on a topic you know. Or why you may have to sit and mull over a paragraph for half an hour at a time.

Some people, when they find that words don't "flow," assume that they have a unique and personal problem: "they don't have a flair for writing, can't spell, don't have a big enough vocabulary, forget grammar." The problem, however, is really with their theory about the writing process. They are expecting the wrong things. The straightforward "put your thoughts into words" theory may capture what writing felt like on Monday, but it fails to mention that on Tuesday it can be a slow, perplexing journey as you try to follow out your ideas. Then on Wednesday it can be like getting to the top of a mountain and finally seeing the whole issue with a new understanding. Composing is like any kind of satisfying mental work: Some days it is hard, some days it is exhilarating, and some days it is simply fun. This means it is neither a dark mystery nor a task that should be simple. Writing is, itself, a thinking process. Choosing how you conduct this process is up to you.

Naturally, some of the writing people do is as simple as jotting down a note or writing in a diary. You don't need a book on writing to help you do that. The writing process I want to talk about is the process behind the significant and potentially difficult writing we all do when we are trying to explain, understand, or argue and we want the reader to see things the way we do.

There are two things to understand about this composing process. One is that it often takes time and energy, because writing is a way of thinking things through. People sometimes hate to admit it, but even experts on a subject find that putting their knowledge into words and sentences forces them to be more explicit. And once their ideas are down in black and white, even experts find that their ideas haven't always passed the acid test of prose—they need to think a little more in order to get it right. So when the words that come out on the page aren't what you intended, don't assume that the problem is with your "writing." Your writing is only showing that you are still working, still thinking things through.

The second thing to understand about your own composing process is that, like any other process, from being a tutor to doing long-distance running, you can learn to observe your own process, to recognize your strategies, to monitor how the process is going, and to change it when you need to. In the next two sections we will look at two aspects of composing: the process of thinking things through and the strategies you use to do it.

THINKING THINGS THROUGH IN WRITING

Thinking takes many forms such as daydreaming, exploring memory, asking questions, memorizing, and problem solving. People turn to problem solving when they have a problem or a goal and they want to figure out how to solve their problem or get to their goal. Problem solving, then, is a form of goal-directed thinking. It is also one of the major thinking processes that helps us get through the day, solving problems such as deciding what to accomplish today, how to get the cat in, whether to get married, and what's the point of this chapter on economic patterns?

A problem is a situation that occurs when you are at Point A and you want to be at Point B and you are not sure how to get there. To solve a problem you must figure out how to get from where you are to where you want to be—how to reach your goals. In Chapter 8 we will look in more detail at how to write a formal problem analysis that puts this process into writing. But for now there are two major things to realize about problems:

1. Problems are only problems for somebody. That is, a problem exists only when you feel a conflict between where you are and where you want to be; that is, between your present state and your goals, or between your own goals. For example, choosing a college is a problem for you only if you feel you should decide on a sensible professional program but you really don't know which profession you would be good at and you feel much more at home at the low-key, but expensive, liberal arts college you visited. The conflicts among your own expectations, your limited knowledge about choices, your even more limited bank roll, and your goal of making an early decision are what make this a problem for you. The problem your parents, spouse, or banker perceive may be quite different. So remember, people define problems.

2. If you can define the problem, you may have solved it. The hardest part of solving many problems is trying to discover what the problem really is and define the conflict that makes it a problem. Writing is a powerful way to think problems through, because it helps you describe and name the conflicting parts of your own thinking. Consider, for example, the problem of trying to understand the point of your economics chapter. Like the college decision problem, your goal is to make sense out of a complicated body of information—in this case twenty pages of facts and figures. Your problem may be a practical difficulty—the chapter assumes a knowledgeable reader, but you don't know some of the major technical terms. Or it may simply be the common problem every reader faces: you must turn those twenty pages of text into a private mental summary of the key ideas and their connections. Or you may pinpoint a problem in your own understanding: You discover, for instance, that you know that two key points are indeed related—the rate of inflation "affects" interest rates—but you realize you don't know how.

Obviously, a clear sense of the particular problem this economics chapter creates for you would make you a better reader by focusing your attention on key issues. Writing is an extension of this defining and focusing process. If you were to write a paper on choosing a college or on economic pattern, the act of writing would, itself, be the act of taking a complex problem and thinking it through. Your writing would be an attempt to find the key issues and make sense out of what you know. In addition, it might clarify your thinking and help you solve the original problem.

WRITING AS A STRATEGIC PROCESS

If writing is a thinking process, what actually happens when you write? Sometimes this question is hard to answer. The writing process, like any other thinking process, has a way of going underground. We can struggle, ponder, write and rewrite for two hours running, then emerge with one page of text in hand and have almost no recollection of what we did all that time. And yet, during those two hours we were not passively waiting for words to come. Instead, we were actively carrying out a whole repertory of thinking processes such as planning, setting goals, generating new ideas, drawing inferences from old ideas, looking for relationships or patterns, creating trial text, evaluating our prose, detecting errors, and diagnosing problems and planning ways around them.

As transcripts of writers thinking aloud show us, much of this process is quite conscious at the time. Writers are constantly giving themselves instructions for how to write and what to do and then monitoring how well their current effort is going. Yet if writing is such a strategic process, why do people often remember so little of it? One reason is that, like all problem solvers, they are absorbed in reaching their goal—in this case in generating things to say. Once that goal is reached, people remember the result but not the process that got them there. Consider, for example all the decisions you make when you are choosing what to order at a restaurant: how much will it cost, when did I last have squid, will it really be fresh in Omaha in December, and how will Aunt Cory react if I do? Yet this complex process of comparing, inferring, evaluating, and appetite testing quickly drops out of memory once the job is done. We could have expressed what we were doing at the time if anyone had cared to ask, but once the task is done, the efficient thing is to remember our order but wipe the details about our decision process off the slate of our working memory.

A second reason people are vague about their own writing process is that they notice the obvious outward events, such as starting to write at midnight, drinking a whole pot of coffee, and pacing the room, but they don't pay much attention to their own inner, mental actions. A writer who spends 15 minutes in a fruitless search for the "right" words is so preoccupied with her goal that she may be giving only a tiny portion of her attention to observing her own strategies and to noting how well they are (or aren't) working. However, being aware of your own composing process and the strategies you use can give you the enormous power of conscious choice—the power to guide, test, and alter your own problem-solving process.

The following transcript shows a writer thinking aloud as she works. Thoughts that are attempts to produce trial sentences are underlined. The rest of her thoughts are devoted to either planning or revising. In parentheses, I have noted some of her basic strategies as they occur. This junior in college is applying for a scholarship that would allow her to spend a month during the summer doing creative writing. Her general plan at this point (after about 10 minutes of work) is to convince the judges that "the way to learn is by doing."

TRANSCRIPT OF A WRITER THINKING ALOUD

. . . Um . . . and so maybe as a writer I don't need . . . to go to classes and have to hack out stuff that won't help me in my development as a writer. (Generating ideas) What I do need . . . I'm just thinking that that's the angle that's coming out (Monitoring and evaluating ideas), that um . . . it's the same old story about I am an artist so help me, feed me, pay me money so I can create and work. (laughs) (Drawing an inference and evaluating) I think. Umm . . . What I do need to say (Sets a goal) . . . I need to be allowed to develop on my own. (Writes text) and to go . . . For some reason, right when I started to write "develop on my own" I thought of Star Trek. The Star Trek Convention just popped into my head (Making associations) and um . . . that reminds me that one of the things I am interested in is . . . finding

out exactly why stuff like that pops into your head. (Generating ideas) I'm thinking this is a good idea and I should get it down. (Monitoring process and setting a process goal) What are the cues that stimulate a person to re-member something? (Generating ideas) How can I put this for those ladies in the pink hats? (Trying to set a goal) Ladies' Club women, want to give a scholarship . . . (Analyzing audience) O.K., the point is I want to learn as a writer how to go looking for those cues in the right place. (Writing trial text) How does that fit in? (Evaluating and trying to organize ideas) Let's see. Well, that's a kind of creativity and you sure have to learn that one on your own. (Drawing an inference; generating ideas) Maybe I should emphasize that instead. (Diagnosing and setting a goal) Like all writers I need to learn to find those cues on my own. (Revising text) O.K., now where am I . . .

As you can see, this writer is not merely turning out sentences; she is rapidly generating ideas, making associations, throwing up trial sentences, evaluating, diagnosing, and guiding her own process. Writing is a mental three-ring circus.

Common Problems

In the rest of this chapter we will look at some common problems writers have as they compose, and then at ways you can track and understand more about your own personal writing process. If your composing process runs into difficulty from time to time, you may be in good company. Here are some of the more common process problems people share:

1. I like to build on a draft, but I can never get started.
2. I can get started, but I just keep starting and throwing it away. I can't build on a draft.
3. The first part comes quickly, but then I dry up. I don't know what to do when that happens.
4. I can't write more than a two- or three-page paper. Once I've said it, I'm done.
5. I often think of good things to say but forget them by the time I sit down to write.
6. I often like my papers—they say what I want to say. But the teacher doesn't like them and I don't know why.
7. I feel that I can't judge whether what I have written is any good. I have actually worried myself into writer's block from the uncertainty.
8. In high school (a previous course, my last job) I got very good at doing one kind of writing (such as personal, expressive writ-ing, five-paragraph themes, or even well-packaged hot air). Suddenly I find that what I know how to do doesn't work any-more and I don't really know how to do what is being asked for

now (such as analyzing an issue, defending a thesis, or writing to an editor's specs).

A lot of these difficulties point to strategic problems—and to the need for a larger set of alternative strategies for reaching goals. Over the years, people sometimes build up a set of rituals—some magic patterns that "worked" in the past and then grow into rigid rules for how to write. When I was in high school I developed a ritual for writing book reports: I saved the final page of the book to read just before I was about to write. Then I sat down and wrote the whole thing in one flash of inspiration and understanding just before it was due. I guess I was lucky; my ritual made life exciting, and it often worked for high school book reports. But it didn't transfer very well to writing research papers. For one thing, it gave me no time to mull things over or to write a draft and revise. If inspiration didn't strike when I sat down "to write the paper," I was stuck. And even when it did, in its fashion, I was always surprised that the writing took longer than I had planned, and once again my paper was late. My ritual of one-draft inspirations had worked so well before that it took me quite a while to realize that it simply didn't transfer to this new, more demanding task. I needed thinking strategies, not magic rituals.

Of course sometimes rituals can be very effective—especially ones such as setting aside time and creating an atmosphere that says "I am going to concentrate." On the other hand, it often seems to me that some popular composing rituals, such as writing in bed, having the TV or stereo on, or writing on the bus at night, are either plainly counterproductive or are proof of the writer's extraordinary ability to write in spite of his or her own rituals. Rituals are often external props. The strategies we will look at now are internal, optional thinking techniques for getting to a goal.

We will now look at two practical problems: the problem of getting stated and the problem of getting stopped, or temporary writer's block. If you have trouble getting started, if you depend heavily on inspiration or the threat of deadlines to motivate you, or if the idea of having to write makes you anxious and you try to avoid it, this discussion should be of some help to you.

GETTING STARTED

Nearly everybody has trouble getting started. Some people procrastinate as far from pen and paper as possible; others sit and stare at a blank page. Getting started is a common problem because it is not simply a question of ability (even good writers have difficulty getting started) or of knowledge about the subject (experts with a lot to say have trouble, too). Getting started is often a strategy problem directly related to how you tackle the task.

Let us look at the thinking process of a writer who is trying to begin a paper. What are some of the strategies and goals this writer seems to have? How well do they work?

TRANSCRIPT OF A WRITER THINKING ALOUD

Trial and error

My name is Jo Banta. I'm trying to write a paper on writer's block. In today's world . . . for today's student, writer's block is a matter of great concern . . . of universal concern. In today's high-pressure education, writer's block is a question that plagues many students. . . . In today's high-pressure education. . . . In the high-pressure education of today, writer's block is a problem of great, of universal concern that plagues. . . . In high-pressure education, writer's block is a matter of almost universal concern. . . . In high-pressure education of today, one problem that plagues many students is. . . .

Perfect-draft block

This is a problem because. . . . Writer's block is a problem because. . . . Due to the phenomenon of writer's block. . . . Because of its omnipresence, many writers fail to hand in assignments on time and thereby lose, . . . and they thereby receive, . . . they get lower grades. Because of the omnipresence, because of writer's block . . . oh what the hell do I know about writer's block. I think Im having it! How can I write about writer's block when I'm in the middle of it!! What an awful assignment. Wonder what dinner will be tonight. Boy, that window's dirty.

O.K., writer's block. . . .

Waiting for inspiration

Words looking for an idea

Brainstorming

Writer's block . . . maybe something will come. Just think about it a while. . . . Although many people fail to recognize it . . . Although. . . . Although what!? I don't know! Oh well. . . . Although many people don't know, don't recognize it, one of the most important determinants of students' grades is . . . is . . . what? O.K. Try again. . . . Not only is writer's block one of the most important, but . . . but . . . but. This is crazy. I'm getting nowhere writing sentences. . . . Let's see, what do I really know about writer's block? Sometimes I get it when I don't know what I'm talking about. Maybe because I don't have anything to say yet. But sometimes I get it when I do know a lot, when there's a lot of pressure, and I've got to turn a paper out, and I want it to be really good, and sound like I've got things covered. . . . All right, writer's block is a universal . . . universal problem for students when under conditions of pressure . . . a universal situation in which students placed under pressures of today's university . . . oh, here I go again . . . what

WIRMI

I really mean is . . . writer's block is a problem for students who have good ideas but can't express them because of . . . O.K., what are my choices . . . because of the

Notation

{
environment
education pressure
pressure of time and grades
limits of time and the pressure of grades

Satisficing   *That's not perfect, but I'll just bracket it as a problem and go on. It's always easier to make those decisions as an editor instead of when you're generat-*
Brainstorming   *ing. O.K., now I haven't done much brainstorming yet, so let's see if I can map out what I do know and what I'll want to think about. It's time to brainstorm. What is a block?*

Notation

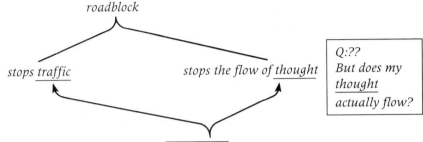

Does writer's block stop | something | *from coming out?*
That assumes that the "something" is already there.
Is it? That's a distinction I might play with. How about writer's blank?

Weak Strategies

The above transcription of a writer's thoughts demonstrates four composing strategies that often cause trouble for writers:

1. *A trial-and-error approach to producing sentences.* One of the first things we notice in this transcript is the almost random way the writer keeps trying to combine words and phrases in the hope that one version will finally sound acceptable. In working out her first major thought, she is trying out six alternative phrasings:

in today's world   *a matter of*
for today's student   *a question that*
in today's high-pressure education   *a problem of*

These trial-and-error stabs at producing sentences often produce only confusion, because in trying to juggle so many alternatives and keep them all in mind at once, the writer is likely to overload her short-term memory. The capacity of human short-term memory— what we might call our conscious attention span—is rather limited. That is why people often fail at tasks such as trying to listen to two conversations and think of something to say at the same time. Because we can consider only a few separate elements at one time (some say the limit is seven elements, plus or minus two), we are unable to simultaneously consider all the alternative versions of a sentence and make an efficient choice. So we keep reviewing the options. This writer's performance is also characteristic of trial and error in that she often loses track of her search and continues to re-produce previously rejected versions.

A trial-and-error strategy is not only confusing, it's slow. Say our writer had continued to hammer away at this one sentence alone, juggling its mere two sets of alternatives. There are at least 104 possible combinations and grammatical transformations—including passive, negative, declarative, interrogative, and so forth—that she might conceivably have had to try! Clearly, one of the first strategies a writer needs is a way to narrow this enormous field of options—of all the possible things one could say—down to a set of things one would want to say.

2. *A perfect-draft strategy.* Here the writer starts at the beginning and writes a perfected final draft in one slow, laborious pass-through. Looking at the first paragraph as a whole, we see that instead of planning, jotting notes, or defining her goals, the writer has started out by trying to produce a perfect set of sentences. She is trying to generate her ideas and language in the flowing sequence of a finished text. The form of the final product is dictating the form of her mental process.

As inefficient as this strategy is, many people depend on it—spending hours trying to perfect their first paragraph or first page. Once they have sweated out that first paragraph, the rest of the paper does indeed come more easily. But why? It is because, in the act of writing those introductory sentences, they have also been planning the point and the organization of the entire paper. As if planning one's ideas wasn't hard enough, these writers are also trying to produce perfect sentences, create just the right tone, and make smooth connections between all their points. All of these things must eventually be done, but a perfect-draft strategy tries to do all of them at once. By jumping into producing finished prose before deciding what they want to say, such writers are unlikely to do either task well. They give themselves their own writer's block.

3. *Waiting for inspiration.* Some writers wait until they see the whole piece clearly in their mind or until words and sentences start "flowing" and they know just what they want to say. This is a chancy but well-known strategy that will be discussed in more detail later.

4. *Words looking for an idea.* The writer is still focusing her attention on producing sentences. In the second paragraph the expressions "Although . . . ," "is . . . ," "Not only . . . , but . . ." sound promising, until the writer discovers she has no ideas to fill in the slots. She has let the momentum of language itself direct composition and lead her down the garden path.

Powerful Strategies

One of the advantages of this simulated transcript is that our writer can suddenly turn very obliging and clever. Once she realizes that the perfect-draft approach isn't working, she switches tactics and demonstrates a set of more powerful strategies that do work. Here are a few:

1. *Brainstorming.* Instead of producing perfect sentences, the writer concentrates on her ideas, jotting thoughts in whatever order they come to her.

2. *Using WIRMI.* WIRMI is a strategy for getting yourself to make a clear and concise statement of your point whenever you find yourself bogged down in trying to perfect a sentence. Simply say to yourself, *What I Really Mean Is* . . . and switch from writing prose to "talking to yourself." Just say what you think, then perfect the prose later.

3. *Using notation techniques.* In trying to write a sentence or get an idea clear, it often helps to get it down on paper so you can work with it visually, not just in your head. For example, it helps to write alternative phrasings under one another, or to use more exotic displays of relationships—flow charts, trees, brackets, boxes, arrows, and so forth. If you don't write down fragments and phrases as they come to you, you are likely either to lose them or to find yourself reproducing them over and over. But to take maximum advantage of your notations and visual displays, you must also leave room to rewrite and make changes on your draft. That means skipping lines and leaving generous margins. Your goal here is to ease the load on your limited short-term memory and let yourself write and edit rather than juggle alternatives in your head.

4. *Satisficing.* When you are writing a first draft it is often useful to accept an adequate, but imperfect, expression or idea in order to get on with more important problems. People have coined a rather odd but very useful word for this notion, which is "to satisfice." Problem-solvers satisfice, as it is called, when they take the first acceptable solution or alternative instead of searching for the very best one. People satisfice very day (to the relief of grocers) when they take the first acceptable peach at the fruit stall instead of rummaging through the entire bin for the very best one. And writers satisfice when they decide to write now and revise later. Things that are impossible to solve in the middle of composing often become simple when you are editing. So satisficing on a first draft can let you make the best use of your time.

❧ GETTING STOPPED AND WRITING UNDER PRESSURE

Most of us write under pressure, whether it's the pressure of deadlines, grades, critical readers, or our own expectations. Some amount of pressure is a good source of motivation. But when worry or the desire to perform well is too great, it creates an additional task of coping with anxiety. When it comes to writing, some people are automatically so anxious that they can't get started, or they avoid the prospect at all costs by looking for courses and jobs that don't require writing.

These are the extreme cases. For most of us, getting stopped or having writer's block is a temporary condition. It comes at the end of a train of thought when we suddenly find ourselves unsure of what to do next, or when words refuse to fall into sentences and we are left stranded in midphrase.

The causes of writer's block vary. Although external forces such as a deadline often create pressure, it is internal forces that produce anxiety and writer's block. In other words, writer's block is an obstacle that writers throw in their own path. Two ways they commonly do this are by having an overly critical Internal Editor or by depending on an inefficient composing method.

People who write well or who wish they did are often their own worst enemy. Their success or failure in the past leads them to set extraordinarily high expectations: "This paper (which really means 'I,' the writer) must be brilliant, creative, original, or beyond criticism." High standards are a good idea (many writers could improve their performance substantially if they bothered or dared to reread and revise). But *unrealistic* expectations often produce nothing more than anxiety.

Here then is the problem. A writer who demands good results can demand them at the wrong time. He or she often sets up a highly critical Internal Editor who pounces on every scrap as it's written, rejecting the writer's half-formed thoughts because they are disorganized or don't sound like a polished piece of writing. Unfortunately, few papers, even good ones, emerge from the writer's mind in their full glory and polished form. Instead they come out in bits and pieces, in stray thoughts that later become important, and in tentative, disorganized sentences. When such unrealistic expectations set up a severe internal critic, this watchdog stops the thinking process before it starts, and the writer ends up with a series of false starts and crumpled, rejected drafts.

Why do writers do this to themselves? What leads them to expect their thoughts to flow out in polished, finished prose? The answer often lies in the assumptions they make about their composing process.

ALTERNATIVE COMPOSING METHODS

Let us look at the advantages and limitations of three major approaches to writing: the perfect-draft, inspiration, and problem-solving approaches.

The Perfect-Draft Approach

As noted earlier, this method, which attempts to produce a paper in one pass-through, can be efficient if it works. But if your ideas are not fully formed and you need to concentrate on purpose, content, or organization, it makes little sense to try to juggle the demands of polished prose at the same time.

The Inspiration Method

When we feel inspired, writing seems easy and exciting. The words seem to flow unbidden and the first draft is the final one. Unfortunately, muses are notoriously unreliable, and this makes inspiration a very poor choice as a standard composing method. Yet many people assume that it is the *only* method open to them if they want to produce a really good piece of writing. The perfect-draft approach and steady work can always turn out words on a page, but good writing comes when, and only when, the writer finally gets his or her "inspiration." Or so the myth goes.

One of the best descriptions of the myth of inspiration comes from poet Samuel Taylor Coleridge's account of how he came to compose his famous, mysterious poem *Kubla Khan*. You may think that the creative process of a major poet has little to do with normal expository writing, but, in fact, the exploits of heroes and artists are often the source of popular myths that tell us how the experience *should* be.

In his account Coleridge says that he had been reading a book called *Purchas's Pilgrimage*, a fabulous account of the marvels seen on seventeenth-century voyages of exploration. He had been taking opium, which he tells us was, of course, prescribed by his doctor. When he woke up, he began his poem with these words:

> In Xanadu did Kubla Khan
> A stately pleasure-dome decree:
> Where Alph, the sacred river, ran
> Through caverns measureless to man
> Down to a sunless sea.

Writing about this experience, and referring to himself in the third person, Coleridge says:

> . . . he fell asleep in his chair at the moment that he was reading the following sentence, or words of the same substance, in *Purchas's Pilgrimage:* "Here the Khan Kubla commanded a palace to be built and a stately garden thereunto. And thus ten miles of fertile ground were inclosed with a wall."

> 1. The Author continued for about three hours in a profound sleep, at least of the external senses, during which time he has the most vivid confidence, that he could not have composed less than from two

2. to three hundred lines: if that indeed can be called composition in which all the images rose up before him as things, with a parallel
3. production of the correspondent expressions, without any sensation or consciousness of effort. On awaking he appeared to himself to have a distinct recollection of the whole, and taking his pen, ink, and paper, instantly and eagerly wrote down the lines that are here preserved. At this moment he was unfortunately called out by a person on business from Porlock, and detained by him above an hour, and on his return to his room, found, to his no small surprise and mortifica-
4. tion, that though he still retained some vague and dim recollection of the general purport of the vision, yet with the exception of some eight or ten scattered lines and images, all the rest had passed away like the images on the surface of a stream into which a stone has been cast, but, alas! without the after restoration of the latter!

Coleridge's account of his experience contains four major elements of the myth of inspiration. This myth becomes a problem when people see it as a description of how the writing process *should* work. In the myth,

1. The vision comes to the writer in sleep. In other words, there is no conscious effort, no preparation or planning, no thinking.
2. The writer's inspiration or vision comes complete and fully assembled. He does not simply have an intuition or an idea that must then be developed; the state of inspiration reveals a "whole" product, in this case two or three hundred lines that we can assume will not have to be revised.
3. The act of composition itself is not the time-consuming task of testing and modifying alternatives. Instead, the author merely remembers and preserves the content of the dream or vision. This is appropriate because inspiration is often seen as a gift from the gods. Naturally you wouldn't expect such a gift to come only half-written. Moses received the Ten Commandments written on tablets of stone. Athena, the Greek goddess of wisdom, science, and the arts, and an appropriate emblem for creative thought, was said to have sprung fully armed from the head of Zeus. These elements of the myth of inspiration are old and well established.
4. The final element of this myth is the most critical one for us. Because the stuff of inspiration is, in a sense, a gift from the gods that appears without conscious effort, it cannot be duplicated or repeated. Once interrupted by a gentleman from Porlock, the vision will be lost forever. Like that proverbial "bolt from the blue," our ideas come from outside instead of from our own efforts to assemble our knowledge into new insights. These elements of the myth of inspiration suggest that writers are passive recipients of visions and that the creative process is a mixture of waiting and luck. Fortunately that's just not true. Although the myth describes the way it often *feels* to create something, it isn't particularly accurate about

what actually happens. The magic of inspiration is the magic of a mind hard at work. For example, literary sleuth John Livingston Lowes has shown how the images of *Kubla Khan* had their source in Coleridge's wide reading. Coleridge's combination and translation of these images were unique—a creative act—but the raw material of the creative process was the knowledge stored in his own mind.

If the myth of inspiration is neither a particularly accurate nor helpful model for the creative process, is there a better one that can also include the subjective experience of inspiration we've all felt? In *The Art of Thought* (1926), Graham Wallas showed that inspiration, or "illumination," is merely the third stage in a four-stage creative process:

1. *Preparation* is the first stage. "Chance," Pasteur said, "favors the prepared mind." This is a mind that has read, thought, and worked on the problem. Sometimes this stage can last for years.

2. *Incubation* is a second, little understood stage. No one knows quite what happens or why, but in periods of rest when the problem is not being actively considered, new combinations are formed, new ideas generated.

3. *Illumination,* the third stage, is simply the result of the previous two, but it is the stage that gets all the press. This may be a dramatic moment, or alternatively a quiet one, when preparation and thought pay off and you see your solution, an image of what you want to do. Unfortunately, most illuminations don't spring from the mind as fully armed Athenas or as completely written texts. What we usually "see" is only a plan or a sketch of what the solution might be. This leads to the next step.

4. *Verification* is the working out of the solution. For writers, this is often the complex and lengthy process of making language say exactly what they want it to say and making sure it says it to readers as well as to themselves. Any approach to composing, then, should recognize all four of these processes, not just the moment of illumination.

A Problem-Solving Approach to Composing

A problem-solving approach to writing differs from the perfect-draft and inspiration methods in two ways. It stresses a goal-directed kind of thinking, and it often draws on a variety of strategies (also known as *heuristics*) to achieve its end.

It may seem odd to think of writing as a "problem" with a "solution," since we often apply those terms to situations for which a precise solution *procedure* is already known, as it is in algebra. A problem, however, is simply any situation in which you are at point A and need to find some way to get to your goal, point B. Problem solving is the act of getting there, of achieving goals.

What sort of problem-solving approaches do you use when you write? Generally speaking, writers have three alternative ways to proceed. They can use (1) rules, (2) trial and error, or (3) heuristics:

1. *Using rules.* Rules tell you exactly what to do when. If you know the time and the rate, you can compute distance by using the rule $T \times R = D$. In grade school many of us learned rules for writing: State your topic; make three main points about it; develop each point in three separate paragraphs, each of which has a topic sentence; then write a conclusion.

The virtue of rules is that they are explicit; anybody can follow them. Their weakness is that they are simple-minded and are inadequate for more complex problems such as solving our energy crisis, fixing a car that won't start, or writing a report on either of these.

2. *Using trial and error.* People like to use trial and error because it seems like a comfortable way to proceed. You don't have to plan or study the problem; you just start writing and see how it turns out. When the problem is small (for example, writing a note to leave on the refrigerator) or the problem solver is lucky, trial and error is efficient. But as we saw in the transcript on pages 45–46, this haphazard method can waste a lot of time if there are too many alternatives.

If your car wouldn't start and you began a systematic trial-and-error search of its 6,000 parts, you would, on the average, have twiddled 3,000 screws, plugs, and wires before you found the trouble. Proceeding without a plan can be easy, but expensive in terms of time.

3. *Using heuristics.* Heuristics—that is, efficient strategies or discovery procedures—are the heart of problem solving. Some of them are nothing more than small rules of thumb that say "try this first" and cut down the number of alternatives you must consider. They reduce the size of the problem. For example, in a typical chess game there are 10^{120} possible moves to make but only 10^{16} microseconds in a century in which to make them. So experts rely on a heuristic procedure such as "try to control the center with your pawn" instead of considering all the possible alternative moves.

Heuristics—or strategies, as I will be calling them—have another important feature. They are powerful; that is, they have a high probability of succeeding. For example, a good heuristic procedure for diagnosing a dead car is: first check the gas, then the battery, then the ignition. A powerful heuristic writers often use is "just try to jot down things without organizing them yet." The problem-solving strategies we will be looking at in this book are simply a set of heuristics or techniques that good writers rely on. Some of these strategies are as old as Aristotle's methods of forming comparisons. Some, such as brainstorming, come from the study of creative thinking done by scientists, inventors, and problem solvers in industry. And some come from recent studies of the thinking processes of writers themselves. In each of these cases, I have tried to translate a heuristic procedure that experts use into a practical strategy writers can learn.

Although heuristic procedures are powerful, they do not come with a guarantee. For example, many good tennis players rely on the following strategy: Try to make a hard, deep shot in order to get a soft return from your opponent, so you can then run up to the net and put the ball away. Unfortunately, as you are charging the net, your proponent might just hit a passing shot that goes right by you. Unlike a rule, which will always produce a "correct" answer if followed, a heuristic procedure is only a high-probability way to proceed, so a writer needs to know a variety of alternative techniques. However, for a complex problem such as writing, heuristics are the most dependable and most creative way to go.

One of the chief differences between good and poor writers, and good and poor problem solvers in general, is the repertory of strategies, or heuristics, on which they draw. Good writers not only have a large repertory of powerful strategies, but they have sufficient self-awareness of their own process to draw on these alternative techniques as they need them. In other words, they guide their own creative process. Although motivation, talent, or experience can strongly affect that process, it is a process writers *can* understand and change. The purpose of this book is to make the intuitive problem-solving process that good writers use more explicit and available to the rest of us.

Let us close this chapter, then, by applying a basic problem-solving principle to the problem of writing under pressure.

❦ PRACTICAL SUGGESTIONS FOR COPING WITH PRESSURE

When you have trouble with getting started or with getting stopped, the cause may lie in the strategy you have chosen. If you can't eliminate external pressure you can cope with it by changing your own writing method. The key is a basic problem-solving principle: Break the large, complex problem of writing down into a set of smaller subproblems that you can concentrate on one at a time.

First, instead of sitting down to produce a paper in its entirety, give yourself a subgoal or separate task such as brainstorming or writing an individual page or paragraph on a topic you are already clear about. It often helps to separate these tasks in time: Tell yourself, "All I have to do this morning is jot down my ideas and make a rough plan for the paper. I don't have to do any writing unless I want to."

By concentrating on a manageable subtask, and only a subtask, you often do it better, and ironically, when the pressure is off, you may find that the writing is no longer so hard to do. By setting up a limited and achievable subgoal, you can seduce yourself into starting to write.

A second way to reduce pressure and create manageable subgoals is to use a "write and revise" method. Plan your writing so you can write a reasonably efficient first draft and satisfice on those places that would slow you down. If you don't know how to spell a word, don't give it a second thought. Just write it down and keep on going. Should you use a colon or semicolon here? If you aren't sure, figure it out later. Make this first draft as coherent and clear as you can; where you need to stop and think about your meaning, do so. But don't get sidetracked into perfecting your prose. Instead, count on revision to be a major second step in your writing process. Give yourself the freedom to just write a working draft.

There are good reasons for doing this. First of all, the fact that it is only a rough draft reduces the extra, internal pressure that causes anxiety and writer's block. Secondly, a two-step process of writing and revising is a smart way to use your time. Many local problems that seem insurmountable when you are in the midst of composing are problems because you are still deciding where you want to go next. If you keep the larger picture in mind while writing, minor problems will fall into place when you later edit and revise.

As a general rule, if you find your writing process becoming inefficient or unproductive, that is a signal that you need to switch tactics and tackle the problem in a new way. The following chapters on steps and strategies in writing will offer you some concrete, alternative ways to proceed.

PROJECTS AND ASSIGNMENTS

1 A self-appraisal of your own writing process. This self-analysis asks you to do three things: first, to look at your own writing process as objectively as a musician, dancer, or athlete would look at his or her performance. What strategies do you typically rely on and how well do they usually work? Second, spend some time collecting data on yourself. What do you really do when trying to write? And finally, how does that compare to your image of what a good writer would do? Jot down your answers on a separate sheet.

a. What are the last four things you have written (excluding short notes), and who read them? We will refer to your writing here as a "paper," but it could have been a college composition, a letter, a memo, an announcement, a proposal, or a report. (In the questions that follow, whenever you find it difficult to decide what is typical for you, refer back to these four events as your norm.)

b. In general, how do you feel about writing?

rather enjoy it   neutral   dislike it

c. Do you find it easy to write papers that say what you wanted them to say? In practical terms, is writing a relatively efficient process for you in which your time is in proportion to your intentions?

d. How many hours did you spend writing (drafting, writing, revising) the last three papers you did? Give number of hours and number of pages written (excluding appendixes). Is this normal?

e. Do you generally try to write a piece in one sitting from the beginning, or do you work on sections separately and at various times?

f. Do you generally end up having to do the actual writing of papers under pressure—that is, under a tight time constraint?

g. When you think of having to write a paper, what are the main things that come to mind for you?

h. Are any of these problems ones you frequently have?

1. Getting started:
   Getting the whole paper ordered in your head before you write.
   Getting a beginning paragraph.
   Getting a first sentence.
   Sitting down to write.
   Turning on the flow of creative ideas.

2. Organizing what you know into a paper:
   Finding a main idea or thesis that fits in all the things you have to say.
   Turning an outline or sketch into a fleshed-out, proper paper with sentences and paragraphs.
   Turning lots of good ideas into an outline.
   Writing a formal paper when you know you could explain it easily if you could just talk to the person.

3. Writing for an audience:
   Knowing what your reader really wants.
   Finding that readers miss the important things you thought were clearly stated.
   Finding that, upon rereading your writing, you don't understand it in the same way you did when you wrote it.

4. Controlling the circumstances under which you write:
   Trying to concentrate with noise and activity around you (the TV, stereo, friends, family).
   Writing when you feel tired or sleepy instead of during the most alert part of your day.
   Being inadequately prepared (you haven't had time to think the problem through before you start to compose).
   Having no time (or less than a day) to let the paper sit between writing and editing it.

i. Do you have any rituals that help you get in the mood to write? Many people depend on private rituals that help them to get started and maintain their concentration as they write. The rituals can vary from mere sharpened pencils to special rooms, desks, or times of day set aside for writing. Some people set subgoals and give themselves rewards when they achieve them. Do you have any private rituals that help you get in a frame of mind to write? If so, jot them down.

j. Once you have completed questions A-I, read over your responses. Try to define as perceptively as you can three major problems you have in writing. Make your definitions as specific as possible. Now develop a practical plan for dealing with each of your problems the next time it comes up.

2 Thinking through a problem. Everyone talks about the problems of the freshman year in college: living in a dorm, adjusting to a new environment, handling academic pressure, learning to budget time. Take one of these problems (or one like it) that you know well and use your writing to think the problem through. What is the real issue—what made/makes this a problem for you? (You may also want to use this paper as an opportunity to study your own writing process.)

3 Experiment: Tracking your own composing process. What happens when you compose? What strategies do you use? To run this experiment on your own writing process, start by making some predictions you would like to test, such as

a. How do I allocate my time? How much goes to planning, to producing a draft or final text, to revising, to avoiding writing?

b. Could I accurately express my main ideas or conclusions at the beginning of writing? What do I learn by writing?

c. What kinds of revisions do I make? Do I fix errors, change ideas, improve organization?

d. What strategies do I use most frequently?

Then, use one of the following tracking techniques to answer your questions. Notice that these different methods tap your process at different levels. Choose the one that will tell you what you want to know.

1. *Thinking aloud.*

   Use either a tape recorder or a partner to observe you as you think aloud on a fresh writing problem. (Start taping as soon as you read the assignment if you want to study your planning strategies.) The only rule is to keep talking out loud. Say whatever is going through your mind, even if it is silly or off the subject. Writing is not always a very rational process. This method will give you the most detailed record of your own thinking. Notice that it does not ask you to think and talk about your writing process itself as you write. Devote all of your attention to the task and just talk aloud to yourself as you work.

2. *An introspective report.*

   Observe yourself composing, and stop from time to time to take notes and make comments on your process. Look for surprising turns, difficult moments, or decision points. This method will tend to interfere more with your process, since you will be trying to pay attention to both the task and yourself performing the task. But it can also lead to some surprising on-the-spot insights.

3. *A process log.*

   At various key points in your composing process—when you begin, when you are in trouble, and when you take a break—make notes about your process. Keep a log with columns for dates, times, what you did, and problems or comments. (See Chapter 13 for an example.) Fill it in anytime you work on the paper, even if you were thinking about it while walking home or talking with a friend. This method will give you a good record of how you spend your time and information about some of the key events over the entire course of writing.

4. *A retrospective account.*

Use a combination of any of these methods as your data, then look back over your composing process and construct a description of how it worked. Use as much factual data as you can, but try to make sense out of what happened and why. Write your account up as a thriller, an intellectual detective story, a sad moral tale, or a romance with a happy ending—whatever fits the data.

IF YOU WOULD LIKE TO READ MORE

If you want to know more about problem solving, creativity, and ways to explore your own writing process, see:

Elbow, Peter. *Writing Without Teachers.* London: Oxford, 1973. / This short and readable book has helped many people get over their worries about writing.

Hayes, John R. *Cognitive Psychology: Thinking and Creating.* Homewood, IL: Dorsey Press, 1978. / This highly readable book traces the history of modern psychology and how it has attempted to understand the mysterious processes of creative thinking. The book covers the major approaches, from introspection to computer simulation, and concludes with current research in cognitive psychology.

————. *The Complete Problem Solver.* Philadelphia: Franklin Institute Press, 1981. / This fascinating introduction to the art of problem solving puts theory and research to practical application. It discusses effective strategies for a wide range of intellectual and practical tasks, from planning to remembering information to decision making and creative thinking.

Koestler, Arthur. *The Act of Creation.* New York: Dell, 1967. / This classic combines a theory of creativity with hundreds of historical sketches and examples of both scientific and artistic creativity.

chapter three

Case Study:
A Personal Profile

In the following chapters we will be looking at nine goals in the composing process and at a variety of strategies for reaching these goals.

PLANNING
Goal 1: Explore the Rhetorical Problem
Goal 2: Make a Plan

GENERATING IDEAS IN WORDS
Goal 3: Generate New Ideas
Goal 4: Organize Your Ideas

DESIGNING FOR A READER
Goal 5: Know the Needs of Your Reader
Goal 6: Transform Writer-Based Prose into Reader-Based Prose

REVISING FOR EFFECTIVENESS
Goal 7: Review Your Paper and Your Purpose
Goal 8: Test and Edit Your Writing
Goal 9: Edit for Connections and Coherence

Each of these nine goals represents a step that you as a writer will need to take. However, these steps are unusual: Unlike stair steps that march straight from A to B, each of these steps may need to be taken over and over in the process of writing. A simple-minded model of the composing process might pretend that writing was a neat, orderly, straightforward set of steps like those in Figure 3–1.

By contrast, the normal process of a writer is not a linear march forward; it is recursive. That is, writers constantly move back and forth among different kinds of writing activities. For instance, in order to revise the wording of a sentence, they may suddenly find themselves going back to planning and asking, what do I really care about here? What *is* my point? Figure 3–2 shows a more realistic graph of what a writer was doing over a 10-minute period. In the circled area the writer was editing a passage he had just written when he realized that there was a gap in his argument. So he stopped editing and returned to serious planning, talked to his roommate, came up with some new ideas which he organized with the

FIGURE 3–1
A Simple-Minded Model of the Composing Process

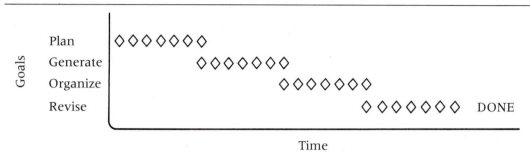

reader in mind, and then revised the whole passage and moved on, planning what he wanted to do next.

The following chapters will describe nine key goals or steps in the process of writing, but the way you move back and forth among them will depend on how your writing develops. Each chapter will offer you a number of strong, but optional, strategies writers use to reach those goals, such as strategies to help you plan more effectively, collaborate, generate better ideas, or revise for specific effects. These strategies, based on the effective strategies experienced writers use, can help you increase your repertoire of problem-solving skills for writing.

It is important to remember that these strategies are not rules or sure-fire formulas for writing. Instead they are simply an organized description of some of the things good writers normally do when they write. Many may be effective strategies you already use but didn't have a name for. Just to make this point more vivid, let us look at a case study of a real writer in action who uses many of the strategies we will discuss.

FIGURE 3–2
Model of a Normal Composing Process

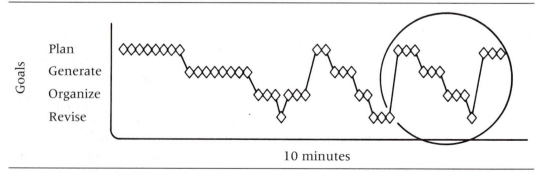

CASE STUDY OF JOAN

This short case study describes the experience of Joan, a real college student who has a writing problem: developing a personal essay for a scholarship application. The process of writing went on for nearly two weeks, from the time she started thinking about the essay until it was mailed. In this process she used a number of the writing strategies that will be discussed in the next few chapters. However, as you will see, she often used them without knowing that she was doing so, or in response to someone else's questions. This case study will let you see how individual techniques such as brainstorming or making analogies are often an instinctive part of the writing process. The only difference is that as a problem solver one has the power of conscious choice.

Joan is a junior in engineering at a large university. She is doing well in her courses, but her real career goal is medical engineering—she wants to combine research and working with people. A year in London would give her a firsthand experience of what medical research is really like before she has to specialize. But she can't afford to go to London on her own.

On day one her writing process starts with the decision to write her application. She has a strong desire to go to London and a good school record to back her up, but beyond that she doesn't know what to say. As a result, her writing process begins with a four-day wait for inspiration that doesn't come. On day five, with her deadline approaching, she sits down after dinner with the empty form, a pad of paper, and the TV, to write something anyway. By 12:30 A.M. there is nothing left to watch and she spends an hour and a half on the first draft.

In the hard light of the next morning the draft sounds alternately pompous ("I feel my achievements in scholastic and extracurricular activities will demonstrate my ability to take advantage of an educational opportunity of this sort. . . .") or it sounds young and naive ("The idea of spending a year at the University of London fulfills some of my oldest dreams. It is the kind of experience I most want. . . ."). The section on her courses and past activities was easier to write and sounded all right but was mostly a list and, she felt, rather dull. Whenever she thought of faculty members of a British university reading this humdrum essay, she felt depressed. There was no way of guessing what they were looking for.

At this point her writing plan had two main goals: to mention all the achievements she could think of and to make sure there were no errors in the essay. The first important change in her strategy came about on day six quite by chance when she stopped by to ask a professor to write a recommendation for her. Although Professor Harris wanted to write a good letter, she knew nothing about medical engineering or the school. She read Joan's first draft and began pressing Joan for information. Joan later said, "It was like being grilled; she was asking me all these questions I couldn't answer. And yet I kept thinking: How can I be applying to this place if I can't answer them?" Here is how their conversation went. The notes in italics refer to strategies you will find discussed in later chapters.

HARRIS: A great idea. Wish I could be in London, too. But now tell me, why do you want to go to this particular place rather than some other city? *(Setting goals)*

JOAN: Well, it's a great opportunity. And I've never been to England, and I'd just like to get out on my own. . . . Well, I guess they wouldn't care about that. Well, . . . it's a very good place to study medical research. . . . I don't know, . . . if you ask me point blank. Anyone would want to go.

HARRIS: Well I sympathize, especially with being on your own, but that hardly seems like a compelling reason for them to put up $5000 for you to study in London. So there's no particular reason. . . .

JOAN: Oh, but wait a minute. You don't see, there is. . . . You see, I want to prepare myself for a rather new field. There aren't many medical engineers yet. And it's important for people with an engineering background to understand what the real problems in medicine are—to really be up to date in medical research and know where technology can help. What's more, this will help me figure out where to specialize after I graduate. Unlike American schools, British schools use a tutorial system that could be tailored to my special interests. And this is the perfect time in my career to do it. You see, I've taken all these courses in preparation. . . . *(Brainstorming)*

Maybe I should put some of this in the essay. I didn't know about the scholarship until a week ago, but I've been preparing myself in a sense for something like this for three years. People think my course schedule is crazy—physiology next to fluid mechanics. But you have to know those things to design an artificial heart.

O.K. now. I guess I do have some sort of answer. I want to go because it would be the best place—I could explain why—to prepare myself for a career in medical technology. This is also the time when I most need to make the bridge to medical research, before I decide where to specialize. *(Stating in a nutshell)*

HARRIS: Sounds good. But if you don't mind my asking, why would they want *you* specifically? *(Simulating a reader's response)* What I want to do in my letter is support, wherever I can, the arguments you are making in your application.

JOAN: This is awful. There will be hundreds of people applying—and lots of people have good grades. I'm not even in medicine. I don't know why anyone would want to give money away anyway, especially to me.

HARRIS: Well, how about looking at it as an investment rather than a gift? What kind of an investment would you be likely to make? *(Thinking by analogy)*

JOAN: Well, if you put it that way, I guess I might really pay off. For one thing, I'm really committed to this. I can show it, too, with my courses and my summer job in the Chicago lab, and I've just finished a first-aid course. I really do care about people; I'm good at engineering, and I've been preparing for this special career for a long time. I guess it also matters that I work hard, not just in classes but on independent projects, too. That would matter a lot for this particular year. *(Brainstorming)*

HARRIS: I'm getting convinced. Maybe if you could just say some of *this* in the application? Somehow all this is more persuasive than your first-draft generalizations, which I'm afraid made me feel, "Ho hum, I've heard this before."

JOAN: Yes, except. . . . Well, I just realized that the real problem here is to convince them that they want to give this scholarship to somebody in engineering instead of medicine. I've got to show them that it's good for undergraduates like me to spend a year in a medical research school. *(Setting goals and subgoals for writing)* That's the real thing. Maybe if your letter could somehow show that I really can bridge that gap between technology and human concerns. Maybe you could mention the project I did. *(Creating a more operational definition of a goal)*

If it's O.K., I'd like to do another draft of this and bring it in on Wednesday. *(Setting a subgoal)* That'll still give me a few more days to sit on it before the deadline. *(Incubation)*

When Joan set out to write the final version, her plan and priorities had changed significantly. First, she had a better idea of what she wanted the essay to accomplish for her. And in this draft, that's all she chose to worry about; polishing could come later. In other words, she broke the large problem of "write this essay" down into a set of more manageable tasks. *(Setting subgoals.)* Since her father had asked a friend in the medical school to look over her draft, she tried writing it with him in mind, trying to anticipate his questions, such as "Do you know enough about medicine yet to benefit from a medical research program?" *(Talking to your reader.)*

According to Joan, this is the first time she had thought this much about her reader, and she was surprised to find out how well the approach worked. In the next two chapters we will pick up the rest of Joan's writing process, using some of her notes to illustrate writing strategies. The final version of her application follows. Notice how she has tried to use the ideas we saw her generating.

National Institute of Health Internship Program

PERSONAL ESSAY

My Purpose in Applying

I am applying for the University of London Internship Program in biomedical research because it would give me firsthand experience in medical research operations and the chance to learn scientific, communication, and personal skills not routinely encountered during an undergraduate education. Furthermore, it is unique opportunity to combine my interests in engineering and biological research and prepare me for a career in medical engineering. The following is a brief description of my education, experiences, and interests that contribute to my ability to take full advantage of this internship.

Academic Studies

As a result of my strong interest in science and math, I am presently completing a degree in engineering. However, I am doing this as part of a self-designed interdisciplinary program that combines engineering and medicine. This has enabled me to pursue my interests in the biological sciences and to gain analytical and problem-solving skills. In addition to studying chemistry, biology, physiology, and basic engineering sciences, such as thermodynamics and mechanics, I have elected engineering courses related to the biological sciences. For example, I am presently studying the electrical biophysics of muscle, nerve, and synapse and am taking a chemical engineering course in the dynamics of biological systems. This knowledge of both biology and engineering would aid me in understanding the scientific theories and techniques employed in biomedical engineering research.

Goals and Practical Experience

As a biomedical researcher, I would fulfill my goal of a career that will help other people while at the same time be challenging scientifically. I had exposure to research while doing a biochemical assay for a neuropsychopharmocologist at _____ Clinic in Chicago. Besides learning the scientific procedures and techniques that are used, I learned how to deal with some of the practical and organizational problems encountered in research. I saw how the lack of equipment and funds often calls for real cooperation between departments and careful planning of one's own project. The experience also helped me develop more of the patience research requires and recognize the enormous amounts of time, paperwork, and careful steps required for testing a hypothesis that is only one very small but necessary part of the overall project.

But besides knowing some of the frustrations, I also know that many medical advancements, such as the cardiac pacemaker, artificial limbs, and cures for diseases, exist and benefit many people because of the efforts of researchers. Therefore I would like to pursue my interest in research by participating in the NIH Internship Program. The exposure to many diverse projects, designed to better understand and improve the body's functioning, would help me to decide which areas of biomedical engineering to pursue. For example, I would be interested in projects emphasizing chemical, electrical, or mechanical knowledge; work performed on a cellular or macroscopic level; and work concerned with the design of machines and products or the discovery of new processes within the body.

Qualities and Skills

Although my academic program has been of central importance, it has not been of single importance. I feel I have learned many nonacademic skills and qualities necessary for research by participation outside of the classroom. My skills in organization and communication have been enhanced by planning programs, keeping records, writing letters, and working with people as an officer of Tau Beta Pi, the National Engineering Honor Society. I have gained leadership skills as a supervisor of a swim club, learned how to handle staff problems and emergency situations, and learned the importance of maintaining accurate and current financial records. I had to analyze problem situations, search for alternatives, make the best decision possible, and then accept and defend it until it was necessary to change. I feel I have learned self-discipline, motivation, and the value of goal-setting by participating for ten years on competitive swimming and basketball teams.

Summary

A scholarship to the NIH Internship Program would give me both new scientific knowledge and practical insight into biomedical research. In addition it would give me the opportunity, at the best time in my academic program, to wisely plan a career in medical technology. I feel that with this scholarship I could help engineering make a significant contribution to the field of medical research.

PROJECTS AND ASSIGNMENTS

1 You have decided to apply for a job, summer internship, or scholarship in your field of interest. As part of your application you have been asked to write a one- to two-page statement of your background *as it is related to* your career objectives, your interests, and your abilities. Since the reader will also have a copy of your résumé with the dates and facts, this statement, or personal profile, is to be your analysis of the meaning of those facts. Select a specific audience for this essay and write a profile that shows how your abilities fit the audience's needs.

You may wish to work on this assignment (and the following one) as you read the next three chapters. Therefore, for help in *planning* your paper, see Chapter 5; for help in *generating ideas*, see Chapter 6; and for help in *organizing ideas*, see Chapter 7.

2 *Checklist: Personal Profile.* The following checklist will help you judge how well you have met three important expectations readers bring to reading résumés and personal statements.

☐ a. *The goal statement.* This statement at the beginning of your profile should include a career or personal goal that is both true about you and relevant to your reader's goals. This statement and/or goal should also preview or tie together the abilities and qualities you later present in the profile.

☐ b. *Use of concepts.* Your task as a writer is to turn a set of facts (which might be listed in a résumé) into a set of qualities and abilities. This means that the profile should present a set of concepts supported by facts. In most cases this means that the topic sentence of each paragraph should contain a concept that ties together the information in the paragraph.

☐ c. *Structure of ideas.* The overall structure of the profile should be a hierarchy. At the top level should be a statement that combines your goals and your reader's concerns. The rest of the profile should support this organizing idea. Each paragraph should present a clear point you wish to make. Avoid writing merely an expanded, elaborated list of the things you have done.

3 Take one of your own abilities or strengths that you find important but difficult to explain. Set aside 15 minutes and begin writing. Free association, partial sentences, odd statements are fine—but keep writing. Get down everything that comes to mind about that ability. Then at the end of 15 minutes (you can go longer but not less), read your raw material. Try to sum up what you know about that ability now in one or two paragraphs. If you haven't said it all, try another 15-minute exploration.

4 If the place to which you are applying doesn't invite a personal statement, write a letter of application to accompany your résumé and adapt the checklist above to this shorter format. In addition to the standard features of a business letter (see your handbook), place a version of your goal statement in the first paragraph. Use the middle paragraphs to present a miniature profile or set of relevant concepts about yourself—help the reader interpret the facts of your résumé in the way you would, if asked. Use the final paragraph to politely request action and aid the reader in contacting you.

chapter four

Planning and Learning

What does it mean when a person says, "I know what I mean, but I can't say it in words"? What do you really "know" that you can't express? One answer is that you don't really "know" anything yet—all you have are vague intuitions or feelings, not actual ideas. Another equally extreme answer is that such intuitions and non-verbal knowing may be an even better, more profound kind of knowing than knowledge expressed in words. I want to offer you a third answer—one that is less evaluative, more descriptive. This answer says that "knowing" is an action, the act of representing information to yourself. And people's mental representation of information can take some dramatically different forms. For instance, some are verbal and some, such as knowing the feel of a good tennis swing, are not.

We often use metaphors to talk about this experience of having different kinds of knowing. For example, we say that people tap different "pockets" of knowledge or that they have notions in the "back of their mind." The underlying fact is that people *create internal, mental representations* of new information in order to remember it and think with it, and these inner representations can be both *verbal and nonverbal.* When it comes to writing, some of these mental images are easily translated into a verbal representation, but some are not.

A writer then is a little like a film director trying to create a scene. The director has built in his mind's eye a representation of that scene in the various languages of film. He can imagine the scene in terms of music, the script, the unstated theme or idea, and the film conventions it uses, as well as the physical and emotional presence of the actors, the sound of their voices, and the visual image created by lighting, staging, and cropping. The writer may find that she has an equal range of mental images in her mind's eye. Her job as a writer is to translate all these different ways of representing knowledge into prose. Her job becomes difficult when her initial representation is not as explicit or detailed as it needs to be to write prose.

Consider the nature of knowledge in this situation: You are walking through an open pine woods in Wyoming when above and behind you, you hear a faint, high scream that turns into a dark shape with spread wings diving through the trees in your direction. As the hawk pulls up, you see a nest in a tall lodgepole pine and a second hawk coming toward you from the right with a similar wonderful but ominous cry. You decide it would be wise to move on.

What do you know from this experience? How much of it is verbal? Back at home, with the help of your field guide, you find a name for this apparition, so you can now talk about seeing a red-tailed hawk, and you infer that there was a pair guarding a nest and that they were, indeed, speaking to you. But until you began to talk about this to yourself or to write it down, much of your knowledge was decidedly nonverbal: the shape of the bird and its wingspan, the arc and sound of its flight, the cry you described as a scream, the feeling of tension in your muscles, the shock running down your back, and that mixture of fear and elation you felt, even as you made sense of the event.

Looking back at your field guide you can see that the authors, Robbins, Bruun, and Zim, have had to struggle with the same problem of translating various kinds of knowing—visual, verbal, and emotional—into formal prose. Furthermore, assuming that one of them "knew hawks," he would have had to select (from all he knew) those features that his reader, wanting to identify birds, would need. A closer look at *Birds of North America* shows us how these writers tried to solve the problem of turning various kinds of verbal and nonverbal knowledge into the kind of written and pictorial representation you could print in a book.*

What does a hawk look like in the field? In Figure 4–1, these authors try to represent such information in three ways: One is verbal (a description of distinctive features), and the other two are visual (a series of paintings and a silhouette of the hawk among other birds). What does each representation accomplish for these writers?

What does a hawk look like? Notice how the authors give us two different kinds of visual information. The paintings are good for showing details of color, pattern, and age and sex differences. The silhouettes, however, are much better at expressing the hawk's relative size, shape, and posture. (Did the needs of the reader/user of this book influence these representations?)

How do you translate your knowledge of a sound into words? Robbins et al. try two ways: They give us a verbal description ("Call is a high scream . . .") and a visual one in the form of a sonagram— little squiggles on a graph showing changes in pitch and timbre over a 3-second period. Why? Finally, consider how you would present the years of data the U.S. Fish and Wildlife Service has collected on the location of these birds. Remember that this knowledge starts out as lists of individual sightings and counts at specific spots across

---

*Chandler S. Robbins, Bertel Bruun, and Herbert S. Zim, *Birds of North America* (Racine, WI: Western Publishing, 1966), pp. 70–71.

FIGURE 4–1
Different Ways of Knowing and Representing Hawks

(a) Verbal Description: A well-known and common buteo [note the author's use of the Latin genus name for hawk]; nests in woodlands and feeds in open country. The uniformly colored tail of the adult—reddish above, light pink beneath—and the dark belly band are the best field marks.... Body is heavier than other buteos', plumage extremely variable. Flying head-on, light wrist area gives impression of a pair of "headlights." Often perches on poles or treetops, rarely hovers.

(b) Visual Representation: Painting

(c) Visual Representation: Silhouette

(d) Verbal Description of Sound: "Call is a high scream, often imitated by jays."

(e) Visual Representation of Sound: Sonagram of red-tailed hawk

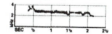

(f) Visual Representation of Range: Map

North America. Robbins et al. solve this problem by translating that information into a map using colors, shading, and lines to show summer, winter, and migratory ranges.

A book like this field guide shows us how writers must often struggle to represent their full knowledge in words. And in some cases, nonverbal representations such as silhouettes are more effective than words. But these writers have come nowhere near representing the full experience of seeing hawks. Compare the representation Robbins et al. created to this one from Henry David Thoreau's journal/essay on living at Walden Pond (*Walden*, 1854). Would you say that one is more precise than the other, or are they trying to capture different aspects of experience?

> Looking up I observed a very slight and graceful hawk, like a nighthawk. . . . It was the most ethereal flight I had ever witnessed. It did not simply flutter like a butterfly, nor soar like the larger hawks, but it sported with proud reliance in the fields of air; mounting again and again with its strange chuckle, it repeated its free and beautiful fall, turning over and over like a kite, and then recovering from its lofty tumbling, as if it had never set its foot on *terra firma*. It appeared to have no companion in the universe—sporting there alone—and to need none but the morning and the ether with which it played. It was not lonely, but made all the earth lonely beneath it.

Thoreau uses prose to describe his nighthawk. In the following poem, written a few years later, Tennyson uses rhyme, a regular meter, and alliteration to "describe" an eagle. Do you think these writers used different verbal forms in order to create different meanings, different representations of experience? How would the poetic devices Tennyson used work for him?

The Eagle

He clasps the crag with crooked hands;
Close to the sun in lonely lands,
Ring'd with the azure world, he stands.
The wrinkled sea beneath him crawls;
He watches from his mountain walls,
And like a thunderbolt he falls.

Alfred, Lord Tennyson (1851)

The point of this set of examples is simple. When you sit down to write, your knowledge may be, like a hawk-seer's, rich and complex but also rather vague and unspecific. In building a prose representation you have the luxury of many alternative ways to do the job. But keep in mind that you are also building new knowledge when you give yourself, and your reader, this new, more elaborate representation of what it means to "see a hawk."

🌿 PLANNING IN WRITING

Planning in writing is the act of calling up mental representations such as these for the purpose of thinking about what you know and what you want to say. Planning for a paper doesn't start when you sit down to write. It may start as you are walking down the hall and begin to tap some of these different pockets of knowledge. The knowledge you find in your own memory may be, in part, visual images, sounds and rhythms, or feelings. Even your verbal knowledge, when you begin to plan, may be rather general. For example, you know that the bird "swooped toward you," but should you think of it or express it as an attack, a threat, or merely anxiety behavior? At this point you may also know that certain ideas are connected, but you may not yet be able to say how. Writing, as a way of thinking things through, is often a process of re-representation—making your knowledge as verbal and as explicit as you can.

Notice that we have answered the question "What do you really know that you can't express?" The answer is that you may know a lot, but writing is a special and particularly demanding way of thinking about what you know. By making things explicit, writing not only lets you remember and communicate your ideas, but it lets you test them. When you write an idea down it is easier to stand back and ask, "Does that version of my knowledge do justice to what I really know?"

Although this analogy isn't always true, I find it helps to think of writing as both a journey and a process in which you are exploring and then restructuring your knowledge into a new representation that someone else can understand. You often start out happily wandering around in ways of knowing that are a long way from finished text, or maybe even from words: images, feelings, memories of events, loosely related ideas, or at best, unconnected fragments of coherent discourse that don't yet add up to a whole. At the other end of this journey you want to end up with polished prose, which is a very powerful, but also a very specialized way of expressing your knowledge. Look, for instance, at some of the features polished prose must have: It must be in words, show logical connections (your private associations are no longer enough), fit some standard format, follow the rules of grammar, use standard spelling, and more. Notice that in planning and writing drafts, you often choose, quite sensibly, to ignore some of these special features of prose. Features such as spelling, word choice, and sentence style are necessary parts of the final "prose" representation, but they aren't crucial early in the journey, or even in some draft stages. In the following example, compare the amount of information contained in these four different verbal representations of my knowledge. In one I have listed only topics, in the second, key words and abstract relations, and in the last two I have tried to express my meaning in prose. What have I been able to communicate by taking on the extra demands of finished prose?

TOPICS
    HEAT   WATER   POLLUTION   ALGAE   FISH

KEY WORDS AND RELATIONS
    Heat + Water = Pollution (= thermal pollution)
    Pollution ⇒ Dead fish
    Cause of dead fish = uncontrolled algae growth

PROSE: With a Focus on the Process
    The heated water from local industries (a form of thermal pollution) kills many species of fish by triggering the uncontrolled growth of oxygen-stealing algae.

PROSE: With a Focus on Definition
    Thermal pollution—a side effect of industrial waste disposal—occurs when industrial wastes heat a river or lake, stimulating the uncontrolled growth of algae, which eventually suffocates the fish. (What would happen if I added just one word and said "unavoidable" side effect, or changed it to "unregulated" side effect?)

The Purpose of Planning: Setting Goals and Getting a Gist

In describing writing as a journey that restructures knowledge, we all have a good image of the final result—polished text—and of the stage before that—a working draft. But what are you trying to achieve as you plan? This question seems hard to answer because planning is work that goes on in the head more often than on paper. It is done when you are walking down the street, going to sleep, or just sitting, thinking, and writing notes. Some people produce outlines, but others don't. So if you can't equate planning with anything that is written, such as a draft, what should you try to produce as you plan?

There is probably no single answer to this question, but experienced writers often concentrate on two main things as they plan. First, they create a sense of their major goals and subgoals. Second, they form a sense of their gist and the general structure of their ideas. These are common-sense notions, but I will define them briefly here, and then use the next section to illustrate some of the different forms these goals and gists can take.

Your **goals** for a paper say how you want to link and present ideas (for example, are you aiming for a forceful argument or a personal reflection), and they might include the effect you want to have on a reader (paragraph by paragraph). Your goals will also be the standards and criteria you want to keep in mind (that is, stick to your point). A genre will always dictate certain conventional goals (for example, news stories have to have a "lead"), but in the planning stage you are also setting your unique goals for this paper.

A **gist** is a summary statement of the essential things you want to say. In order to have such a top-level statement of the main points or the big idea, you have to have explored your own knowledge and/or done some reading and have figured out what is important. The gist is the guiding idea. It also includes a tentative sense of structure: knowing how your important ideas are related to each other. The first goal of planning, then, is to be able to walk up to someone and say (in fifty words or less), "I'm writing a paper that basically says: (gist), because what I want to do is (goals)." A detailed outline of the paper itself is only an optional end result of planning.

Here are some maxims that sum up some of the critical features of planning:

1. Plans are made to be broken.
2. Any plan is better than no plan (Minsky's Maxim).
3. Plans are instructions you give yourself, so give yourself good ones. (Note: The form doesn't matter. You can talk to yourself in doodles, outlines, or full-color images; if it works, it is good.)
4. Good plans are detailed enough to argue with and cheap enough to throw away.
5. Bad plans are plans you can't use (even if they look great on paper).

In order to make our discussion of planning more concrete, I would like to show you some snapshots from the planning process of Joan, the writer discussed in Chapter 3. We will look at the planning that led to her third paragraph, the one on her goals and experience. This paragraph is interesting because it involves so many different kinds of knowledge, from images to narrative memories to goals and gists, before it becomes polished prose.

Joan's planning for this section really began when Professor Harris asked her, "Do you have any experience in this area?" and she tried to answer by telling the story of her summer job at the Chicago Clinic. Notice how her knowledge starts with a strong visual image and is structured around a memory for people, events, and her own feelings. These memories will be the raw material for her later planning.

CONVERSATION: Well I tried to get some experience in my summer job. I can still see that lab book. I lived with it—all those little boxes you filled in, every detail about the experiment: times, dates, measurements. You wouldn't believe the detail. And you couldn't guess or fill it in later like you do in high school. (Note the visual image. How would you translate this memory into a statement about her "work experience"? What does this knowledge "mean" given her writing task?)

And the Clinic itself was a zoo. This guy Ranjar ran the adjacent lab. When I came he was really nice to me and always asked me how things were going in my lab. He looked like your father—this silver hair—but, I don't know, you had to watch out. He was a fox. One time we were working on a test that had to be done at 12-hour intervals, and there was never enough money and equipment for each lab to have its own machines. I came in early one Wednesday to run the fourth test and the equipment was gone. I finally tracked it down to Ranjar. Apparently he needed it, and he was all sorry, friendly, and slick. Promised to get it back. Well, he didn't. I had to run the whole series over. Some of the people there were really building empires. But you just had to cooperate to get things done. The competition hurt everyone. (Note the narrative memory of people and events. What does Joan "know" about her "work experience"?)

In Figure 4–2, you will see another way we can represent some of the knowledge in Joan's memory. This memory network is a schematic diagram of some of the concepts in her memory, such as Ranjar and fox. The lines that link these concepts are named: **is** indicates a definition (Ranjar is not good); **isa** indicates that something belongs to a larger class of things (having insufficient equipment is an example of a realistic situation); and **has** indicates a property or feature (having a fatherly look is a property of Ranjar). In this system for representing knowledge in memory, episodes and events are named with a verb, such as "missing," and put in an oval circle. Actions are linked to agents (which cause things to happen) and to objects (which receive the effect of an action).

What does this representation show us that a narrative doesn't? Notice first that major ideas in this network are ones that have a lot of links—all roads lead to Rome. Ideas with many links in memory

FIGURE 4–2
A Piece of a Memory Network

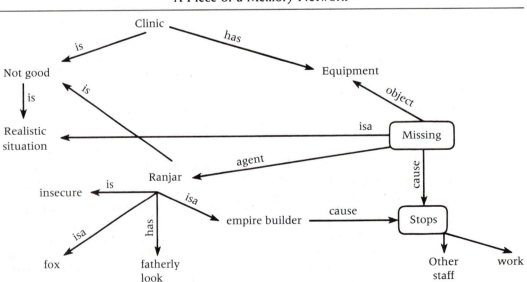

are easy to get to; you are likely to remember them. Ideas that have few links may be things that you "know" but have trouble remembering. They may be knowledge you have but don't use because you don't call it up when you need it. Finally, this network shows how people like Joan can hold concepts that may actually conflict with one another—how can Ranjar be both a "fox" and a "father"? Thinking or writing about this knowledge may make this conflict more apparent and lead Joan, as it does in her narrative, to try to make a new link. In this case we can imagine a revised network in which both "fox" and "fatherly look" are connected by a new idea such as "looks are deceptive."

This network tells us one more thing about knowledge: Much of what people know is probably stored in an abstract form, much like these memory networks. That means that most of the information in our memory is not stored in sentences or even in words and phrases. Instead it is stored as complex "concepts" that may not even have a name. For example, imagine all of the nonverbal feelings attached in Joan's memory to the concept we have labeled "not good." In addition, we may have a strong sense that two ideas like "fox" and "father" are connected, but we may not be able to say in words just what that connection is. Writing is a process of trying to think about those connections and make them explicit. In trying to write, you actually learn new information by forging new links between the concepts you already have.

In order to write, Joan has to translate these memories, images, and abstract connections into more explicit ones that are relevant to her purpose: to show that she has useful experience. We can see this happening by looking at how she plans the text itself. Notice how her plans and her notes are in fact a new and different image of knowledge: they re-represent what she knows in a new form.

PLANNING THOUGHTS: I've got to show what I got out of all this. What can I show for this. . . . It's experience, but it has to be something I've learned. I sure learned how to keep records. So what, I'm not applying for bookkeeper. But, . . . yeah. Scientific, being scientific. That careful . . . all those steps you have to go through. And then mention records and testing. OK.

Notes

Records = (*Scientific*)

- *steps*
- *records*
- *testing*

If we look closely we can see that even the scribbled notes themselves are full of information. The equals sign and the large circle are graphic, or nonverbal, ways of saying that the meaning of "records" is not the records themselves but the idea they support: the notion that she learned to be "scientific." The line tells us that she is going to elaborate that idea and the dots are a graphic way of saying "cover these ideas in this order."

These notes with their combination of key words and structural information capture the *gist* of what Joan wants to say. Notice what happens to this gist when she elaborates it into a complete text (pp. 64–65). Then consider another piece of her planning.

> PLANNING THOUGHTS: Ranjar, oh boy. Well, actually I learned how to work around him. Maybe it is important to let them know I'm not naive or inept here. I know that there are people problems even in pure research. Some people are a real headache and you have to . . . you have to get results anyway. Guess I don't really want to say that here, maybe in the interview or something. My point is, what? I got to see the problems of working in an organization. Money, records, all those are practical problems, but you also learn to cooperate, share equipment—or die—and to plan. OK, organizational problems.

Joan's planning also creates a number of goals. In the above excerpt, for instance, she decides to achieve her major goal—demonstrating her experience—with a pair of subgoals to show she is neither naive nor inept. Her initial plan is to tackle the "naive" subgoal by talking about people problems, but then she decides that "people problems" is a better topic for an interview. So her main subgoal then becomes to show what she can do by discussing both the practical problems and the skills of research. Notice how her goals also form a tree structure that has the most inclusive goals at the top supported by subgoals beneath (see Figure 4–3).

To sum up, Joan's planning shows a writer working with many different ways of representing her knowledge. She starts with visual images, a memory of a personal experience, and some partially connected concepts. She creates notes that contain both visual and verbal information. As she plans, she translates her knowledge into a set of goals and a gist adapted to her purpose in writing.

PROJECTS AND ASSIGNMENTS

1   In this chapter we looked at the way the writers of *Birds of North America* dealt with the problem of representing some very different kinds of knowledge about hawks. As writers in the popular Golden Guide series of field guides, they also had the problem of adapting their knowledge to the needs of the reader. Think about some alternative ways of writing about a bird and examine the choices these writers made. Did the needs of the reader

FIGURE 4–3
Joan's Goals

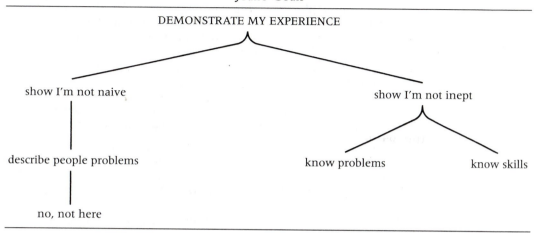

have any effect on the information they selected and the way they presented it?

2   This exercise is a journal entry you might do to help you with a paper you are currently working on. Start planning as Joan did by jotting down notes about visual images, remembered experiences, or conversations. Use your writing to recall your knowledge, however it may be represented in your own mind. Try pictures, notes, dialogues, stream of consciousness—whatever taps your best knowledge. Then given your purpose in writing, try to express your knowledge as a **gist**—say what it means. Secondly, show how this meaning fits your **goals**—say why you want to use that information and what you want it to do for you.

3   Have you ever had an experience that was hard to capture in words? Consider, for instance: being at a concert, a sports event, or a tense social situation; appreciating the style of someone's performance in any of those; making music, or doing something athletic, physical, or social yourself. Create a small portfolio of perspectives on this experience. Feel free to use or create photos, drawings, audio tapes, *and* a variety of verbal representations (such as, a blow-by-blow account, a dramatization that highlights key features, a speculative reflection on the meaning of the experience, versions of the story that you would give to different people).

Look at some of the interesting ways the representations in your portfolio differ from one another. As you write a commentary on those differences, speculate about an answer to this question: Are some ways of representing your knowledge especially adapted to (or good at) capturing certain aspects of experience?

4   Do you think historians, writers, and media people give us qualitatively different representations of common public events or just additional facts? Consider an event (large or small) that has made the news (historically or yesterday). Create a portfolio of representations (see Assignment 3 for ideas). Consider not only TV, radio, and newspapers, but historical accounts, reviews, commentaries, and interviews. For example, if your event were a scene from a local play, you could use the performance, the text, program notes, current and historical reviews, scholarly criticism, and a talk with an actor. These accounts will naturally contain different factsand conclusions, but do they also represent different aspects of experience, including emotion, values, implications, personal meaning, logical connections, or causation? Write a paper in which you think about this question: Do some of these representations seem to offer a distinctive way of knowing that event that the others can't (or don't) provide? If some people only saw one or two of these accounts, would these differences have any implications?

5   This writer is trying to describe the unique discourse community created in her drawing class by the weekly "crit" or critique in which student work is analyzed by the instructor and the group. But how do you talk about a visual experience, especially when you are still learning to see things in a special way?

To analyze how this writer did it, apply four of the concepts from this chapter to the paragraph. Is it possible to see (or infer) any **goal(s)** she had for this paragraph (beyond giving a description)? Can you state the **gist**? (What features of the text were your "tip-offs" to her goals and gist?) Finally, sketch a quick version of what her **memory network** for a "strong" and "weak" drawing appears to include. (How many connections do you see?) Now look at the particular ways she *chose* with each sentence to **represent** those perceptions and relations in prose. Could you have done it differently?

The crit goes on as we begin to pick the drawings we want to discuss. Drawings are discussed by speaking about their strong and weak points. A strong drawing means that its composition or the way its parts are put together to make up its whole work well, or it is visually pleasing. An example of a drawing that is not visually pleasing or which doesn't work well could be a drawing done with some very dark shades of grey and some very light grey tones but no middle tones. Drawings like this tend to be spotty. If middle shades of grey are added to the drawing, it helps it to flow together and connect its parts making it into a whole. Another example of a weak drawing could be one whose negative space, the space or air around a subject, is too large for the subject. Let's say the subject is a drawing of a frog. If the space around the frog is too big, then the teacher may suggest that the drawing be cropped. Cropping a drawing means to cut off some of the negative space. Things like these are discussed throughout the critique, teaching the students how to see and how to change their own drawings.

IF YOU WOULD LIKE TO READ MORE

If you would like to know more about how people build mental representations, see:

Anderson, John R. *Cognitive Psychology and Its Implications.* San Francisco: W. H. Freeman, 1980. / This book describes the controversy over how people think with images.

Flower, Linda, and John R. Hayes. Images, plans, and prose: The representation of meaning in writing. *Written Communication* 1 (January 1984), 120–60. / This paper looks at how writers must often translate from one representation to another.

Lindsay, Peter, and Donald Norman. *Human Information Processing: An Introduction to Psychology.* New York: Academic Press, 1972. / These authors provide an entertaining but rigorous introduction to the theory of memory networks, which they in fact helped develop.

chapter five

Making Plans

GOAL 1
EXPLORE the rhetorical problem

Decide how you are going to represent this rhetorical problem to yourself.

> *STRATEGY 1*   **EXPLORE YOUR IMAGE OF THE PROBLEM**
> *STRATEGY 2*   **EXPLAIN THE ASSIGNMENT TO YOURSELF**

GOAL 2
MAKE a plan

Sketch out an initial plan to guide your thinking. As you compose, return to this plan, changing and developing it as you go along.

> *STRATEGY 1*   **MAKE A PLAN *TO DO* AND A PLAN *TO SAY***
> *STRATEGY 2*   **MAKE YOUR GOALS MORE OPERATIONAL**
> *STRATEGY 3*   **LISTEN TO INTUITION AND CHANGE YOUR PLAN**
> *STRATEGY 4*   **REVEAL YOUR PLAN TO THE READER**
> *STRATEGY 5*   **USE COLLABORATIVE PLANNING**

If good writers and problem solvers have a secret power, it is planning. Trial and error can often generate useful results, but if you rely solely on this method you are taking blind luck as your guide. Problem solvers rely on plans. The twenty minutes you spend planning can save you hours in writing. And good planning, as you shall see, can also have a dramatic effect on the quality of your paper. In this chapter we will look at two steps in planning: exploring the rhetorical problems and planning your response.

GOAL 1

EXPLORE the Rhetorical Problem

A rhetorical situation or rhetorical problem is like a rather large, uncharted territory that contains you, your reader, your ideas, and all the things you possibly could do. As you make a mental tour of this territory selecting the goals that matter and the strategies you will use, you are building your own image or representation of the task. For example, consider the way two car owners I know see the task of "washing the car." In owner A's image, you need to wash the car when the dirt is so thick you can't see the color and somebody has written "wash me" on the back window. His goals: save the body, save face, remove the top layer of dirt. This job is saved for weddings and funerals. His strategies: wait for a warm day, give it a hose, and sponge once over—a 12-minute task. In owner B's image of "washing the car," this task is called for when a salt spray, an afternoon shower, or a dusty road sullies his cream puff. His goal: to see his reflection. His strategies: go to the high-priced car wash for hot soap and a blow dry, vacuum the carpets, do the windows, dust the ashtray, hose the underbody, wax the chrome wheels, and touch up with PolyGuard. If two representations of a simple task like "washing the car" can differ so much, what happens when people have to represent a more complex rhetorical problem to themselves?

For instance, when you are given a writing assignment in a college class, how do you represent the task to yourself? The answer may seem obvious: "I just read the assignment and do what it says." But, in fact, it is more accurate to say that writers *create* their own image or representation of every task they do. That is, they decide which goals (of all they could set) are most important, which ideas (out of many) are relevant, and which text conventions seem most appropriate. It turns out that this "creative" process matters because different writers, reading the same assignment, can have strikingly different images of what is appropriate.

 ## *STRATEGY 1*   **EXPLORE YOUR IMAGE OF THE PROBLEM**

Although we have looked at various kinds of writing from feature articles to memos and applications, most of the writing you will do in college could be defined as "academic discourse." But do you always know when you have met the expectations of that community? What is your image of this task called "academic writing"?

What Is "Academic Discourse"?

Here are some "mystery texts" that come from different discourse communities, including academic discourse published in journals and student writing for courses as well as popular journalism and professional writing. Read each mystery text and decide: is it an example of "academic discourse" or not? Was it written by a professor, a graduate student, an undergraduate, or a nonacademic writer? Make a note of at least *three features* in each text that you saw as "tip-offs."

Mystery Text 1. Looking at a finished paper, a reader has no feel for what went on before. But for a writer, first drafts and throwaways are all a part of the final work. Revision for many writers can be a way to reevaluate their thinking.

Mystery Text 2. Recent research about the way experienced writers approach the revision process reveals some surprisingly consistent findings. It suggests that experienced writers tend to pay more attention to preliminary planning, to setting goals, to suiting subject matter to these goals, and to writing several drafts in which they make major changes that affect the meaning of the discourse, not just the style.

Mystery Text 3. Revision, the establishment asserts, is a powerful, generative process. Many students, however, seem to operate with a different definition. . . . If teachers and professionals are right about the nature and power of revision, why are students slow to take advantage of such a good thing?

Mystery Text 4. The method I used is not perfect; no research method is. . . . My purpose and my method reflect a logic of exploration and discovery, which is necessary in order to increase our understanding of a very complex human activity.

Mystery Text 5. I like to compare my method with that of painters centuries ago, proceeding, as it were, from layer to layer. The first draft is quite crude, far from being perfect, by no means finished; although even then, even at that point, it has its final structure, the form is visible.

Mystery Text 6. The schools are not always hospitable environments, however. Some teachers actually penalize critical thinking, says Richard Paul, director of California's Sonoma State University Center for Critical Thinking and Moral Critique: because the system tends to value the answer more than the process, a student who ably defends a socially unacceptable belief often gets a lower grade than one with an unreflective but safe view.

Have you made your decisions and jotted down your reasons? To get the most out of this mystery, discuss it with other members of your class. I will reveal the "answers" later because the real purpose of this mystery is to let you take a look at your own assumptions about your images of "academic writing." For instance, look at the three reasons you jotted down. Which features did you look for to evaluate these texts?

Formal features. Are you looking for the formal features of the text, such as sentence length, word choice, style? Are you focusing on conventional rules?

Content. Are you basing your decision on the content: on what is said, on the position the writer takes?

Rhetorical features. Are you using the rhetorical features of the text to make your decision: looking at the writer's purpose, the apparent context for the text, and the writer's relationship with the reader?

These mystery texts let you uncover some of your own assumptions about academic writing and how to evaluate it. If you look at your own private mental image of an "academic" text, what is in the foreground; in other words, what is the focus of your image: words, rules, and local stylistic features or rhetorical ones? When you switch from evaluating a text to writing one, you will find that focusing on rhetorical features may be more useful to you. Do these mystery texts let you speculate on different ways people in this particular discourse community—academic discourse—seem to use writing?

How Do You Represent a Reading-to-Write Task?

Let's now look at an actual college assignment that asks you to read-in-order-to-write-a-paper. Read the assignment and the excerpt from the source materials and ask yourself, how do I represent this task to myself?

Assignment: Here are some notes, including research results and observations on time management. Please read and interpret these data in order to make a brief (1–2 page) comprehensive statement about this subject. Your statement should interpret and synthesize all the relevant findings in the text.

Excerpt from the Reading Notes:

The key to success, according to efficiency expert Alan Lakein in his recent book *How to Get Control of Your Time and Your Life,* lies in pacing and planning. The average worker has two kinds of "prime time" to plan: external time and internal time. External time is the best time to attend to other people. Internal prime time is the period in which one works best.

Noted philosopher and psychologist William James found that most people do not use their mental energies in sufficient depth. He advocated continued concentration in the face of apparent mental fatigue: "The fatigue gets worse up to a certain critical point, when gradually or suddenly it passes away, and we are fresher than before. We have evidently tapped a new level of energy."

In his guide to intellectual life, Jean Guitton stresses the importance of preparation for peak performance, asserting that it is vital to rest at the least sign of fatigue and to go to work with a relaxed attitude. Find a place that is at once calm and stimulating. Tolerate nothing that is not useful or beautiful.

In a recent survey, students reported some of the following as their standard strategies for getting through assignments and minimizing some of the debilitating effects of long-range pressures.

Do what's due; postpone big projects.
Create a crisis.
Allow the minimal estimate of time it will take to get a project completed.
Read the material once; don't try to remember it until it's needed.

Now write your statement about time management based on your interpretation of these data.

What do you think this read-to-write assignment calls for? And do you think everyone would see it as you do? A group of teachers and researchers at the Center for the Study of Writing asked 72 freshman students to do the expanded version of this assignment and report back on their representation of the task. Below is a checklist of the major options people considered. Mark your choices and your predictions for what the freshmen chose. For instance, under Source of Information, some people said, "the text," while others said, "what I already knew." Under Text Format and Features, some students thought this sort of assignment just called for a short summary with an opinion paragraph added on at the end; whereas others assumed the "appropriate" format was standard school theme with an introduction, a few paragraphs, and a conclusion. And still others had the conventions of a more formal, publishable essay in mind. Perhaps the most important decision people made was a decision about the Organizing Plan, since it led some students to write a careful summary, while for others the sources became a springboard for a personal reflection on the topic. Some writers created a synthesis, organized around a concept they defined, such as, "advice for students" or "alternative theories of time management." And still others used the sources for a purpose of their own, such as raising the question of whether time management is teachable at all, given all this contradictory advice. Are all of these decisions a reasonable response to the task?

Some Options for a Read-to-Write Assignment

MAJOR SOURCE OF INFORMATION
☐ Text
☐ Text + My Comments
☐ What I Already Knew
☐ Other Texts

TEXT FORMAT AND FEATURES
☐ Notes/Summary Paragraph
☐ Summary + Opinion Paragraph
☐ Standard School Theme
☐ Persuasive Essay

ORGANIZING PLAN FOR WRITING
☐ Summarize the Readings
☐ Free Response to the Topic
☐ Organize around a Synthesizing Concept
☐ Interpret for a Purpose of My Own

The teacher and students who conducted this study found that people didn't agree on what this "typical college assignment" called for. Each student built his or her own representation of the task—assuming it was the "right" or "obvious" representation—but the person in class beside him or her was assuming something quite different. Here are some results: Under *Source,* 32% said "text" and 52% said text plus comments; under *Format,* 50% picked the "standard theme" (which leaves 50% with other ideas); under *Organizing Plan,* 43% chose to do a "summary," 25% a "synthesis," and only 11% an "interpretation with a purpose."

Can you spot the different organizing plans from some introductory sentences?

"Basically, time management is broken into two parts, planning and pacing. Also an important factor is efficiency."

"I found that this research was relevant to my endeavors. I do plan ahead, but procrastination always occurs when an assignment is due. I find myself writing late at night when I am tired and concentration just isn't there because the only thing I'm thinking about is sleep."

"There are several theories as to the most efficient theories of time management. Some say. . . . But others say. . . ."

"The basic problem of time management for college students involves changing schedules and finding a good working environment. As Lakein says. . . ."

"Based on the research and self-help books, I feel the solution to the problem of time management will have to be a compromise among the opinions of these professionals, many of whom disagree with each other. In fact, many of their 'helpful hints' based on business workers are really obstacles to many students."

Now, you may be asking, is there a "right" answer to this assignment? We can respond to this question in two ways.

1. When you receive a "typical" assignment, do you know what your instructor expects? For instance, many instructors want you to summarize the readings to show you understand them. But other instructors "assume" that a good paper will synthesize information, that is, that you, the writer, will create a new concept to which all the key ideas in *your* essay are linked. Those instructors want you to make sense of your reading, organize your observations, and maybe even come up with a new controlling idea. And still other instructors

may expect a good paper to go one step further and apply the reading to some topic or problem being discussed in the course.

In academic writing all of these organizing plans are valuable—there are times you need to summarize, times to synthesize, times to interpret and apply. But each plan produces a very different sort of paper. If you and your instructor represent the task differently without realizing it, you could turn in a "good summary" but a "poor synthesis"—a paper that failed to show what you really can do. One always wishes that teachers, supervisors, and clients who ask for writing would be more explicit about what they want, but as a writer it is your job to explore the rhetorical situation before you plunge in.

2. On the other hand, what if the "best" representation is not dictated by the situation; what if it is up to you? This study showed us that the most important thing is to realize that *you* are making the choice—that you are building your own representation. Many students in the study did not realize how many different options there were. It may help to look at your choices in terms of the costs and benefits to you.

Making Your Own Choices

For instance, a *summary* helps you remember the reading and if you had lots of practice doing summaries in high school, it may be easier to write a good summary than a good synthesis. However, there are hidden costs in deciding to summarize: you aren't developing any ideas of your own and readers in the academic discourse community often expect to learn something new from a text—they are likely to be bored by a mere summary.

Think about some of the costs and benefits of using *synthesis* as an organizing plan. It lets you introduce your own ideas and experience and come up with a new way to look at your sources. But what if the sources are like Lakein, James, Guitton, and the students and don't provide a ready-made synthesizing concept? One cost of this plan is that you will have to create your own concept. You will have to look for links and try to define an interesting connection (or organizing concept). Finding a good concept that does justice to all of your key points and says something worthwhile can require thought. For instance, the teachers who read the time management essays decided that a topic sentence such as "There are many ideas about time management" didn't really qualify as a new synthesizing concept. Although it was a tidy way to link all the paragraphs, it seemed too obvious and uninteresting to these academic readers to qualify as a new concept.

Interpreting the sources for *your own purpose* gives you much more independence and opportunity to think about something you care about. (The examples on pp. 100–101 are all organized by a purpose the writers themselves set.) However, as we know, defining one's purpose and using it to organize a whole text often takes thought and revision—it has a cost. For me as a writer, adapting outside sources to my own purposes is almost always worth the effort, but there are times when it is not. When somebody asks me to write a short report on a project, I have the choice simply to cut and paste material from an old report (lowest cost), to summarize off the top of my head or synthesize around some obvious concepts (moderate costs; more benefits), or to write a special report adapted to what my readers need or to what I especially want them to hear (highest cost and highest potential benefit). Although academic writing places a premium on new knowledge and using knowledge to address an issue or problem, the most important fact for you as a writer to know is that *you create your own goals.* Exploring the rhetorical situation will let you make the most sensible decision for yourself.

❧ *STRATEGY 2*   **EXPLAIN THE ASSIGNMENT TO YOURSELF**

Assignments are a special kind of rhetorical problem in which certain parts of the problem are already specified. But even in an assignment, many parts of the problem are implied—the professor assumes you will fill in the unstated pieces of the puzzle. Knowing how to explain an assignment to yourself by elaborating its assumptions, key terms, and unstated criteria is a critical skill in writing. It can mean the difference between writing a successful paper and writing one that doesn't succeed, because it solves the wrong problem.

Let's suppose that you are enrolled in a History of Western Civilization course and your teacher has just asked you to write a short paper on the question: "Why was Erasmus considered to be the Prince of Humanists?" How would you develop the paper?

When an assignment asks a direct question, there is a temptation to do a **memory dump**—that is, simply to write everything you can remember about Erasmus. But that is not what the question asks for, and such an answer will often earn a low grade.

One step up from the memory dump is the **definition + example** type of answer: after defining Humanism, one then explains what Erasmus did that made him a famous humanist. This strategy addresses the two parts of the question and it fits Erasmus into the Humanist tradition. But it does not *answer* the question.

To answer the question, you need a **definition + comparison + context answer.** That is, after you define Humanism, you must think about why Erasmus was more of a humanist than anyone else. Consider what a **comparison plus context** might entail: Was he more humane, more kind, more virtuous? Is being the Prince of Humanists a matter of *quantity*—did he write more letters and books, learn more languages, know more theology, have more friends than any other humanist? Is it a matter of *quality*—did he write better books, have more interesting friends, and so on? Is it a matter of *primacy*—was Erasmus the first humanist, or did he influence more people than any other humanist? Or is it a matter of *notoriety*—did he get into more trouble or make more enemies than any other humanist? Or is the answer a combination of these? Or something else? (And who gave Erasmus this title, anyway?)

The point is, to answer this question, one must do three things. First, one must define Humanism. Then, one must analyze the meaning of "prince," which suggests "best," or "most," and consider what that comparison means. Finally, one must create a basis for that comparison. To explain why Erasmus was the "Prince of Humanists," one must know something about the people who were lesser humanists. The question really asks you to place Erasmus and the Humanist movement in a *context*. Your teacher will not believe that you understand this material unless you can talk about not only the aims and ideals of Humanism but what it came out of, what it was a reaction to, and perhaps what opposition the people who belonged to it faced. If you know these things, you can explain why Erasmus embodied the ideals of the movement more than anyone else did.

It is possible to say most or all of these things in a "memory dump" answer. Yet such a response will usually receive a lower evaluation than will a definition + contrast + context answer, because in the second kind of answer the information is focused. After all, when instructors ask questions such as this one, what do they want to know? Beyond factual information, they want to know whether you can *use* the facts—that is, think about them and connect them for yourself. Instructors know that rote memory knowledge, the kind displayed in the "memory dump" answer, is shallow and transient. Deep knowledge, of the kind meant by the word "education," is usable knowledge. That is why assignments ask you to reorganize ideas around a question, and why instructors use words such as *define, analyze,* and *compare*.

One way to read an assignment is to predict that it will probably ask you (in one way or another) to do three major mental actions: to define something, to make a comparison, and to connect something to its context. So when you read an assignment, look for the terms or clues that say what you should define, what you should compare, and what context you should discuss. You can do this even for short questions. One reason they are short is that they have left the task of explaining or interpreting the assignment up to you. For example, you can rewrite the assignment "What was enlightened about the Enlightenment?" to say,

Define "enlightened."
Compare it to its opposite or to other ways of conducting society.

Show what effect its context, the period called the Enlightenment, had on the idea of being "enlightened."

Understanding an assignment, then, is often a process of rewriting
and expanding a question into a set of **actions** you could take. Many
keywords in assignments suggest actions:

compare   List or discuss similarities in order of importance (usually most to least).

contrast   List or discuss differences in order of importance.

evaluate   Judge the worth of something by measuring (comparing
and contrasting) its key features against a standard; the standard may be either what is *normal* or what is *ideal.*

how   "By what means does it happen that . . ." asks for cause/ef-
fect (*not* narrative!).

justify/support   Corroborate with reasons, explain the rationale
for each reason, and support the rationales with facts.

significance   "Give/tell/show the significance of . . ." means describe the important consequences or implications (the cause/
effect relationships).

summarize   Restate the main facts or points concisely, using your
own words.

superlatives   "Prince," for example, asks for comparison or contrast.

why   "For what reasons . . ." asks for cause/effect.

Sometimes questions will ask you to do even more "rewriting" and
to supply the key terms and actions yourself. For example, how would
you answer the question "Imagine that Plato is reading Thomas
Paine's pamphlet *Common Sense.* What would he say about it?"

If you decided that this question asks you to compare and contrast
the ideas of Plato and Paine and to express these comparisons in
terms of Plato's response to Paine, you are right. If you know anything about the ideas of these two philosophers, you probably also
realize that a good answer would involve definitions of key terms
(*citizen,* for example) and that your comments about Plato would
probably be based on his book *The Republic.* The question also implic-
itly asks you to distinguish important concepts from less important
ones and to evaluate Plato's probable response to Paine's pamphlet.
Your knowledge of the times and circumstances in which Paine and
Plato wrote—the context of fourth-century Greece and eighteenth-
century America—will help you evaluate this response and explain
why these philosophers agree and disagree.

People often define the same question in quite different ways.
Consider this assignment: "Analyze some aspect of the relation between politics and culture in the twentieth century." Compare your
interpretation with the problem/purpose statement of the writer in
Example 1 at the end of this chapter.

GOAL 2

MAKE a Plan

Goals state where you want to end up. Plans say how you are going to get there. One of the virtues of a plan is that it is cheaper to build than the real solution would be. Therefore, architects start with blueprints rather than concrete, and writers plan a twenty-page paper before they write. As an inexpensive representation of your solution, a plan lets you test and discard ideas as you work. So a good plan needs to be detailed enough to test, but *cheap enough to throw away.*

Minsky's Maxim may be right—any plan is better than no plan. But some plans are also a lot better than others. For instance, compare these two plans:

Topic-Based Plan	*Goal-Based Plan*
I'm going to write a paper on the psychological effects of noise.	I'm going to show my readers (college students and professors) how noise can affect their mood and productivity. Then I'll use the research I've found to suggest strategies people can use to cope with noise.
One effect is. . . . Another effect is. . . . Effect #101 is. . . .	That means I'll want to start with a vivid demonstration of how noise actually affects us, then survey the history of the study of noise. . . .

One of the chief virtues of setting goals is that it lets you cut enormous problems down to size. So instead of covering the topic of noise, you choose the information you need in order to meet your goals. Traditional outlines are often merely topic-based plans, or arrangements of information, unrelated to the writer's goals. Figuring out your goals is obviously more difficult than just naming or outlining a topic (for example, "I'm writing about noise"). But of the two procedures, it's the one that will actually help you write. Outlines, especially premature ones, are often dominated by the structure of the available information (all the things that could be said about noise), whereas a goal-based plan is governed by the writer (what *you* want or need to say to explain a new idea, stimulate your reader, or perhaps change his or her mind). Frequently, an outline is a list of the topics you might want to cover in your paper, whereas a goal-based plan is an expression of what you want to do by writing.

Look at planning as a goal-directed attempt to make two kinds of plans fit together: plans for what you want **to do** and plans for what you want **to say.**

◆ STRATEGY 1   MAKE A PLAN *TO DO* AND A PLAN *TO SAY*

In the case study of Joan in Chapter 3, we imagined her group of goals. A practical planning technique is to actually sketch your own plan for what you want **to do**—an outline of your goals and your plan for achieving them. The special feature of this kind of outline is that instead of focusing on your topic, it focuses on what you want to do with the information you have.

Start by writing down one of your top-level goals: What do you expect this piece of writing to do for you? Think of the text as a stand-in actor that will go to the reader in your place. What exactly do you want the reader to see, to think, or to do?

Figure 5–1 shows a plan sketched out by a college student who wanted to get a summer job as a legislative aide. Instead of merely listing his courses and extracurricular activities ("I want to describe things I've done"), he established a goal ("I want to convince the congressman I'm the best candidate"). He then made the goal operational by exploring *how* he could convince the congressman. Notice how he used the facts about himself to create the effect he wanted to have. In his final letter of application, he began by showing how his desire to be a legislative aide was part of a larger career plan and how he had chosen his college and his courses in light of that career.

FIGURE 5–1
Goal-Based Plan for a Letter of Application

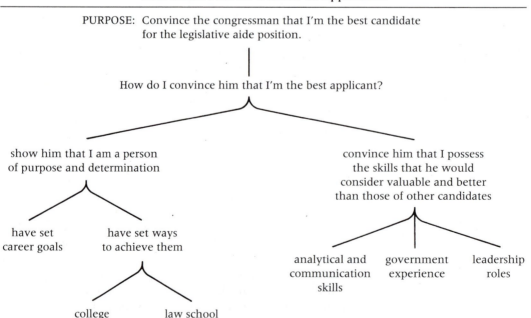

PURPOSE: Convince the congressman that I'm the best candidate for the legislative aide position.

How do I convince him that I'm the best applicant?

show him that I am a person of purpose and determination

convince him that I possess the skills that he would consider valuable and better than those of other candidates

have set career goals

have set ways to achieve them

analytical and communication skills

government experience

leadership roles

college   law school

In making your own goal-based plan, ask yourself, "How am I going to accomplish my goals? What will I have to do?" The writer in the example spent some time figuring out how he could convince his congressman. In the process, he threw away a number of alternative plans, including one to describe his own student senate campaign and the crazy, successful stunts they pulled. It sounded, he decided, like a great plan for a story but a bad plan for convincing a congressman.

Once you have formed even a tentative plan for what you want **to do,** it is easier to start a plan for what you will need **to say.** Let the two kinds of planning feed on each other. A plan to do something lets you do a more goal-directed search of your own memory and other resources as you go after the information you will need. At other times, knowing something you wish **to say**—whether it is a key word, a good phrase, or a whole argument and set of facts—can help you see a potential new goal. Figure 5–2 is a nice example of how plans are a way of playing around with your ideas and considering things you might do. Sometimes, when you are trying to juggle

FIGURE 5–2
Preliminary Sketch for a Magazine Article

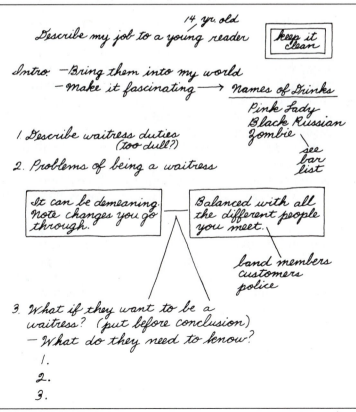

many options and ideas in your head, it helps to express them visually on paper, whether you use flow charts, diagrams, trees (as in Figure 5–1), or just doodles and connecting lines. Figure 5–2 shows a plan sketched out by a writer as she began an article for *Seventeen* magazine on her job as a cocktail waitress. Notice how her plan combines both goals and content and how it visually indicates the structure of her ideas, revealing main points, supporting details, and a balance between the pros and cons of the job. Although the plan is very rough, you can see how the writer uses it to adapt her knowledge about the job to the needs and interests of her reader. This sketch is not just a simple printout or outline of the *information* she has stored about this job. It is the beginning of a plan for what to do with that information as a writer. A good plan contains both content and goals for using that content.

Plans take many forms, from mental notes to informal sketches done on the backs of old envelopes to well-developed written plans such as outlines and proposals. The most useful plans are ones that combine topic information (what you want **to say**) with goals and plans for using that information (what you want **to do**).

 ### *STRATEGY 2* **MAKE YOUR GOALS MORE OPERATIONAL**

Let's suppose you have set up a goal: "I'm going to write a letter of application requesting a summer job." You realize that merely stating your request probably isn't enough. But what else can you do to meet your goal? To write that letter you need to make your goals more specific, or more operational. An operational statement is one that specifies actions—it tells you how to operate, what to do. For example, a more operational goal would be: "I'll try to arouse the reader's interest enough so that he or she will read my résumé, will remember at least two things about me, and will then ask me for an interview." Note that once you have established this set of subgoals or steps in accomplishing your overall goal, every paragraph in the letter you write will have a function. You will expect it to affect your reader in some specific ways, not just list the facts about you.

Goals that aren't operational are often highly abstract, such as: "I want to discuss team sports," "I'd like to impress my reader," "My aim is to do well in this course." They don't give you a clue about *how* to do it. Operational goals are more concrete and specify a set of separate subgoals you can achieve along the way. For example, compare these two goal statements, one abstract, the other with a set of operational subgoals.

1. I intend to become rich and famous.
2. I intend to study probability and statistics so I can get rich quickly in Las Vegas, then study writing and become famous by writing a best seller on how I did it.

We can apply this same process to writing. Let us suppose you were going to write a paper on the role of nonverbal communication in classrooms. In general, your goal is to be persuasive: "to convince the reader to see things my way." You might then define this more operationally as "I'll try to forcefully argue both sides of this controversy in order to show the reader that I have pinpointed the crucial issues and also to pave the way for my own ideas." For this particular paper you might then set up a number of subgoals such as:

1. Define nonverbal communication.
2. Use examples to show how it works in the classroom (perhaps putting this section at the beginning for dramatic effect).
3. Review the conflicting studies on whether or not a teacher's nonverbal communication can affect students' IQ or achievement scores.
4. Argue for your position, supporting it with your own observations of the specific ways children respond to nonverbal communication in the classroom (describe Head Start experiences).

When do you need to use this strategy and make your plan more "operational"? Maybe never. An operational plan, like a good road map, lets you decide where to turn next. But sometimes you don't need a map. You may want to start out with a good intuition or a rather vague goal and wait to see what comes out when you write. Plunging in can open the door to discovery. But it can also get you lost. This strategy of *trying to be operational*—of trying to figure how you might reach your goals—is particularly valuable under three circumstances. One is, of course, at the beginning when you want to make a good plan as usable as possible. The second is when you feel momentarily stuck or uncertain. That feeling is a signal to look at your plan (not at the word or sentence you may be stuck on) and try to spell out how such a plan could operate, what you might do next. A third time to get operational is when you want to think over your own options for a given assignment, as in the situation below.

The students who wrote the papers on time management discussed earlier had a number of practical strategies for doing this assignment. Let me describe in an operational way four strategies which I observed writers using in this read-to-write assignment and ask you to compare the costs and benefits of these plans for yourself.

Some students used a familiar "gist and list" strategy. To do this you go through the readings to find key words and figure out the "gist" or main idea of each passage. Once you have notes that summarize each authority, you use this list of "gists" to write your paper, maybe adding comments of your own as you go along or at the end of the paper. In class, we began to call this the "efficiency" strategy.

Do you see some costs and benefits? Will this strategy help you learn the material? Yet what role does this "operational" plan give to your own ideas? What would a reader who liked a "gist and list" paper have to want?

Other students used a strategy we named the "TIA" strategy, for the words True, Important, and I Agree. To use this method, you go through the readings looking, not for the gist, but for ideas that seem True, Important, or ones with which you Agree. You pick out ideas you find interesting or relevant, even if they are not related to each other or to the author's main idea. From this pool of TIA ideas you write your paper, commenting on what you found interesting. Taken alone the TIA won't let you write a synthesis, but it can build a foundation.

One problem with the TIA way of planning a paper is that it can lead a writer simply *to select familiar ideas* without thinking over contradictions to those ideas, evidence for or against them, or what the authors in the source are trying to say. So some students we observed added a "dialogue" strategy in which they would argue with the text in their own thoughts. They would think about their own experience, pull in other information, and talk to the author. And then they would let the author talk back, as they tried to imagine another point of view. For instance, a student might "dialogue" with William James by thinking, "Yeah, that is true, it's like getting a second wind when I'm running. But it doesn't always work—if it's 3:00 A.M., you don't remember what you read even if you do push on because you aren't alert. But maybe if he means mental fatigue, not lack of sleep, then this would make sense." Notice how the dialogue lets you include your own ideas and still come up with a more balanced and qualified response. (Notice the little words such as "true," "but," "if," "maybe," "sometimes, but not always," "then," and "because." These are signals that you are building a more conditional, qualified, balanced idea of what is "true." Look for them in your own thinking and in your prose.)

Finally, a few students added a "constructive" strategy to their planning. In addition to selecting ideas they wanted to use, they spent some time actually thinking about their goals for the paper and what might be a good way to get to those goals. As one writer said to himself part way through: "Unless I just restate a lot of this stuff, talk about the fact that, you know, it is important. . . . But that's not what they want. They want me to assimilate this, to come up with some conclusions—and I guess they should be related to something. So . . . Yeah, I'm gonna deal with the problem, yeah, the problem of how to attack time management. This is good."

When you spend time like this writer thinking about your options, about how to construct a paper, and how to guide your own process, you have just made your goals more operational. Does the benefit of planning seem worth the cost?

STRATEGY 3   **LISTEN TO INTUITION AND CHANGE YOUR PLAN**

Do the examples of planning you have seen so far look more rational and neat than your plans look (even given the fact that a textbook must be as clear as possible)? Or have you found that even when you had a well-developed plan, like those in Strategy 1, that you still hit a roadblock part way into writing? If so, your experience is perfectly normal. In fact, experienced writers who use private mental dialogues and see their writing as part of the ongoing conversation Burke described in Chapter 1 expect changes, just as you expect a live conversation to affect your thinking. There are many paths to a good paper. Here are three common ones:

1. *Plan and write.* This path lets you start with the big picture, build a plan that takes your own goals and your reader into account, and carry out that good plan in writing. A good plan may only exist in your head and it may be messy and vague at spots, but it is a map that charts your journey.

2. *Plan, abandon, and replan.* However, if your rhetorical problem is complex or you have high standards for this paper, you are likely to take a different path. Although you started with a good plan and may have written part of the text, your intuition tells you it isn't going to work as you intended. Or perhaps you have discovered a new organizing idea or you realize your own purpose and goals have changed as the result of planning and writing. This is the point to abandon your plans, follow your intuition, and build a new and better plan to guide your writing. That new plan may even save some of the text you wrote or it may send you back to the drawing board. Plans are made to be abandoned when a better plan comes along.

3. *Write and then plan.* Sometimes the best course of action is simply to start writing. If the topic is new, if it seems perplexing, or if you are feeling blocked for one reason or another, use writing itself to discover what you might have to say about a topic. Techniques such as freewriting and brainstorming, discussed in Chapter 6, let you ignore matters such as spelling, complete sentences and even organization in order just to get your thoughts down in writing. Then, when you can look back at what you are thinking, build a plan based on your best ideas.

As you probably already know, the hardest part of planning is not getting plans or writing text, but being willing to give both of them up when you discover things, as writers normally do, through writing.

 STRATEGY 4   **REVEAL YOUR PLAN TO THE READER**

Having a good plan makes a paper easier to write. It also makes it easier for a reader to read, particularly if you indicate your plan early on. Revealing your plan is like showing the reader a road map;

it helps him or her follow the discussion, see your point, and grasp the importance of what you are saying.

One of the best ways to do this is to open your paper with a **problem/purpose statement.** Such a statement is a concise, informative introduction that does two things. First, it sets up the problem, issue, or thesis on which you will focus. Second, it states the purpose of your particular paper—that is, it tells the reader what you are going to do with your topic and what he can expect to get out of reading further. A good problem/purpose statement not only informs but motivates. It convinces the reader that there is a reason for what you have written—and a reason for him to read it. As you can see, a problem/purpose statement simply combines the introductory problem definition, which was discussed in Chapter 1, with a statement of your rhetorical purpose.

A problem/purpose statement is often simple and direct, as in the examples below. It could be a paragraph or a page long; it could be labeled "Introduction" or "Background," or it could just come at the beginning. It might be embedded within a dramatic example or an interesting lead-in to your discussion. The particular form your problem/purpose statement takes is not important. Just be sure the information is there, because your reader will be looking for it.

Here are some sample beginnings of papers. The purpose statements are underscored. Notice that in Examples 2 and 3 the beginning sentences define a problem that the reader is also concerned about. And Example 3 includes a preview of how the paper is organized, giving the reader a helpful plan for reading.

A finished problem/purpose statement looks simple and straightforward but is sometimes hard to write, for this reason: In order to adapt your statement for the reader, you must switch roles, from being a researcher to being a writer. For example, a psychology student who has been researching the theories of Carl Jung may discover, when formulating her purpose statement, that her implicit purpose has been to "show all the things I know about Jung." Yet she realizes that the intended reader, her professor, will be less interested in the quantity of details she has accumulated than in whether she fully understands Jung's theories. A more realistic purpose for her paper would be "to show I have a clear grasp of Jung's concepts and can contrast them with several other important theories," and her revised statement should reflect this plan.

Problem/purpose statements help not only the reader but the writer. Working on a purpose statement can bring a writer back to the questions of "What is my goal?" and "Who is my reader?"—questions that should always govern the writing process. The importance of designing for a reader and writing reader-based prose will be discussed further in Chapters 9 and 10.

Writers use various conventions or text patterns to express their plan. Although the names for these text conventions often have more than one meaning, here are the standard terms:

The word **theme** is sometimes used to refer simply to the **topic** of the paper (for example, the theme of Chapter 9 in *Word Play* is naming). Other times the term theme refers to the **main point** or **gist.** It describes what you might want readers to think or remember if they summed up your paper. This second, more complex definition of theme, which involves the writer's point of view or conclusion about the topic, is more useful.

The term **topic sentence** is used in the same two ways as "theme" when talking about paragraphs. Sometimes a topic sentence simply announces the topic (such as, "Dictionaries work in many ways"). At other times it states the gist or point the writer wanted to make *about* the topic (as in, "Despite what most people believe, dictionaries do not give 'meanings' of words, but present 'meaning' by offering a selection of synonymous words and phrases").

The term **purpose** can refer to a conventional purpose—such as describe, argue, define, and so on—or it can refer to the unique rhetorical purpose behind a given text or even a given paragraph (for example, "I want to show why a dictionary definition fails to capture a word's 'meaning in use'").

In general, readers want to know the topic, the theme or point of the text, and the writer's purpose as soon as possible. If this information isn't actually stated, they will infer it, even though they may guess wrong. If your prose is clear and under control, your reader should be able to state both the gist of what you have to say and your thesis or major claim. To make sure that readers get these things right, writers depend on three standard text conventions.

One is the familiar **topic sentence** that gives the gist of the paragraph. The second is the **thesis statement** that not only states the writer's claim or thesis, but signals the reader that this claim is the major one. Some of the most common signals include putting the thesis statement in the form of an assertion, putting it at the end of an introductory paragraph, or putting it at the end of a "Some people think, but, in fact . . ." argument. (We will discuss the process of building a thesis in more detail in Chapter 8.)

The third convention, shown in these examples, is the problem/purpose statement. A **problem/purpose statement** is a specific sentence (or group of sentences) in the text which lays out the problem or issue under discussion and reveals what the writer proposes to do in this paper. As with the thesis statement and topic sentence, writers use various conventions of placement and wording to help the reader recognize the problem/purpose statement. (We will look at problem definitions in more detail in Chapter 8.)

Do these three text conventions ever appear in the same sentence? A writer could simply assert a thesis without defining a problem or indicating the purpose of the paper. In that case, there would be no overlap. But if the writer's main purpose were to explore, evaluate, or argue for a given thesis (as in Example 1 below), then the problem/purpose statement might contain a statement of that thesis within it. Notice how the underlined statement in Example 1 presents the problem or conflict that sparked this whole discussion, a thesis about German art and politics, and an indication of the purpose which will organize the essay (to understand why people followed Hitler) and a purpose which might motivate us to read (to have a more complete history). But also notice how the first and second paragraphs begin with their own, more local topic sentences about political movements and the role of artistic images. Each of these could have been the thesis for an entire essay—but they weren't. Could you as a reader have picked out the problem, purpose, and thesis if it hadn't been underlined?

Example 1
Essay for a Course in Western Civilization

Wagnerian Opera in Hitler's Germany

Political movements often seem abstract to the people who live during them. For that reason, people will often view the movement in terms of some specific image, often an image of a group of people. For example, people who lived in the northern United States during the 1850s and 1860s tended to see the problems of the time in terms of slavery, as described in Uncle Tom's Cabin, rather than in terms of economics. In the same way, Germans during the 1920s and 1930s found it easier to think of Germany's economic problems as being caused by an international conspiracy headed by Jews rather than as being caused by a world-wide depression.

The images people use to understand the times they live in are often provided by artists and musicians. Sometimes the artists create these images spontaneously and deliberately, as Wagner did in his operas during the mid-1800s. At other times, a government may choose an image that it likes, as Hitler chose Wagner's mythic images of the German people—fifty years after Wagner's death. Either way, the artists and the images they create give people specific symbols to which they can attach their feelings about social problems, and which they can use in deciding how to act. In this way, artists help people to participate in the events of their time. The pictures of heroic-looking soldiers and vicious Jews created by Hitler's artists increased anti-Semitic feeling in Germany. At the same time, Hitler's personal friendship with the revered Wagner family linked him and his growing war machine with musical images of Aryan supremacy. Thus, Hitler's patronage of Wagner's operas encouraged the German people to see themselves as direct descendants of the gods and heroes in those operas. Although it may seem incongruous to discuss a political movement such as the Third Reich in terms of the art it encouraged, no history of the Reich can be complete without such a discussion, because without it we cannot fully understand whey the German people followed Hitler into World War II.

Example 2
Report to the College Placement Director

Many students perform poorly in job interviews even though they are skilled in their subject area and well qualified for the job. The most frequent problem in such interviews is that students are unnerved by certain kinds of questions. Although they can answer any technical questions concerning their field of study, they have difficulty answering questions about personal motives, weaknesses, and strengths. In addition, they lack experience in interviewing situations. The purpose of this paper is to propose a program for giving students an introductory experience in interviewing and answering the personal questions interviewers regularly ask.

Example 3
Guide to Dealing with Rent Hikes

Recent inflation has created an increased conflict between realtors and tenants in our area. Landlords need higher rents to pay for rising costs and to make a profit from their business. Tenants are also faced with increasing prices and want to keep rents as low as possible. When landlords raise rents sharply, tenants are faced with the problem of deciding how to react, since no action is itself a response.

The tenants' reaction to a rent hike consists of two steps: (1) making the right choice among the alternative actions available, and (2) given that choice, executing it in the best possible way. This report explores the tenants' options, the factors to consider in choosing an option, and the procedures tenants should follow for each kind of response.

STRATEGY 5   USE COLLABORATIVE PLANNING

Of all the strategies in this book, collaborative planning is probably the most powerful—that is, it can make dramatic improvements in a text, it can be adapted to your specific needs or problems, and it can help you discover important things about yourself as a writer. Collaborative planning comes at the end of this chapter not only because it is the most important, but because it is a place to pull the other strategies together. Working with a collaborative partner is one of the best ways to explore a rhetorical problem and talk over an assignment. Talking to another person can help you make a **plan to do** by making your goals more operational and letting you talk through a problem/purpose statement with a potential reader.

COLLABORATION AND INDIVIDUAL AUTHORSHIP

But, if you are like many writers in college, you may be skeptical about the idea of collaboration. After all, weren't we taught in school that getting ideas from other people was cheating? Doesn't our romantic image of writers picture a lonely individual, up in a garret? Or maybe you have worked in groups and found that group work could be frustrating. On the other hand, you may find that you already do a lot of informal collaboration that plays an important role in your writing. Use the brief survey above to look at the ways you use collaboration and then compare your experience with that of other members of your group—either people you survey or other members of your course. Check a box if you have done the activity two or three times. How many of these do others use? When you tally up the results, figure out what percent of your group uses each strategy and where you fit in the picture. Is informal collaboration a "common" or a "rare" event?

Activity	You	Your Group
1. Interpreting an assignment or analyzing the rhetorical situation with someone you know.	☐	☐
2. "Talking over" or "trying out" your plans and ideas for a text in informal conversation before writing.	☐	☐
3. Meeting for a deliberate planning session or conference with an advisor, instructor, or friend.	☐	☐
4. Submitting a written plan for comments before you begin a writing project.	☐	☐
5. Engaging as you write in a sustained mental "dialogue" with the author of another text or an imagined reader, who gets to "speak back" in your imagination.	☐	☐
6. Getting feedback on a text from your peers, classmates, or co-workers.	☐	☐
7. Getting feedback on a text from a mentor, instructor, group leader, or manager.	☐	☐

Activity	You	Your Group
8. Negotiating with advisors, editors, instructors, readers, and peers about the plan or text you want to write.	☐	☐
9. With whom do you typically collaborate? ☐ Friends ☐ Family ☐ Classmates/Co-workers ☐ Instructors/Supervisors	☐	☐
10. What are the problems you have encountered in collaborating?	☐	☐
11. Did the people you noted in question 9 differ as collaborators? What makes a good supporter?	☐	☐

If you were to ask professional people, including college teachers and researchers, whether they write alone or in collaboration, what would you find? When Andrea Lunsford and Lisa Ede asked 1,400 such people about their writing on the job, the first response they got was, "I write alone." But as they discovered, many people assumed that collaboration meant two people drafting sentences together on a co-authored text. When Lunsford and Ede asked more about what people were really doing, they found that 87% of these engineers, city planners, chemists, psychologists, academics, managers, and technical communicators depended on some form of collaboration in their writing. Informal collaboration is a normal way to get things done for experienced writers and for professionals who write on their job. Informal collaboration plays an important role for many college writers, too. However, you will find that using the slightly more structured **collaborative planning strategy** described below will let you get a lot more out of this normal process, without giving up its informal and social nature.

COLLABORATIVE PLANNING: THE BASICS

Collaborative planning is an informal session in which you (the **planner**) meet with a friend (the **supporter**) to talk over and develop your plans for your current piece of writing. As the **planner,** you schedule this meeting whenever you feel you have a plan you can share, but before your plan or a text is "cast in stone." That is, call up your **supporter** when you have ideas, notes, maybe even some draft text, but be prepared to walk away from your session with a new, expanded, or revised plan. (Most writers will probably want to use some of the strategies for generating and organizing ideas which we discuss in the next two chapters *before* coming to a collaborative session.) Or you may collaborate to re-plan a paper after getting feedback. The timing depends on what you want to accomplish.

Find a quiet place where you can talk without distractions. Plan to spend 15–20 minutes on your paper, and then switch roles and give your partner the kind of support he or she gave you. But be warned. Many writers find these discussions so helpful they go on far longer than expected.

As the planner, your job is to explain your ideas for your paper, to talk about any problems or questions you are having, and, in the process of explaining, to build a more developed image of your rhetorical situation and of what you want to do. Your partner, or supporter, will support your thinking and help you extend this plan by listening carefully, trying to understand, asking questions, and at times raising problems or suggesting possibilities. Collaborative planning differs from peer review in that the focus is on developing your plan, rather than evaluating your text. It differs from an ordinary discussion in that your attention is focused on a rhetorical problem and on building a **plan to do.** Collaborative planners use a prompt called the Planner's Blackboard (which we will describe below) to help them move from **plans to say** to **plans to do** by focusing attention on their purpose, key point, audience, and text conventions.

Finally, when you come to your session, bring a tape recorder and a tape for each person. You will soon learn to ignore the taping. The tape of your discussion is invaluable for two things: It lets you review the ideas you generate, and it lets you reflect on your own collaboration and planning strategies. If the setting doesn't allow you to tape your session, try to take notes during and immediately afterward. However, you are much more likely to make surprising discoveries when you can make independent observations from the tape.

THE ROLE OF THE PLANNER

When you initiate a Collaborative Planning session, your role as planner is to explain and elaborate your plan to your partner, to make your partner see what you are doing and why. But instead of just repeating the content of your paper, your job is to convey what your *key points* are, to reveal some of the *reasons and purposes* behind what you are doing, to predict how you think your *readers* will respond, and to think through some of the *conventions of written text* you might use to achieve your purpose or meet readers' expectations. Because these are key parts of your rhetorical problem, a good plan needs to bring all of these things into the picture. If your partner looks confused, that is probably not a sign that there is something wrong with your partner, but that *your plan* is not yet clear or coherent. The session is also a time for you to raise problems and to talk over alternatives and difficulties that may be at the back of your mind. Because ideas can fly by quickly in a collaborative session, it is wise to take notes on possibilities as they come up. Don't assume you will remember even your own good ideas!

Another part of your role as planner is to set the agenda for this session. What sort of help do you need at this time? Do you need to talk over the task itself—how to interpret the rhetorical situation or what someone expects? Do you need to brainstorm ideas in an open-ended way? Or do you want your supporter to play the role of a specific reader and give you feedback on how your argument or presentation will work? As planner, it is up to you to organize this collaborative session to be the most help to you. If it isn't working, stop, talk over how the session is going, and consider redesigning the focus of the session.

And finally, as the planner, it is your job to be prepared to talk— to have a plan that is developed enough to discuss, even if you have problems or are still in early stages. Your supporter will only help you develop what is already there. On the other hand, if you meet after your ideas are firmly fixed or the text is done, and you have no desire to change it, you will also be wasting your time. Good sessions depend on your ability to explore a rhetorical problem and consider options. As you will find, collaborative talk when you are in an exploratory stage will give you very different help from a session held when you have detailed plans or a draft you want to test. Both kinds of sessions can be useful in different ways. Designing a collaboration is up to you.

AN EXAMPLE OF COLLABORATIVE PLANNING

As you may recall, you have already seen an example of collaborative planning in Chapter 1. The discussion between Carter and Jennie comes from a transcript of a collaborative planning session these two writers taped in their freshman year of college. Their session was used in Chapter 1 to illustrate a rhetorical situation that included an assignment, plans, text, and readers' responses and because Carter had some smart things to say about the problem of moving into an academic discourse community. When we tuned in to their discussion at turn 30, Carter had a pretty clear idea of his main point, but let us look now at how that idea developed. When the session begins, Carter is telling Jennie about the differences between the papers he does for the composition course they are both in and for another course called Technology and People. Carter has a lot *to say*, but it isn't until turn 30 that he really gets down to the point this paper will make. As you read the transcript, notice what parts of this plan Carter and Jennie are trying to develop. The boldface type emphasizes some of their rhetorical thinking.

14 CARTER: And the problem that can come out of this is trying to decide what style to use for different classes, because when you first start taking the class, you really don't know what to expect, so you might not know what writing style to use for that class.

15 JENNIE: Yeah, yeah. I definitely see how different classes require different things from you. And I think that in itself can be a problem for writing, just because each class will like kinda put you in a mold of what they want and you have to fill those requirements, and you know they're gonna have limits on you, which will be a problem in writing when you want to express something in a different way, and you just can't do that. So that's gonna be like **your main focus and key point,** right?

16 CARTER: Right.

17 JENNIE: Well, what are **some of the main points** that you're gonna bring out **in this paper?**

18 CARTER: I'm gonna try to, well, **convince the reader** that these differences do exist for a lot of people. I'm sure that they don't exist for everybody, because probably a lot of people write the same way for everything—they don't really have a difference.

19 JENNIE: I don't know.

20 CARTER: You don't think? I think some people, you know, they might.

21 JENNIE: Well, it depends.

22 CARTER: They might not care. I mean, they might just write the same way for everything and not really care. I'm sure no students here *(laughs)* do that but. . . .

23 JENNIE: Yeah, yeah. That's what I mean. Well, **who's your audience for this?**

24 CARTER: My **audience** would probably be college students. It would really be **of interest probably to freshmen** because they're switching from high school and starting out college writing.

27 JENNIE: I see. Well, Carter, if your **audience** is gonna be **a college student,** I think every college student, you know, has to go through this change. I can see if your paper is to the **general public**—some people really don't write too much, and really write for one specific purpose, which would be the same all the time. **But if it's for a college student, I think** you should focus that it *does* change, not that it *might* change.

28 CARTER: Okay. You're right, I guess. You're always right.

29 JENNIE: *(Laughs)* Well. . . . nah, I'm just kidding.

30 CARTER: And my **audience,** they're probably gonna expect a lot of examples. I'm gonna have to use **a lot of examples to prove to them** that different writing styles exist, and **I want my audience to be able to relate their own experiences to this,** and maybe see how it affects them.

31 JENNIE: So what kind of examples are you gonna use? **Can you give me an example?**

32 CARTER: Um, okay, I'll give you a real big example. Switching from high school writing to college writing.

What makes this a successful session? We don't see dramatic breakthroughs or changes; Carter doesn't walk away with a brand new plan. What we do see is a writer who starts with a description of two college classes and ends up with a usable (operational) plan for a smart paper. And what does his supporter contribute? Although Jennie's question at turn 31 elicits some important new information that Carter hadn't thought of, Jennie doesn't add new ideas herself. What she does do is help Carter *turn his own ideas into a focused plan for a paper* that is organized around a few main points and tailored to what his particular audience is likely to expect.

THE ROLE OF THE SUPPORTER

It takes both energetic listening and imagination to be a good supporter. Although the supporter's main job is to help the planner elaborate his or her plan, supporters can play different roles.

The Questioning/Reflecting Role. This role is designed to draw out ideas and hold up a mirror to the planner's own thought. Like a good counselor, this kind of partner offers support and encouragement, rather than advice, and reflects back the planner's own ideas, with comments like: "Yes. You seem to be saying. . . ." (And here the supporter restates what he or she is hearing in his or her own words.) Or "Are you saying that your real purpose here is . . . ?" In the low-effort version of this role, the supporter is merely a laid-back "yes-man" who prompts the planner, but doesn't help extend the discussion. Writers soon become frustrated working with a low-effort supporter. But in the high-effort version, the supporter is a careful, active listener, on the lookout for connections and implications in the planner's own talk that the planner may not have seen. Reflecting can be a powerful strategy for helping planners explore their own ideas and discover gaps between what they meant and what they said. Notice how Jennie plays this role in turns 15 and 17.

The Problem-Finder Role. This kind of supporter listens carefully for potential problems: gaps in the argument, parts he or she can't understand, claims that are open to question. The problem finder also brings up alternative ways of reading the task, other goals that haven't been considered, and negative responses readers might have. This supporter helps the writer deal with potential problems early, in the planning stage before the writer is committed to text. In the low-effort version, the partner is a nit-picker or sweeping critic (neither of which writers seem to enjoy). In the high-effort version, the supporter works to help define what the problem really is and what some possible responses could be. Notice how Jennie senses a problem at turns 19 and 21, expresses her doubt and then at 23 asks for more information about the audience. Raising this problem in turn leads Carter to think about who he really wants to address.

The Collaborator Role. This kind of supporter joins in the planner's effort to interpret the task, to develop a plan, to think of alternatives, to anticipate problems, and to evaluate opinions. This supporter may suggest new ideas or help the planner play around with various ways to organize a section or format a document. Although this may sound contradictory, in the low-effort version the supporter contributes by doing what is easiest—saying what he or she would do, as if this were the supporter's paper. The low-effort supporter simply lectures at or argues with the planner. In the high-effort version, on the other hand, the supporter has to listen carefully to the planner's intentions and needs, and works to help the writer do what he or she is trying to accomplish. In turn 27, Jennie offers a suggestion, much as she did in turn 37, which we read earlier (p. 8). Although she is happy to contribute her ideas, notice how she always ties them to Carter's goals as she understands them. And when she offers suggestions, she often starts by trying to restate or make sure she understands what Carter is trying to do.

When you are a supporter, pay attention to which role you are taking. Do you tend to take the same role all of the time? Try to get some feedback from your planner about what he or she finds most useful. If, when you become the planner, your supporter is stuck in one role and you need another, ask the supporter to switch strategies.

STARTER QUESTIONS FOR SUPPORTERS

Here are some questions/comments that let you take different roles as a supporter.

- Listen carefully and reflect back the **gist** of what you heard: "What I hear you saying is that _____. Am I hearing you right?"
- Ask the planner to **elaborate.** "You just said _____; tell me more about _____ (what you mean or why you said that)."
- Ask for more information about key parts of the **blackboard** that the planner has only explained in a sketchy way. (See the Planner's Blackboard in Figures 5–3 and 5–4 for a guide.) "If your purpose is _____, how are you going to do that? What are your other goals?"
- Ask—from time to time—how different parts of the plan are **connected,** especially when you see possible links or problems. "If your key point here is _____, how do you think your readers will respond to that?" Or "Is there any link between your purpose and the format you plan to use?"

- Let the writer know when you feel confused or see a **problem.** You don't need to have a solution; just give feedback about how the plan works for you. "I feel lost at this point; why did you say that?" "I don't know what you mean when you say _____." "Can you tell me how this part of the paper is linked to that part?" Your feedback as a "live reader/listener" (rather than as a critic or advice-giver) can help the writer begin to imagine how other readers might respond and start to plan with them in mind.
- **Share** your perception of the task or alternative strategies the writer might consider. "I saw the assignment a little differently; let's talk about what our options are." Or, "You might use an example here." Or, "That's an important point you could emphasize."

ENCOURAGING CONFLICT IN COLLABORATION

Some people go to great lengths to avoid conflict between themselves or others. And some types of conflict are rarely productive. *Interpersonal* conflict—focused on disagreement between people—leads to bad feelings and defensive attitudes. A second kind of conflict, *procedural* conflict—focused on what we should do and how to do it—can lead to a group that gets bogged down over the question of what road to take rather than getting somewhere. But sometimes, talking over alternative procedures and roads can save a lot of time and get you to a much better place. Finally, collaborators can engage in *substantive* conflict—focused on different ideas about the matter at hand. This kind of conflict, which can be carried out with a warm and supportive attitude among partners, can be highly productive.

People who cultivate substantive conflict are willing to delay closure; they don't seek immediate agreement or a snap decision. Instead they try to consider alternatives, problems, other perspectives. They ask probing questions such as "why is this *not* the best plan?" and "what else is involved?" When they do come to a decision, they do so with the sense that they have considered some alternatives and have chosen this as the "best" plan, not because it was the "only" plan they came up with.

Collaboration opens up the possibility for productive substantive conflict; but it doesn't ensure it will happen. One study of business students planning a co-authored text found that sometimes one partner tried to dominate the discussion or another took the role of a passive yes-man. Either move tended to squelch conflict.* Another problem to look out for: Sometimes a person's cultural background or upbringing makes him or her feel that expressing conflict is

*Rebecca Burnett, *Conflict in the Collaborative Planning of Co-Authors: How Substantive Conflict, Representation of Task, and Dominance Relate to High-Quality Texts.* Doctoral dissertation (Pittsburgh, PA: Carnegie Mellon University, 1991).

inappropriate. Many women are socialized to be agreeable, whatever they are thinking. When this happens in your group, people with good ideas may be reluctant to express a difference of opinion. Try to deal with any of these problems in a direct but tactful way. Expressing different perspectives is both a way to support other people and an important thinking strategy. It may be important for you and your partner or group to look at your own patterns of interaction, to acknowledge your different attitudes about conflict, and to discuss ways you can use it best.

THREE PRINCIPLES OF COLLABORATIVE PLANNING

Although collaborative planning shares some obvious features with peer editing, teacher conferences, and group sessions, it differs from them in some significant ways. Writers can use collaborative planning before they write, in the middle of a draft, or as a part of reviewing a text. However, when they design their planning sessions, three principles should apply:

- Authority (and the "floor") belongs to the writer as a planner and thinker.
- The aim of this planning process is to explore options and build a more elaborated plan To Do that involves all four areas of the Planner's Blackboard.
- The supporter's role is to help the planner develop a plan and become more aware of his or her own writing strategies.

🖋 MOVING FROM PLANS TO SAY TO PLANS TO DO

Talking and working with other people is a powerful strategy. But collaboration alone won't help you develop a good plan. Nor is it enough simply to know something to say about your subject. To build a **plan to do** something, you will also need to consider the conventions of the discourse you are entering, your own point and purpose, and how your reader will respond. The Planner's Blackboard can help you think strategically and focus your collaborative talk on these key rhetorical issues.

PLANS TO SAY

The first goal of many writers is to develop a **plan to say,** that is, to get a notion or even an outline of ideas and language they want to see in final text. To make this idea more concrete, think of your mind as a mental blackboard (see Figure 5–3) on which you can jot

FIGURE 5–3
Planner's Blackboard for a Plan to Say

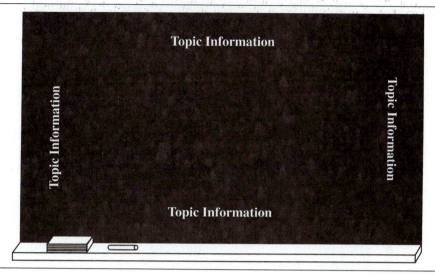

notes, draw connections, sketch maps or outlines, and post ideas, headings, transitions, and wording that will go in your text. Strategies like brainstorming, nutshelling, and issue trees are all good ways to generate ideas and language.

In working on a **plan to say,** you are spending time posting notes on a metaphoric Topic Information blackboard. Some writers spend all of their planning time thinking about what to say. If the task is simple or if their knowledge is already adapted and organized around what the reader needs, then this **plan to say** can do the job by itself. But unless you are writing a short-answer exam, plans dictated by what a writer knows about the topic are usually not enough. In academic writing, readers generally expect you to use your knowledge to address an issue, explore a problem, or answer a question.

PLANS TO DO

Experienced writers do more than build **plans to say.** They start by reading the situation, reading the assignment and in a sense mapping out the problem space. Experienced collaborative planners, for instance, are likely to start by analyzing and interpreting the rhetorical situation with each other—why was this task assigned, how does it fit in the larger context of a course or a project, who is involved and what are their expectations, what are the features of this kind of discourse?

Second, experienced writers go on to build more elaborated **plans to do.** They look at their text as a rhetorical move in a transaction, and they ask themselves, what do I want to accomplish in this situation—what do I want my words *to do?*

Imagine the mental blackboard of an experienced writer. In addition to the Topic Information blackboard that is filled with things to say, there are three additional blackboards on which these writers are posting and revising ideas (see Figure 5–4). These writers spend time thinking and talking about three key areas:

Purpose and/or Key Point.   A text may make lots of "points," but the "key point," the gist, or the main claim is what gives coherence and an organization to the text. But why is the writer making *that* key point, and what is she trying to accomplish with that paragraph? What is her reason for using an illustration here instead of a list? The answer to all of these questions lies in the author's purpose or goals. An experienced writer not only can tell you about the general purpose (such as recommending policy guidelines), but about a whole cast of supporting goals and "how to" plans for doing something in text. The writer sees the different parts of the text as moves, each of which is designed to accomplish some purpose, and can tell you the reasons behind these moves.

Even more important, the writer recognizes that most professional texts have multiple purposes or a number of goals related to different readers. Sometimes these goals come in conflict with one

FIGURE 5–4
Planner's Blackboard for a Plan to Do

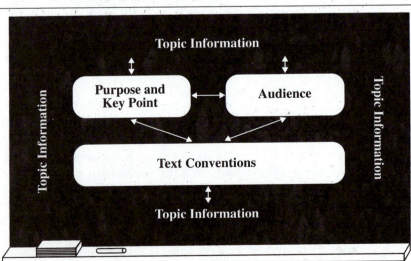

another. Planning is the place to recognize and begin to negotiate these conflicts before they lead to a disjointed text.

Notice how much Carter is trying to accomplish in his text. As he says in turn 30, he wants to convince some skeptical freshmen that these different writing styles really do exist (remember Matt in Chapter 1 who wasn't even impressed that this was a problem when he started to read Carter's paper). If his goal is to "prove" that differences exist, his current plan for doing that is to use lots of examples. But later Jennie adds another goal—she wants a "specific example from his life" because she thinks this argument needs to "become more real." On top of that, Carter has an even more ambitious goal—he wants to affect how his readers read this text; he wants them to actually relate his ideas "to their own experiences . . . to see how it affects them." Given these purposes (which are only part of the goals Carter sets for himself), what do you think about his plan for achieving them? Would you have advised him to consider any other goals?

Audience.   As you might predict, experienced writers generate ideas about who their readers are, what they know (or don't know) and what they need or expect. But an even more important strategy they use is to imagine how those readers might respond to the writer's own ideas or text. These writers then post a lot of ideas on their Audience blackboard that give them direct help in revising their developing plan and shaping their text. Here is where supporters, as a stand-in for the reader, can be especially helpful.

Notice how Carter's plan to convince people that different writing styles exist hinges on how his readers will respond. Some people might not pay any attention to this difference. And other people might not care. And his target audience, the new college freshmen, might not realize this will happen to them. Would you make the same sort of argument for these different readers?

Text Conventions.   As every writer knows, setting goals and imagining readers will not write the text for you. Experienced writers spend thinking time translating these more abstract plans into specific text moves. That is, they look at different ways they could carry out their goals in text—ways to emphasize a key point by placing it in a topic sentence or in bold; ways to convince a reader by offering evidence or dramatizing the point with a personal example; or ways to make a recommendation more effective by turning it into a procedure the reader can follow.

We use the term *text conventions* here to cover a broad range of alternative text features writers consider which are part of the established *conventions of written text*. When you think about it, many of these conventions are familiar to all of us; the genre features of a journal entry or an editorial, organizing plans such as comparison/ contrast, rhetorical techniques such as examples and quotation, and ways to format and present a text such as using headings to organize, italics to emphasize, or bullets to list. The difference is that experienced writers talk and think about these features as if they had a tool kit of alternative conventions they could use on this text to carry out their multiple purposes, develop their key point, and adapt to their readers.

When Carter and Jennie start thinking about some of the text conventions Carter will be using, the idea of a conclusion comes up. But Jennie's expectation that the conclusion should offer a *solution* doesn't fit Carter's intentions. Notice how Carter decides to use another convention for concluding—a convention which is a better fit to his original goals.

71 JENNIE: How about a concluding paragraph?

72 CARTER: Yeah. A concluding paragraph. It'll definitely be in there. That's a necessary in an Introduction to Writing paper.

73 JENNIE: Well, let's talk about your conclusion then.

74 CARTER: Okay. My conclusion . . .

75 JENNIE: Like, are you gonna try to offer a solution to this problem, or just talk about it?

76 CARTER: I might give them ideas on how to at least try to give ideas on how to, you know, keep these things straight.

77 JENNIE: Well, how could you really solve those problems?

78 CARTER: I don't think you really can solve it. All I said is, I might give ideas to maybe help, you know, nurse along.

79 JENNIE: Help what?

80 CARTER: Help people catch on to these differences sooner than I did. I learned the hard way.

81 JENNIE: Okay. Okay. Yeah, I see that.

Making Connections.   The small arrows on the Planner's Blackboard in Figure 5–4 visualize another distinctive move experienced writers make. As they plan and talk, they not only elaborate their plan in the four areas symbolized by blackboards, they also consciously try to build *links* between these different parts of their plan. For example, they talk about text conventions they could use to draw attention to their key point. They generate ideas that anticipate questions a reader might have. And they develop their own goals and plans by imagining what their reader already knows or thinks or expects.

In the long exchange about Carter's audience (turns 18–30), he was not only imagining who his readers (audience) were and how they would respond to his ideas (topic information), but was deciding on what it would take (text conventions) to convince them (purpose). Turn 30 is striking as a single turn in which all these concerns come together in a single comment. Sometimes these connections across the blackboards just come naturally. But experienced writers often stop and deliberately look for links between the parts of their plan and the ways they can use text conventions and their knowledge of the reader to meet their goals.

Using the Planner's Blackboard

The Planner's Blackboard is a visual metaphor that draws attention to three key facts. One is that inexperienced writers often find it difficult to tear themselves away from the Topic Information blackboard and end up developing only **plans to say.** Second, that even if you intend to work from a **plan to do,** these mental blackboards are empty until you post information on them—until you take the time to generate and elaborate specific ideas and plans. Even skimpy plans with a few ideas are better than no plans, but if your mental blackboards only have a few sketchy notes, there is probably a lot of the problem out there that you haven't thought about—and might need to consider. And finally, this metaphor reminds us that building links between purpose, audience, text, and topic information is one of the most important moves writers make. Even though some of these links are already "built into" the conventions of any given discourse (like the way a news story is adapted to answer readers' questions about "who, what, when, where, and why"), many of these links need to be created as part of a good rhetorical plan.

When you are doing collaborative planning, you and your supporter can use the Planner's Blackboard as a reminder or prompt to help you think about these areas, to test how well you have developed or elaborated your plan in each area, and to look for places you could try to forge a link between the ideas on two different areas. Your goal is a mental blackboard filled with scribbled notes and links. For this reason, it is important that your supporter be more than just a friend you talk over a paper with. Your supporter needs to have a conception of what a rhetorical **plan to do** involves and how to support your effort to develop one.

Some writers use the Planner's Blackboard as a kind of outline, actually writing little notes to themselves in the different boxes. You may find that helpful the first time you experiment with this strategy. However, the danger is that you will end up using the metaphor as a simple checklist, like a recipe or a short-answer test. Writers who do that say that it becomes a rather rigid straitjacket on their ideas, and they prefer the freedom of talking out ideas and taking notes in a more normal way. Think of the Blackboard, then, as a metaphor and a general-purpose prompt that you can adapt to your own needs and collaborative planning. Below is a small list of ideas that writers often try to develop in each area:

Topic Information Blackboard
- Interesting ideas, relevant points you want to include.
- Specific words, phrases, draft sentences.

Purpose and Key Point Blackboard

- The main purpose of the paper.
- The supporting goals, how-to plans, or things you hope to accomplish in each part.
- The key point you want to get across.

Audience Blackboard

- Things your reader expects or needs to know.
- What you want someone to think after reading the paper.
- Ways your reader might respond to what you have just said.

Text Conventions (the How-to-Do-It-in-Writing) Blackboard

- Features of different genres that fit your purpose (a problem/purpose statement, list of recommendations, dialogue, a news "lead," executive summary, a graph, an anecdote or case in point, budget breakdown).
- Conventional patterns of organization, development, and support (topic sentences, summaries, definitions, comparisons, reasons, examples, transitions).
- Visual cues to the reader (headings, sections, italics, bullets).

Links Between Blackboards

- Ideas that involve Information, Purpose, Audience, and/or Text.
- Reasons for one plan based on another blackboard (setting a goal or using a text convention because of the audience).

Setting a Context-Sensitive Agenda for Planning

As you can see, the Planner's Blackboard is a generic, all-purpose prompt that does not say much about what a specific **plan to do** might look like in a history course, for a literature paper, or for an assignment with a special purpose. What if you have a special problem you want to work on? There are many times when you will want to adapt the Planner's Blackboard to your own agenda or to a particular genre. For instance, if you are writing an analysis of a problem, as Carter was, you might want to focus your discussion on a special goal such as the goal "finding and defining a genuine problem" and on the text convention of writing a "problem/purpose statement." You might also want to tell your supporter to help you brainstorm different text conventions you could use to make something "seem more real." Or you may want that supporter to act as a skeptical reader so you can test out an argument. If your supporter is a friend, roommate, spouse, or family member who is not in your writing class, you may need to spend some time teaching this person how to be a supporter. A friendly discussion never hurts, but an active supporter can give you much more.

The important thing to remember in using collaborative planning is that it is up to you to make it useful. You are free to focus the session and to re-design the strategy to make it work for you.

REFLECTING ON YOUR OWN STRATEGIES

You may have wondered how making a tape of your collaborative session would contribute to your planning. It may have even made you nervous the first time you did it. However, some of the most important things you can learn about planning will not come from this book or an instructor, but from what you teach yourself. You are the one who must figure out ways to adapt general principles and strategies to specific situations. Reflecting on your own successes, problems, discoveries, and strategies is the best way to become a more flexible, strategic thinker. But simply recalling what you think you did in the heat of writing misses a great deal. You are likely to "remember" what you already thought you did and unlikely to discover surprises. The tape from a collaborative planning session can give you insight into a telescoped period of focused thinking. It can let you see how you use collaboration—and how you might design it to be more useful. And when the tape, as an independent record, is combined with your own memory, it lets you catch a glimpse of some of your own assumptions, expectations, and effective strategies. It can help you give a name to things you were aware of but didn't really control—which can include some of your most problematic and most powerful strategies for writing.

Reflection is most likely to lead to discovery when you write about it. Listen to your tape and write a brief, personal "observation and reflection" statement. Use the observation part to sketch out an interesting feature of your own planning session: Describe in concrete terms something that you found revealing, perplexing, or simply interesting about what you did. Then take a brief space to reflect on what that means, why it happened, or to draw some inferences about what it suggests to you.

Then in your class (if that is possible) or in your planning group, share your observations and reflections. When you share reflections, some things to listen for are:

- What problems did people encounter the first time they did collaborative planning? Why?
- How do other people plan to redesign their session next time; what discoveries have they made?
- What did other people see as most successful about their session?
- What did other people discover about being a supporter?
- What specific strategies are other writers using? Are some of these ones you share? If so, what is the source of these strategies?
- What assumptions or expectations are other people bringing to their writing? If so, what do you think is their source? Is there a reason to question any of these assumptions?

Here are some examples of discoveries other students have made. In addition to the insight these writers have into their own thinking, these observations show writers who are actively negotiating the demands, deadlines, and expectations they face as they take control of their own writing.

This writer moves from a detailed observation of what happened to a surprising interpretation of what it means:

My second collaborative session wasn't nearly as helpful as the first one had been. I arrived with the arguments I had worked on over the weekend fully thought out and presented them in a logical manner. At first my partner couldn't find any points that needed clarification, and since I didn't think I had any problems left, I didn't have any questions. I had a final paper in my mind which made it difficult to accept suggestions. And then she did find a major discrepancy that didn't fit neatly into my argument. If my paper had not been so etched in stone in my mind, I would have been more receptive and could have created a far better place for this idea than I did.

My reasons for writing a final draft were legitimate, though. We couldn't meet until Monday, and I didn't want to risk starting to write Monday night and not getting it revised to my standards in time. A "real" session would have been better, but in college where five classes are screaming for attention, it boils down to a problem of negotiation. Facing a deadline, I went back to my "tried and true" plan of early draft and revision. On the other hand, comparing these two papers, it seems that when I get help collaborating earlier in the planning stage (as I did on the first one) I produce better papers.

This observation, which comes after a writer's second collaborative session, tests his expectations against his experience:

One other thing that I observed was that when I was following through some thought process in my writing, my reasoning could go off tangentially. I was still following a thought process, but it had nothing to do with my initial problem. When talking aloud with my collaborators, as soon as I got off the subject, they would want to know what my purpose was in taking that particular line of reasoning.

In general I would say that collaboration helps. My initial inclination was that it was just a good exercise to develop an internal collaboration skill. While I think I can still improve my ability to collaborate internally, it is impossible for me to objectively view my own writing and thinking. No matter how vividly I can imagine a reader's response, it is good to have some empirical data as well. Talking to a person is easier than just talking to a wall.

Here is a writer coming to new images of what collaborative sessions can do:

One interesting feature is that as Chuck and I spoke about our plans, we seemed to be talking in circles. We would get surprisingly far along in explaining the details of what might work as a way to [apply schema theory] in our papers, and then loop back to find ourselves asking again, "what exactly is a schema?" or "do people share schemas or just conclusions they've made?" or "I'm not sure that's a schema though, what do you think?" In other words, we got off to these running starts, in the midst of which we were forced to question our basic understanding of schemas in order to continue.

After listening to the tape, it is fair to say that our knowledge of schemas was not as strong, initially, as it should have been. However, the confusion was, in my opinion, beneficial in that it forced us to look for answers in [the articles on schemas], where we stumbled on new ideas we wouldn't have explored otherwise.

Another interesting observation was that . . . it wasn't long before I took over in asking scores of questions about my own paper. As I listened to myself doing this on the tape, I realized that I was asking Chuck the same questions I would have been asking myself had he not been there. Only his answers often led to new ideas.

PROJECTS AND ASSIGNMENTS

In doing the writing assignments below, use this chapter to help you begin your plan, but as you work, you may also wish to read the chapters on generating and organizing ideas which follow.

1 In responding to the "mystery texts" on page 83, some students found that they assumed that "academic writing" was, by nature, "stuffy, boring, bland, limited, strictly factual, impersonal, and not creative." If you have to do academic writing, this is a pretty discouraging image of the task. Do you think this image is *necessarily* true? Do some of the features of academic discourse, for instance, work quite well for "insiders" but not for new readers?

If you could imagine an "ideal academic essay," that could be written by a student and also meet the needs of the academic discourse community, what would it be like? Use a text (from an academic journal, a textbook, or a student paper) to help you describe your ideal by supplying examples of features you would keep or change. See if you can convince other students and your instructor that your ideal version is the one worth writing.

[Here, by the way, are the sources of the mystery texts: (1) An undergraduate student's paper based on readings on revision. (2) A graduate student's paper on the same readings. (3) A report from a collaborative research project on revision by Linda Flower, John R. Hayes, Linda Carey, Karen Schriver, and James Stratman (all teachers and researchers) published as "Detection, Diagnosis and the Strategies of Revision" in *College Composition and Communication* 37 (Feb. 1986), p. 16. (4) A paper titled "Pre-Text and Composing" also published in *CCC* [38 (Dec. 1987), p. 397] by Stephen Witte (who is a researcher, teacher and also the editor of another scholarly journal, *Written Communication*). (5) From an interview with the novelist Alberto Moravia in *Writers at Work: The Paris Review Interviews,* ed. Malcolm Cowley (NY: Viking Press, 1957), p. 220. (6) From the Education section of *Newsweek* (Jan. 27, 1986) in an article titled "Why Johnny Can't Reason," signed by William D. Marabach with Connie Leslie in New York and bureau reports.]

2   Rewrite one of the mystery texts on page 83 (or a short piece of your own) to belong to a different kind of discourse: adapt the format, the voice, the purpose, and conventions you use for a different group of readers. Test your old and new mystery texts on real readers: Can they guess the type of writing from your samples; can they spot the original? Keep notes on the decisions you made in order to revise and on the clues your readers used to predict who was who. Discuss what you now see as the key features of "academic writing."

3   Look back at a paper you have written for another class. Use the Read-to-Write list of options on pages 85–86 to analyze what you did. Did you make some choices consciously on that paper and just assume others; what were the costs and benefits of your decision?

4   This assignment is a thought experiment that looks at why people treat (seemingly) simple tasks in such different ways. Look at the assignment (pp. 84–85) that the college freshmen were given and imagine it was assigned in the English class you had most recently. Given the options on pages 85–86, what do you think you would have done and why? Now compare your prediction of what you might have done with the text handed in by a freshman in that class. What do you think her goals were; what was going through her mind? This is the complete text:

> I have tried to incorporate these ideas into my statement but I have been wandering in circles long enough. To continue to struggle for words would not be an efficient use of time and wasting excessive time does not seem appropriate, especially on a paper about time management.

Now, as the third step in this thought experiment, can you think of any way to account for the difference between the decisions you might have made and the one this writer did make?

5   Give yourself the task of interpreting a text by using it for your own purpose. Read your source text, and instead of summarizing or synthesizing what the author(s) said, try to apply whatever seems relevant in the sources to understanding a problem you bring or to carrying out a purpose of your own. Try to signal your purpose to the reader in your problem/purpose statement and stick to that purpose by making each paragraph contribute to your plan. (To create a realistic academic conversation, your instructor may suggest an issue or sources that could be shared with your class. But the purpose of this paper is up to you.)

6   Explain the following assignments by translating them into actions you might take as a writer.

   a. Name an economic liberal and explain why and how his ideas place him in the category of liberals.

   b. Analyze the meaning of the raft in *Huckleberry Finn*.

   c. In what ways did the Romantic movement affect nineteenth- and early twentieth-century society?

   d. "Although history is often seen in terms of great individuals, looking at it in that way can give a seriously distorted understanding of the time and events in which that individual participated." Discuss this statement as it applies to Napoleon Bonaparte.

7   *Checklist: A Problem/Purpose Statement.* Write a problem/purpose statement and ask someone else to role-play the part of your intended reader. Have him (or her) respond by telling you what he would want from such a paper and what your statement has led him to expect. Or evaluate your statement using the checklist below.

☐ a. Have you defined a problem, a critical issue, or a thesis on which your paper will focus?

☐ b. Have you told the reader the purpose of your paper?

☐ c. Have you given the reader any preview of how your paper is organized, any road map for reading?

8   Good ideas and better plans have a habit of developing while you are writing a draft. Can you help this writer out? Here is her initial problem/purpose statement.

> In a discussion of "linguistic chauvinism," Peter Farb asserts that "English is a sexist language" and many of his examples show sexual bias in the university (p. 142). He also shows how other linguists dispute whether this bias exists or if it is a serious problem. However, student writers have to evaluate the implications of these different viewpoints. If they hope to reach an audience that includes a significant number of women (including professors and other students), they need to learn ways to express their thoughts that do not "make women invisible."

This seems like a good beginning, however, because this writer made a planning tape (as described in Chapter 2), we can see how her plan developed.

> I'm ready to take a break and I find I'm having a lot of trouble getting my paper to hold together. As I've been writing I've gradually decided that what I'm trying to say here is that I agree with Farb's basic argument, but I think he stops short. Let's see, when was this written . . . oh, 1974. Oh, . . . he just seems to throw up his hands at some point and say language can't change the system. It's like the system has to change first. There's nothing you can do. And I think that ignores some . . . some good alternatives for avoiding sexist language. And that seems to be what I have ended up writing about most, all the alternatives. Yeah, that's the point. I guess my focus has just changed. Now what?

Can you help this writer take advantage of her expanded sense of the problem? Rewrite or expand her initial paragraph and problem/purpose statement to include this new view of the problem and to make it preview both sets of ideas.

9   In his book *Word Play* (New York: Knopf, 1974, p. 6) Peter Farb says: "The language game shares certain characteristics with all other true games." He names five characteristics of a language game: (1) It has a minimum of two players. (2) Social pressure may force even bystanders to play. (3) Something must be at stake for both players. (4) Players are usually distinguished by their particular style and by their ability to shift styles if needed (as in shifting from formal to folksy speech). (5) Finally, like all games it is structured by rules people learn unconsciously as part of a discourse community (such as who speaks when, what not to say, how to make your point, and expressions or attitudes that show you are an insider).

How well does this theory fit your experience of language in action? Write a paper in which you interpret and apply Farb's ideas to this question. Think of a language game in which you are relatively expert (such as, talking like an insider about music and musicians, about football, feminism, or computers) or take an everyday game such as counseling friends or negotiating with parents, roommates, teachers, or dates. Play the game to get a fresh observation and some notes, then use Farb's five rules to help you analyze the language game you just played. Keep at least two purposes in mind as you write your paper: Try to explain your own language game to an outsider and try to test Farb's theory. Address your paper to other people in this academic conversation who have also read Farb and wondered about his theory.

(As a journal entry, you might wish to keep notes on how your task representation of this assignment develops as you work. These notes will help you on assignments in Chapter 8.)

10 Is informal collaboration a "common" or a "rare" event? Use the collaboration questionnaire described under Strategy 5 to conduct a survey of ten people who form a group of some sort (such as business versus art majors, commuting students, people at work). Check off a strategy if your respondent has used it at least two or three times, then tally the percent of your group which uses each strategy. When you compare your results with the rest of your class:

- Compile all your results to get a picture of the whole. Which activities are common, which are rare across the people surveyed?

- Do certain groups differ in clear ways from the "norm" of your sample as compiled by the whole class?

- Did questions 10 and 11 (about problems and good supporters) turn up any shared experiences or frequent answers?

- Did you learn anything interesting or surprising either from these patterns or from doing the survey itself?

- Write your own analysis of how writers use collaboration, based on your observations.

11 To introduce yourself to Collaborative Planning, I suggest you experiment with it in three phases: one focused on making **plans to do,** a second focused on the dynamics of being a collaborator, and a third focused on your own observations and reflections. Although reading about this strategy helps, experimenting and reflecting with a group will show you much more.

MEETING 1: MAKING A PLAN TO DO

Let's start with a rhetorical situation that provides a reason to plan and write. Look back in Project 4 at the short text written by a real freshman for her composition course and recall your theory about her goals and intentions. Because Darlene (a pseudonym for a real student) and her class were part of the Reading-to-Write study, we can also look at a taped transcript of Darlene thinking aloud in her dorm room as she was writing that paper. It may surprise you to find that in spite of her short text, Darlene spent a long time on this assignment. Here are some of the things she was actually thinking at different points in this long session. Do you see any assumptions or strategies that may have been the source of her trouble? (Underlined text is being written as Darlene talks.)

(1) *I'm just going to treat this like a journal, I think, and just write a statement. It's not going to be graded, I think. I don't think I have to worry too much about it.*

(2) (Later, after more reading) *And so the ones who get things done manage their time wisely, but what do I have to say about it? . . . These readings just don't do anything for me, and I don't even know what I'm supposed to be doing. I feel like such a wuss. What do I do?*

(3) (Later, rereading assignment) *So I'm just gonna—I don't care, I'm going to interpret them the only way I can interpret them. . . . Let's just put what the authors agreed on.* <u>*Authors agree*</u>*—If at least two of them concur, then we'll say they agree.* <u>*Authors in general agree that*</u> *. . . . But then they don't agree. There's nothing you can say about this.*

(4) (Later, writes a beginning sentence) <u>*I had a difficult time writing a*</u> (put it in quotes) <u>*"comprehensive statement" about time management because the notes I read didn't help.*</u> *. . . . It's not that they didn't help, 'cause I guess they helped. They didn't write the essay for me, is the problem . . . they didn't seem to make a clear statement.*

(5) (Near the end) *Great, I have 5 lines. . . . Send a telegram. Hello. Stop. I don't know what to do! Exclamation. How can I possibly make this into anything? Now I sound like one of the kids in the survey. Yes, I put it off till the last minute. But I did not. It's 12:58 p.m. It's noontime. I'm sitting here thinking about rehearsal tonight. I'm sitting here thinking about anything but—that's not true. I'm thinking about time management. And I'm thinking that I'm not doing well, but I don't know why.*

Your Planning Problem

Given your experience and any class discussion you may have had about Darlene, what could you write that might help her (or other freshmen) deal more effectively with college writing? The purpose of Meeting 1, then, is to build the best plan your group can for responding to Darlene on the issue of "What should freshmen know about writing after high school." The second goal of this meeting will be to reflect on your own planning and what you did.

Start by developing a plan for your response to Darlene (or to entering freshmen at your own college) working as a collaborative planning group. Begin with a free-ranging discussion, but ask the person recording your ideas on the blackboard to try to group your ideas into the different areas of the Planner's Blackboard as they come up. Don't worry if your recorder is uncertain about where an idea fits—keep your attention on generating a rich set of plans and alternatives.

However, after you have come up with a good set of ideas, take time out to reflect on the state of your plan and what you have been doing as planners:

- First of all, where have you spent your attention? Do some blackboards have more information, more developed plans than others?

- If you were the one delegated to sit down and write this text right now for the group, is the plan you see adequate or would you like more help in specific areas? For example, do you know what the text would look like? Do you know what points should get priority and how you will do that in the text? Is this a well-developed **plan to do**? How do you know a good plan when you see one?

- Do you see any ideas that really fit in more than one blackboard? That is, did your planning make links across the blackboards with ideas that joined audience and purpose, for instance? Or did you come up with text convention ideas that solved a problem or helped you meet one of your goals? Do you see places you could generate links now if you thought about it?

- How many alternative plans or options did you come up with? Were you, as a group, willing to entertain potentially conflicting ideas? If so, can you track on the blackboard what emerged from those alternative plans or ideas? Or, on looking for them now, do you see any alternatives or generative conflicts in your ideas that might lead to a better plan?

Wrap up this experiment with rhetorical planning by reviewing the strong points of this process. What do you want to carry over into your own planning? In preparation for your second meeting on collaborative planning, spend 15 minutes sketching out your own plan for a response to Darlene. Bring whatever notes, outlines, or text fragments you find useful. Be prepared to explain to your supporter not only a plan for what you want **to say** but your plan **to do**. In addition, bring your responses to the survey questions on your collaborative experience and review the roles of planner and supporter.

MEETING 2: COLLABORATING AS PLANNER AND SUPPORTER

Meeting 1 focused on what it means to build a rhetorical plan **to do**. Use this second meeting to experiment with the roles of planner and supporter and to share your experiences with collaboration. You might start by discussing your own response to the surveys on collaboration or the results from the more formal Project 9 above.

When you review the different types of supporters discussed in the text or by your survey respondents, what do you prefer? Did the people you noted in question 9 on the survey differ in their style of collaboration? What makes a good supporter?

Use the rest of this meeting to experiment with and reflect on working as a planner or supporter. Do a short planning session on your response to Darlene with a partner. Then before you switch roles, spend a few minutes to discuss what you observed during this short trial run. Here are some questions you might ask about your session:

- How did you organize your discussion? Did you follow an outline, go through the Blackboard Planner areas, or go directly to the key points of the plan or to a problem?
- Did you develop a **plan to do** or a **plan to say?**
- Which area did you most need to concentrate on?
- Who had the floor?

- Which strategies did the supporter use and what effect did they have?
- How would you redesign a real session?

Share your responses to these questions with the group. What did you learn from this brief experiment you could use in a real session? Now switch roles, try the process again, and share your observations and reflections.

Use Collaborative Planning on Your Next Writing Task

Make an appointment to meet with your partner as soon as you have a plan (and probably some notes) which you are ready to talk about. Make sure to schedule your meeting far enough ahead of the due date that you have time to rethink your plan and write.

Have a tape recorder and a blank tape for each person at the session. Being nervous about the tape will soon wear off. Try to capture everything, even the informal talk, since that can be an important part of your session. Reviewing the tape later will let you recapture good ideas and let you reflect on your own successful strategies and on ways to guide your collaborative sessions.

MEETING 3: REFLECTING ON YOUR OWN PLANNING

Reflection may be your most important step, since here is your chance to learn from your own experience. Listen to the tape from your collaborative planning session to observe and reflect on what you learned. The first time you do this exploration you may want to focus on what you observed about the collaboration itself. But by the second or third time you carry out this reflection, you will probably want to focus on what you can discover about your own writing, assumptions, and strategies. In reflecting on your own strategies, look for things that work for you, but don't be afraid to look at problems, uncertainties, and difficulties, too, since those are also important places to learn about writing.

When you present your observation and reflection in class, try to distill the "interesting feature" that will let you and other members of the class share your experiences, problems, and discoveries.

Write a one-to-two-page "observation/reflection statement" in the form of a memo to the rest of your writing group to comment on your own experience as a collaborator, problem solver, and writer. Use the tape of your collaborative planning session to review what actually happened and to succinctly describe your observations—be specific, use examples, details, quotations from your tape, notes, and text. Combine this observation with your reflections or inferences about what you learned. Here are some possible topics for the Subject Line of your memo:

Subject: An Interesting Feature of My Planning and/or Our Collaborative Process
This open-ended question lets you focus on what this particular experience revealed, given your own interests and curiosity.

Subject: Using a Collaborative Process
Some questions you might consider: How did my partner carry out the different roles a supporter can take? Which of the roles sketched earlier

in this chapter would describe us? Did we allow substantive conflict to occur; was it productive? What was the most/least useful feature of our collaboration? Did the three principles of collaborative planning describe our experience?

Subject: Building a Rhetorical Plan to Do

How far did our session take me toward the goal of building a better rhetorical plan? Did we move from the Topic Info Blackboard to the three rhetorical BBs? Where did we spend most of our attention: on representing the task or on one of the three BBs? What were the most productive problems we turned up? Did we develop, expand, or improve the planner's initial plan?

Subject: Designing an Effective Collaborative Session

Given this experience how would I redesign my next collaborative planning session to make it more useful to me? What would I do before meeting? What would I ask my supporter to do?

Subject: Comparing Sessions

Now that I have done collaborative planning two or three times and can make some comparisons, what have I figured out about my planning strategies? What do I do? What surprised me?

IF YOU WOULD LIKE TO READ MORE

If you would like to know more about the nature of plans and exploring your rhetorical problem, see:

Farb, Peter. *Word Play.* New York: Knopf, 1974. / Farb turns the research on how people use language into an adventure story.

Flower, Linda, Victoria Stein, John Ackerman, Margaret Kantz, Kathleen McCormick, and Wayne Peck. *Reading-to-Write: Exploring a Cognitive and Social Process.* New York: Oxford University Press, 1990. / This book tells the story of the Reading-to-Write Project discussed in Strategy 1 and of Darlene quoted in Projects 4 and 11.

Flower, Linda, David Wallace, and Rebecca Burnett (Eds.). *Making Thinking Visible: Writing, Collaborative Planning, and Classroom Inquiry.* Urbana, IL: NCTE, 1994. / In this introduction to the theory and practice of collaborative planning, inquiries by high school and college teachers document what they learned about the planning strategies of their own students.

Miller, George, Eugene Galanter, and Karl Pribram. *Plans and the Structure of Behavior.* New York: Holt, 1960. / This stimulating book shows the manner in which planning works as a moment-to-moment feature of everyday thinking.

chapter six

Generating Ideas

GOAL 3
GENERATE new ideas

Use the strategies of creative thinking to explore your own knowledge. Your goal is to discover useful ideas stored in your memory and to create new ideas by forging connections among the old.

STRATEGY 1	**TURN OFF THE EDITOR AND BRAINSTORM**
STRATEGY 2	**TALK TO YOUR READER**
STRATEGY 3	**SYSTEMATICALLY EXPLORE YOUR TOPIC**
STRATEGY 4	**REST AND INCUBATE**

Generating and organizing ideas are like two sides of a coin. They represent two different kinds of thinking every writer needs to do. In this chapter we will take up creative thinking, which is a form of mental *play:* It asks you to plunge into the problem and seek out ideas without trying to edit or tidy them up. This sort of energetic intellectual play lets you be a more creative and productive thinker. Compared to the method of grinding a paper out, creative play can do three things. First, it helps a writer break his or her mental "set" and get out of those well-worn thought patterns that often stifle new ideas. Second, it captures those elusive intuitions that are often censored and lost when a writer only pays attention to fully formed ideas. Finally, it helps a writer to draw inferences and discover new, surprising connections among his or her own ideas.

If creative thinking is a form of *play,* organizing ideas (which we will discuss in the next chapter) is a way to *push* your ideas for all they are worth. Organizing is equally powerful because it lets you work in a systematic, logical way to test out ideas, determine their implications, and fit them into a meaningful whole. And planning, as we have discussed, lets you create the goals that direct both the generation and organization of your ideas. Taken together, planning, generating, and organizing form a creative trio. Good writers constantly shift back and forth from one mode of thought to another as they work on a problem. In the heat of writing you can remind yourself to switch strategies by remembering this three-step formula: plan, play, push.

GOAL 3

GENERATE New Ideas

The four strategies discussed in this chapter cover a wide range of creative techniques. They range from the goal-directed-anything-goes process of brainstorming to the venerable rhetorical method of Aristotle's "topics" and the modern systematic art of tagmemics, to end finally in the only too pleasurable strategy of "rest and incubate." The point of this chapter is simple: There are many ways to get good ideas, and the more alternative strategies you know and can use, the better.

STRATEGY 1   TURN OFF THE EDITOR AND BRAINSTORM

Once you have a sense of your goal and the problem before you, brainstorming is a good way to jump in. Brainstorming is a form of creative, goal-directed play. Your brainstorming can take any form you wish, whether it is jotting down notes such as we saw in the planning chapter, or writing out fragments or even whole passages, as long as your goal is to energetically generate ideas.

My writing inevitably starts with brainstorming. I sit down with clean paper—a fair pile of it—good pencils, and some time officially set aside for just brainstorming. I have no obligation to produce prose, not even a draft. I'm just trying to think up a storm and get down all the things that seem relevant to my problem. Sometimes I just produce notes and a plan, sometimes I write out whole sections of the discussion as I follow a train of thought. For some reason, knowing that all you have to do is brainstorm for the next half hour or so makes it easier to get started even when you have small blocks of time. And I often find that I have written some important pieces of the paper when I am done. At the very least, I have a better image of the territory I want to cover.

The purpose of brainstorming is to stimulate creative thought, so as a procedure it has three rules that try to protect those half-formed suggestive ideas we often censor. The first rule then is: Don't censor any possibilities—just write them down. When you come up with an idea or a phrase that isn't quite right, resist the temptation to throw it out and start again. Just write it down. You may come back later and see what it really meant.

The second rule is: Don't try to write "polished prose" when you are brainstorming. Don't stop to perfect spelling, grammar, or even phrasing. Keep working at the level of ideas whether you are jotting notes, drawing sketches, or writing out a monologue as you talk to yourself.

Finally, try to keep your eye on the question or the problem you have set for yourself. Brainstorming is not free association; it is a goal-directed effort to discover ideas relevant to your problem. So when your flow of thought begins to slow down or dry up, don't worry about having lost your "flow" or inspiration. Associative flows always dry up eventually. Just ask yourself, "What else do I want to consider here; what else do I know?" Then return to the problem at hand.

Brainstorming is a goal-directed search for ideas. This is what makes it different from either freewriting or writing a first draft. In writing a draft, you are always under pressure from your draft to start from the most recent paragraph and extend the current text, even if you have hit a dead end. The text locks you into its own pattern very early. Freewriting, as its name says, is a freely associative technique rather than a goal-directed one. It depends on the rich associative power of words to unlock new connections.

If you are writing an essay, especially one that explores your own thoughts and feelings, freewriting can be another excellent way to get started. In freewriting, you try to write out whatever comes to mind just as though you were taking dictation from your imagination. But keep in mind that freewriting is not the same as writing a draft. It is a technique for generating ideas that has it own rules: Start with the topic that is on your mind and begin to write. Don't worry about correctness, but do keep writing. In fact, if you go blank, just keep writing "I feel a blank" until something comes. Let the words tumble out and let associations come as you use your own words to elicit other words and ideas. Then—and this is the crucial step—go back to that rambling text and try to discover your key ideas and build a new gist out of your own writing.

Freewriting is especially valuable when you feel blocked or when you feel insecure about your writing or your ability to say anything sensible on the topic. At such times, simply tell yourself to sit down and write for 10 minutes by the clock, writing whatever comes. By letting your thoughts wander in the storehouse of your memory, calling on the enormous associative power of words, freewriting often offers amazing proof of what you do have to say and gets the process started again. Bear in mind that it is often hard to edit associative freewriting into a paper. So use it as the basis for writing a new, more focused draft and as a smart technique to get yourself going, even when you are feeling stumped.

 ## *STRATEGY 2* **TALK TO YOUR READER**

People often come up with their best ideas and most powerful arguments when they are engaged in a face-to-face discussion. You can give yourself this same advantage by acting out such a discussion in your own mind, especially if you play all the parts. Everyone has a natural ability to play various roles, such as the role of the "mature and responsible person" we try to project at a job interview. And with a little thought, we can play the role of our interviewer as well. That is, we can switch parts, take on a hard-nosed, "show me" attitude, and carry on our own simulated discussion.

You can use role-playing to help you get better ideas and *to get them down in words*. Instead of staring at blank paper, imagine yourself walking into your reader's office: You have three minutes to tell this person what you have to say, and you want to make him or her listen. So talk it out and write it down. Or, imagine yourself giving a lecture to fifteen high school students who can't wait to talk back. As you go along, simulate the responses of your various readers and listeners: Make them ask you questions (basic and difficult ones), raise objections, or make their own interpretations. For example, what would your reader's first response probably be, and what would you say back to him? To get extra power out of this technique, give yourself different audiences with distinct expectations: a professor or supervisor listening carefully to your logic, a prospective employer looking to see what you can offer her, an enthusiastic audience of beginners sitting in on your lecture, or a friend listening to you over a cup of coffee.

This technique works for two reasons. First, by putting you in a realistic situation with a "live audience" it helps you choose the things you *need* to say out of all the things you *could* say. Secondly, it lets you switch to a "talk" strategy, muttering to yourself as you walk around the room, instead of trying to write finished prose. Whenever you do this, you may have to edit the result a little later. But you are reducing some of the constraints on yourself, and the words and ideas should flow more easily.

❧ *STRATEGY 3* **SYSTEMATICALLY EXPLORE YOUR TOPIC**

Ever since Aristotle, people have been devising ways to think systematically about complex topics. In classical rhetoric this was called the art of invention. Conducting a systematic exploration of your topic has two important advantages. First, it leads you to see your topic from various points of view, many of which would never have occurred to you. That is, it leads you to see new connections and invent new ideas. Secondly, a powerful systematic procedure not only directs your attention by asking questions but it asks the right questions. For example, the familiar "Who? What? Where? When? Why? How?" formula of journalism leads you to the heart of an event by asking you to consider its most important features.

We are going to look briefly at three systematic approaches to the art of invention: Aristotelian topics, modern tagmemics, and the use of analogy. Like any serious systematic procedure, these methods work best when you understand and know them well. In-depth coverage of the methods is outside the scope of this book; my purpose is simply to introduce each approach and the kinds of questions it asks, then indicate where you could learn more.

Imagine the following situation. You are working on a paper about reading strategies and have already done a good deal of research and thinking about reading itself. You've decided to focus on the notion of the "active reader" and want to systematically explore everything you know about the subject. Let us see how each of our three methods of exploration could be used in approaching your problem.

First, consider Aristotelian "topics." *The Rhetoric* of Aristotle was designed to instruct public speakers of fourth-century Greece in what Aristotle called the "available means of persuasion." Taken together, these patterns of argument are called the "topics." Each "topic" represents a way of organizing ideas, or arguing for a position that most listeners will find logical or persuasive. As you will see from even this short list, Aristotle's "topics" cover some of the basic ways people think about a subject and organize their ideas. Here is how a writer might use the "topics" to explore the subject of the "active reader."

Aristotle's "Topics"	*Ideas*
Definition	Active reading is a constructive process in which a person seeks information and builds a coherent meaning from a text.
Comparison and contrast	It is unlike passive reading, in which the reader works on the principle of the sponge, trying to absorb each word or sentence in the hope that it will all make sense in the end.
Cause and effect	Active reading leads to greater comprehension because the reader is actively hooking each new idea to things he or she already knows.
Support from evidence	A number of studies show that even brief training in active reading increases both speed and comprehension of complex prose.

A modern method for systematic thinking is called *tagmemics*. It is a powerful tool for analysis because it is both simple and comprehensive. This method is built on the premise that one of the best ways to understand the true nature of a thing is to see it from various perspectives. In particular, it helps to look at your problem or subject as a *particle* (a thing in itself), as a *wave* (something that changes over time), and as part of a *field* (an element within a larger context). Although simple on the surface, tagmemics is a rich and complex approach to generating ideas and well worth learning. With regard to our subject it could lead us to observations such as these:

The Three Perspectives of Tagmemics	*Ideas*
See your topic as a particle (as a thing in itself)	Active reading is made up of a number of processes, including previewing the text to set up expectations and questions that reading will fulfill; searching for key information as one reads; summarizing the gist of the passage to oneself; and making connections as one reads.
See your topic as a wave (a thing changing over time)	The method of active reading changes with the difficulty of the text and individual passages. Skimming often works for newspapers, but with textbooks, active readers switch from fast previewing and brisk reading of introductions and examples, to slow, careful reading and summarizing of difficult passages.
See your topic as part of a field (as a thing in its context)	Active reading is part of the larger process of comprehension, which includes not only recording new information but integrating it into the elaborate patterns of knowledge the reader already possesses. Active reading makes these intellectual processes more accurate and efficient.

The third technique we will look at depends on the generative power of analogies. It has a simple basic premise that much research on the psychology of creativity supports: namely, one of the best ways to understand a new problem is to see an analogy between it and things you already know. One systematic method that uses analogies, called *synectics,* was developed by a think-tank group of inventors, artists, and psychologists who were trying to find creative new solutions to practical problems. Using synectics, a group or individual tries to generate four kinds of analogies to the problem at hand: personal analogies, direct analogies, symbolic analogies, and fantasy analogies. By its very nature, the approach leads you to come up with offbeat, impossible ideas in the hope of finding one startling new insight.

The Four Analogies of Synectics	*Ideas*
Personal analogy (imagine you are the topic or the solution to a problem)	As an active reader I see myself trying to make each idea my own personal possession. Or it is as if I were trying to explain the text to a child who kept asking questions.
Direct analogy (compare it to something concrete)	It's like using an erector set to build a structure (of meaning). The author gave me the materials and a blueprint, but I built the final structure.
Symbolic analogy (compare it to an abstract principle)	Active reading works on the principle that for every action (the author's), there is a separate and equal reaction (the reader's).
Fantasy analogy (anything goes)	It's like walking right inside the writer's head and getting him or her to answer your questions (even if the author helped draft the questions you want to ask).

Another mode of thinking-by-analogy is simple to change your vocabulary: Use the language and concepts from one area you know to understand another. Say your problem is to analyze what your college has to offer, but the college catalog vocabulary of "intellectual community" and "integrated programs" doesn't let you say what you want. If you are familiar with systems engineering, you might assess your college in terms of its work flow and productivity. Or you might switch to the outlook and special language of marketing, asking such questions as "What 'commodities' do colleges typically promise to deliver?" and "How could one test the college's 'advertising claims'?" Often a change in your vocabulary will bring about a change in your "idea set," or way of viewing the problem. By changing terms you tap different pockets of your own knowledge.

 ## STRATEGY 4 REST AND INCUBATE

Sometimes this can be the most productive strategy of all, but only if you do it correctly. That is, before you stop work, make sure you have formulated the next unsolved problem you want to be thinking about. There needs to be something in the "incubator" if it's going to hatch.

People agree that incubation works; nobody understands quite why. The folklore is that your unconscious mind goes to work and solves the problem while you sleep. A more recent explanation of the process says that before people explore a problem in detail, they often create a rather limited or ineffective plan for solving it. Working on the problem, they learn a great deal that doesn't fit into their original plan. What happens in incubation is that people simply *forget* or abandon their old, inadequate plan and are then able to take advantage of all they've learned. For example, after working on the problem and doing a first draft, they come back to their writing with a new, more powerful plan that can work.

Incubation, then, is a strategy you can actively use. Sometimes even half an hour can make a difference. So starting a paper early is a practical decision; otherwise you simply lose the benefit of one of the easiest strategies available, and you will probably spend more actual time on the paper. When you use incubation, keep two points in mind: Return to your unfinished business from time to time so as to keep it *actively* simmering in the back of your mind; then, when a new idea or connection comes to you, *write it down*. Most experienced writers carry around note cards of some sort for just this purpose. Don't expect inspiration to knock twice.

PROJECTS AND ASSIGNMENTS

1   Hold an in-class workshop to try out the idea-generating strategies described in Step 3. Working in a group or with a friend, try out each of the strategies on some common problem. For example, you might take this as your problem: "Writing is a lot like talking, yet many people who can tell you something have trouble writing it. Why? In particular, why is it that even students who know the material thoroughly have trouble writing papers in college?"

☐ a. *Brainstorming.* You are the member of a think-tank or professional problem-solving group. Use brainstorming and try to come up with fifteen good ideas on the problem within the next 5 minutes. Don't just jot down code words, but try to explain briefly what each idea means.

☐ b. *Talking to the reader.* Break up into two groups to generate ideas for a reader. For example, if your problem were "Why Writing Is Difficult," you could tell the group that they have a late paper and must prepare a statement for a professor explaining why writing is difficult. Let the other group decide what they would say about the same problem to a friend. Then compare your two sets of ideas. Are they different? How?

☐ c. *Systematic exploration.* Break into three groups and analyze a common topic from the three different perspectives of Aristotle's "topics," tagmemics, and analogy. Use each of these systematic methods to create new ideas and develop insight into your subject. Then compare your results. What would you say are the special strengths of each method?

2 Use the creative thinking strategies of Step 3 to write a paper that explores both sides of an issue. Choose an issue about which you yourself have conflicting feelings: for example, the value of grades versus a pass-fail system, the decision to ask a friend out on a date, or the choice of a profession. In one form or another, use all four strategies discussed in this chapter to generate ideas and argue both sides of your question.

3 After you have done Assignment 2, compare your notes from each strategy to your final text. Write a brief commentary on which strategies did the most (or the least) for you and why.

IF YOU WOULD LIKE TO READ MORE

If you would like to know more about creativity and other strategies for generating ideas, see:

Aristotle. *The Rhetoric.* Trans. Lane Cooper. New York: Appleton-Century-Crofts, 1932. / This is the work that established the study of systematic idea generation called, in classical rhetoric, the art of invention. Aristotle's "topics" are still powerful.

Gordon, William. *Synectics: The Development of Creative Capacity.* New York: Harper & Row, 1961. / This book describes how the system of synectics was developed and has proved its worth in industry, both as a way of producing new inventions and as a method for creative problem solving.

Young, Richard, Alton Becker, and Kenneth Pike. *Rhetoric: Discovery and Change.* New York: Harcourt Brace Jovanovich, 1970. / A groundbreaking work in the field of rhetoric, this book presents the tagmemic method for exploring complex problems.

chapter seven

Organizing Ideas

GOAL 4
ORGANIZE your ideas

Use these strategies to develop and focus your ideas. Your goal is to turn good intuitions into precise, well-developed ideas that you can express in clear, logical relationships to one another.

> *STRATEGY 1* **EXPAND YOUR OWN CODE WORDS**
> *STRATEGY 2* **NUTSHELL YOUR IDEAS AND TEACH THEM**
> *STRATEGY 3* **BUILD AN ISSUE TREE**

Getting good ideas is half the battle. The other half is making sense out of what you know. The techniques we discussed in Chapter 6 will help you generate a wealth of ideas, but sometimes those ideas will seem more like intuitions than clearly stated arguments. Or they will be in the form of key words or brief notes to yourself that you will have to flesh out in detail for a reader to understand. And sometimes you will end up with a rich but unfocused body of ideas whose only organization is the order in which they occurred to you. This chapter will help you turn such intuitions into clearly stated ideas and then organize and develop those ideas into a logical, well-supported argument.

GOAL 4

ORGANIZE Your Ideas

Each strategy in this chapter suggests ways you can use your own plans, notes, or drafts to develop and organize your ideas. Strategy 1 helps you expand your own loaded expressions into a more meaningful discussion, while Strategy 2 helps you pull key points or concepts out of such a discussion. Strategy 3 gives ideas for organizing all these elements in a clear, logical way. And, as you will notice, these strategies help you start taking your reader into account, even as you explore and organize what you know.

STRATEGY 1   EXPAND YOUR OWN CODE WORDS

Many times writers find that their important, key words in a passage are really "code words." That is, these words carry a great deal of meaning for the writer that they would not carry for the average reader.

For example, what does the expression "problem solving" mean to you? To some people it means nothing more than the process of doing an algebra problem. But for me, "problem solving" is not only a basic thinking procedure that gets people through everyday life but a process that leads to bursts of creative thinking and new insight. And it is also a branch of psychology.

Thus, for me the term evokes a large, complex network of ideas. But just because "problem solving" is a loaded expression for me—a code word I think with—I cannot simply use it and expect most of my readers to fully understand me, to make the same connections I make. When I use such code words, I must explain and develop the meaning I really have in mind.

A writer's code words can be jargon, special terms such as "problem solving," or simply complex concepts such as "persona" that some readers wouldn't understand. But often they are merely abstractions, as in the remark "He has a very interesting job." Here "interesting" is a kind of mental shorthand that stands for a body of related ideas—ideas that may be evident to the writer but are unlikely to be perceived by the reader. In fact, such words may sound like nothing more than vague generalizations or hot air.

Your own code words, then, can sometimes create a problem because they mean much more than they actually express. However, they can also open the door to a very effective strategy for developing and focusing your ideas. Only you, the writer, can tell empty abstractions from solid concepts. For example, ask yourself "What did I really mean by 'interesting'?" One of the best ways to develop your writing ideas and fill in the gaps for the reader is to show or explain what you mean by your own code words. This strategy is especially useful when you feel you need to develop an argument or reinforce a point but aren't sure what else to say.

The strategy is simple. First go through your notes or a draft of your paper and locate some of the key words or phrases (ones that you intend to carry much meaning in your paper). Look both for abstractions and for key words and complex concepts that you depend on. Then see if they might also be working as code words, ones that may not convey all your intentions to the reader. Look for words that stand at the center of a whole network of ideas and experience that are *unique to you*. Then ask, "What do I mean by this code word or term?" Try to push that complex meaning into words, using it as a springboard for developing your own ideas. Then transfer this new understanding to your paper.

Example 1 shows just how many interesting and important ideas can be buried beneath a code word or phrase. In her first draft of a geology paper, the writer had asserted that Alfred Wegener's 1912 theory of continental drift was a "major breakthrough" in the field of geology. She knew this was a strong point she needed to support and develop. After fruitlessly searching for quotes that would support it, she realized that it would be far more effective simply to explain in her own words what she meant. So she used her intuition and her code words as starting points for exploring what she really meant by saying that the theory was a "breakthrough."

Example 1
The Buried Meaning in Code Words

The theory of continental drift was a major breakthrough in geology.

It drew on enormous amounts of information from different fields, including paleontology and physics as well as geology.

It contradicted major assumptions everyone had made about the rigid nature of continents.

It led to new kinds of studies, such as ones that described and dated the life cycles of continents. It changed the way people studied geology.

It gave us a whole new image of the earth's surface as plastic and dynamic.

All in all, it changed both the study of geology and popular notions about the earth. (Note: Use this idea to organize the paragraph.)

Above are some of the ideas she jotted down and eventually worked into her paper. They show how much information she already had on the topic when she began seriously to probe her own network of ideas.

Think back for a moment to the writer's original assertion. Would you as a reader have been able to fill in all of the ideas behind "breakthrough" that the writer knew but didn't tell you? As a geology instructor, would you have assumed that the student knew all the supporting facts she didn't express? Code words are like intuitions. They offer a starting point for thinking about the reader and for developing your own ideas.

Example 2 demonstrates how this strategy can lead you back through the entire process of planning, generating, and organizing your ideas. The passage below comes from a draft of the scholarship application that Joan was writing in Chapter 3. She has underscored a few of the key terms that are loaded with information for her but are in danger of just seeming abstract to a reader. Play the role of a reader on the scholarship committee wondering if this applicant really understands research well enough to benefit from the scholarship. How would you interpret the terms that are underscored?

The response of a friend to whom Joan showed the draft wasn't very encouraging. According to the friend, "It sounds OK—it's organized and everything—but I felt as if I'd read it before. It's saying things that 'couldn't be wrong,' but I don't have a sense of what you think or what you have actually done. What is a 'relevant area' for you? I don't know, and this draft gives me the feeling you may not know either."

Now look at the notes Joan jotted down (see Example 3) as she thought about one of the phrases underscored in her draft. Then review her revised draft (Example 4), with new material underscored. You will notice two interesting things. First, the revision contains the kind of additional, specific details that make Joan's key words meaningful and convincing. In addition, the very process of developing her own code words has led Joan to express a new idea about the benefits of research that was an important but unstated part of her own personal network of ideas. Her code words provided a leaping-off point for generating new ideas.

Example 2
Finding Code Words in Text

I want a career that will help other people and at the same time be challenging scientifically. I had the opportunity to do a biochemical assay for a neuropsychopharmacologist at _____ Clinic in Chicago. Besides learning the scientific procedures and techniques that are used, I learned how to deal with some of the <u>problems encountered in research</u>. This internship program would let me pursue further my interest in research, while currently exposing me to <u>relevant and diverse areas</u>.

Example 3
Excerpts from the Writer's Notes as She Worked on
One of the Underscored Phrases

<u>problems encountered in research</u>

practical {
Hard to see how research at the Sleep Center tied in with overall program of the Clinic. But you needed to see the big picture to make decisions.

No definite guidelines given to the biochem people on how to run the assay.
}

Lots of paperwork for even a small study.

organizational ⎰ Difficulty getting equipment
1. Politics between administrators; Photometer at the University even though the Clinic had bought it.
2. Ordering time; insufficient inventory; had to hunt through boxes for chemicals.
3. Had to use personal contacts to borrow equipment. Needed to schedule and plan ahead to do so.

But breakthroughs do occur—pacemaker, artificial limbs, and so on.

Example 4
Revised Draft with Additions Underscored

Besides learning the scientific procedures and techniques that are used, I learned how to deal with some of the practical and organizational problems encountered in research. I saw how the lack of equipment and funds often calls for real cooperation between departments and careful planning of one's own project. The experience also helped me develop more of the patience research requires and recognize the enormous amounts of time, paperwork, and careful steps required for testing a hypothesis that is only one very small but necessary part of the overall project.

But besides knowing some of the frustrations, I also know that many medical advancements, such as the cardiac pacemaker, artificial limbs, and cures for diseases, exist and benefit many people because of the efforts of researchers. Therefore I would like to pursue my interest in research by participating in the NIH Internship Program. The exposure to many diverse projects, designed to better understand and improve the body's functioning, would help me to decide which areas of biomedical engineering to pursue.

STRATEGY 2   NUTSHELL YOUR IDEAS AND TEACH THEM

Find someone, a fellow student or a long-suffering friend, who is willing to listen as you explain the essence of your argument. Then, in a few sentences—in a nutshell—try to lay out the whole substance of your paper. Stating a gist practically forces you to distinguish major ideas from minor ones and to decide how these major ideas are related to one another. Expressing your argument in a nutshell helps you put "noisy," supporting information in its place and focus on the essentials of what you have to say. For example, the outline at the beginning of this chapter conveys in a nutshell what the main ideas of this chapter will be.

Besides helping people to separate main points from interesting but merely supporting ones, nutshelling has another benefit. In trying to condense their thoughts, people often synthesize or combine ideas and create a new concept that expresses or encompasses all they have in mind. For instance, Joan did this in Example 3, when she looked at her notes and decided that a number of points could be grouped and labeled an "organizational" problem. This process of conceptualizing is probably the writer's most difficult yet also most creative action. Stating the gist of your argument helps you do it.

The second part of this strategy, teaching, takes the process one step further. Once you can express your idea in a nutshell to yourself, think about how you would *teach* that idea to someone else. How would you have to introduce or organize your brief discussion so someone else would understand and remember it? Like nutshelling, trying to teach your ideas helps you form concepts so that your listener gets *the point*, not just a list of facts. Furthermore, as a teacher you have to think about which concepts will be most meaningful to your reader. In explaining the dangers of germs to a five-year-old, for example, you would probably find "dangerous things" a more effective organizing concept than "public health problems." Nothing helps you stand back, evaluate, and reorganize your ideas more quickly than trying to teach them to someone else who doesn't understand.

Even if you don't have a live audience to talk to, there is an easy and practical way to use this strategy of nutshelling and teaching when you write. Simply imagine your intended reader sitting before you, think about what you want that person to learn or do when you're through, and then try to teach your ideas in writing so that you get results.

🌿 *STRATEGY 3* **BUILD AN ISSUE TREE**

Most of the idea-generating strategies described so far ask you to think and write without the straight jacket of an extensive outline. However, one of your goals is to produce a paper with a tight, logical structure. Experienced writers resolve this dilemma in the following way: they try to *pull* an outline *out* of the ideas they generate, rather than write to *fill* an outline *in*. Building an issue tree is a technique for organizing the ideas you generate.

WHAT IS AN ISSUE TREE AND WHY USE ONE?

As noted in Chapter 1, an issue tree is a sketch like an upside-down tree that puts your ideas in a hierarchical order. As you know, in a hierarchy, the top-level idea is the most inclusive. All the other ideas are a response to it or a part of it, like subsystems in a larger system. This does not mean that they are less important (a subsystem of the body, such as the brain, can be crucial), but they are less inclusive.

Issue trees have two main things to offer writers. First, they let you sketch or test out ideas and relationships as you write. At the same time they let you visualize the whole argument and see how all the parts might fit together. Issue trees can also help you generate new ideas. A traditional outline, written before you start the paper, only arranges the facts and ideas you already know. An issue tree highlights missing links in your argument and helps you draw inferences and create new concepts.

In the sections that follow we will look at ways of using an issue tree to organize your brainstorming, to develop a paper, and to test the organization of your first draft.

Using an Issue Tree to Organize Your Brainstorming

To show how useful an issue tree can be in organizing ideas, we will watch a writer in action using a tree to organize his ideas and write an essay. Here is the assigned topic:

> In England there is a saying that every Englishman is branded on his tongue. Is this true in the United States? Do a person's speech traits—from pronunciation, to pitch, to choice of words—mean anything in the American social system?

Figure 7–1 shows the first three steps a writer might take in answering this question.

1. Generate some ideas on the problem. At this point the writer's goal is simply to answer the question "Do speech traits communicate anything to me?" and generate some ideas. These are jotted down like a list.
2. Find a key word or phrase for each idea.
3. Put the key words in a hierarchically organized tree.

In Figure 7–1, the line connecting "speech traits are social markers" and "education" simply tells us that there is a general relationship between the two. It will be up to the writer to eventually make that relationship more explicit (for example, is education a cause or

FIGURE 7–1
Organizing Brainstorming into a Tree

Brainstorming	Key Words
As with the British, Americans' traits differ according to upper, middle, and lower class	class
They are like social markers or tags that identify people	social markers
Affected by education	education
Biggest source must be the region one grows up in	region

Tree

SPEECH TRAITS ARE SOCIAL MARKERS

class   education   region

an effect of speech traits?). As we will see, an issue tree can help you create concepts that give order and meaning to your own ideas.

Sometimes the best organization of one's ideas is self-evident, as it was for the ideas in Figure 7–1. But when it isn't, when things seem confusing, an issue tree can help you spot the missing links in your thinking and generate new concepts that will organize your ideas. For example, Figure 7–2 shows a set of ideas our writer generated after reading a number of studies on people's responses to voice. These ideas didn't neatly fit onto the tree. "Breathiness," "throatiness," and "pitch" are clearly related to the top-level idea of speech traits as social markers, but they certainly do not belong on the same level with "class," "education," and "region." Nor are they subordinate to (a part of) those larger categories. Taken as a group, however, they add up to another kind of social marker that would be comparable to a regional or class trait. The question is, what should the writer call it?

The writer's task is to generate a new concept that sums up these facts. In other words, he must examine the material and propose a new unifying idea. In this case the unifying idea he arrived at was that speech traits also suggest or reflect a person's sex role (see Figure 7–3).

Creating a unifying idea or concept from facts is something we do all the time. The problem is that in the heat of writing, when ideas just don't seem to jell, people often continue to flounder rather than stop, think, and *create* new organizing ideas. At such times the writer needs to turn from searching his or her memory for the "right" word (because it isn't there) and start looking for relationships and developing new ideas. An issue tree helps do this.

FIGURE 7–2
Using an Issue Tree to Spot Missing Concepts

Brainstorming   *Key Words*

Breathiness is considered a "sexy" trait in women.   breathiness
Throatiness (i.e., a husky, quite deep voice) is considered "unfeminine" in   throatiness
    women but mature in men.
A wide pitch range is heard as "effeminate" in men and as "flighty" or   pitch
    "frivolous" in women.

Trees

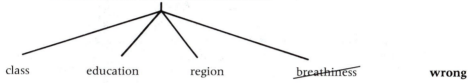

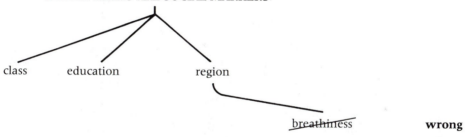

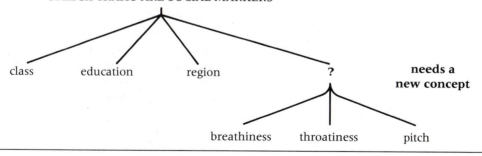

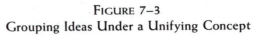

FIGURE 7–3
Grouping Ideas Under a Unifying Concept

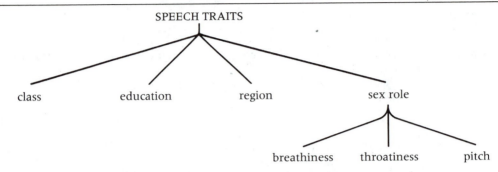

Speech traits are an important means of communication in the United States. First of all, *listeners* use them to determine someone's social identity, especially in the areas of class, regional background, and sex role. In addition, *speakers* use them, either deliberately or unconsciously, to communicate certain things as well.

(what things? to project a self-image maybe? or fit in with a group?)

Using an Issue Tree to Develop a Paper

You can also use an issue tree to help develop or flesh out a paper. As you think and write, your issue tree will keep changing, reflecting your developing set of ideas. For example, our essay writer eventually decided not to treat the issue of education and decided that he had two major ideas to discuss on the subject of speech traits. Here are his notes for the beginning of the essay.

As Figure 7–4 shows, the writer's working tree reflects this two-part reorganization of his ideas. And it shows exactly where he needs to support those ideas with more evidence and examples. So again he turns to brainstorming, now with the goal of refining and supporting his major points. Notice how his thinking is working in two directions, from the bottom up and from the top down. Sometimes he starts with an inclusive idea such as "listeners interpret regional speech traits" and tries to work from the top down to support that idea with more facts and examples. Sometimes he starts with facts and examples, such as the facts about New Yorkers, and works from the bottom of the tree up, finding relationships and creating a new idea.

The revised tree shows how much of the writer's final argument was created in the process of organizing and developing his ideas, that is, in the process of building a tree. An issue tree, then, offers a writer three important things:

1. It is a flexible tool for thinking that develops as your ideas develop.

FIGURE 7-4
Developing a Paper

Working issue tree

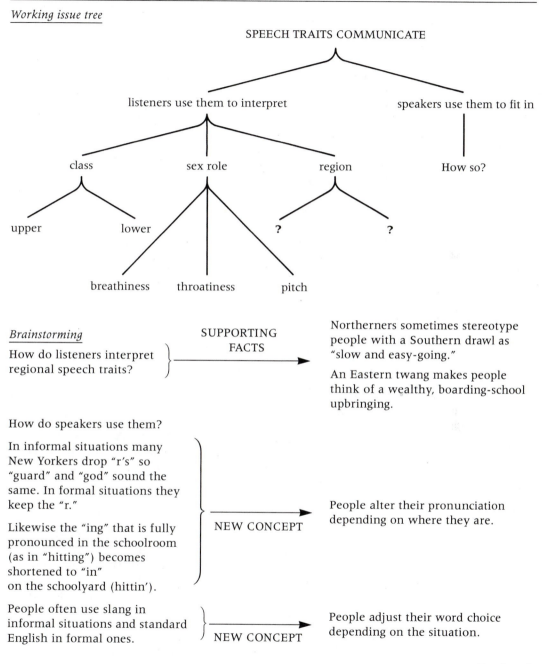

SPEECH TRAITS COMMUNICATE

listeners use them to interpret

speakers use them to fit in

class   sex role   region   How so?

upper   lower   ?   ?

breathiness   throatiness   pitch

Brainstorming

How do listeners interpret regional speech traits?

SUPPORTING
FACTS

Northerners sometimes stereotype people with a Southern drawl as "slow and easy-going."

An Eastern twang makes people think of a wealthy, boarding-school upbringing.

How do speakers use them?

In informal situations many New Yorkers drop "r's" so "guard" and "god" sound the same. In formal situations they keep the "r."

Likewise the "ing" that is fully pronounced in the schoolroom (as in "hitting") becomes shortened to "in" on the schoolyard (hittin').

NEW CONCEPT

People alter their pronunciation depending on where they are.

People often use slang in informal situations and standard English in formal ones.

NEW CONCEPT

People adjust their word choice depending on the situation.

(Continued)

FIGURE 7-4 (continued)

Revised issue tree

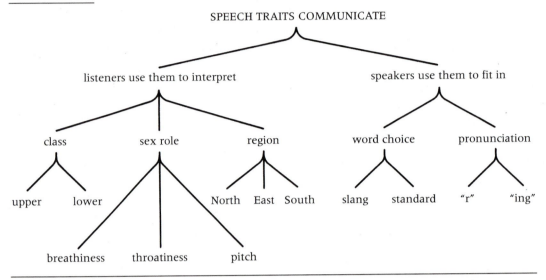

2. It helps you visualize, organize, and support the ideas you have.
3. It signals when you must stop to look for relationships and create new unifying ideas.

By this point in the writing process, the issue tree has done its job and the writer is well into writing paragraphs, but knowing as he writes how each part fits logically into the whole.

Using an Issue Tree to Test Your First Draft

One of the best ways to compare your *thought* with what you actually *wrote* is to do a tree of your own first draft or, if you can, ask a reader to do this for you. The procedure is simple: From your draft, pull out all the main ideas (use a brief phrase such as "statistics show decline"). You might jot these down in the margin of your paper. Make sure you don't include any ideas that are in your head but not on the paper. Although you can expect readers to see connections and fill in *some* organizing ideas as they read, you can't expect them always to arrive at the same interpretation you did. By building an issue tree, you can find out what your paper is actually saying. The tree will reveal the focus and underlying structure of your prose.

Example 5
Draft with an Uncertain Focus

The Writing Problem

America has a writing problem. Like the Constitution, American education is based on democratic principles, which means it is committed to teaching reading, writing, and arithmetic to everyone as a basic right, like the right to vote. The history of American education is the history of an attempt to turn these principles into practice for everyone. In 1975, *Newsweek* magazine, in a famous exposé article entitled "Why Johnny Can't Write," started a crusade against poor writing. The vivid, even shocking examples in this article came from colleges all over the country. Other disturbing findings on writing skills have come from various sources, including the National Assessment of Educational Progress, the College English Education Board, and the Department of Health, Education, and Welfare. However, many people have been most appalled by the statistics on basic literacy itself. These statistics are especially revealing. The majority of Americans use only the simplest sentence structures and the most elementary vocabulary.

Many things have led to this decline—the schools themselves, television, and our changing social values. In an attempt to create relevant, attractive courses, many schools have understressed the old-fashioned basics of reading and writing. The long-term impact of television has lulled people into a more simplistic speaking style. Writing, on the other hand, is essentially book talk, which goes as far back as the invention of movable type. But today students spend time watching television that they might have spent reading 20 years ago. Studies have shown that many students watch more than 8 hours of TV per day. TV has in fact replaced books, newspapers, and even movies as our primary source of entertainment and information. Instead of actively participating in learning, people prefer the more passive experience of watching "the tube." According to Marshall McLuhan, "literary culture is through." It belonged to the world of the printing press. And who wants to watch a printing press?

In the next example, a tree diagram is used to look at the underlying structure of individual paragraphs. When you apply this technique to a whole paper, you might want to work in larger units and

let each point on your tree summarize the point of an entire paragraph. The two paragraphs in Example 5, taken from the beginning
of a student's paper, demonstrate two of the most common problems
a tree will uncover: a top-heavy or unfocused organization (seen in
the first paragraph) and a runaway branch (seen in the second). Read
the first paragraph and then look at Figure 7–5, which shows the
structure of the discussion as a reader saw it.

Consider the first paragraph of this draft. It is hard to see the paragraph's focus. Is the main idea the democratic ideal and the failure of
education, is it the decline of writing skills, or is it the drama of the
Newsweek crusade? According to the writer, he really had intended to
focus on how American education was failing to teach writing. Figure 7–5 compares the tree the reader saw with the tree the writer
really wanted to produce. Notice that all the reader saw was a list of
facts, whereas the writer really had intended to use those facts to
support the idea that skills had declined.

In sketching his intended tree, the writer uncovered another problem. Although he felt his comments about democratic ideals were
relevant, he really didn't want to discuss that issue in this paragraph.
He realized it would make more sense to discuss it in a later section
about how the writing problem is also a failure to meet the historical
goals of American education. Sketching out a tree of the paragraph
helped the writer take a bird's eye view of his organization and compare his private mental tree (or the one he would like to have) with
the idea structure his prose actually presented to the reader. Example 6 is a revision of the first paragraph in which the writer tries to
keep a clear focus and show the reader how each sentence and point
are connected to his main point.

Example 6
Revised Draft with a Strong Focus

The Writing Problem:
A Failure of American Education

According to the startling *Newsweek* article of 1975 ("Why Johnny
Can't Write"), the U.S. educational system is failing to equip its
students with sound writing skills. The article displayed a number of
examples of poor writing from colleges all over the country. But more
definitive support came from test results reported by the National
Assessment of Educational Progress, the Department of Health,
Education, and Welfare, and the College English Education Board.
These were supported by the even more appalling statistics on basic
literacy itself; for example, the majority of Americans use only the
simplest sentence structures and the most elementary vocabulary.

FIGURE 7–5
The Opening Paragraph: The Tree the Reader Saw Versus the Tree the Writer Intended

The reader's tree

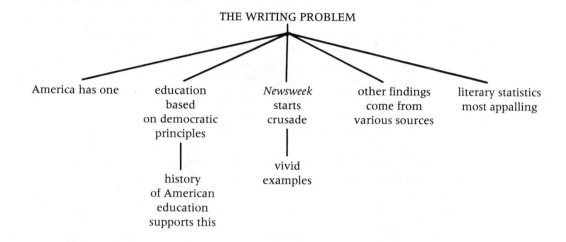

The writer's intended tree

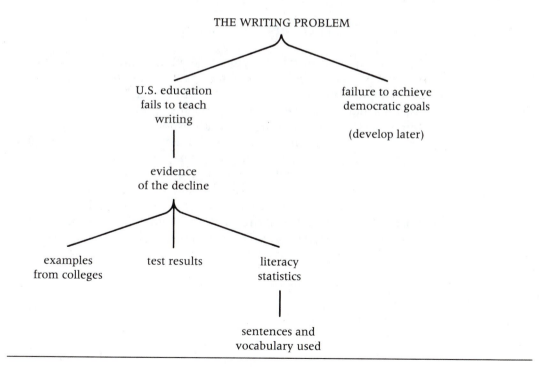

A second problem that a tree will reveal is the presence of a long, trailing branch. In the second paragraph of Example 5, the author began discussing causes of this decline, and one idea led to another, to another, and yet another. Each idea was a response to the one before, but they got further and further from the writer's top-level idea. The branch simply ran away with the writer and produced an unbalanced paragraph in which very little time was spent on his major, top-level topics. In the process of composing, the writer remembered a number of interesting ideas about television and other media, so his ideas did seem to "flow" as he wrote. But in sketching the tree, he realized that he had given too much space to one supporting idea (watching television) and little or no space to his points that schools neglect basics and that changes in social values are causing the decline.

Figure 7–6 gives a vivid picture of the structure of this paragraph and places it in the context of the other major points the writer wanted to cover, in both the paragraph and the entire paper. As you can see, he intended to focus on American schools and education, but the interesting topic of television simply ran away with his paragraph.

Whether you actually sketch a tree or read your prose looking for its underlying hierarchical structure, you can use this technique to test for the focus and connections your reader is likely to see.

USING QUESTIONS TO DEVELOP AN ISSUE TREE

Sometimes a writer will develop a skeleton of an issue tree but not know where to go from there. One way to break this block is to start asking questions about each item in the tree. This method simply makes a natural process more systematic. When you write you are often carrying on a question-and-response dialogue with your reader or yourself. Children, as we all know, can build endless chains of reasoning with the single question "Why?" or "How?" Other questions that frequently arise in a reader's mind are "What do you mean?" (which asks for a more expanded definition) and "Such as?" (which is a reaction to a vague, overly abstract idea that lacks supporting examples). As a writer, you can anticipate the reader's questions, as well as generate more material, by asking such questions of yourself. Some useful ones are:

What do you mean?
How so?
How do you know?
Such as?
Why?
Why not?
So what?

FIGURE 7–6
The Second Paragraph: A Runaway Branch

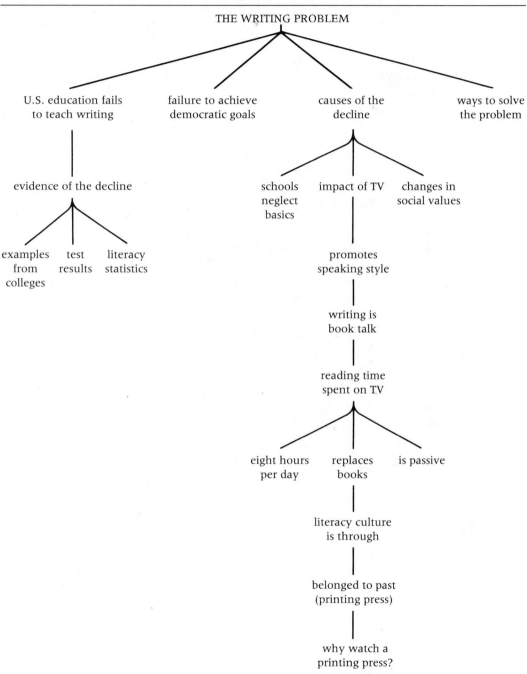

The questions that are most applicable will depend on the type of paper. A journal article exploring a question of scientific fact will rely heavily on the question "What evidence?" ("How do you know?"), whereas one concerned with pragmatic or technological issues would probably concentrate more on asking "How?" "Why?" and "So what?" Figure 7–7 shows how a writer has used the questioning method to develop ideas for a paper on running. Notice how each new point is a response to the point above it. Unlike an outline,

FIGURE 7–7
A Tree Generated Through the Questioning Method

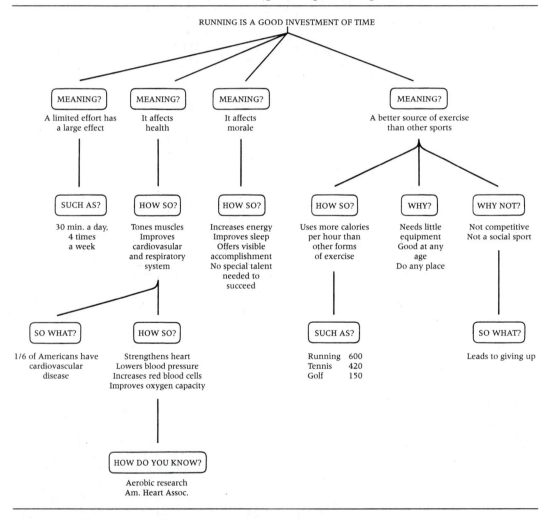

an issue tree allows you to keep adding more points one under the other, in any direction you wish.

This technique, also called *issue analysis,* is often used in a formal, systematic way to examine large policy questions such as "Should we build more nuclear power plants?" Issue trees help people deal with such enormous problems because they offer a way of systematically stating and organizing all the major points such a decision should cover. In addition, a systematic use of questions such as "Why?" and "So what?" helps people to reason carefully about an issue by considering it from a variety of viewpoints.

PROJECTS AND ASSIGNMENTS

1   Use the strategies in Step 4, "Organize Your Ideas," to help test and improve the first draft of a paper on which you are currently working.

    a. *Expand code words.* Go through your first draft and circle three or four words that are functioning as code words for you. Then, on a separate sheet, brainstorm all the things that come to your mind when you use those expressions. Use your brainstorming to go back and develop and clarify those ideas for your reader.

    b. *Nutshell and teach your ideas.* Try to state the main points of your paper in a nutshell, then try to teach those ideas to another person. You might also test how well you communicated by having your listener tell you back, in her own words, what she thought you meant. If she didn't see your point, try again. Then use this experience and your own new ideas to go back and focus your paper better for a reader.

    c. *Develop an issue tree.* On a separate sheet of paper, do an issue tree of the draft you have just written. Then find someone who is familiar with the issue-tree concept and ask him to read your paper and from it develop his own tree. Tell him to write items down in his own words as much as possible and to tree your argument as he sees it on the first reading. If he is at all confused in trying to follow the paper, you want his tree to reflect that. Ask him not to put down any of his own ideas on what he thinks you should have said. Then compare the two trees and try to account for the differences. What happened and why?

2   *Checklist: Recognizing Code Words.* Only you can tell your own rich code words, but here are some words and phrases you should test for hidden, unexpressed meanings:

    ☐ a. Important-sounding, three-syllable words with Latinate endings (such as *-ion, -ment, -ance*), since these are often abstractions (for example, a performance situation).

    ☐ b. Good sounding but vague phrases (for example, relevant and diverse areas).

    ☐ c. Important words you would emphasize or pause after in speaking but haven't developed in the text (for example, breakthrough).

☐ d. Words that name a list of things your reader might want the specifics of in addition to your generalization (for example, problems encountered in research).

☐ e. Words that say a lot to you when you read the text (if someone asked, you could give a five-minute, on-the-spot elaboration).

3 Take a controversial question such as "Should smoking be allowed in public places?" Or, "Is a liberal arts education still one of the best preparations for any career?" Do a systematic analysis of the issue, using the questioning method ("How so?" "Why?" and so on) outlined earlier. Make sure your analysis looks at both the pros and the cons. Then write a short paper that takes a stand and argues for one side while acknowledging the strengths of the other. Use an issue tree to focus and organize your ideas, and be sure to give your reader an introductory problem/purpose statement that previews your paper (see Chapter 5).

4 *Checklist: The Overall Structure of a Paper*

☐ a. *Problem/purpose statement.* Have I given the reader an introductory problem/purpose statement that sets up a problem or thesis on which my paper will focus? (This idea will be at the top of your issue tree. Also review the problem/purpose statement checklist in Chapter 5.)

   ☐ If I talk about various aspects of a problem, have I signaled what I see as the *central* conflict or issue?

   ☐ If I make a number of assertions, is my *major* claim or thesis signalled?

☐ b. *Paragraph focus.* Is each paragraph organized around an idea, not just a list of facts? (If not, you can use an issue tree to help create the missing, higher-level concept under which all your points will fit.)

   ☐ Have I used a topic sentence or some other convention to signal my main idea in each paragraph?

   ☐ If it is a complex idea, have I stated the gist directly at some point?

☐ c. *Overall hierarchy.* Can you and your reader see the overall hierarchical structure of your paper? Does each section, paragraph, and idea fit into the structure in a logical way? (If it doesn't, you probably need to rethink some of your top-level unifying ideas. Try using an issue tree to play with other possible organizations and concepts.)

5 The organizing techniques in this chapter, such as nutshells, issue trees, and questions, are really techniques for making sense out of the unstructured pool of ideas people often bring to writing. The following is an example of just such a body of data on the topic "Time Management and Efficient Student Strategies." It comes from two sources: List A, the "Real Experience" data, is based on students' comments about their own problems managing time for studying and writing papers. It lists the things people really do. List B, the "Good Advice" data, lists a number of suggestions for managing time. When you have read and thought about a topic for a while, your own knowledge may look like these rich but unordered lists of ideas. You know a lot, but you need to organize it in order to make meaning.

Real Experience	**Good Advice**
Once it's read, forget it.	Don't procrastinate!
Do what's due.	Set a sub-deadline; make a commitment to someone.
Do it all in one sitting.	The Executive Move: What is the best use of my time right now?[1]
Postpone big tasks.	
Don't reread notes until finals week.	Plan around special times or places.
Wait for inspiration.	Pace yourself.
Use minimal estimates of the time it takes.	"Planning is decision-making."[2] So decide how to use your time.
Don't talk to the teacher.	The Judo Move: Use fear constructively: What knowledge or action would neutralize it?[3]
Never mark up a book.	
Don't eat breakfast; stay up all night.	
Assume you will understand sooner or later.	Have a positive attitude.
Panic!	Learn your learning style.
Remember: You hate school!	Pace yourself!
Wait for the weekend.	Confer!
Avoid courses with writing or math.	The Swiss Cheese Strategy: Identify and do one tiny task each day; reduce your mountain to a Swiss cheese by biting off small bits whenever you have a minute.[4]
Reread texts for tests.	
Create a crisis.	
Teachers never want as much as they ask for.	
	Planning can be as important as doing.
	Set priorities.

a. As you read the "Real Experience" list for problems, you probably noticed that they fall into clumps. For example, some of the data clump together as a low-payoff, low-probability strategy that could be called:

	Allow minimal time.
"Lie to Yourself a Little"	Assume you'll know it later.
	Teachers don't want as much as they ask for.

What would be some other ways of grouping these experiences into an issue tree? (You may want to add some new "Real Experience" data of your own.) Give an appropriate title to each new group or tree. Notice how your title forms the top-level node on your small issue tree.

---

[1] Alan Lakein, *How to Get Control of Your Time and Your Life* (New York: New American Library, 1973), p. 109.
[2] Lakein, p. 109.
[3] Lakein, pp. 131–32.
[4] Lakein, pp. 100–5.

b. Look at your series of small issue trees and try to sum up each one in a nutshell. Then look at the larger picture: can you say how these strategies are related? Try to sketch an issue tree (you will probably have to think up your own top-level ideas) that brings your previous ideas or trees together and shows one way they could be related to each other. Test your new tree by trying to explain, in a nutshell, to someone else how you see this problem of managing time. (Do you predict that your nutshell will be the same as other people's?) You have now organized that unorganized list of experiences into a meaningful analysis of a problem.

c. Now look at that "Good Advice" column. What items of advice seem to you most useful in addressing the experience problems that you're working with? Take one of the pieces of good advice. Imagine that you could interview the person who gave this advice and ask questions about that strategy, for example, "How does it work?" and "Why should I use it?" Try the questions discussed on page 154, and use an issue tree to keep track of your points.

d. You have now analyzed the problem as "Real Experience" sees it and have explored and developed what some of the "Good Advice" could mean. Now try to put these two groups of ideas together in a brief paper. What good advice might help solve the problems you have defined? In organizing your ideas, look for ways to relate these ideas as cause and effect or a problem and solution. (Use issue trees to try out different possible organizations.) Then consider how you want to present the whole discussion—what is your own top-level organizing idea for understanding the problem of "Time Management and Efficient Student Strategies"?

IF YOU WOULD LIKE TO READ MORE

If you would like to know more about strategies for organizing ideas, see:

Simon, Herbert. The architecture of complexity. *Proceedings of the American Philosophical Society,* 106 (December 1962), 467–82. Reprinted in Herbert Simon, *The Sciences of the Artificial.* Cambridge, MA: M.I.T. Press, 1969. / This essay, by one of the creators of information processing theory, discusses the role of hierarchical structures in human thought.

Wojick, David. Planning for discourse. *Water Spectrum,* Winter, 1975–76 and Summer, 1978. / This offers an introduction to issue trees in their original setting, the analysis of complex policy issues.

chapter eight

Analyzing a Problem and Building a Thesis

Why write? One of the most basic reasons for writing, which students, academic writers, journalists, and business people share, is to discuss and deal with problems. This chapter will explain how to go about analyzing a problem, then show you one way to express your thinking in a written problem analysis, and finally, show how you can use the process of problem analysis to develop the thesis of an expository or persuasive paper.

Problems occur when you are in one state, or at some Point A (let's say you are broke and have two papers to write) and you want to be in another state, or at a Point B (let's say you want to take off for spring break next week). What is the real problem: money, time, your priorities, your work habits? People define their own problems and good answers depend on a good analysis of the problem.

Defining and solving is also a major part of many jobs. If you have ever been a group leader, teacher, or a coach, you have probably been in a situation in which something—as yet undefined—wasn't going as well as it should. And it was your job to understand or define that problem and solve it—to move the situation from point A to a new, better point B.

Understanding a problem often means discovering a conflict that creates the problem or that keeps you from your goal. However, the conflict or critical issue at the heart of a problem is often hard to see. For example, why isn't your club working up to its potential? What is the conflict that underlies the situation? Do its members have multiple goals that don't mesh? Or take a famous problem raised in Shakespeare's *Hamlet,* namely, why does Hamlet delay? For years people have tried to define the social and psychological conflicts within Hamlet that prevent him from revenging his father's death. We can ask a similar question about Shakespeare himself: What broad human problems in his own mind was Shakespeare trying to dramatize when he wrote the play? Finally, what problems does *Hamlet* raise for us as readers; what unresolved issues does it create in our own minds? The play *Hamlet,* then, really involves a set of problems and conflicts existing in the minds of Shakespeare the author, Hamlet the character, and each of us as readers.

In literature, history, science, or education, much of the writing people do is an attempt to put their finger on the key issues in a situation involving a conflict. They write to define and help solve a problem. Whether you are a historian studying urban decay, or a hospital administrator writing a proposal to reorganize county clinics, or a student in either field, you will often depend on the skill of problem analysis. In this chapter we will look at a five-step process you can use to analyze problems and to communicate your understanding to a reader.

FIVE STEPS IN ANALYZING A PROBLEM

Problem analysis is a form of detective work. It is the act of discovering key issues in a problem that often lie hidden under the noisy details of the situation. The process of analysis begins when people encounter what is called a "felt difficulty." That is, you feel that something doesn't fit, you feel a conflict. Sometimes that conflict is obvious: two people disagree, or you discover that you yourself hold two contradictory ideas on a subject such as marriage. Many times both sides of a conflict will have merit, as in the federally required testing of new drugs for long-term dangers, which prevents their immediate use by those who would benefit. At other times the conflict will be harder to see; for example, you may feel that there is some as yet unspecified "organizational problem" at the place you work or in an organization to which you belong.

The question in all of these cases is, "What exactly is the problem?" In trying to answer that question an analyst would normally do the following five things:

1. Define the Conflict or Key Issue

A problem analyst's first job is to discover the critical conflict or key issue that lies at the heart of any felt difficulty. In trying to understand a problem, bear in mind the difference between defining a problem (finding a conflict) and merely stating a topic or describing a situation such as "pollution." Although everyone might agree that pollution is harmful and unpleasant, there was a time when it was seen not as a problem but as a sign of industrial prosperity. Problems are only problems for someone. Pollution is only a problem when people want clean air but drive cars that pollute, or when society wants both a clean environment and maximum industrial productivity.

An even clearer example is the much publicized "energy problem." Energy per se is not a problem; it is a topic. Even the dwindling supply of fossil fuel is only a situation. However, when we juxtapose this supply against the American tradition of high consumption at low cost, we have begun to isolate a problem. We have found one of the central conflicts that create a problem.

We often like to think of a conflict in terms of good versus evil, but in most human organizations it is a conflict between two goods (a high standard of living and a beautiful environment) or between the legitimate needs of two groups (the farmer versus the food consumer). This is what makes real problems so hard to solve.

2. Place the Problem in a Larger Context

As we have seen, the first step in problem analysis is to zoom in on a problem for a close-up look at its critical issues. The second step is to pull back for a broader view. Now you must try to see the problem in a larger context and fit it into a category of similar problems. This will let you describe the same problem at two different but complementary levels: close up and in context.

Sometimes the larger problem will seem obvious or implicit—for example, making a good career decision. But it is always important to look at the big picture, not just the immediate conflict. For example, is the "energy problem" a technological problem (production can't meet demand) or a social and economic problem (our wasteful consumption endangers our balance of trade)? The context you choose—and you may see more than one—will have an enormous impact on the solutions you propose. For example, should we treat energy as a technological problem and pump money into developing solar energy for the year 2020, or tackle the social problem and start rationing gasoline tomorrow?

Another way to step back and put your problem in perspective is to look for a larger concern you and your reader share. For example, one student whose paper compared statistics textbooks saw a conflict between what students needed and what textbooks offered and placed this problem in the context of trying to get through a statistics course. If she had been writing to a group of teachers, she might have defined the problem in terms of effective teaching. Either way, her approach would be to step back and put the textbook problem in a broader perspective.

In a sense, students do the same thing when they step back to get perspective on an assignment an instructor has given. They may ask themselves "Why was I assigned this paper?" or "What is the point behind this lab experiment?" or "What is the larger issue or question my work should address?"

3. Make Your Problem Definition More Operational

Steps 1 and 2 help you create a two-level definition that defines a conflict or key issue and puts it in its larger context. If your goal is to understand a complex phenomenon, such as a Shakespearean play, these are the crucial steps.

But perhaps your problem is a practical one: Someone needs to act, or you wish to persuade him or her to act. Here you can improve your analysis by making your definition more *operational*. This means stating the problem or your goals as specific operations—as actions or tasks you could actually perform. An operational problem definition is more useful than an abstract one because it suggests possible courses of action or the features of a good solution. For example, you could make an abstract definition—such as "The problem is that Americans need to lower their energy consumption"—more operational by saying, "The problem is, how can we lower consumption by increasing fuel prices, without at the same time putting an unacceptable burden on the poor?"

Sometimes an operational problem definition contains details that work as miniature plans for tackling the problem. Let's compare different ways a smoker could define his or her problem:

1. My problem is cigarettes (overly abstract problem definition; no identification of conflict or key issue).
2. My problem is that I want to cut down on smoking but just can't do it (more specific problem definition with identification of conflict).
3. My real problem is how to stop smoking at parties or when I'm out with friends (more operational definition).
4. My real problem is how to break a long-standing habit of smoking around my friends without feeling left out or unsociable (an operational definition that suggests a number of places to act).

In defining your problem, try to make the conflict and context as operational as you can.

> **Note:** The series of boxes in this chapter give guidelines for turning the ideas you generated through problem analysis into written form.
>
> The format of a written problem analysis follows the thinking process in a number of ways. The format treated here, which we will call the basic problem analysis, is widely used in business and organizational communication (examples on pages 7–9). In addition, the elements of a basic problem analysis are the core of most research papers, essays, and reports, although the elements are often rearranged and subordinated to a thesis.

> ### Writing a Problem Analysis
>
> #### State Your Operational, Two-Level Problem Definition at the Beginning
>
> In writing a basic problem analysis, give your reader a clear, two-level definition of the problem somewhere near the beginning of your paper. In a short, one- or two-page paper, most readers will expect you to define the problem (on both levels) in the very first paragraph. Come immediately to the point so your reader will know the key issue. This is also the place to reveal the purpose or point of your paper. Stating this directly at the beginning isn't always easy to do, but your reader will be looking for it.
>
> In many cases you will want to present the larger context or shared problem first, as a way of orienting the reader or catching his attention with a subject you and he care about. Then state the key conflict or issue that is at the heart of your problem.

Here is an example for an operational, two-level problem definition written as an introduction to a paper on creativity. Although this example makes the problem definition more operational by adding detail in an example, the question "How operational is my problem statement?" applies to the whole statement. It is a relative judgment about how easy it would be to act on the problem as you have defined it.

Context for larger problem
Critical conflict or key issue
More operational definition of the conflict (added as example)
Preview of purpose of the paper

According to Brewster Ghiselin *(The Creative Process),* "One might suppose that it is easy to detect creative talent and to recognize creative work. But the difficulties are considerable." Because every creative act in some way violates an established order, it is likely to appear eccentric, if not patently unreasonable, to most people. How, for example, could anyone be sure Freud's insights into the human mind weren't motivated—like the bizarre "insights" of his patients—by hidden psychological forces? And how could his contemporaries judge the validity of such startling and novel explanations of behavior? The careers of Sigmund Freud and Karl Marx show us how society deals with this problem of recognizing creative work.

4. Explore the Parts of the Problem

Once the problem is defined you need to explore the various subissues or subproblems within it. This helps you break a complex problem

Writing a Problem Analysis

Isolate and Define the Major Subissues or Subproblems Within the Problem

Make the overall hierarchical structure of your discussion clear. Once you have told the reader what the problem is, you will need to discuss it in more detail. However, instead of simply describing the situation, organize your discussion and your paragraphs around a set of subissues or subproblems within your problem. In other words, you should be able to name the major issues your analysis will address and the reader should be able to see which issue each paragraph or set of paragraphs is talking about.

In a short paper, you might use this organization:

First paragraph: TWO-LEVEL PROBLEM DEFINITION

Body of paper: Issue Issue Issue

Final paragraph: CONCLUSION

Notice that by defining a problem and a set of subissues or subproblems, you have created a hierarchical organization of ideas. Your problem definition is the top-level, most inclusive statement. The discussion and subproblems or subissues grow out of it, and your conclusion at the end will work like a new top-level idea in that it will respond to the entire discussion. Make sure your reader sees this hierarchical organization of your ideas.

down into manageable parts. For example, a smoker might decide that the major subissues within the problem of stopping smoking are "health," "costs," "strength of habit," "social pressure," and so on. In isolating subproblems the analyst needs to see how they fit into the hierarchy as parts of the larger problem.

5. Come to an Open-Minded Conclusion

In the conclusion, you come to a solution or a new definition of the problem. But you will know whether your answer is best only if you have considered other good answers. The chief weakness of most problem solvers is that they leap too quickly to a solution. Upon seeing the first strong alternative, they breathe a sigh of relief, say "this is it," and look no further. However, your conclusion will look strong to your readers only if they know you have considered and rejected with reason other logical solutions or ways of viewing this problem. For example, some people feel that smoking should not be viewed as a public health issue at all but as an example of the exercise of individual rights. Show that you have seriously considered the alternatives.

A good conclusion takes a stand, but it is open-minded in yet another way. It recognizes that any position has its own assumptions and implications. Real problems rarely go away; current solutions are often only a temporary fix. Your conclusion stands on a precarious boundary between a problem clamoring for a solution and the *implications* and consequences of that solution stretching out into the future. A solution with unrecognized implications may only be a new problem in the making. Your job as an analyst is to alert your reader to those implications that he or she must foresee if your solution is to have a real and beneficial impact. For example, giving up smoking can lead to an increase in eating and frequently cause withdrawal symptoms. Prepare your reader to deal with these implications.

Writing a Problem Analysis

Tie Your Conclusion to the Problem and to the Foregoing Analysis When Appropriate, Show That You Recognize Alternatives, Assumptions, and Implications

Your conclusion will be a new idea, but one that takes account of all the discussion that has gone before. Make sure your conclusion isn't simply a package plan you tack onto the end. It should be directly related to the problem *as you defined it*— and you should make that connection clear to the reader. Show how your conclusion deals with the problem and with the subissues or subproblems you defined. In your conclusion you must take a stand, which means offering a solution or presenting a summation of your new view of the problem. You can support your conclusion not only by offering evidence but by showing the reader that you have given open-minded consideration to alternatives and the implications of your own position.

To write a good conclusion, then, you must do three things: (1) seriously consider alternatives, (2) recognize the implications of your own position, and (3) then take a reasoned, open-minded, but solid stand. It can be uncomfortable to live with the knowledge that no response is absolutely right, but real problems rarely have simple answers. So decide what you think, even if no answer is perfect, and support it with the best evidence you can find.

EVALUATING YOUR FINAL WRITTEN PROBLEM ANALYSIS

Sometimes people have an intuitive understanding of a problem and arrive at a well-supported solution, hypothesis, or new view of the problem. But in actually sitting down to write the paper, they may let intuition take over and lose sight of the reader's probable reactions. It is one thing to understand a problem intuitively and well. However, if you want your understanding to make any difference, you must be able to communicate it to someone else. Having a good or even the "best" solution to a problem only matters if your analysis convinces someone else. A written analysis, unlike an intuitive one, demands both conceptual clarity as a thinker and rhetorical skill as a writer.

Use the checklist below to evaluate your written analysis. How well have you handled each of the following seven important features a reader will expect?

The Problem Definition

1. Is there a shared problem or larger context?
2. Is the central conflict or key issue defined?
3. Is the problem definition operational?

The Overall Structure

1. Are specific subissues or subproblems clearly defined?
2. Is the overall hierarchical structure of the discussion clear?

The Conclusion

1. Does the conclusion reflect an active consideration of alternatives and an open-minded sense of the assumptions and implications of your own position?
2. Is the solution clearly tied to the problem defined initially and to the bulk of your discussion?

Often, consulting such a checklist can help you see weaknesses or missing portions of your basic problem analysis. Here is a first draft of a problem analysis written by a student who had worked for two summers at a firm called Timmerman Landscape Company:

Where is the problem? Timmerman Landscape is a local nursery that has recently moved into doing landscaping. They have a year-round staff of around ten people, but in the summer they hire a lot of summer help to meet peak summer workloads. Most of the summer help are college students. There is a waiting list for these jobs because the pay is good and the **Subproblem** work is outdoors but not as heavy as construction work. Or at least it shouldn't be. But because many new summer workers don't know how to move large trees, the best ways to handle the equipment, handle **Is this the key issue or conflict?** the trucks, or the large plants, or dig holes, their job is much harder. But Timmerman does little to help summer employees in these areas.

Subproblem One problem is that unloading large trees and shrubs can be difficult, even dangerous if you don't know how to position the truck and use the planks. And positioning large plants in the hole is very time-consuming if you don't know how to gauge depth and position **Subproblem?** before unloading. Word-of-mouth publicity is very important to Timmerman, but when neighbors come over to ask summer help about the names of plants, conditions they like, or care they need, the new workers usually have no idea, or make a blind guess.

Subproblem? **Conclusion—not tied to problem definition; doesn't recognize alternatives and implications** By my second summer, I had learned a lot about plants and realized that many, even expensive, trees and shrubs were damaged by incorrect rough handling and incorrect planting—in holes too shallow, too close to a house, with air left around the roots. In conclusion, I think Timmerman should develop a handbook for new employees that would be used as part of a brief orientation program for new summer workers.

In analyzing his draft, the writer realized that his problem definition was too long in coming and did not convey the conflict underlying the problem, nor was it very operational. He found that his subproblems were not organized hierarchically; one even appeared before the problem definition. He also decided that his conclusion seemed "tacked on": It did not clearly proceed from what had come before or recognize the alternatives and implications of his proposed solution. Here is his revision:

Large problem **Operational problem definition including identification of conflict** Timmerman Landscape is a local nursery that has recently moved into doing landscaping. In the summer they need to hire extra help—many of them college students—to meet peak workloads during that season. Most summer workers like the job because the pay is good and the work is outdoors, but problems arise because Timmerman, in order to save money, spends no time on training them in procedures and techniques that would make them more efficient.

Subproblem   This lack of training affects both the students themselves and Timmerman's profitability. The work is hard for summer employees if they don't know the best ways to move large trees, handle the equipment and trucks, handle large plants, or dig holes. It can even be dangerous, if someone is unloading large trees and shrubs and doesn't know how to position the truck and use the planks.

Subproblem   Further, the lack of training causes reduced productivity, plant damage, and loss of business for Timmerman. Untrained workers waste a lot of time: for example, positioning a large plant in a hole is very time-consuming if you don't know how to gauge depth and

Subproblem   position before unloading. Many trees and shrubs, including expensive ones, are damaged by incorrect rough handling or incorrect planting— in holes too shallow or too close to a house, or with air left around the

Subproblem   roots. Finally, Timmerman depends on word-of-mouth publicity, but when neighbors come over to ask summer help about the names of plants, conditions they like, or care they need, the new workers usually have no idea, or make a blind guess.

Recognition of   Apparently Timmerman cannot afford to have its regular help
alternatives   spend much time training summer workers. I think the best solution
Conclusion   is for Timmerman to develop a handbook for new employees that
Recognition of   would be used as part of a brief orientation program for summer
implications;   workers. While this would involve some time and expense, it is a
conclusion tied   one-time project that could help both the nursery and the new
to problem   summer workers.
definition

 ## PITFALLS IN PROBLEM ANALYSIS

In trying to write a good analysis, people may encounter difficulty in any of the three major areas: problem definition, structure, or conclusion. Here are some examples of typical pitfalls to watch out for in your own writing. These come from responses to an assignment, to analyze and evaluate textbooks.

The Definition Pitfall

Instead of defining a problem, the writer in Example 1 is simply discussing his topic and describing a situation. He is telling us what he observed, instead of presenting key issues and concepts.

EXAMPLE 1:   Of the three textbooks I surveyed, Brace's offers the most detailed coverage of modern history—1340 pages to carry every day.

Howard's book is easier to read and half the length. Unlike most history books, it is organized around topics rather than strict chronology. Levine's is the oldest and is outdated on some recent topics. Each book has unique features.

The Structure Pitfall

The writer of Example 2 has given us a useful top-level idea: The book fails to provide background. However, the rest of the paragraph is simply a list of facts, all of which seem equally important but unrelated. The writer needs to reorganize this list into two or three major subproblems, such as the book's lack of social, biographical, and literary contexts, and then use the facts to support her organizing ideas.

> EXAMPLE 2: The poems in this anthology are harder to understand and remember because the book doesn't provide any context for them. There are no footnotes to say when a poem was written and only a sentence or two about the author. Many poems refer to historical events or unfamiliar customs that most students wouldn't know about. If you wonder about why the poem was written, or why it was written the way it was, the anthology offers no help. Although it has a large number of sonnets, it never mentions the nature of sonnets, what kinds of people wrote them, or when.

The Conclusion Pitfall

The writer of Example 3 started with a well-defined problem: The current French text is not organized for easy review, even though that is a necessary part of learning the material. But her conclusion shows two common pitfalls. First, the solution is a prepackaged, unrelated assertion that does not address the problem she defined. Secondly, it is the kind of conclusion that "can't go wrong." As with a statement supporting Mom and apple pie, no one will probably disagree with it, but then no one will bother to listen either.

> EXAMPLE 3: In conclusion, students need to be able to learn at their own pace and still cover the material required by the course. For many students this will involve not only more time spent studying, but more chance to speak and use French in the classroom.

MOVING FROM A PROBLEM TO A THESIS

In this chapter we have been discussing the art of problem analysis—the art of thinking through a complex situation. You may now be asking, "How does problem analysis help in writing a typical college paper in which you must state and support a thesis?"

Problem analysis can help in two ways. First, the thesis of many papers is simply a claim that a problem or an issue exists, that the conflict is important, interesting, unnoticed, or that we should do something about it. As you can see in the examples following, this claim or thesis is put in the spotlight and the paper is organized around it. But the main parts of a problem analysis are still the core of the paper as you discuss this problem and its subissues.

Writers can move from a problem to a thesis in another way. If pondering over and analyzing a problem has led you to a conclusion, a solution, or a new idea, that conclusion can become your thesis. Notice the irony in this: In order to find a good thesis (and to write the first paragraph of your paper which contains the thesis) you may need to write much of the paper first. That is, you may need to do a problem analysis in order to arrive at your conclusion. But when you do, that conclusion can be moved to the head of your paper as the thesis you want to support. In fact, this is how experienced writers often work. They may start with only a vague or tentative thesis; however, they fearlessly write this tentative thesis down simply to get started. Their first paragraph may say nothing more elegant than: "This paper is going to argue that . . . (a sketchy thesis). . . ." This lets them start writing about their problem and in the process come to a conclusion that will become the thesis.

It is important to recognize the difference between a topic, a problem, and a thesis. In the textbook assignment discussed on page 168, the topic was "textbooks and the differences among them." A topic simply names a field, a body of knowledge, or a situation (for example, textbooks differ). Given only a topic, you could simply write a description of different textbooks. But what would you choose to say, how would you order it, and why would you be writing (other than to turn in the paper on time)?

By contrast, when you define a problem *within* the topic, you are identifying a key issue or conflict that you and your reader care about. For example, in writing about textbooks you might define the problem as "Textbooks often don't meet students' needs." A problem analysis is, by definition, an exploration of a problematic situation. As a result of such an analysis, you might conclude that textbook writers are making the wrong assumptions and thereby making their books hard to use; that textbooks should build on the students' exist- ing skills; or that the current statistics course is a failure. It is at this point that you have a thesis.

A *thesis* can be defined as an assertion about a topic that you believe to be true and that you intend to support and explain in your paper. If we could follow the thinking process of a writer, we would see that it often follows this path from topic to problem to thesis. The following examples show three ways in which writers turned the fruits of a problem analysis into a thesis. The first two kinds of theses focus on the problem itself, the third on its solution.

Theses that assert that a problem exists:

The textbook in our course is causing real difficulty for many students.

The continued fruitless search for the "missing link" in man's evolution suggests that the theory of slow, steady evolution needs to be reconsidered.

Theses that assert a hypothesis or new understanding of the problem:

Students are failing to grasp the basic principles in our course because the textbook tries to build on knowledge most students don't have.

The relatively sudden and widespread appearance of early man eliminates the possibility that man evolved by the time-consuming mechanism of competition and survival of the fittest.

Theses that assert a solution to a problem:

Instructors of large, required courses should consider pretesting their texts with a representative group of students.

In order to unlock the mysteries of man's development, we should explore the genetic factors that govern two key features of man: the rapid growth of the brain and the slow process of maturation.

 ## THE PROCESS OF BUILDING A THESIS

What happens when you have to build a thesis from scratch? Let me sketch a typical process writers go through and describe some milestones to look for in your own process. Although your path on a given paper may look quite different, this example shows some of the decisions that often go into creating a good thesis.

The assignment we will work with is an open-ended one which reads:

College students have to move among many different discourse communities which include those created by family and friends, by college organizations, by classes. Students must operate not only within the academic discourse community itself but within the special discourse of different fields, different professions, and even different courses. Moving among these groups can be like going to a foreign country. When you cross the border both the language and the expectations of the audience change.

The fact that different discourse communities exist is, of course, only a situation. Does this situation ever create a problem for students as writers or readers? What does it mean to enter or succeed in a given discourse community at your school?

Write a paper on this issue, using your reading and own observation to develop and support a thesis. Define the audience you will address as a part of your plan.

How might you go about developing the thesis this situation calls for?

At the Beginning

1. Although the assignment requires a thesis, no one would expect you to have a claim already in mind, unless you had been previously working on the problem. So in fact, the best place to start is with your own experience and intuitions about the *problem*. For example, have you ever seen a problematic situation in which a student was trying to talk with a professor or in which an expert was trying to explain his or her knowledge? Do the writing strategies that work in one class work in all? In your own major, do people write and talk in special ways? Have you ever seen the fact of discourse communities create a problem you would like to understand?

Here is where all your skills of problem analysis play a role. Build a picture of a problem you want to discuss.

2. In addition to exploring your own knowledge, explore the *assignment* and think about what your thesis will need to accomplish. As an academic writer, you will be expected to add something new to the conversation—not a staggering new theory, but an interesting idea based on your own close observation and outside reading. And because a thesis makes a claim, your readers will be looking for evidence and arguments that support your claim. But remember that academic readers also put special value on a skeptical argument that recognizes evidence on both sides of a question—so you can present a qualified thesis if you are not sure a flat assertion is really true. Your goal is to add to the conversation, not end it.

Along the Way

3. Don't go with the first attractive thesis that comes along. As you start to read a lot, to gather data and think a lot, a number of possible claims will occur to you. But chances are you will need to go through a longer thinking process before you see a thesis that can do justice to your best ideas. This is normal, and waiting is a smart way to proceed.

4. Decide on your *preliminary definition* of the problem. What is the issue here; what is the conflict you see? What is at stake? And what are some of the subproblems? (See the checklists on pp. 121 and 166.)

5. Create a *tentative thesis*. You probably won't keep this one, although some writers find it very difficult to give up their first idea or feel afraid they may not get another one. But doing research means you will learn so much that your later vision of the problem and your thesis are likely to be much better. However, this tentative thesis plays a big role in reaching the next two milestones.

Testing a Thesis

6. Given your sense of the problem and your tentative thesis, see if you can now describe your *purpose and audience* in writing. You will have passed an important milestone when you know what you want to accomplish. Do you want to create a controversy, help professors understand students, help students enter the conversation, figure out what makes the discourse in your field distinctive or . . . ? Where are you headed? Who would appreciate your discovery? Who needs to hear about it?

7. Once you have a tentative thesis you can read in a more purposeful way: look for connections which will support it and look just as energetically for ideas which will test it. Finding evidence against your tentative thesis does not spell doom. It only makes you wiser. In the process of testing you are likely to see ways to *qualify or change your thesis.* You may even discover a whole new way of seeing the situation. If so, cheerfully abandon your tentative thesis—it did its work—and tell the reader about your new, more carefully tested and qualified claim and the evidence that makes it worth considering.

This process of *developing* a thesis—of starting with a problem or issue, of resisting the first idea that comes along, and of changing your tentative thesis until it fits your purpose and your evidence— means you spend a little more time planning and less time throwing away text that didn't work. As you probably know, leaping into writing with a "good" idea that fizzles out because it is too small to support a full argument can guarantee frustration. Having a thesis you have tested and having a purpose behind that thesis can make the time spent writing not only more productive but personally satisfying.

Here are excerpts from two papers stimulated by the assignment to explore a discourse community. Is it possible to locate both a thesis and a problem definition in each of these papers or not? Notice the form these statements take.

WRITING WITHIN A DISCOURSE COMMUNITY

When writing for a certain discourse community such as chemistry, does the author accommodate a text to the type of audience that is going to read it? To answer this question, I took three introductory textbooks in chemistry and compared them to two advanced textbooks. Does the writer of the simplified textbook, while "watering down" the information keep the basic principles intact, or will the reader have to relearn the information when he moves to a higher level book? I found that the authors definitely structured the books to simplify the text and theories for the novice reader. But they distorted the information as little as possible by simply leaving certain things out.

This first difference between the introductory and advanced books can be seen by just looking at them. The easier books are not as thick and have much simpler covers. A very thick chemistry textbook with fine print, lots of detail, many charts and tables, and atomic diagrams on the cover will most likely scare off the first-time chemist.

C. S. WORLD

The bright gray, black, and white screen flashes highlighted parts of the program I just typed and prints the message **PROGRAM NOT COMPI-LABLE** at the bottom. Clicking through the list of problems it has found, I see the computer is giving me messages that have become too familiar: **This is not a Val Parameter, This is Not an Expression, Type Clash and Mismatch.** I re-compile the program I am trying to write, to find yet more errors revealed. I clench my fists and stiffly beckon to one of the tutors in the room while contemplating breaking the little machine in front of me and taking the course next semester. The small, possibly cute screen has added a new and potent source of stress to my relatively new life as a college student.

The tutor understands his job too well and answers by asking me a question: What type of parameter do you think needs a Var or Value?" The tutor uses words like "program decomposition" and "control structures" that I don't recall being in the reading assignment. I ask a student who is typing away confidently next to me if he could help me with my program for a minute. I remember having seen him in some of my other classes and thinking that he was rather quiet. I was surprised at how talkative, confident and comfortable he seemed in the computer science world. He knew Pascal and told me what to type, but gave no explanation for what I was punching into the computer. The program worked, so I handed it in and closed the door to the sound of typing without a sense of accomplishment.

Computer science, since its birth, has created and refined a language that is unique for a reason. It is cryptic to an outsider, but it has a definite purpose as a useful tool in its world. . . .

These two writers relied on different conventions for combining a problem analysis with a claim or thesis. Look back to find as many different conventions used here as you can (see the glossary below for ideas). On the basis of your list, would you conclude that both of these papers are examples of academic discourse or not? Do they speak to the same community? (If you and other members of your class disagree, you might want to compare how you are defining a discourse community.)

PROJECTS AND ASSIGNMENTS

1   A literary problem. Many works of literature show us two sides of an important question—two conflicting attitudes toward love or honor or madness or imagination. Or they embody, in two characters, alternative ways of feeling or acting. In a book you are reading, describe this conflict—that is,

what is at issue either within the world of the book, within the author's point of view, or within you as a reader?

2   A personal problem. Michael B. is a college sophomore who commutes to school. He feels he is missing much of the experience of college by living at home with his parents and seeing primarily high school friends who didn't go to college. He wants to live on campus next year but knows that if he does that, he will have to ask for the money from his father, who feels Michael should be working instead of going to college, and saving money rather than spending it. The conflict has left Michael unable to act. Can you analyze this problem and offer useful suggestions?

3   A professional problem. Jim Grayson and Tom Brand both work for the Ford Motor Company in Chicago. One is a spot welder on the assembly line, the other a plant manager. In his book *Working*, Studs Terkel interviewed both men, asking them to talk about their jobs, and turned up some interesting contradictions.* You have been hired as a trouble-shooter and consultant by Ford with the long-range goal of satisfying the needs of both the employees and management. These interviews, on pages 164–68 and 171–81 of *Working* are your raw data. Analyze them and write a one-page problem analysis to the vice-president in charge of production. No one expects the problem to be a simple one; at the same time, your reader needs to be able to act on the recommendations you give.

Alternatively, you could read the interview with Steve Carmichael, also in *Working* (pp. 341–43), and write your own analysis of this situation in a one- to two-page report to the district superintendent, who needs to act on this personnel problem.

4   Your own problem. Generally the most fruitful problems to analyze are your own. Think of a problematic situation in which you find yourself right now. Remember, a problem is only a problem when someone feels caught between two sides of a question. Examine the key conflict in your situation and write an analysis of the problem, giving alternatives, assumptions, and implications.

5   The set of six projects and assignments which follow suggest various ways you can analyze problems and develop your own theses about how people use language. You can use one or more of these projects as a "method" to collect information for the discourse community assignment described on page 171. If you choose to address your paper to someone other than those of us already interested in how discourse communities work, indicate who your reader is.

Here is a brief glossary of terms you may find helpful in researching that topic. Add to this glossary some important terms from the discourse community you are observing or elaborate this glossary with specific examples from your area.

---

* Studs Terkel, *Working* (New York: Pantheon, 1972).

discourse: language in use, both written and spoken.

discourse community: a group of people who can comfortably use the conventions of a particular discourse and who share certain expectations about content, language, and style (see Chapter 1).

discourse convention: a familiar pattern or feature of a text which both writers and their readers recognize as meaningful. Such conventions can range from the discipline-specific patterns expected in scientific argument, to general rhetorical patterns such as comparisons and examples, to text features such as topic sentences, thesis statements, and italics (see Chapter 1).

academic discourse: a set of conventions used to carry out and to share the results of research and scholarship and to carry on conversations about ideas. Different disciplines create their own communities within academic discourse (see Chapter 5).

problematic situation: a situation which contains some conflict, often in people's goals, values, or expectations.

problem definition: a statement which locates and describes the conflict itself or which defines the issue or question which underlies a problematic situation.

thesis: a statement or a claim, usually made in response to a problem or an issue, that will be supported with evidence.

preliminary problem definition and tentative thesis: good ideas created on the way to better ones.

6 Create a list of technical terms or confusing concepts from a course you have taken. In "Politics and the English Language," George Orwell argues that language is an instrument people create and use for their own purposes. In "If Black English Isn't a Language, Then Tell Me, What Is?", James Baldwin takes a less neutral stance; he argues that language is a political instrument; it is both a means and proof of power.

Consider these ideas as tentative theses and at the same time find out more about your chosen terms. Then develop and support your own thesis on how these words *evolved* or how they *work* within their discourse community.

7 Have you ever noticed what happens when insiders and outsiders to some discourse meet? Try to overhear (or stage) such an encounter and write a dialogue of your own which portrays the situation. Then take on the hat of a drama critic and write a short review that interprets and comments on your scene. (You may need to read some examples of both dialogues and drama reviews to sound like an insider yourself.)

8 Find two discussions of the same topic in a popular and a technical source (for example, a discussion of a historical event, a book, or a new product in a magazine article and a professional journal). Or compare the presentation of a concept in an introductory and advanced textbook. Use these comparisons to draw a portrait of the readers in each group: what do they know; what do they seem to expect; why?

9 In her article "Teacher Talk," Shirley Brice Heath says that teachers have special ways of asking questions that aren't really questions, but requests or commands. Her research suggests that questions are used to teach and socialize children into the appropriate patterns of response expected in school. John Braxton and Robert Nordvall claim that you can characterize a college by whether its teachers ask "why" and "how" questions (which he sees as desirable) or "what" questions (which simply ask students to parrot information). How do questions function in your classes? Can they tell you anything about how the discourse in those classes operates?

You can use some of the standard methods of classroom research to analyze teacher/student discourse. On two different days keep a detailed log on every exchange in a 10-minute period. Set up a system to note who initiated the exchange; who talked; what was the purpose; and what was the outcome. If you picked a course that causes difficulty for some people, you might ask: Did teachers and students seem to have the same expectations about this discourse? [Sources: S. B. Heath, "Teacher Talk: Language in the Classroom," *Language in Education: Theory and Practice 9* (Washington D.C.: Center for Applied Linguistics, Georgetown University, 1978). S. B. Heath, "Questioning at Home and School: A Comparative Study," ed. George Spindler, *Doing the Ethnography of Schooling* (New York: Holt, Rinehart & Winston, 1983). J. Braxton & R. Nordvall, "Selective Liberal Arts Colleges: Higher Quality as Well as Higher Prestige?", *Journal of Higher Education 36* (Sept.–Oct. 1985), pp. 538–54.]

10 Do different readers really see the same thing when they read a text outside their experience? Do your own observational research to get an answer. You will need a short (1 page) but demanding article from your field, a reader from outside the field, and a tape recorder. Give your reader the following instructions:

I'm going to give you a passage from ——— (a drama review, an automotive road test, an economics text). I would like you to read it out loud and say, as far as possible, whatever you are thinking as you read. After every few sentences I will also ask you to stop and tell me how you interpret the passage so far. At the end I will ask you a few questions about what you have read. Don't worry about "getting it wrong" or not understanding what the passage means. The purpose of my observation is to explore *different* ways readers interpret what they read.

Ask your reader how he or she "interprets" the text every few sentences, and if the reader falls silent, prompt your reader with, "Can you tell me what you are thinking now?" but don't interfere or explain. At the end you might ask your reader to summarize the text or to explain its main points to check his or her comprehension. For comparison, you may wish to repeat your observation with a reader in your field.

Look at your data. What did your reader do? Does this close look at the interpretive process help you see any problems readers might have who are trying to "enter the conversation of a field" as we talked about in Chapter 1? Use your data and any other information you have to analyze that problem.

11 Many of the preceding assignments ask you to experiment with different kinds of discourse, to collect and ponder information in order to understand a problem or develop a thesis. This gives you a good opportunity to observe your own process unfold. Keep a log in which you track how your definition of the problem and your thesis develops. Each time you work jot down a note about:

1a. Date   Time   Hours worked

1b. My *current* sense of the problem/my purpose/my tentative thesis is:

1c. What I Did/Interesting Observation:

When you are done, write a journal commentary on how your ideas seem to develop.

IF YOU WOULD LIKE TO READ MORE

If you would like to know more about problem analysis and designing your written analysis for a professional audience, see:

Mathes, J. C., and Dwight Stevenson. *Designing Technical Reports: Writing for Audiences in Organizations*. Indianapolis: Bobbs-Merrill, 1976. / This book shows how to use problem analysis to write effective technical reports within an organization. It gives an excellent introduction to professional writing in all kinds of organizations.

Young, Richard, Alton Becker, and Kenneth Pike. *Rhetoric: Discovery and Change*. New York: Harcourt Brace Jovanovich, 1970. / The authors of this important book on rhetoric explore the entire process of problem analysis and inquiry. They analyze what it means to think about problems through the act of writing, and in doing so they lay the groundwork for a modern theory of rhetoric.

chapter nine

Designing for a Reader

GOAL 5
KNOW the needs of your reader

The first step in designing your writing to be read is to understand the needs, attitudes, and knowledge of your particular reader, and to help that reader turn your written message into the meaning you intended.

> **STRATEGY 1 ANALYZE YOUR AUDIENCE**
> **STRATEGY 2 ANTICIPATE YOUR READER'S RESPONSE**
> **STRATEGY 3 ORGANIZE FOR A CREATIVE READER**

First drafts are often satisfying; they seem to say just what one meant. But when writers come back a day, a week, or a year later, they often discover a gap between what they were thinking and what their writing actually conveyed. If you are writing to be read, it is what you communicate to your reader that finally counts—not what is in your head. If you want to be understood, it is usually not enough simply to *express* your ideas. One of the secrets of communicating your ideas is to understand the needs of your reader and to transform writer-based thought into reader-based prose. The next two chapters will help you design your writing so someone else not only will read it but will understand and remember it.

In trying to design for the reader, one question people often ask is "How soon should I start thinking about my reader? Where does this step fit into the total writing process?"

The answer is that it can fit nearly anywhere. It may occur during planning, when you try to identify the audience; during idea generation, when you may develop your code words to help the reader understand; and during organizing, when you nutshell and teach your ideas with the reader in mind. Thus, designing for the reader occurs during many stages of the writing process. It could be said that this step is nested, or embedded, within other phases, much as a set of Chinese boxes is nested within one another.

Nesting also occurs on a broader level. The general steps of planning, generating, organizing, and editing are often performed "out of order" or one within the other. As you know from your experience, writers use the steps we have been discussing in this book but do not always use them in a 1, 2, 3 order like stair steps to a finished paper. They may generate ideas first, then go back to plan, then organize and edit while revising some of their plan, and so forth.

The process of designing for a reader, which will be discussed in this and the following chapter, is one that occurs throughout the act of writing. You may use the process as part of one particular step, such as planning, or you may stop between steps—say, between generating and organizing—and decide to focus on your audience before proceeding further. Therefore, designing for a reader is nested not only within each writing step but within the total writing process; you turn to it whenever you feel a need to pause and concentrate in depth on your reader. That moment could come in the middle of planning, while you are organizing ideas, or before you begin the second draft of the paper. Whenever such a time comes, Steps 5 and 6 will help you think and write for your reader.

GOAL 5

KNOW the Needs of Your Reader

The goal of the writer is to create a momentary common ground between the reader and the writer. You want the reader to share your knowledge and your attitude toward that knowledge. Even if the reader eventually disagrees, you want him or her to be able for the moment to *see things as you see them*. A good piece of writing closes the gap between you and the reader.

STRATEGY 1   ANALYZE YOUR AUDIENCE

The first step in closing that gap is to gauge the distance between the two of you. Imagine, for example, that you are a student writing to your parents, who have always lived in New York City, about a wilderness survival expedition you want to go on over spring break. Sometimes obvious differences such as age or background will be important, but the critical differences for writers usually fall into three areas: the reader's *knowledge* about the topic, his or her *attitude* toward it, and his or her personal or professional *needs*. Because these differences often exist, good writers do more than simply express their meaning; they pinpoint the critical differences between themselves and their reader and design their writing to reduce those differences. Let us look at these three areas in more detail:

1. *Knowledge.* This is usually the easiest difference to handle. What does your reader need to know? What are the main ideas you

hope to teach? Does your reader have enough background knowledge to understand you? If not, what would he or she have to learn?

2. *Attitudes.* When we say a person has knowledge, we are usually referring to his conscious awareness of explicit facts and clearly defined concepts. This kind of knowledge can be easily written down or told to someone else. However, much of what we "know" is not held in this formal, explicit way. Instead it is held as an attitude or image—as a loose cluster of associations. For instance, my image of lakes includes associations many people would have, including fishing, water skiing, stalled outboards, and lots of kids catching night crawlers with flashlights. However, the most salient or powerful parts of my image, which strongly color my whole attitude toward lakes, are thoughts of cloudy skies, long rainy days, and feeling generally cold and damp. By contrast, one of my best friends has a very different cluster of associations. To him, a lake means sun, swimming, sailing, and happily sitting on the end of a dock. Needless to say, our differing images cause us to react quite differently to a proposal that we visit a lake. Likewise, one reason people often find it difficult to discuss economics and politics is that terms such as "capitalism" conjure up radically different images.

As you can see, a reader's image of a subject is often the source of attitudes and feelings that are unexpected and, at times, impervious to mere facts. A simple statement that seems quite persuasive to you, such as "Lake Wampago would be a great place to locate the new music camp," could have little impact on your reader if he or she simply doesn't visualize a lake as a "great place." In fact, many people accept uncritically any statement that fits in with their own attitudes—and reject, just as uncritically, anything that does not.

Whether your purpose is to persuade or simply to present your perspective, it helps to know the image and attitudes that your reader already holds. The more these differ from your own, the more you will have to do to make him or her *see* what you mean.

3. *Needs.* When writers discover a large gap between their own knowledge and attitudes and those of the reader, they usually try to change the reader in some way. Needs, however, are different. When you analyze a reader's needs, it is so that you, the writer, can adapt to him. If you ask a friend majoring in biology how to keep your fish tank from clouding, you don't want to hear a textbook recitation on the life processes of algae. You expect the friend to adapt his or her knowledge and tell you exactly how to solve your problem.

The ability to adapt your knowledge to the needs of the reader is often crucial to your success as a writer. This is especially true in writing done on a job. For example, as producer of a public affairs program for a television station, 80 percent of your time may be taken up planning the details of new shows, contacting guests, and scheduling the taping sessions. But when you write a program proposal to the station director, your job is to show how the program will fit into the cost guidelines, the FCC requirements for relevance, and the overall programming plan for the station. When you write that report, your role in the organization changes from producer to proposal writer. Why? Because your reader needs that information in order to make a decision. He may be *interested* in your scheduling problems and the specific content of the shows, but he *reads* your report because of his own needs as station director of that organization. He has to act.

In college, where the reader is also a teacher, the reader's needs are a little less concrete but just as important. Most papers are assigned as a way to teach something. So the real purpose of a paper may be for you to make connections between two historical periods, to discover for yourself the principle behind a laboratory experiment, or to develop and support your own interpretation of a novel. A good college paper doesn't just rehash the facts; it demonstrates what your reader, as a teacher, needs to know—that you are learning the thinking skills his or her course is trying to teach.

Effective writers are not simply expressing what they know, like a student madly filling up an examination bluebook. Instead they are *using* their knowledge—reorganizing, maybe even rethinking their ideas to meet the demands of an assignment or the needs of their reader.

Sometimes it is also necessary to decide who is your primary audience as opposed to your secondary audience. Both may read your paper, but the primary audience is the reader you most want to teach, influence, or convince. When this is the case, you will want to design the paper so the primary reader can easily find what he or she needs.

A SAMPLE AUDIENCE ANALYSIS

Margo Miller, a college student who works in the bookstore at her university, has been asked by the new store manager to write a job description of her position as an administrative assistant in the paperback department. The manager, Dot Schwartz, said she wanted to know what tasks the position involved and needed information that would help in evaluating Margo's performance and in hiring and training an eventual replacement should Margo leave the position. Dot mentioned that new trainees might be shown the description for guidance in performing the job.

Margo's audience chart in Figure 9–1 pinpoints the critical features of her primary reader, the store manager, Dot Schwartz. Although there is much more Margo could find out about Dot, such as age and education, and so forth—observe how her notes and thinking focus on the critical facts—the facts most relevant to her purpose in writing.

Figure 9–1
Audience Chart for Primary Audience: The New Store Manager

CRITICAL FEATURES OF THE READER

Knowledge	*Attitudes*	*Needs*
Has general knowledge of bookstore operations but not a detailed understanding of how thing work here.	Sees it as a student job—no responsibility.	General list of tasks.
	Assumes I'm temporary.	Time they take.
Doesn't know what tasks I've added to my job description.		Background or experience required.
		Needs info to give new trainees.

KNOWLEDGE: Dot Schwartz, the new manager, knows a lot about bookstore operations in general, but she probably doesn't know what, exactly, I do as an administrative assistant and what tasks I've added to my job since I've been here. In terms of the tasks I've added, the amount of *new knowledge* I'll need to convey will be rather small, so that aspect of the report should be easy to handle.

ATTITUDES: When I took this job it was mostly a matter of typing and filing. However, through my own efforts I've now often become responsible for dealing with salespeople, ordering certain paperbacks, and designing window displays. I suspect Dot's image of my job is an inadequate one that doesn't recognize the importance of what I'm doing. She may see it as simply a part-time student job, but I see it as a training position that's allowing me to gain increased experience and responsibility. This difference in our images of the job could be critical when I ask for a raise in the fall. So in this report I need to revise Dot's inadequate image of my job and close the gap between our differing attitudes.

NEEDS: If asked, I could give a very detailed account of my job: exact facts, figures, people, and procedures. But I don't think that's what my reader needs. Dot asked for the report in order to carry out her overall job as a bookstore manager, not to get involved in minutiae. She's interested in the basic tasks involved, how long they generally take, and, since trainees may be coming in, what kinds of background or experience to look for.

Clearly the reader's needs here dictate a quite special organization of Margo's knowledge.

Margo also has a secondary audience for this report: the new trainee who will eventually read it. This reader is quite different in some ways from the manager, as Margo's audience chart in Figure 9–2 shows. Again, here are Margo's notes and thinking:

KNOWLEDGE: This reader probably won't know the difference between a back order and an O. P. title, so I'll need to explain procedures and terms in more detail.

FIGURE 9–2
Audience Chart for Secondary Audience: The New Trainee

CRITICAL FEATURES OF THE READER

Knowledge	*Attitudes*	*Needs*
Probably won't know basic terms or procedures.	May think of it as a "simple" part-time job. Might not recognize the opportunities or demands really involved.	Needs to know what to do and how to do it: an operational description of the job.

ATTITUDES: Given the official description of this as a part-time job, a new trainee may not realize the opportunities it offers or the amount of planning and organization required to do it well.

NEEDS: The new assistant may be using this report to learn the job, so, unlike the manager, he or she will need a report organized around when and how to do things. However, since the manager is still my primary audience, I probably should put this detailed information in a chart or separate section at the end.

By analyzing her audiences and their particular needs, Margo now knows enough to design a report that not only will achieve her ends but will be effective for her two quite different readers.

What about other situations, when you must write for a general reader? In the following example, Margo has decided to adapt her thoughts about her job to a very different use. She wants to submit an article to the *University Times* for a series the paper is running on jobs at the university. Even though this audience represents a cross-section of the university's students, faculty, and staff, Margo's audience analysis turns up some concrete ideas that will help her plan the paper. Here are her thoughts about the article:

These readers may have a limited knowledge of what it means to run a bookstore beyond selling books (knowledge). *Furthermore, as with the store manager, their image of my job will be colored by their conception of part-time jobs* (attitudes). *Since I want to show how part-time jobs can be good career training, I'll have to deal directly with those attitudes. Finally, these readers will also need to expect something from the article* (needs). *Some people might want to learn things relevant to themselves, or might simply want some entertainment. Many people are reading the series in order to find out about various types of jobs they might like to apply for. It may be possible to meet all these needs if I structure the article well.*

Margo also needs to keep in mind her secondary audience, the *University Times* editor. Although the editor is himself seeking to meet the needs of his audience, he also has special requirements the writer must meet. For example, he needs articles under 1,000 words that are focused on the series topic and are written in an engaging, partly journalistic style. To be successful with both her audiences, Margo needs to meet them halfway.

We can sum up this discussion of audience analysis by noting three things you can do:

1. Find out who your reader will be. If you have more than one, decide which audience is primary. Which reader or kind of reader will your paper be designed primarily for?
2. Then begin to explore what you know about your reader's knowledge, attitudes, and needs. Locate these characteristics of your reader that will be critical in light of your purpose in writing.
3. Then plan how you are going to close the gap between you and your reader to make your paper effective.

STRATEGY 2   ANTICIPATE YOUR READER'S RESPONSE

Let us now shift focus from a particular audience or type of audience to the reader's actual process of understanding. When you think about it, we ask a great deal when we expect people to translate a few words presented on a page into a complex meaning or an image that resembles what we originally intended. As we all know, merely reading a message is not the same thing as understanding, much less remembering, it.

The question then is, what happens when a reader tries to turn a *message* into a *meaning?* And what can a writer do to increase the chances that the reader will comprehend and retain the *writer's* meaning?

HOW DOES THE COMMUNICATION PROCESS WORK?

We often talk about communication as if it were a physical process rather like sending goods in a delivery truck to the reader. We say that a writer *conveys* his message, *expresses* his ideas, or *gets* his point *across.* In this view, the writer's duty is simply to pack all his meaning into the message before it is delivered. Then the reader supposedly gets the message and sees the writer's point of view. Figure 9–3 depicts this concept of communication.

One problem with this model is that it turns the writer into a delivery boy. Communication, it seems to say, is the same as simply expressing what's on your mind. If your meaning has been placed (somewhere) in the message, then the reader can dig it out. But unfortunately readers can, and quite often do, read information yet fail to get your meaning or your point. This model of the communication

FIGURE 9–3
Delivering an Idea: A Simplified Model of Communication

idea transmitted to reader

writer puts idea   reader gets the
into words   picture; no loss
                                                          of meaning

process misleads us by suggesting that a writer's meaning or ideas can simply be transferred intact to someone else.

During World War II a more sophisticated version of the communication process was developed by electrical engineers who were trying to increase the amount of information transmitted through electronic equipment such as radios and telephones. This model of how communication works (see Figure 9–4) depicts the writer as a combination of a radio announcer and a transmitter that sends the messages out on air waves.

In this model the writer, or sender, has a meaning in mind. He "encodes" that meaning into a message, and it is this message that is sent to the reader. The message could take the form of a signal sent out on air waves, a hastily scrawled note tacked on the back door, or a twenty-page paper with pictures and graphs. The point is that the sender has to *encode* his meaning in some form in order to send it. And some senders are better at turning meaning into code than others. A powerful radio transmitter sends off a good-quality signal; a

FIGURE 9–4
A Model Based on Communication Theory

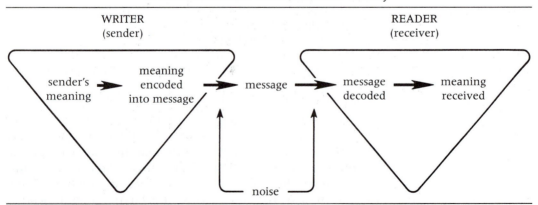

good writer is able to send messages that accurately express his or her meaning. The first hurdle in the communication process, then, is turning meaning into a message.

This model also reminds us that there are many opportunities for *noise* or interference in this process. While the radio operator may worry about thunderstorms, the writer must worry about everything from misspellings and bad grammar to poor organization and fuzzy thinking—all the things that make his coded message a little less clear.

When the message finally reaches the reader, he, like a radio receiver, must repeat the process of decoding the message back into a meaning. The reader, like a secret agent with a cryptogram, must interpret a meaning. And again the chance for noise enters; if the reader is tired, is confused by the subject, or misses a key word, the communication process breaks down a little more.

As you can see, it is a long way from the meaning the sender had in mind to the meaning that the receiver eventually decodes at the end of the line. The value of this model is that it graphically demonstrates that no matter what you *mean,* and even no matter what message you *send,* all that finally counts is the decoded meaning that the reader finally *receives.*

This model, however, has a limitation: It can't help us understand how readers actually decode messages. To know that, we would need a cognitive or mental model that describes some of the thinking strategies readers use to transform messages into meanings as they read. The discussion that follows will show that readers are not passive recipients who simply *see* the writer's point. In order to comprehend a message, they actually create a meaning in their own mind.

THE CREATIVE READER

What happens when readers go about decoding messages and creating meanings? The first thing to notice is that they just don't *remember* all the things we tell them. (Imagine trying to repeat every major and minor idea that was presented in the preceding chapter of this book.) Instead of remembering all the details, readers do something much more creative—they draw inferences as they read and use the writer's ideas to form their own concepts. In other words, readers remember not what *we* tell them, but what they tell *themselves.* You can demonstrate this process for yourself with the following exercise.

Here is an excerpt from the "Personal Experience" section of Henry Morris's application for a summer job in accounting. As personnel director, you have been asked to evaluate six such applications. Your job is to read each one and come up with a set of distinctive qualities that characterize each candidate. How would you characterize Henry Morris from his statement below?

During high school I managed the concession stand for our home basketball games. Later I worked at the nearby A & W Root Beer stand during summers, and for three years I kept the books at my father's local
soda bottling plant. I have taken a number of math courses and have had
two courses in acounting. I am currently taking courses in small business managment.

Before reading further, write down several sentences that you would
use to characterize this applicant.

You now might want to compare your reactions to those of a
group of students who were shown the statement. First they listed in
the left column the main facts about Henry they all agreed were important (see Figure 9–5). Then everyone proceeded to describe the
Henry they had just read about. Here are some of the conclusions
they reached about Henry:

LISA: He seems like a good bet for the job—first, because he's had a lot
of practical accounting experience. And then he's had a couple of
courses on the subject, plus the math. On top of that, he seems pretty
enterprising to have taken all those courses and gotten himself those
summer jobs.

JOSE: It sounds as if he's had accounting experience all right, but all
he's done is work at his father's plant. And maybe he only had the job at
the concession stand because of his father's plant. He doesn't seem very
enterprising if he hasn't gone out and found another accounting job to
get more varied experience.

TIM: His accounting experience does look impressive: three years
is a lot of experience for a young guy coming into a summer job. But
his application is so sloppy. He misspelled both "accounting" and

FIGURE 9–5
Drawing Inferences from Facts

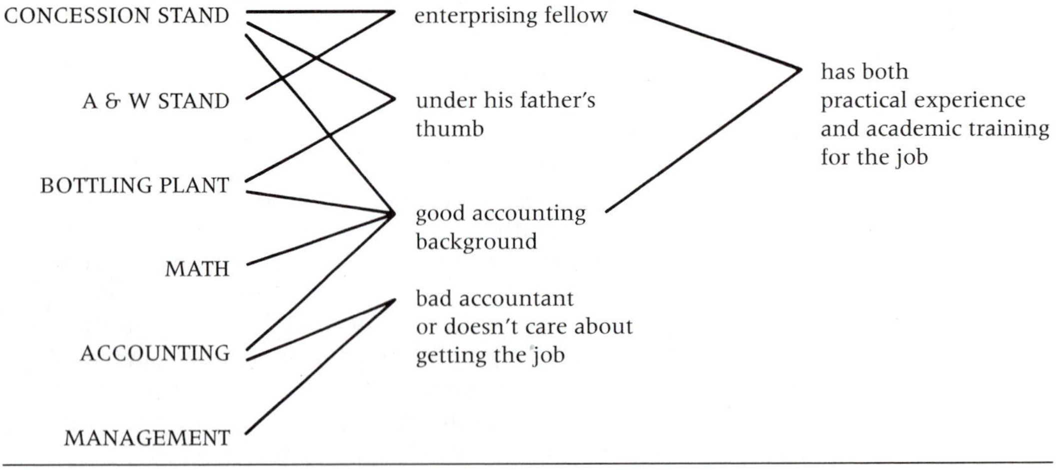

"management" in just that one paragraph. Accountants are supposed to be good with details. Maybe he didn't proofread the statement before he sent it, but in that case he seems very careless or not really interested in the job.

Note that from even small details in the text, such as misspellings, the students had arrived at some sweeping conclusions. Furthermore, the chances are good that a real personnel director might have the same response. As you can see from this example, when people are trying to understand a passage, they constantly are drawing inferences and making their own meanings.

This experiment demonstrates two things. The first is that readers do not passively absorb a writer's information; they make meaning as they read. Second, the meanings they make are often surprising leaps of imagination. The obvious question, then, is why are readers so creative with our prose? Why must they draw inferences and form concepts?

The Problem of Conscious Attention

One reason for this phenomenon is the limitation of our conscious attention, which forces us to "chunk," or group, information in order to understand it. When it comes to reading, or in fact processing any kind of new information, people are remarkably inefficient. This is because our conscious attention (or short-term, working memory) can handle only a limited number of inputs at one time. This is in contrast to the apparently unlimited storage capacity of long-term memory.

Imagine yourself sitting in a lecture. All incoming information— the voice of the speaker, the words on the blackboard, that idea you were trying to remember, and the person smiling at you across the room—all this information clamors for a portion of your limited conscious attention. We are often caught like jugglers with too many balls in the air.

To test the limits of your own short-term, working memory, multiply 12×14 in your own head. Now try multiplying 789×678 in your head. Do it now.

Notice how difficult it is to keep track of your partial answers, carry-overs, and the current multiplication task at the same time. You can see why one of our major limitations as thinkers and problem solvers is the nature of our short-term memory. Although we must deal with highly complex problems, we are unable to actively hold in mind and consider more than a few separate items at a time. Cognitive psychologists set the critical limit at 7 ± 2 bits of information.

Furthermore, in comparison with other processing systems, such as a computer, we are neither particularly fast nor accurate. As a communication channel the human voice can process 25 "bits" of information per second, whereas most electronic channels are designed to process between 10^4 and 10^5 bits in that same second. According to cognitive psychologist George Miller, it is a charity to call us a channel at all. We are more like a bottleneck.

Fortunately, we human beings have another trick up our sleeve that makes us remarkably good at thinking. This is the ability to "chunk" information—to look at a whole milling array of facts and perceptions, all shouting for immediate individual attention, and to reduce that throng to a single chunk. ("Oh, that's one of those whatchamacallits again.") A chunk may be a concept, a category, a term—anything that enables a person to organize miscellaneous data. Telegraph operators use this process when they learn to perceive a string of rapid dashes and dots as meaningful chunks such as words and phrases. You and I do it when, instead of thinking "There are forty-eight individual cars (in Aztec Red, Seafoam Green, Harvest Gold, and so on) jammed up around the 5th and Penn Avenue intersection honking their horns at 5:34 P.M. Tuesday afternoon . . . ," we simply think to ourselves, "rush hour traffic jam," and go on with our conversation. In order, then, to compensate for the limitations of short-term memory, people sort information into chunks they can manage.

Drawing Inferences/Remembering Gists

One way to make a chunk is to draw an inference. An inference is a new idea *we create* from previous ideas. (Sometimes, however, people such as the résumé readers may not realize they have drawn an inference and think they are simply stating the facts.) In slow motion, the process would look like this: We look at two or more facts or ideas and ask ourselves, "What single new idea (or chunk) would connect (or contain) those facts?" Our inference, such as "he's a good accountant," is a creative interpretation of the information. Another way to chunk information, which we have already discussed, is to summarize it into a gist. These inferences and gists often form the top-level ideas in a hierarchy. And these top-level ideas are what readers remember best.

But what determines *how* the reader will chunk new information and *which* inferences they will draw? We naturally like to think that readers carefully mine our prose for *the* meaning we intended. But much recent research in psychology shows that it is more accurate to think of readers as hard at work using our information like a set of tinker toys, to build an idea structure of their own. And if our writing doesn't help them build it, that final structure may or may not resemble our own. In attempting to read and understand a message—to make meaning—a creative reader

1. *Uses context.* The reader will try to fit your new information into a context or framework he or she already knows.

2. *Makes predictions.* Readers make predictions about what should follow, and they use these expectations to interpret the text—even when they are wrong.
3. *Creates gists.* Readers consolidate new information into more manageable packages or chunks. These gists are what they remember.
4. *Organizes ideas.* Readers sort and structure ideas into an unconscious hierarchical structure built around key concepts or gists (as they see them).

Let us look at these processes of the reader in more detail.

Readers Need a Framework, or Context, for New Ideas. In 1938, Orson Welles threw thousands of people into panic with a radio broadcast reporting a Martian invasion of New Jersey. Why? Because his audience had the wrong framework. Those who tuned in during the middle thought they were hearing a news broadcast, not a mere radio drama called "The War of the Worlds."

Readers make sense out of new information by putting it into context. When they aren't given a clear context for such information, they are likely to do two things. First, they supply their own context. A worried reader, anticipating disagreement and afraid that no one likes him, will interpret your helpful suggestion as yet another criticism. Second, they will not understand you at all. Even the simplest information may be hard to understand and impossible to remember if the reader has no context for making sense out of it.

To demonstrate this for yourself, try this experiment. Read the following passage through once (and only once).

The procedure is actually quite simple. First you arrange things into different groups. Of course one pile may be sufficient depending on how much there is to do. If you have to go somewhere else due to lack of facilities that is the next step, otherwise you are pretty well set. It is important not to overdo things. That is, it is better to do too few things at once than too many. In the short run this may not seem important, but complications can easily arise. A mistake can be expensive as well. At first the whole procedure will seem complicated.

Soon, however, it will become just another fact of life. It is difficult to foresee any end to the necessity for this task in the immediate future, but then one never can tell. After the procedure is completed, one arranges the materials into different groups again. Then they can be put into their appropriate places. Eventually they will be used once more and the whole cycle will then have to be repeated. However, that is a part of life.*

---

*John D. Bransford and Nancy S. McCarrell, A sketch of a cognitive approach to comprehension, in *Cognition and Symbolic Processes,* ed. Walter Weiner (Hillsdale, NJ: Erlbaum, 1974).

Now shift your attention for a minute or so by saying the alphabet backwards or reading a page at random from this book. Then, without looking at the passage again, try to write down all you can remember about the passage.

How much did you remember? When psychologists John Bransford and Nancy McCarrell ran this experiment they found that their subjects did very poorly, even though the passage describes a very common activity for which everyone has a framework: washing clothes. When another group of subjects was given the passage and told at the beginning that it was a description of washing clothes, the subjects had an immediate framework. Not only did they appear much less frustrated with the task, but they remembered much more of the passage. By creating a context for their readers, Bransford and McCarrell were able to more than *double* their readers' comprehension and recall.

Professional writers and magazine editors often go to great lengths to establish a context for their articles. Consider the article shown below, from the March 1979 issue of *Ms.* magazine. It creates a context in five different ways, each one more specific than the last.

1. The heading tells us we are reading the magazine's monthly column on *money*.
2. This month it will be on money and *housing*, the picture says.
3. In particular it's on *buying* your own house, we learn from the title.
4. Buying, that is, with a *low down payment*, the subtitle adds.
5. And it is especially pertinent if you are a *woman*, we learn in the first sentence.

MONEY

How To Buy A House on Your Own...with a Little Help from Uncle Sam

Under one government program, you can buy a house for $1 down.

BY EMILY VAN NESS

I never dreamed that as a single woman I would ever be able to own a house. Like many women, I assumed that on my salary (about $14,000 a year) and with today's staggering new-home prices, I would continue to be a "renter" all my adult life—unless I struck it rich or decided to get married and pool my resources.

Then, while apartment-hunting last year in New Jersey, I came across an ad in a local paper for a three-story, brick house in Trenton for only $30,000, 10 percent down, and an unbelievably low 7½ percent mortgage. (Today most conventional lenders are requiring a cash down payment of at least 20

Consider the difference if the article had had an ambiguous title or heading and had started out with "While apartment hunting last year in New Jersey, I came across an ad in a local paper for a three-story brick house in Trenton. . . ." Unless you knew it was a short story (and had faith that it would get better soon), your reaction would probably have been "So what? Why should I read this?" As you can see, a context not only helps a reader make sense of things, it also creates expectations that lure him or her on. And this brings us to the second point about readers.

Readers Develop Expectations and Want Those Expectations Met. General context, as we have seen, gives readers a rough idea of what is coming by setting up a framework with empty slots waiting to be filled. Sometimes the very type of article or paper arouses firm expectations. For example, whenever I read a movie review I expect to find some discussion of the theme or plot, some background on the actors, and an evaluation by the critic—but not a description of the ending. If you depart too greatly from your genre—whether it is a stockholders' report, a highly structured essay assignment, or a résumé—you are likely to confuse or disorient your reader.

Although you can sometimes use expectations readers already have, as a writer you also have the power to create expectations in the reader's mind. Exam graders, for example, are strongly influenced by a dazzling first answer or a weak beginning. If an article or paper begins in a vague fashion, the reader's expectation may be: "This paper sounds as if it's going to be full of hot air, so I can just skim." Perhaps the writer is building slowly up to a point or plans to save his best ideas for last, but it is hard to overcome the powerful effect of a reader's initial expectations.

Cues in the text—whether they are key words you introduce, "teaser" sentences that suggest interesting material to come, or simply a preview of the contents—help generate expectations. But cues can backfire, too. In Henry Morris's accounting application (see p. 188), certain readers saw Henry's misspellings as evidence that he would be a poor accountant. Readers often generate expectations from relatively small, and sometimes inadvertent, cues in the text. These expectations may be so strong that the reader simply won't see what you have to say.

Once a reader's expectations are aroused, they actively clamor to be fulfilled. So it is important to follow through on what your initial paragraphs promise. A reader quickly becomes impatient with wandering prose that seems not to be moving toward the points initially previewed.

Setting up and fulfilling expectations also serve another very important function—they make people remember things. The best way to make your point vivid and memorable is to set up a strong expectation and then fulfill it. Expectations are a valuable way of circumventing short-term memory. If you know what you are looking for, it is much easier and faster to process all that information. Plus, by giving the reader a context and building up expectations, you are equipping him with a set of hooks for retaining what you want him to know.

Readers Organize Ideas into Gists and Natural Hierarchies. A final way readers understand and remember what you tell them is by organizing your discussion in a general hierarchical way. If you don't do it for them, they will do it themselves—and the result may be far from what you had intended.

The important things about hierarchies, as you know, are that they create a focus by distinguishing major points from minor ones and they show how ideas are related to one another. In general, a reader will want to get a feel for the structure of any discussion very quickly; it is hard to hold many unrelated ideas in mind for long. A writer, on the other hand, might want to present all the facts first and then reveal his point, hoping the reader will keep everything in mind until he does so. Unfortunately, when readers don't see the focus and structure of your ideas, they will probably just build an organization of their own to comprehend the discussion. And the structure they build may not be the one you had in mind at all.

To demonstrate for yourself just how creative readers can be, try the following "headless paragraph" experiment. The six sentences listed below come from a paragraph written by a student on the topic of "The Writing Problem of College Students." Without a topic sentence and without the transitions and connections between the sentences, it is hard to see just how the ideas in this paragraph were organized. Read the six sentences and then jot down in a sentence or two what you think the main point of the paragraph was.

The Headless Paragraph

Students aren't practicing.
College atmosphere produces tension.
Students are afraid of getting a "D."
Writing is time consuming.
Writing is usually done under time pressure.
Writing courses are not required, so students must take a heavy
    course load to learn how.

When this experiment was conducted with a group of eighteen college sophomores, the results were surprising to the student who had written the paragraph containing these ideas. Out of eighteen readers, no one came up with the same organizing idea she had had in mind. Three had concepts that accounted for much of the paragraph, such as: "Students have difficulty in writing due to the pressures imposed upon them by grades, time, and the tension of college life." Three other readers focused on an inclusive or high-level idea, pressure, but neglected other points such as practice.

Altogether, only six of the eighteen came up with an organizing idea that could incorporate most of the information in the paragraph. Of the other twelve readers, four came away with concepts that accounted for only a limited part of the paragraph, such as "Students don't have enough time." And seven ended up with ideas that were not contained in the sentences at all! For example, these readers thought the topic sentence should be "Students aim to please teachers," or "There is too much competition in college," or "Writing should not be required," or "Writing should be required in college." These readers simply took the writer's information and hooked it onto a framework of their own. They used it to support something they already believed. The final reader in this group of eighteen even dropped the subject of writing altogether and said that the major idea of the paragraph was that "Students are more interested in grades than in learning. Their selfishness produces artificial pressures." This statement came as quite a shock to the original author.

As you can see, some readers created a focus or structure that was at least close to what the writer had intended. Their topic sentence created a tree that was at least able to account for most of the information. But some of the readers, in their need to create some sort of organization, interpreted the paragraph in unexpected, even drastic ways.

Here, for comparison, is the paragraph that the writer finally developed after receiving input from her classmates. Note how she employed a topic sentence to create expectations and used cues along the way to show how the ideas were related.

> Students often have trouble writing in college because of a combination of bad habits and high pressure. To start with, students don't practice. This is partly because of time limitations: learning to write is time consuming, and since writing courses are not required, students have to take a heavy load in order to learn how. Some students do have the time to practice but fail to do so because writing in the high-pressure atmosphere of college produces anxiety and tension. Many students are so afraid of getting a "D" that they avoid writing altogether—until the day before the paper is due. Furthermore, college papers are usually done under time pressure, which simply increases the tension of writing.

STRATEGY 3   ORGANIZE FOR A CREATIVE READER

Creative readers are a fact of life, because reading, like writing, is an active process of making meaning. For example, I expect you, my reader, to mentally rewrite this book as you read, making it your own with your own examples and associations and using it for your own purposes. On the other hand, I want my version of the ideas to be clear to you, too—even if you choose to remember your own. As writers, one of the major tools we have for speaking to our creative readers and for helping and guiding them as they read is organization.

A clear organization lets readers do three of the four actions described on pages 190–91 make predictions, create gists, and organize ideas.

In the next few chapters we will look closely at ways to plan and test for a coherent and reader-based organization. But of all the techniques we will look at, probably the three most time-tested rules of thumb are the following ones.

1. State Your Main Idea Explicitly in the Text

This is harder than it sounds, because it often means that you must look at a paragraph and say, "What is my main idea?" You have to create the gist you want the reader to remember. You can place this main idea in various places. The most common ones in a paragraph are at the beginning and at the end. Notice, however, the distinction between a mere *topic* and a *gist*.

A topic merely names the subject or issue you are talking about. In the student example above, the topic is "students' writing troubles." A topic sentence that names the topic is indeed helpful to the reader, but that is not the same as stating your main idea.

A main idea or a gist is a statement about the topic—that is, it makes a claim or a comment on the topic of "writing troubles." The main idea or gist of the paragraph above is that these troubles are caused by bad habits and high pressure. In our example paragraph, the topic sentence not only announces the topic but summarizes the main idea of the entire paragraph in explicit terms and then places that statement of the gist in the powerful first-sentence position. When you test your own paragraphs, don't confuse a mere topic with an explicit statement of your main idea—your comment on that topic.

2. Focus Your Paragraph on the Topic or Main Idea

Assume that the reader will try to see each paragraph as one chunk. Are all the sentences connected to your main idea, and can they be summed up into a single gist? If not, you may have a headless paragraph the reader will rewrite.

3. Use a Standard Pattern of Organization

You can help the reader make good predictions by organizing your ideas into a familiar paragraph pattern. Such patterns, which are discussed in Chapter 12, include these ways of organizing: Describe something: Stick to your topic if you use this one. Compare two things: Show how they are alike and different. Show cause or effect: You can work backward or forward. Present a problem and a solution: This can be dramatic.

The following set of data presents a real-life problem in doing all the things discussed in this chapter. This is part of a survey conducted among students to discover their assumptions about writing and to see whether their assumptions had any relation to the kind of writing they did. What does it mean? In order to understand these data, we will walk through some of the things you as a writer might do:

1. Chunk related facts together and draw an inference.
2. Group those inferences together in order to interpret each student's assumptions about writing in physics.
3. Compare those assumptions to each other, to the instructor's assumptions, and to the student's success in writing in physics.
4. Build your own interpretation and set of main ideas or inferences from these data.
5. Apply your inferences, if you wish, to related kinds of writing.
6. Present your main ideas to a reader, using the data and your inferences to support your interpretation, and creating a context and a structure the reader can follow.

JOE'S SURVEY PROJECT

Professor Grapevine, a teacher of freshman composition, has asked her students to do a survey among the students in some class that has writing assignments (other than freshman composition), for the purpose of learning on what standards the students in that class think their work is being evaluated. Dr. Grapevine wants her students to compare, as far as possible, their view of what teachers look for when they evaluate writing with the views of the students in the course being investigated.

Joe Scholar, a student in Dr. Grapevine's class, has decided to use a section of Physics 50, taught by Professor Orangeblossom, for his survey project. Joe has chosen Physics 50 because he took the course last semester and he has dark memories of struggles with lab notebooks and written explanations of homework problems. Since it is early in the semester, Joe wonders whether this group of students is having the same difficulties he had. After considerable thought, Joe produced the following form.

Pilot Survey for Physics 50

What 2–4 things in writing lab reports for Physics 50 have hurt your grade the most?

1.

2.

3.

4.

What is your grade in Physics 50 so far? _____

What is your academic major? _____

What is your grade in school? (circle one)

Fresh   Soph   Jr   Sr   Grad

Is this your first physics course? (yes/no) _____

When Joe begins to read the data from his pilot survey, he finds a sheet with the following responses on it. From these data, what inferences could you draw about either Student S or about what effective writing means in Physics 50?

Student S

1. didn't use graph paper
2. didn't use two-column data/comment format
3. didn't number the steps
4. used #4 pencil

Course grade so far: D

Academic major: Criminal Justice

Year in school: Freshman

Is this your first physics course?   yes

How did you interpret that set of facts? How did you, as a creative reader, arrive at your interpretation? In this case study of Joe's project, we are going to walk through the process of looking at facts (or statements or observations) and then draw an inference that will sum up or interpret those facts with a new idea. We will try to slow down this process of inference making, which normally happens so quickly that we don't even realize we have done it. As we follow Joe's inference-making process, bear in mind that there are no right or wrong answers. We are looking at his interpretation. We are watching a writer in action.

From these data on Student S, Joe draws several inferences. First, he notices that Student S's comments all deal with matters of form: using certain paper, using a soft lead pencil, using columns, and so on. (The little $\Rightarrow$ is a symbol for an inference, which you can read as "means.")

- wrong paper   (means)
- wrong format $\Rightarrow$ form matters most
- unnumbered steps   (inference)
- wrong pencil

Apparently Student S believes that the most important feature of well-written homework is its form, or that form is what Professor Orangeblossom is grading for. Joe's inference, to the right of the arrow, sums up S's four comments with the phrase "form matters most."

Having taken Physics 50, Joe remembers that the theory "form matters most" was one that many freshman students held at the beginning of the year. However, looking back, he realizes that it is possible to draw a different inference (or interpretation) about what Professor Orangeblossom was looking for if one thinks about other possible causes for the same results. Here are Joe's inferences, which add up to a very different conclusion:

                              (means)
- unnumbered steps ⇒ the order of the discussion
                              is hard to follow
                                     (inference 1)   clearly showing
                                                             the steps in your
                                                          ⇒ solution matters
                                                             (inference 3)

- #4 pencil ⇒ the fuzzy handwriting
                     is hard to read
                     (inference 2)

We now have two conflicting sets of inferences: those Joe attributes to Student S and his own. How do we know which is best? Inferences are interpretations that both writers and creative readers constantly make in order to make sense out of things. But what makes a good or a better inference? Here are two rules of thumb you can use to test your own inferences.

1. A good inference accounts for all (or more) of the data.
2. A good inference follows closely from the facts.

Put in the negative, if you have to make a large leap of imagination to get from observation to inference, or if someone else has trouble seeing the connection, be suspicious. You may have made a greater inference (a bigger leap) than the facts allow.

At this point Joe asks himself whether the rest of the data support his current inference. For instance, what might be the relevance of the two-column data/comment format? Here is his interpretation:

- no data/comment format   S gave either no   showing
                               ⇒ comments or   your reasons
                                  very brief   ⇒ matters
                                  comments   (inference 5)
                                  (inference 4)

In support of this theory, Joe remembers that when he began learning physics principles, he often misapplied them because he didn't understand how questions about different parts of the same problem could call for the application of different principles. When he wrote out his reasons for choosing a principle and his decisions about how to use it, he learned a great deal, especially when he read Professor Orangeblossom's comments. Joe remembers that Orangeblossom gives credit for a reasonable solution process even if you get the wrong answer.

Putting together all these observations and inferences, Joe has come up with his own theory about what effective writing means in Physics 50:

- showing the steps matters
- showing reasons matters ⇒
- a good attempt counts

showing your thinking and having a clear problem-solving process matter most in physics writing (inference 6)

How well do you think these inferences account for the data?

Here are three more sets of data, from Students Y, Z, and Q. What inferences can you draw about why each student is earning the grade reported on the form? If you look at all four sets of data, what inferences can you make about Professor Orangeblossom's grading standards?

Student Y

1. late papers
2. used wrong principals for the problems
3. mispelled physics terms
4. comments too short

Course grade so far: C–

Academic major: engineering

Year in school: freshman

Is this your first physics course?   no

Student Z

1. Although I can usually think of 2 or 3 ways to approach a problem,
2. I can't always tell why one is better than the others.
3. Also, I frequently can't make any one of them work.
4. When an approach does work, I'm not always sure why it worked when another one didn't.

Course grade so far: B–

Academic major: Chemistry

Year in school: Freshman

Is this your first physics course: no

Student Q

1. bad math
2. bad handwriting
3. diagrams unclear
4. personality conflict with teacher

Course grade so far: C−

Academic major: Math

Year in school: Freshman

Is this your first physics course? no

After conducting his survey and tabulating the results, Joe decided to interview Professor Orangeblossom to learn what criteria he used when grading and how well his criteria matched those of his students. Here is how Dr. Orangeblossom answered the survey:

1. mechanical, unthinking approaches to problems; no explanation of why a particular approach was chosen
2. not showing clearly all the steps of the work
3. sloppy work—leaving out steps, writing hard to read, solution spread haphazardly all over the page and out of order
4. late papers

Regarding his first answer, Dr. Orangeblossom said,

I suppose it's cheating to give two answers to #1, but the first thing is what I encounter in all students. To get them past it, I have to insist on explanations for approaches and on clearly presented problem-solving processes. Of the two, the explanations are most important because they are where I can make the most direct contact with the students' minds, where I can comment in ways that will teach them how to think about physics problems. I had to mention late papers because I get so many of them that I have to grade down for lateness, but really, that doesn't matter to me as much as the first three answers matter. They are about communication, or failure to communicate. That's what really bothers me about students' writing, failure to communicate.

Then Joe gave Dr. Orangeblossom a list of the problems most commonly cited by students in the survey and asked him to rank them. Here is his ranking:

1. not showing all the steps of the work
2. giving few comments

3. using physics terms incorrectly
4. getting wrong answers or using incorrect principles
5. using incorrect format (for example, numbering the steps of solutions to physics problems)
6. using the wrong kind of pen or pencil
7. misspelling words

You have now seen a sample of the data from Joe Scholar's study, "Writing in Physics." As you have probably noticed, it is included in this chapter because it raises two questions about writing for a reader.

Problem 1: In Writing for a Physics Professor or Writing Lab Reports, What Matters Most?

To answer this question, you must examine the rest of the data, just as Joe did, and draw your own inferences. Remember, an *inference* is a new idea that connects or accounts for previously learned facts. But notice that a good inference must account for a number of facts. *A good inference is supported by the evidence.*

The following questions might help you draw inferences as you examine the data in this problem (that is, the comments by four students, Joe's inferences, and the professor's input).

1. How consistent are the subjects' grades with Dr. Orangeblossom's comments? Does Orangeblossom really seem to be grading for the things that he says he's grading for?
2. How does Dr. Orangeblossom's comment about communication help explain his answers to the two survey forms? What inferences can you draw?
3. Certain things appear to matter very much to Dr. Orangeblossom, and other things matter relatively little. What can you reasonably suppose are the reasons for this?
4. Why do some things that are important to Dr. Orangeblossom not even appear in the pilot survey results? And why do Orangeblossom's students place so much emphasis on matters that their teacher thinks are fairly trivial?
5. What attitudes, theories, and features of the writing itself matter most in writing for physics?

If you draw an inference that you think is right but don't have enough evidence to support it, you can try to get more information. When Joe asked Dr. Orangeblossom to explain his comment about communication, he received the following answer. How does it affect your reasoning about the last question?

You see, Joe, physics is as much a way of thinking about the relationships among forms of matter and energy as it is knowing sets of facts. In fact, the thinking may be more important. I'm trying to teach people how to think about these relationships. I can't show them how to improve their thinking if they don't tell me *what* they're thinking. That's why I give up to 80 percent credit to an answer that is mathematically wrong if it's well thought out and clearly expressed—that is, if the student used the appropriate physics principle for the right reasons in the right ways. I believe that if you can't express what you're thinking, then you don't really *know* what you're thinking.

Problem 2: Writing for Your Own Reader

After thinking about this material, could you give Students S, Y, Z, and Q some advice on how to raise their grades on the physics lab reports in Dr. Orangeblossom's class?

Remember, you have creative readers who want to see the main ideas and see the relevance to themselves. As you write for these readers, think about their attitudes and needs:

1. What do some of your readers already believe?
2. How can you present and support your own inferences or top-level ideas? Help your readers to see not just the facts but your interpretation of them.

PROJECTS AND ASSIGNMENTS

1   Thinking about the reader while you are composing is a good way to make decisions about what to include, what to emphasize, and how to organize it. The writer in the following transcript is using the reader for that purpose as he composes a section of a new staff handbook for the Timmerman Landscape Company. This section will introduce inexperienced summer staff to the surprisingly complex task of planting a tree. (You can see the original proposal for this project in Chapter 8.) As this writer uses the audience in this planning, he also creates a slowly growing portrait of those readers—as he sees them. Using his comments, try to reconstruct this writer's "mental image" of his readers.

First, you might look at which of the readers' features he actually considers: knowledge, attitudes, or needs. (The initial episodes in his planning have already been annotated.) Then compare his assumptions about his readers to the discussion on pages 180–82. Does he see his audience as creative readers? How does he expect them to read or process information or to respond to what they read?

Draw a verbal portrait of the reader (as this writer sees him). Then decide whether this is a realistic portrait. Will his plans, based on that reader, work?

Transcript About Writing a Manual

reader's knowledge

OK, the most important thing in this manual is how to plant trees. And I don't want people to make the mistakes that Larry and I made.

need to know

Our biggest problem was the holes—we made them too small.

reader's response/
need to know

And here I wonder if it will confuse people to have different directions for evergreens and deciduous trees right together? Or if I give separate sets of directions, will they read the first set and miss the second set? Hmm. The only difference is the treatment of the root ball. So maybe I'll keep all that together and just give separate directions at that one point, and use big labels.

OK, now, the hole. I'm going to need a drawing. I can tell them to make the hole twice as big as the root ball, and I will tell them in what order to put in the drainage stuff, manure, and dirt. But a drawing is clearer, it lets you see everything in proportion to the tree.

OK, what else? The dirt—it has to be new dirt, not the customer's subsoil. I have to explain that. And we supply it.

Oh yes. CALL THE CUSTOMER! Essential step; I'll have to put it early in the manual. So why is it an essential step? They'll need a list of reasons here:

—to verify the order
—to make sure he's home when they deliver
—so he can supervise where they dig the hole
—so he can call someone if they hit a pipe, or there's some other kind of trouble
—so he can pay them and save us sending a bill.

That reminds me—I have to explain about not planting trees too close to the house, the street, the driveway.

This could be long. Will they read it? Diagrams—they'll look at pictures with big headings and not much print. So I'll also need a diagram for bushes—or maybe combine bushes & trees into one diagram? Yeah—make this one chapter on planting bushes *and* trees. Because who needs different chapters for every little thing?

OK, good. Now, the list of stuff for the truck: wire cutters, spade, pick, canvas, stakes, pieces of garden hose. Burlap, twine, wire, pruning hooks, clippers, bucket, 2 hoses. I should say that they can't expect to use the customer's things, or even expect the customer to have a hose. Most of this is pretty obvious. Except maybe the canvas. If I tell them step by step how to plant and stake the tree, they'll see why they need these things. So I won't explain; this will be a checklist they can use when they go out on jobs. So it will go up at the top, even before calling the customer. And the step-by-step directions will be real short.

I wonder if I'll need a picture of how the tree should look when they've wrapped the trunk and staked it?

2 You are writing an article on eating out for people who are following a low-carbohydrate diet, and you plan to include a paragraph on fast-food restaurants. Use the data in the following table for source material, and write a paragraph tailored to your audience. How will you chunk the data? What inferences can you draw?

NUTRITIONAL CONTENT OF POPULAR FAST FOODS

Item	Calories	Protein (Grams)	Carbohydrates (Grams)	Fat (Grams)	Sodium (Milligrams)
HAMBURGERS					
McDonald's Big Mac	541	26	39	31	962
Burger Chef Hamburger	258	11	24	13	393
FISH					
Arthur Treacher's Fish Sandwich	440	16	39	24	836
Long John Silver's Fish (2 pieces)	318	19	19	19	not available
OTHER ENTREES					
McDonald's Egg Muffin	352	18	26	20	914
Taco Bell Taco	186	15	14	8	79
Dairy Queen Brazier Dog	273	11	23	15	868
SIDE DISHES					
Burger King French Fries	214	3	28	10	5
Arthur Treacher's Cole Slaw	123	1	11	8	266
McDonald's Chocolate Shake	364	11	60	9	329
McDonald's Apple Pie	300	2	31	19	414

Source: The New York Times, September 19, 1979. Copyright © 1979 by The New York Times Company. Reprinted by permission.

Now use the table for a different purpose. You are giving a talk to a group of heart patients who must follow a low-fat, low-salt diet, and you plan to mention fast food. Write a paragraph advising them of good and poor fast-food choices. A third way you could chunk the information in this table is in terms of food value per dollar. A survey of fast-food places in Pittsburgh in April of 1984 and again in January of 1988 turned up these prices (1988 prices are in parentheses): a Big Mac is $1.30 ($1.54); Arthur Treacher's Fish Sandwich is $1.19; Long John Silver's Fish is $1.81 ($2.10); an Egg McMuffin is $.99 ($1.16); a Taco Bell taco is $.73 ($.79); and a

Dairy Queen Brazier Dog is $.79 ($.79). Write a discussion of fast foods in terms of the best food for your money.

IF YOU WOULD LIKE TO READ MORE

If you want to know more about readers and how to design your writing with them in mind, see:

Bransford, John D. *Human Cognition: Learning, Understanding and Remembering.* Belmont, CA: Wadsworth Publishing, 1979. / This is an excellent introduction to the most recent research and theories about human thinking processes.

Farnham-Diggory, Sylvia. *Cognitive Processes in Education.* New York: Harper & Row, 1972. / This book offers a good introduction to the many psychological issues that affect education and learning.

Mathews, J. C., and Dwight Stevenson. *Designing Technical Reports: Writing for Audiences in Organizations.* Indianapolis: Bobbs-Merrill, 1976. / This book gives excellent guidance on professional writing in all kinds of organizations, with special emphasis on the writing of technical reports. It also offers a very detailed and effective way of analyzing one's readers in a technical organization.

Miller, George. The magical number seven, plus or minus two: Some limits on our capacity for processing information. *Psychological Review,* 63 (March 1956), 81–96. In *The Psychology of Communication,* New York: Basic Books, 1967. / This is a witty and well-written introduction to the research that has been done in information processing, authored by one of the pioneers in the field.

chapter ten

Writing Reader-Based Prose

**GOAL 6
TRANSFORM writer-based prose into
reader-based prose**

Use your knowledge of the reader's needs to develop a strategy for communicating, not just expressing, your ideas. By identifying a goal you share with the reader and adapting your knowledge to your reader's needs, you can also achieve your own goals as a writer.

> *STRATEGY 1* **SET UP A SHARED GOAL**
> *STRATEGY 2* **DEVELOP A READER-BASED STRUCTURE**
> *STRATEGY 3* **GIVE YOUR READERS CUES**
> *STRATEGY 4* **DEVELOP A PERSUASIVE ARGUMENT**

As we saw in Chapter 9, simply expressing yourself isn't always enough; it's no guarantee that you are actually communicating with someone else. This chapter will focus on specific rhetorical strategies you can use to design your writing for a reader.

Some people are rightly suspicious of the notion of rhetorical strategy when they equate it with such things as "mere rhetoric," empty eloquence, or the sophist's art of persuading by any means available. The rhetorical strategy we will discuss is, instead, an attempt to fulfill your goals by meeting the needs of your reader. It is, in essence, a plan for communicating.

Why is such a strategy necessary? We have already looked at one reason: The creative reader needs the help of a context, a clear structure, and guiding expectations to effectively read your prose. Writing a message down is one thing; communicating your meaning is an art that requires planning. Shortly we will look at a second reason for conscious strategy, which grows out of the private nature of the writer's own composing process.

GOAL 6

TRANSFORM Writer-Based Prose into Reader-Based Prose

Good writers know how to transform writer-based prose (which works well for them) into reader-based prose (which works for their readers as well). Writing is inevitably a somewhat egocentric enterprise. We naturally tend to talk to ourselves when composing. As a result, we often need self-conscious strategies for trying to talk to our reader.

 STRATEGY 1   **SET UP A SHARED GOAL**

The first strategy for adapting a paper to a reader is to create a shared goal. Try to find a reason for writing your paper and a reason for reading it that both you and your reader share. (Remember that your desire to convey information will not necessarily be met by your reader's desire to receive it.) Then organize your ideas and your arguments around this common goal. You will need to consider the knowledge, attitudes, and needs of your reader, as discussed previously.

A shared goal can be a powerful tool for persuasion. To illustrate, try this exercise:

> You have just been commissioned to write a short booklet on how to preserve older homes and buildings, which the City Historical Society wants to distribute throughout a historical section of the city in an effort to encourage preservation. Most of your readers will simply be residents and local business people. How are you going to get them, first, to read this booklet and, second, to use some of its suggestions?

Take several minutes to think about this problem, then write an opening paragraph for the booklet that includes a shared goal.

To test the effectiveness of your paragraph, consider the following two points about shared goals:

1. A shared goal can *motivate your audience* to read and remember what you have to say. Does your paragraph suggest that the booklet will solve some problem your reader faces or achieve some end he or she really cares about? An appeal to vague goals or a wishy-washy generalization such as "our heritage" is unlikely to keep the reader interested. Use your knowledge to fill some need your reader really has.

In a professional situation think of it this way: Your reader has ten letters and five reports on her desk this morning. Your opening statement with its shared goal should tell her why she would want to read your report first and read it carefully.

2. A shared goal can *increase comprehension.* People understand and retain information best when they can fit it into a framework they already know. For example, the context of "home repair" and

"do-it-yourself" would be familiar and maybe attractive to your readers. In contrast, if you defined the goal as "architectural renovation" or "techniques of historical landmark preservation" you would make sense to members of the historical society but would have missed your primary audience, the local readers. They would probably find that context not only unfamiliar but somewhat intimidating.

Offer your readers a shared goal—one for which they already have a framework—that helps them turn your message into something meaningful to them.

Here are examples of three different introductory paragraphs written for this booklet. After reading each one, consider how you would evaluate its power to motivate and aid comprehension. Then read the reaction of another reader, which follows each paragraph.

1. This booklet will help you create civic pride and preserve our city's heritage. In addition you will be helping the Historical Society to grow and extend its influence over the city.
   A reader's response:
   I suppose civic pride is a good thing, but I'm not sure I'd want to help create it. This paragraph makes me feel a little suspicious. What does the Historical Society want from me? I'll bet this is going to be a booklet about raising money so they can put up city monuments.
2. This booklet is concerned with civic restoration and maintenance projects in designated historical areas. It discusses the methods and materials approved by the City Historical Society and City Board of Engineers.
   A reader's response:
   I guess this is some booklet for city planners or the people who want to set up museums. "Methods and materials" must refer to all those rules and regulations that city contractors have to follow. I wouldn't want to get mixed up with all that if I were doing improvements on my own home.
3. If you own an older home or historical building, there are a number of ways you can preserve its beauty and historical value. At the same time you can increase its market value and decrease its maintenance costs. This booklet will show you five major ways to improve your building and give you step-by-step procedures for how to do this. Please read the booklet over and see which of the suggestions might be useful to you.
   A reader's response:
   This might be a good idea. I don't know if I'd want to buy the whole package, but I think I'll read it over. What is it—five things I could do? I might find something useful I could try out. I'm particularly concerned about the maintenance costs. Maybe I can find something here on insulation.

Note that in the final example the writer not only has identified shared goals but has given the reader a sort of mental map for reading and understanding the rest of the booklet.

Sometimes a shared goal is something as intangible as intellectual curiosity. But it is the writer's job, in whatever field, to recognize goals or needs that his reader might have and to try to fulfill them. Philosopher Bertrand Russell set forth his shared goal in this way in his introduction to *A History of Western Philosophy:*

> Why, then, you may ask, waste time on such insoluble problems? To this one may answer as a historian, or as an individual facing the terror of cosmic loneliness. . . . To teach how to live without certainty, and yet without being paralyzed by hesitation, is perhaps the chief thing that philosophy, in our age, can still do for those who study it.[1]

To sum up, the first step in designing your paper for a reader is to set up a shared goal. Use it in your problem/purpose statement, and you might also use it as the top level of your issue tree when you generate ideas. A good shared goal will motivate your reader by providing a context for understanding your ideas and a reason for acting on them.

❦ *STRATEGY 2* **DEVELOP A READER-BASED STRUCTURE**

Most of us intend to write reader-based prose, to communicate with our reader. But for various reasons, people often end up writing writer-based prose, or talking to themselves. For example, the following excerpts are from letters written by students applying for summer jobs. They had been asked to include some personal background and experience.

Do some detective work on these paragraphs and try to describe the hidden logic that you think is organizing each one. Compare the paragraph to some other way you could write it. Why did the writers choose to include the particular facts they did, and why did they organize them in these particular ways?

> *Terry F.:*
> I was born in Wichita, Kansas, on December 4, 1962. After four years there my family moved to Topeka, Kansas, where I attended kindergarten. The next year my family moved to Rose Hill, Iowa. I went to first grade there and my family moved again. I started second grade in Butler, Pennsylvania, and finished it in Pittsburgh, Pennsylvania, where I still live today. . . . I took the college curriculum in high school, which included English, history, Science, French, and mathematics, and am currently a college sophomore.
>   I would like this job for two reasons. First, I could use the money for school next year. Second, the experience would be very helpful. It would help me get a job in that specific area when I graduate.

---

[1] Bertrand Russell, *A History of Western Philosophy* (New York: Simon & Schuster, 1945), p. xiv.

Katherine P.:
As a freshman I worked as a clerk in a student-managed store, Argus.
. . . I became acquainted with the university personnel manager and was
offered the position of Argus personnel manager for the semester beginning August, 1979. I accepted and held the job until December of 1979,
when a managerial position was eliminated. With managerial staff reduced to two people, responsibilities were adjusted and I was offered
the position of purchasing agent. Again I accepted.

Notice that in these examples there is a logic organizing each
paragraph, but it is the logic of a story, based on the writer's own
memories and, in Terry's case, personal needs. The needs of the
reader have not been considered. This is writer-based prose—writing
that may seem quite clear and organized to the writer but is not yet
adequately designed for the reader. In each case, the potential employer probably wants to know how the applicant's background and
experience could fit his or her needs. But neither paragraph was organized around that goal.

Why do people write to themselves when they are ostensibly
writing to a reader? One reason is a natural mental habit that psychologists call "egocentrism": thinking centered around the ego or
"I." Egocentrism is not selfishness but simply the failure to actively
imagine the point of view of someone else as we talk or write. We
see this all the time in young children who happily talk about what
they are doing in a long, spirited monologue that has many gaps and
mysterious expressions. They may speak in code words or private
language that, like jargon in adults, is saturated with meaning for
the user but not for the listener. Although a bystander may be totally in the dark, the child seems to assume everyone understands
perfectly.

Part of the child's cognitive development is growing out of this
self-centeredness and learning to imagine and adapt to another person's state of mind. But we never grow out of our egocentrism en-
tirely. When adults write to themselves, it is usually because they
have simply forgotten to consider the reader.

There is another very good reason adults write writer-based prose.
If you are working on a difficult paper, it is often easier to discover
what you know first and worry about designing it for a reader later.
An interesting study called the New York Apartment Tour experiment demonstrated people's tendency to explain in a self-oriented
way.[2] The experimenters, Charlotte Linde and William Labov, posed
as social workers and asked a number of people to describe their
apartments. They found that nearly everyone gave them a room-
by-room verbal tour and used similar procedures for conducting it.

---

[2] Charlotte Linde and William Labov, Spatial networks as a site for the study of language and thought, *Language,* 51 (1975), 924–39.

Although neither the experimenters nor the speakers were actually in the apartments, the descriptions were phrased as though they had been. For example, the description typically starts at the door; if the nearest room is a big one, you go on in ("from the left of the hall you go into the living room"); if the nearest room is small, the speaker merely refers to it and makes a comment ("and there's a closet off the living room"). Then the speaker suddenly brings you back to the entrance hall ("and on the right of the hall is the dining room"), without having to retrace steps or repeat previous rooms. The intuitive, narrative procedures used in conducting this verbal tour were very efficient for remembering all the details of the apartment.

Linde and Labov found that 97 percent of the people questioned used this sort of *narrative* tour strategy. Only 3 percent gave an *overview* such as "Well, the apartment is basically a square." The reason? The narrative tour strategy is a very efficient way to retrieve information from memory—that is, to survey what you know. In this case it allows you to cover all the rooms one by one as you walk through your apartment. Yet it is almost impossible for another person to reproduce the apartment from this narrative tour, whereas the overview approach, which only 3 percent used, works quite well. As in writing, an organization that functions well for thinking about a topic often fails to communicate that thinking to the listener. A strategy that is effective for the speaker may be terribly confusing to a listener.

Note, however, that in draft form, writer-based prose can have a real use. Since this type of writing comes naturally to us, it can be an efficient strategy for exploring a topic and outwitting our nemesis, short-term memory. If a writer's material is complicated or confusing, he may initially have to concentrate all his attention on generating and organizing his own knowledge. He might simply be too preoccupied to simultaneously imagine another person's point of view and adapt to it. The reader has to wait. But you don't want to make the reader wait forever.

You can usually recognize writer-based prose by one or more of these features:

1. An *egocentric focus* on the writer.
2. A narrative organization focused on the writer's own discovery process.
3. A *survey structure* organized, like a textbook, around the writer's information.

There are times, of course, when a narrative structure is exactly right—if, for example, your goal is to tell a story or describe an event. And a survey of what you know can be a reasonable way to organize a background report or survey. But in most expository and persuasive writing, the writer needs to *re*organize his or her knowledge around a problem, a thesis, or the reader's needs. Writer-based prose just hasn't been reorganized yet.

A READER'S TEST

Following are two drafts of a report that will be used as a test case. The writers were students in an organizational psychology course who were also working as consultants to a local organization, the Oskaloosa Brewing Company. The purposes of the report were to show progress to their professor and to present a problem analysis, complete with causes and conclusions, to their client. Both readers—academic and professional—were less concerned with what the students had done or seen than with *how* they had approached the problem and *what* they had made of their observations.

To gauge the reader-based effectiveness of this report, read quickly through Draft 1 and imagine the response of Professor Charns, who needed to answer these questions: "As analysts, what assumptions and decisions did my students make? Why did they make them? And at what stage in the project are they now?" Then reread the draft and play the role of the client, who wants to know "How did they define the problem, and what did they conclude?" As either reader, can you quickly extract the information the report should be giving you? Next try the same test on Draft 2.

As a reader, how would you describe the difference between these two versions? Each was written by the same group of writers, but the revision came after a discussion about what the readers really needed to know and expected to get from the report. Let us look at the three things that make Draft 1 a piece of writer-based prose.

Draft 1

Group Report

(1)   Work began on our project with the initial group decision to evaluate the Oskaloosa Brewing Company. Oskaloosa Brewing Company is a regionally located brewery manufacturing several different types of beer, notably River City and Brough Cream Ale. This beer is marked under various names in Pennsylvania and other neighboring states. As a group, we decided to analyze this organization because two of our group members had had frequent customer contact with the sales department. Also, we were aware that Oskaloosa Brewing had been losing money for the past five years, and we felt we might be able to find some obvious problems in its organizational structure.

(2)   Our first meeting, held February 17th, was with the head of the sales department, Jim Tucker. Generally, he gave us an outline of the organization, from president to worker, and discussed the various departments that we might ultimately decide to analyze. The two that seemed the most promising and more applicable to the project were the sales and production departments. After a few group meetings and discussions with the personnel manager, Susan Harris, and our advisor, Professor Charns, we felt it best suited our needs and Oskaloosa Brewing's needs to evaluate their bottling department.

(3)   During the next week we had a discussion with the superintendent of production, Henry Holt, and made plans for interviewing the supervisors and line workers. Also, we had a tour of the bottling department that gave us a first-hand look at the production process. Before beginning our interviewing, our group met several times to formulate appropriate questions to use in interviewing, for both the supervisors and the workers. We also had a meeting with Professor Charns to discuss this matter.

(4)   The next step was the actual interviewing process. During the weeks of March 14–18 and March 21–25, our group met several times at Oskaloosa Brewing and interviewed ten supervisors and twelve workers. Finally, during this past week, we have had several group meetings to discuss our findings and the potential problem areas within the bottling department. Also, we have spent time organizing the writing of our progress report.

(5)   The bottling and packaging division is located in a separate building, adjacent to the brewery, where the beer is actually manufactured. From the brewery the beer is piped into one of five lines (four bottling lines and one canning line) in the bottling house, where the bottles are filled, crowned, pasteurized, labeled, packaged in cases, and either shipped out or stored in the warehouse. The head of this operation, and others, is production manager Phil Smith. Next in line under him in direct control of the bottling house is the superintendent of bottling and packaging, Henry Holt. In addition, there are a total of ten supervisors who report directly to Henry Holt and who oversee the daily operations and coordinate and direct the twenty to thirty union workers who operate the lines.

(6)   During production, each supervisor fills out a data sheet to explain what was actually produced during each hour. This form also includes the exact time when a breakdown occurred, what it was caused by, and when production was resumed. Some supervisors' positions are production-staff-oriented. One takes care of supplying the raw material (bottles, caps, labels, and boxes) for production. Another is responsible for the union workers' assignments each day.

These workers are not all permanently assigned to a production-line position. Men called "floaters" are used, filling in for a sick worker or helping out after a breakdown.

(7)   The union employees are generally older than thirty-five, some in their late fifties. Most have been with the company many years and are accustomed to having more workers per a slower moving line. . . .

Draft 2

MEMORANDUM

TO: Professor Martin Charns

FROM: Nancy Lowenberg, Todd Scott, Rosemary Nisson, Larry Vollen

DATE: March 31, 1977

RE: Progress Report: The Oskaloosa Brewing Company

Why Oskaloosa Brewing?

Oskaloosa Brewing Company is a regionally located brewery manufacturing several different types of beer, notably River City and Brough Cream Ale. As a group, we decided to analyze this organization because two of our group members have frequent contact with the sales department. Also, we were aware that Oskaloosa Brewing had been losing money for the past five years and we felt we might be able to find some obvious problems in its organizational structure.

Initial Steps: Where to Concentrate?

After several interviews with top management and a group discussion, we felt it best suited our needs, and Oskaloosa Brewing's needs, to evaluate the production department. Our first meeting, held February 17, was with the head of the sales department, Jim Tucker. He gave us an outline of the organization and described the two major departments, sales and production. He indicated that there were more obvious problems in the production department, a belief also suggested by Susan Harris, the personnel manager.

Next Step

The next step involved a familiarization with the plant and its employees. First, we toured the plant to gain an understanding of the brewing and bottling processes. Next, during the weeks of March

14–18 and March 21–25, we interviewed ten supervisors and twelve workers. Finally, during the past week we had group meetings to exchange information and discuss potential problems.

The Production Process

Knowledge of the actual production process is imperative in understanding the effects of various problems on efficient production. Therefore, we have included a brief summary of this process.

The bottling and packaging division is located in a separate building, adjacent to the brewery, where the beer is actually manufactured. From the brewery the beer is piped into one of five lines (four bottling lines and one canning line) in the bottling house, where the bottles are filled, crowned, pasteurized, labeled, packaged in cases, and either shipped out or stored in the warehouse.

Problems

Through extensive interviews with supervisors and union employees, we have recognized four apparent problems within the bottling house operations. The first is that the employees' goals do not match those of the company. . . . This is especially apparent in the union employees, whose loyalty lies with the union instead of the company. This attitude is well-founded, as the union ensures them of job security and benefits. . . .

Narrative Organization

The first four paragraphs of the draft are organized as a narrative, starting with the phrase "Work began. . . ." We are given a story of the writers' discovery process. Notice how all of the facts are presented in terms of *when* they were discovered, not in terms of their implications or logical connections. The writers want to tell us what happened when; the reader, on the other hand, wants to ask "why?" and "so what?"

A narrative organization is tempting to write because it is a prefabricated order and easy to generate. Instead of having to create a hierarchical organization among ideas or worry about a reader, the writer can simply remember his or her own discovery process and write a story. Papers that start out, "In studying the economic causes of World War I, the first thing we have to consider is . . ." are often a dead giveaway. They tell us we are going to watch the writer's mind at work and follow him through the process of thinking out his conclusions.

This pattern has, of course, the virtue of any form of drama— it keeps you in suspense by withholding closure. But only if the audience is willing to wait that long for the point. Unfortunately, most academic and professional readers are impatient and tend to interpret such narrative, step-by-step structures either as wandering and confused (does he have a point?) or as a form of hedging.

Egocentric Focus

The second feature of Draft 1 is that it is a discovery story starring the writers. Its drama, such as it is, is squarely focused on the writer: "I did/I thought/I felt." Of the fourteen sentences in the first three paragraphs, ten are grammatically focused on the writers' thoughts and actions rather than on the issues. For example: "Work began . . . ," "We decided . . . ," "Also we were aware . . . and we felt. . . ." Generally speaking, the reader is more interested in issues and ideas than in the fact that the writer thought them.

Survey Form or Textbook Organization

In the fifth paragraph of Draft 1, the writers begin to organize their material in a new way. Instead of a narrative, we are given a survey of what the writers observed. Here, the raw facts of the bottling process dictated the organization of the paragraph. Yet the client-reader already knows this, and the professor probably doesn't care. In the language of computer science we could say the writers are performing a "memory dump": simply printing out information in the exact form in which they stored it in memory. Notice how in the revised version the writers try to *use* their observations to understand production problems.

The problem with a survey or "textbook" form is that it ignores the reader's need for a different organization of the information. Suppose, for example, you are writing to model airplane builders about wind resistance. The information you need comes out of a physics text, but that text is organized around the field of physics; it starts with subatomic particles and works up from there. To meet the needs of your reader, you have to adapt that knowledge, not lift it intact from the text. Sometimes writers can simply survey their knowledge, but generally the writer's main task is to *use* knowledge rather than reprint it.

To sum up, in Draft 2 of the Oskaloosa report, the writers made a real attempt to write for their readers. Among other things the report is now organized around major questions readers might have, it uses headings to display the overall organization of the report, and it makes better use of topic sentences that tell the reader what each paragraph contains and why to read it. Most important, it focuses more on the crucial information the reader wants to obtain.

Obviously this version could still be improved. But it shows the writers attempting to transform writer-based prose and change their narrative and survey pattern into a more issue-centered hierarchical organization.

Consider another example of how a writer transformed a writer-based paragraph into a reader-based one. The first draft below is full of good ideas but has a narrative organization and an egocentric focus. We can almost see the writer reading the book. Her conclusions (which her professor will want to know) are buried within a description of the story (which her professor, of course, knows already).

Writer-based draft:
In *Great Expectations,* Pip is introduced as a very likable young boy. Although he steals, he does it because he is both innocent and good-hearted. Later, when he goes to London, one no longer feels this same sort of identification with Pip. He becomes too proud to associate with his old friends, cutting ties with Joe and Biddy because of his false pride. And yet one is made to feel that Pip is still an innocent in some important way. When he dreams about Estella, one can see how all his unrealistic, romantic illusions blind him to the way the world really works.

We know from this paragraph how the writer reacted to a number of things in the novel. But what conclusions did she finally come to? What larger pattern does she want us to see?

Reader-based revision:
In *Great Expectations,* Pip changes from a goodhearted boy into a selfish young man, yet he always remains an innocent who never really understands how the world works. Although as a child Pip actually steals something, he does it because he has a gullible, kind-hearted sort of innocence. As a young man in London his crime seems worse when he cuts his old friends, Joe and Biddy, because of false pride. And yet, as his dreams about Estella show, Pip is still an innocent, a person caught up in unrealistic romantic illusions that he can't see through.

The revised version starts out with a topic sentence that explicitly states the writer's main idea and shows us how she has chunked or organized the facts of the novel. The rest of the paragraph is clearly focused on that idea, and words such as "although" are used to show how her observations are logically related to one another. From a professor or other reader's point of view, this organization is also more effective because it clearly shows what the writer learned from reading the novel.

Below is a good example of a writer who has focused all his attention on the object before him. He has given us a survey of what he knows about running shoes, although the ostensible purpose of the paragraph was to help a new runner decide what shoe to buy.

Writer-based draft:
Shoes are the most important part of your equipment, so choose them well. First, there are various kinds. Track shoes are lightweight with

spikes. Road running flats, however, are sturdy, with $\frac{1}{2}''$ to $1''$ of cushioning. In many shoes the soles are built up with different layers of material. The uppers are made in various ways, some out of leather, some out of nylon reinforced with leather, and the cheapest are made of vinyl. The best combination is nylon with a leather heel cup. The most distinctive thing about running shoes is the raised heel and, of course, the stripes. Although some tennis shoes now have such stripes, it is important not to confuse them with a real running shoe. All in all, a good running shoe should combine firm foot support with sufficient flexibility.

In this draft the writer has focused on the shoe, not the reader who needs to choose a shoe. How would we decide between leather, nylon, and vinyl? Or judge what is "sufficiently" flexible? Why does it matter that the soles are layered; was the writer trying to make a point?

Reader-based revision:
Your running shoe will be your most important piece of running equipment, so look for a shoe that both cushions and supports your foot. Track shoes, which are lightweight and flimsy, with spikes for traction in dirt, won't do. Neither will tennis shoes, which are made for balance and quick stops, not steady pounding down the road. A good pair of shoes starts with a thick layered sole, at least $\frac{1}{2}''$ to $1''$ thick. The outer layer absorbs road shock; the inner layer cushions your foot. Another form of cushioning is the slightly elevated heel, which prevents strain on the vulnerable Achilles tendon.

The uppers that will support your foot come in vinyl, which is cheaper but can cause blisters and hot feet; in leather, which can crack with age; and in a lightweight but more expensive nylon and leather combination. The best nylon and leather shoes will have a thick, fitted leather heel cup that keeps your foot from rolling and prevents twisted ankles. Make sure, however, that your sturdy shoes are still flexible enough that you can bend 90° at the ball of your foot. Although most running shoes have stripes, not all shoes with stripes can give you the cushioning and flexible support you need when you run.

Notice how the revision uses the same facts about shoes but organizes them around the reader's probable questions. The writer tells us what his facts *mean* in the context of choosing shoes. For example, vinyl uppers mean low cost and possible blisters. And the topic sentence sets up the key features of a good shoe—cushioning and support—which the rest of the paragraph will develop. The reader-based revision tells us what we need to know in a direct, explicit way.

CREATING READER-BASED PROSE

In the best of all possible worlds we would all write reader-based prose from the beginning. It is theoretically much more efficient to generate and organize your ideas in light of the reader in the first place. But sometimes that is hard to do. Take the assignment "Write about the physics of wind resistance for a model airplane builder." For a physics teacher this would be a trivial problem. But for someone ten years out of Physics 101, the first task would be remembering whatever they knew about wind resistance or friction at all. Adapting that knowledge to the reader would just have to wait.

In general, write for your reader whenever you can, but recognize that many times a first draft is going to be more writer-based than you may want it to be. Even though the draft may not work well for your reader, it can represent a great deal of work for you and be the groundwork for an effective paper. The more complex your problem and the more difficult your material, the more you will need to transform your writer-based prose to reader-based prose. This is not an overly difficult step in the writing process, but many writers simply neglect to take it.

In order to transform your paper to more reader-based prose, there are four major things you can do, all of which should be familiar by now:

1. Organize your paper around a problem, a thesis, or a purpose you share with the reader—not around your own discovery process or the topic itself.

2. With a goal or thesis as the top level of your issue tree, organize your ideas in a hierarchy. Distinguish between your major and minor ideas and make the relationship between them explicit to the reader. You can use this technique to organize not only an entire paper but sections and paragraphs.

3. If you are hoping that your reader will draw certain conclusions from your paper, or even from a portion of it, make those conclusions explicit. If you expect him or her to go away with a few main ideas, don't leave the work of drawing inferences and forming concepts up to your reader. He or she might just draw a different set of conclusions.

4. Finally, once you have created concepts and organized your ideas in a hierarchy focused on your reader and your goals, use cues—which we will discuss shortly—to make that organization vivid and clear to the reader.

STRATEGY 3   GIVE YOUR READERS CUES

Part of your contract with a reader, if you seriously want to communicate, is to guide him or her through your prose. You need to set up cues that help the reader see what is coming and how it will be organized. This means, first of all, creating expectations and fulfilling them so that when your point arrives, your reader will have a well-anchored hook to hang it on. This was discussed in Chapter 9 (on pp. 193–94). In addition, you want the reader to know which points are major, which are minor, and how they are related to one another. By using various kinds of cues and signposts, you can guide the reader to build an accurate mental tree of your discussion.

Readers, of course, come to your prose with built-in expectations about where these cues will be. For example, they expect to find

1. The most important points of a discussion stated at the beginning and summarized in some way at the end.
2. A topic sentence that tells them what they will learn from a paragraph.
3. The writer's key words in grammatically important places such as the subject, verb, and object positions.

It is to your advantage to fulfill these expectations whenever you can.

Writers have a number of tools and techniques they can use to *preview* their meaning, *summarize* it, and *guide* the reader. Figure 10–1 lists some of the most common. Check this list against the last paper you wrote. How many of these tools did you take advantage of?

The conventions of format on a page also work as familiar cues to the reader. Figure 10–2 shows a typical format for papers and reports.

FIGURE 10–1
Cues for the Reader

Title Table of contents Abstracts Introduction Headings Problem/purpose statement Topic sentences for paragraphs	*Cues that preview your points*
Sentence summaries at ends of paragraphs Conclusion or summary sections	*Cues that summarize or illustrate your points*
Pictures, graphs, and tables Punctuation Typographical cues: different typefaces, underlining, numbering Visual arrangement: indentation, extra white space, rows and columns	*Cues that guide the reader visually*
Transitional words Conjunctions Repetitions Pronouns Summary nouns	*Cues that guide the reader verbally*

FIGURE 10–2
Common Format for Typewritten Paper

THIS IS A TITLE: THE SUBTITLE QUALIFIES IT

The first sentence in this paragraph is a topic sentence, which
announces the topic and previews the argument or point of the
paragraph. The remainder of the paragraph often previews the rest of
the paper, introducing the main points to be covered.

THIS IS A MAJOR HEADING

Major headings are placed flush left, often set in caps, and, in
typewritten manuscript, usually underlined. In print they are often
set in boldface type. Ideally a reader should be able to see the shape
of your discussion simply by reading the title and major headings.
Make the wording of major headings grammatically parallel, if you can,
as the major and minor headings are in this example.

This Is a Minor Heading

Unlike a major heading it is indented and typed in capital and
lowercase letters. It should be clearly and logically related to the
major heading that precedes it.

> The fact that this passage is indented says it is either
> a long quotation or an example. The additional space around
> it and the single spacing signal that it is a different kind
> of text, and lets readers adjust their reading speed and
> expectations.

Draft 2 of the Oskaloosa Brewing memo (pp. 215–16) is a good
example of how headings, topic sentences, and previews of conclusions can provide reader cues. Here is another piece of writing that
was designed with the reader in mind. It comes from Thomas Miller's
book *This Is Photography,* in a chapter called "Action."[3] One of the
first previews the reader sees on the page is a photo of a pole vaulter
effortlessly sailing over a bar and a place kicker completely off the
ground with his right foot at the top of his kick. The caption reads,
"These look like top speed but. . . ."

In the passage below, I have italicized and footnoted certain portions for discussion later. As you read the italicized parts, try to figure out what effect the writer was hoping to have on you by using
the cues he did.

---

[3] Thomas Miller and Wyatt Brummitt, *This Is Photography* (Rochester, NY: Case Hoyt
Corp., 1945).

Poised Action[1]

In many sports,[2] particularly in races, movement is constant enough to permit picture making in terms of calculated speeds. *But there are other sports*[2] in which the action is spasmodic, defying calculation. *In those sports,*[2] the instants when action is poised are, pictorially, just as vivid and interesting as the moments when action is wildest. *Take pole vaulting, for instance.*[2] At the very top of the vault, with the vaulter's body flung out horizontally over the bar, action is relatively quiet—yet it's the best pictorial moment in this field event. This peak instant can be "stopped" with much less shutter speed than either the rise or fall.

Baseball[3] has a number of moments which are full of *poised action.*[3] The pitcher winds up and *then*[4] unwinds to throw his speed-ball. *In that instant,*[4] between winding and unwinding, action is suspended, yet a picture of it tells a story of speed and power. *An instant later,*[4] having released the ball, the pitcher is *again*[4] poised—all his energy having gone into the delivery. *There's another pictorial moment.*[5] *To picture either of these moments you need to work swiftly, but a high shutter speed is less important to your success than an understanding of the sport and of the personal style of the athlete before your lens.*[6]

Even in boxing,[7] a good photographer gets his pictures as the blows land, not as they travel. *There was that famous instance*[8] at the Louis-Nova fight in '41. Two photographers, on directly opposite sides of the ring, saw a heavy punch coming and shot just as it landed. Both used Photo-flashes, of course, but one of the lamps failed to work. The photographer whose light had failed discovered, on developing the film, that he had a picture—a most unusual and vivid silhouette—*made by the light of his competitor's flash.*[9] The fighters hid the other man's flash bulb, so the silhouette effect was perfect—and dramatic. *The only moral to this yarn*[10] is that experience teaches pressmen and other pro's that there are right instances for any shots. The photographers on opposite sides of the ring were right—and right together, within the same hundredth of a second.

Here are comments on the writer's cues:

1. In the original, this heading is set in boldface type.
2. These cues make the relationship between each of the sentences explicit. They lead us along; many sports are contrasted to other sports. We are told something additional about "other sports" and then given an example.
3. A topic sentence ties a new subject, "baseball," to the old topic, "poised action."
4. These words and phrases reinforce our sense of the timing and sequence of the action.
5. The writer recaps his discussion by redefining it not just as an action but in the larger context now of photographs representing "pictorial moments."
6. This sentence is a recap on an even larger scale. In it the writer draws a conclusion based on both this paragraph and the

preceding one, and ties the paragraphs to the larger goal of the book and the chapter: how to take good action photographs.

7. This topic sentence and its introductory phrase are performing two functions: They introduce a new subject, boxing, and tie it neatly to the old framework with the words "even in."

8. We are told to see this as an example of the writer's point. He doesn't let us simply be entertained by the story; he uses it.

9. This line was also in italics in the original, to emphasize how unusual the occurrence was. Note that in the phrase just before this one—"a most unusual and vivid silhouette"—the writer used dashes to highlight the significance of the facts. Both italics and dashes are attention-getting cues, though they can be overdone.

10. The writer draws a particular conclusion from all of this that is tied to the point of his book, and he signposts his conclusion quite clearly so we won't miss it: "The only moral to this yarn is . . .".

 STRATEGY 4 **DEVELOP A PERSUASIVE ARGUMENT**

People often write because they want to make something happen: They want the reader to do something or at least to see things their way. But sometimes expressing a point of view isn't enough, because it conflicts with the way the reader *already* sees things. We are faced with the same old problem of communication: Your image of something and your reader's are not the same. What kinds of arguments can you use that will make him or her see things *your* way? In this section we will look at the nature of arguments and at one type, the Rogerian argument, that can help you persuade another person to see things differently.

WINNING AN ARGUMENT VERSUS PERSUADING A LISTENER

When people think of arguments they usually think of winning them. And the time-honored method of winning an argument is by force ("You agree or I'll shoot.") or, in its more familiar form, by authority ("This is right because I [your mother, father, teacher, sergeant, boss] say it is."). The problem with force or authority is that, short of brainwashing, it often changes people's behavior but not their minds.

A second familiar form of argument is debate. Yet many people who learn to debate in high school discover that in the real world their debate strategies can indeed prove their point—but lose the argument. Debate is an argumentative contest: Person A is pitted against person B, and the winner is decided by an impartial judge. But in the real world, person A is trying not to impress a judge but to *convince* person B. The goal of such an argument is not to win points but to affect your listener, to change his or her image of your subject in some significant way. And, as you remember, that image may be a large, complex network of ideas, associations, and attitudes. The goal of communication is to find a common ground and create a shared image, but debate typically polarizes a discussion by pitting one image against the other.

Let us look for a moment at the possible outcomes of an argument or discussion in which the two parties have firmly held but differing images. Ann has decided to take a year off to work and travel before she finishes college and settles on a career. Her parents immediately oppose the idea. To them, this plan conveys an image of "dropping out" and wasting a year, with the possibility that Ann might not return to school. Furthermore, they have saved money to help put her through school and see this prospect as an indication that she doesn't value their plans, hopes, and efforts for her.

For Ann, on the other hand, taking a year off means getting time and experience that would enable her to take better advantage of college. She hopes it will help her decide what sort of work she wants to do, but more importantly she sees it as a chance to develop on her own for a while. In her mind, the goal of going to college isn't getting a degree but figuring out what things you want to learn more about.

Clearly Ann and her parents have very different images of taking a year off. Assume you are Ann in this situation. What are the possible outcomes of an argument you might have with your parents?

One outcome, and usually the least likely one, is that you will totally reconstruct your listeners' image so they see the issue just as you do. You simply replace their perspective with yours. Reconstruction can no doubt happen if your audience has an undeveloped image of the subject or sees you as a great authority, but argument strategies that set out to reconstruct someone else's ideas completely—to *win* the point—are usually ill-founded and unrealistic. They are more likely to polarize people than to persuade them.

A second alternative is to modify someone else's image, to add to or clarify it. You do this when you clarify an issue (for example, taking a year off is not the same as "dropping out") or when you add new information (Ann's college even has a special program for this and might give her some course credit for work experience). As a writer this is clearly the most reasonable effect you can aim for. In doing so you respect the other person's point of view while striving to modify those features you can reasonably affect.

The third possible outcome of an argument may be the most common: no change. Think for a minute of how many speeches, lectures, classes, sermons, and discussions you have sat through in your life and how many of those had no discernible effect on your thinking. If we think of an argument as debate in which a "good" argument inevitably wins, we forget that it is possible for even a "correct" argument to have absolutely no effect on our listener.

To sum up, the goal of an argument is to modify the image of your listener—and that this is not the same as simply presenting your own image. A successful argument is a reader-based act. It considers attitudes and images the reader already holds.

However, a great roadblock stands in the way of modifying a listener's image. Many people perceive any change in their image of things as a threat to their own security and stability. People's images are part of themselves, and a part of how they have made sense of the world. To ask them to change their image in any significant way can make people anxious and resistant to change. When this happens, communication simply stops.

Arguments that polarize issues often create just this situation. The more the speaker argues, the more firmly the listener clings to his own position. And instead of listening, the listener spends his time thinking up counter-arguments to protect his own position and image. So the critical question for the writer is this: How can I persuade my reader to listen to my position and maybe even modify his or her image without creating this sense of threat that stops communication?

ROGERIAN ARGUMENT

Rogerian argument, developed in part from the work of Carl Rogers, is an argument strategy designed not to win but to increase communication in both directions. It is based on the fact that if people feel they are understood—that their position is honestly recognized and respected—they may cease to feel a sense of threat. Once the threat is removed, listening is no longer an act of self-defense, and people feel they can afford to truly listen to and consider other ways of seeing things.

The goal of an argument, then, is to induce your reader at least to consider your position and the possibility of modifying his or her own. One way to make this happen is to demonstrate an understanding of your listener's position *first*. That means trying to see the issue from his or her point of view. For face-to-face discussions, Carl Rogers suggested this rule of thumb: Before you present your position and argue for your way of seeing things, you must be able to describe your listener's position back to your listener in such a way that he or she *agrees* with your version of it. In other words, you are demonstrating that you not only care about your listener's perspective but care enough to actively try (and keep trying) to understand it. So Ann in our example would have begun the discussion with her parents by exploring with them their response to her leaving college and the reasons behind their feelings.

What does this mean for writers who don't have the luxury of a face-to-face discussion? First, you can use the introduction to your paper, including your shared goal, to demonstrate to your reader a thorough understanding of his or her problems and goals. This is your chance to look at the question from your reader's point of view and show how your message is relevant to them.

Secondly, try to avoid categorizing people and issues. This puts people into camps, polarizes the argument, and stops communication. For example, Ann may well have felt that her parents were being old-fashioned and conventional to resist her idea, but establishing that point would have done little to change their minds. A Rogerian argument, by contrast, would begin by acknowledging the parents' plans and hopes for her and recognizing the element of truth in their fear of her "dropping out." They know that, despite good intentions, many people don't come back to college. In taking a Rogerian approach, Ann might also begin to understand the issues more clearly herself. One of the hidden strengths of a Rogerian argument is that, besides increasing one's power to persuade, it also opens up communication and may even end up persuading the persuader. It increases the possibility of genuine communication and change for both the speaker and listener.

The first draft of Ann's letter started like this:

Dear Mom and Dad,

    I wish you would try to see my point of view and not be so conventional. Things are different from when you went to school. And you must realize I am old enough to make my own decisions, even if you disagree. There are a number of good reasons why this is the best decision I could make. First, . . .

Although this letter created a "strong" argument, it was also likely to stop communication and unlikely to persuade. Here is the letter Ann eventually wrote to her parents, which tries to take an open Rogerian approach to the problem.

Dear Mom and Dad,

    As I told you the other night on the phone, I want to consider taking a year off from college to work and be on my own for a while. I've been thinking over what you said because this is an important decision and, like you, I want to do what will be best in the long run, not just what seems attractive now. I think some of your objections make a lot of sense. After all the effort you've put into helping me get through college, it would be terrible to just "drop out" or never find a real career that I could be committed to.

I know you're also wondering if I recognize what an opportunity I have and are probably worrying if I'm just going to let it slip through my fingers. Well, in a way I'm worried about that too. Here I am working hard, but I don't really know where I want to go or why. It's time for me to specialize and I can't decide what to do. And it's that opportunity I'm afraid of losing. I feel I need some time off and some experience so I can make a better decision and really take advantage of my last year here.

But there's still the question of whether I would be dropping out. The college actually has a program for people who want to take a year off, and they even encourage you to enter it if you have some idea of what you'd be doing. So, as far as the school is concerned, I'd be in a well-established leave of absence program. But the fact is, people do drop out. They don't always come back. What would a whole year away from school do to me? You're right, I can't really be sure. But I think my reasons are good ones, and I'm working on a plan that would let me earn credit while I work and come back to school with a clearer sense of where I want to go. Can you offer me any more suggestions on ways I could plan ahead?

Love,
ANN

PROJECTS AND ASSIGNMENTS

1   Here are some mini-cases, dealing with a college environment, in which you need to create a goal that both you and your reader share. Write an introduction that sets up a shared goal and then discuss why you think it would work.

   a.   You would like the chairperson of your department to contribute some money to a fund that would allow coffee hours and socials for majors in the department. You know she has a rather tight budget this year. What can you say to her?

   b.   You would like the faculty members in your department to coordinate their exams and papers better so that students' work will be spread out more evenly over the term. For them, this would be just one more thing to try to plan their syllabus around. They have given you five minutes to talk at the faculty meeting.

   c.   You have been given the responsibility of getting voluntary compliance to the "no smoking" rule in the redecorated conference classrooms, which are rather small and cozy and used for group meetings. Find a shared goal.

2   The following paragraph comes from a student paper analyzing a form that was currently being used for student evaluation of the department's courses. See how many characteristics you can find that make this a writer-based discussion. Then reread the paragraph, decide what the main ideas are, and try to transform it into a piece of reader-based prose. Remember you will need a topic sentence that previews the main points for the reader and transitions that show how sentences are related.

> In order to improve the course evaluation form, it was first necessary to know how the current form is viewed by students and faculty, so the following survey of opinion was taken. From the faculty viewpoint, the form seems subjective. Many feel that the goals of their course are not as simple as the form sets them out to be. And the form has the aura of a popularity contest. When students were asked about the purpose of the form, a majority felt it was designed to mollify disgruntled students. Only a few marked the box "improves faculty performance" on the questionnaire. It also appeared that many students fill out the evaluation form just to let off steam. Attitudes about the form's effectiveness were further indicated by the questions students often asked while the survey was being conducted. The most common of these were "Why aren't the results published?" and "How does the administration use these evaluations?"

3   Write a brief narrative that describes your first experience with something new, such as moving into an apartment, going to a new class, joining Weight Watchers, or learning to play squash. Then think of some group of readers who might benefit from your experience. Contemplate what they are like and write a short, reader-based article or essay that adapts your knowledge and experience to their needs.

IF YOU WOULD LIKE TO READ MORE

If you want to know more about readers and their responses, see:

Clark, Herbert, and Eve Clark. *Psychology and Language: An Introduction to Psycholinguistics*. New York: Harcourt Brace Jovanovich, 1977. / This is a readable and wide-ranging survey of the ways language works.

Holtzman, Paul. *The Psychology of the Speakers' Audience*. Glenview, IL: Scott, Foresman, 1970. / This writer describes communication in terms of the listener's experience.

Linde, Charlotte, and William Labov. Spatial networks as a site for the study of language and thought. *Language*, 51 (1975), pp. 924–39. / This article contains the original discussion of the apartment tour experiment.

chapter eleven

Revising for Purpose and Editing for Style

GOAL 7
REVIEW your paper and your purpose

Check over your paper in a goal-directed way, testing it against your plans and your reader's probable response.

> *STRATEGY 1* **REVIEW YOUR GOALS, GISTS, AND DISCOVERIES**
> *STRATEGY 2* **DETECT, DIAGNOSE, AND REVISE**

GOAL 8
TEST and EDIT your writing

Edit your paper to achieve a clear, direct prose style.

> *STRATEGY 1* **EDIT FOR ECONOMY**
> *STRATEGY 2* **EDIT FOR A FORCEFUL STYLE**

Writers who depend on inspiration are often reluctant to reread their papers. Their image of the writing process assumes that when ideas finally come, they should not be altered or need improvement. Perfect-draft writers have spent so much time laboring over their sentences that they simply don't want to see them again. But a problem-solving writer treats editing and revising as useful steps in composing because they break up the process and make it much easier to handle. Many of the problems that could block a writer are easily solved when the writer returns to revise. Even more important, revising is an inexpensive method (in terms of time and effort) for making dramatic improvements in your writing. Like strategies for designing for a reader, revising lets you concentrate on *communicating*.

GOAL 7

REVIEW Your Paper and Your Purpose

In no other area of writing does the difference between experienced and inexperienced writers seem so clear as it does in revision. A number of studies on writers suggest that the experts, the people with lots of experience, are simply giving themselves a different task to do than are the novices, the writers with less experience. Both say they are revising, but they do different things. Here is a brief profile of these two kinds of revisers. See where you fit.

The goals of a novice: Inexperienced writers often use revision to proofread, to clean up their prose, and to correct errors. Almost all of their revisions focus on individual words or phrases (rather than whole sentences, paragraphs, or the top-level ideas of the text). Their major technique is deleting words (rather than adding new material). The most common diagnosis or reason the writers give for the changes they make is that the current text "doesn't sound right" or that it is "incorrect."

The process of a novice: Inexperienced writers typically begin to revise as soon as they begin to read. They work through the text in a straightforward manner, diagnosing and revising word by word. This is a very methodical process, but it also means that they are usually looking at or evaluating small pieces of text, such as a sentence, rather than a whole idea, paragraph, or discussion.

The goals of an experienced writer: Experienced writers expect to rework a first draft, because the one-two combination of write-then-revise is the fastest way to produce a good paper. They are likely to see that draft as merely a springboard to the final text, using it to try out and develop ideas. In addition, they go into revising a first draft with the goal of expanding, reorganizing, or changing not just words and sentences, but the gist of a paragraph, an argument, or even the whole paper. Their attention is focused on the main ideas; their top priority is the organization and effect of the entire paper.

The process of an experienced writer: Because experienced writers divide their writing time between planning, drafting, and revising, they spend less time writing and perfecting the first draft. Because revising is a strategic move, they also make decisions about what to look for and how to go about it. They may decide to skim the whole text first for organization or persuasiveness, or to work in two passes, reading once for ideas and once for mechanics and style.

Experienced writers also divide their time between **global** and **local** revision. **Local** revision is the familiar process of evaluating individual words, phrases, and sentences. Local changes affect only a small, local part of the text. They don't alter the gist or the overall structure of the text. Even with extensive revision, the top levels of the issue tree stay the same. Local revision often makes a text more "correct" according to the rules of spelling, grammar, and punctuation, or it makes it fit the conventions of good usage and polished style, or the conventions of format and presentation a given discourse community expects.

Global revision affects how the paper works as a whole. Global revision (even if it physically alters only a few sentences) involves changes in the purpose, in the gist, or in the major ideas; it may alter the logic of an argument or the writer's stance toward the reader. These changes, which affect the gist, the structure, the overall tone, or purpose of the piece, may also involve a number of local changes. But the important thing is that they are all part of a more global plan of revision. Writers need both global and local revision strategies.

In order to do global revision, writers must have a clear sense of their own goals or purpose and of the gist of what they wanted to say. Only then can they compare the text they wrote to what they really intended. However, even at the end of writing a draft many writers still find it hard to say exactly what their purpose is or to state the gist of their paper. They have been so involved in writing individual parts, they would find it easier to describe all the details to you than to put it in a nutshell. How, then, can they do global revision? Experienced writers solve this problem by actually reviewing their own work like a new reader to get a sharper picture of their intentions, which in turn guides revision.

In the section that follows we will walk through a four-step procedure for revising that involves review, detection, diagnosis, and revision. Although I will present it as a step-by-step procedure to make the process clear, these strategies are meant to be customized and adapted to your own situation. You will need to develop your own ways to review and diagnose, and you must decide when a given strategy is likely to help. (Chapter 13 will give you another view of this process.) Remember, one thing experienced writers do is to manage and adapt the revision process to suit their needs.

STRATEGY 1 REVIEW YOUR GOALS, GISTS, AND DISCOVERIES

In a nutshell, what is your plan for this paper? And how do each of these sections (or paragraphs) fit into that master plan?

The first thing to notice about this strategy for getting the big picture is that you may want to start by *not* looking at your text. You need a fresh look that isn't captured by the words on the page, and you need to resist the temptation to plunge into local revision. So to start out, sit back and think for a moment: What do I want to do or to say? What do I want my readers to think (and what do they expect)?

Since the plan you made earlier (see Chapter 5) may have changed, it helps to jot a few notes or sketch an issue tree. Or skim over the text quickly to review your plan. Or read the introductory section carefully and sketch the issue tree you have in mind and promised the reader. A more systematic approach for reviewing an argument or complex discussion is actually to make small notes on the gist or point of each paragraph or section of the paper right there in the margin. How good was your review? Test it by trying to give a three-minute overview of your purpose and your main points to someone else. Can you tell them how each paragraph or section is supposed to function in your plan?

Admittedly, reviewing before you review may take four or five minutes and sometimes a little hard thinking, but it has some real rewards. First, you are now ready to test your paper against your personal goals, not just against the conventions and rules of standard usage. Secondly, you will often discover something in your own thinking that has developed during the process of writing. Look for conclusions, for observations, for inferences you have drawn as you wrote. These discoveries are often found at the end of a first draft, at the end of paragraphs, or even buried in the text or in your head. At the same time, look for ideas you now question, for contradictions you can now see. (Remember, recognizing ideas that seem to contradict or that let you qualify your argument is valued in academic discourse.) Discoveries made while writing often turn out to be important insights that let you organize the paper around your best ideas and your real purpose. Revising lets you move these ideas out of the writer-based position (where they occurred to you during writing) and promote them to a more clearly signalled position as an organizing idea, a topic sentence, a named concept, or a more fully stated conclusion. Small changes based on these discoveries often make a large difference to readers.

STRATEGY 2   DETECT, DIAGNOSE, AND REVISE

Some revisions are triggered by happy discoveries—you revise the text to fit your new vision of things. Most revisions are triggered by problems. But if you have only a vague intuition that something doesn't sound right, you may spend time rewriting but never find or fix the real problem. The three-step process of Detect, Diagnose, and Revise may help you turn your intuitions into a more workable, "operational" plan for revising. Detecting lets you find possible problems—ones you might overlook otherwise. Diagnosing helps you pinpoint the source of the problem and lets you revise to fix that problem rather than just rewrite and hope it goes away. (Again, I will present this as a step-by-step procedure for clarity, but expect to customize these strategies to fit your needs.)

STEP 1. DETECT

Assuming your review (above) has given you a good sense of your goals, now is the time to read through your text trying first to detect global problems. At this point all you need to do is to detect that a problem exists, not fix it. So read through at your regular speed like a first-time reader, try to follow the structure, listen to your argument unfold, note how you respond—and listen to your intuitions. Did you stumble anywhere, did you feel confused at the end of a sentence, did you reread, did something sound awkward, did one idea not follow the next here and there? If so, that's normal. Listen for any signal, even a faint one, that you have detected a problem and simply put a note in the margin, a bracket about a paragraph, or a line under a phrase and go on. These are the possible problem spots you will return to later.

Concentrating on detection *only* works well for both global and local problems. For instance, you may hear a faint warning bell for misspelled words and faulty punctuation, even when you don't know exactly what is correct. Just mark the spot as a possible detection and go on. But you will improve your chances of detecting problems if you concentrate on global and local problems in two separate passes. It is hard to see the big picture when your attention is riveted to spelling and equally hard to look closely at words when the argument is racing along.

Try reading the passage below like a detector, marking all the places you hear a faint signal of a possible problem. It is the second paragraph from a handout written to get undecided freshmen women involved in college sports. The first paragraph described available varsity sports, so think about the context and start your detector working as you begin the paragraph. Remember, mark global and local problems, but don't stop to fix them.

> *Problem text* (paragraph 1 was about varsity sports):
> I don't want to infer that the only chance women get for participating in sports is on varsity teams. Intramural sports are not quite the same as varsity sports, in which the rules are better, equipment is better, and with the techniques of the players being more developed. Irregardless, IM sports may be the choice for many women—they can be just as much fun and take less time.

If you can compare your problem spots with those of other people in your class, notice if you were near the group average in number of detections; were there common spots everyone chose? I will show you the choices of one experienced writer shortly. You may find that because readers bring different goals for what the text should do, they will agree on the local problems, but see quite different global ones.

STEP 2. DIAGNOSE THE PROBLEM

At this point in the process, some writers simply say to themselves, "that doesn't sound right" and they leap in and begin to rewrite.

Leaping in can work well if you have a new discovery to add or need to experiment with language, or if you feel something is missing. But we have observed that rewriting without diagnosing often takes more time in the long run (especially for global problems); it can create new problems; and it may fail to solve the original difficulty.

Look back at all the problems you have detected on the intramural sports paragraph. Go through each one and try to diagnose what it was in the text that triggered your detection. What is the cause of the problem; what is its effect on the reader; is it a category of problem you recognize? A diagnosis is a descriptive analysis of the problem. Think of the difference between a mere detection and a diagnosis this way: If a friend looked at you and said, "Say, I think you need some rest," you might be happy he cared and even detected your terminal condition. However, if your doctor said the same thing after you had dragged your sorry case to her office, you might well be annoyed, since from a doctor you expect a *bona fide* diagnosis with specific information and a recommendation for what to do (such as, "You have infectious mononucleosis with a white blood count of 12,000. What you need is to have no alcohol and 10 hours of sleep a night for the next two weeks."). A diagnosis, in that setting, is a problem description that you would be willing to pay for.

Some local problems such as run-on sentences and wordiness become easy to diagnose once you know them by name and know how to spot them. We will look at some familiar problems of this sort later in the chapter. A handbook is another good source of diagnoses for standard, sentence-level problems. But as you will see in the sample diagnosis below, some diagnoses are really a theory about why this text won't meet its own goals or about how a reader might respond. In order to diagnose a global problem, you often have to go through the very process we discussed in Chapter 1 and Chapter 8— you have to become a problem solver, draw inferences, and define the problem for yourself. How does your diagnosis of the intramural sports paragraph differ from that of the writer below? Did you bring the same goals to your diagnosis?

Well, I tossed out infer because it's used incorrectly—just a matter of usage—"infer" for "imply." But the whole sentence is just so—so wordy. For instance, "not quite the same as" doesn't say a thing; in what way are they "not the same"? What's the point of making that kind of a remark? But what I really wanted to fix was all the negatives—the "don't infer," and "not the same" and that awful "irregardless." I think that's not the way a recruiting document should be. I think you should put in positive statements. Talk about positive things. Now secondly, both of these sentences are really lead-ins that don't get you anywhere. You want to get to where you tell what it is rather than what it's not. This sentence structure is just a delaying tactic. So what I tried to do was jump in and talk about what I was going to talk about, which is intramural sports, not varsity. And put the varsity stuff in a subordinate clause. These sentences are just on the wrong subject.

Notice some of the strategies that make this writer an expert reviser. Although he does know the rule about "imply and infer," he sees that error as secondary to the larger problem. He first diagnoses the problem with a maxim about style and "wordiness." But he then goes on to diagnose the real problem in terms of the goals of the text. Handouts, he thinks, should be positive; they should tell people what they need to know and get to the point. Notice, too, how this writer keeps thinking about the problem, trying to be more and more explicit. As his diagnosis develops, it becomes focused more and more on the text's more global purpose and problem. He then uses that diagnosis to plan his revision.

STEP 3. REVISE

Once you diagnose a problem, especially a global one, you often find there are multiple ways to revise it. You need to think about how the changes you make to a given paragraph might affect other parts of the text. Look at your options and plan the best revision you can think of. The important feature of this third step—revision based on a diagnosis—is that you are making changes for a reason. Here is our diagnoser's proposed revision for the intramural paragraph.

Proposed revision:
Even more than varsity teams, intramural sports attract a growing number of women. Intramurals focus on developing skills; they are less competitive and take less time, but they can be just as enjoyable and valuable as playing on a varsity team.

Can you think of another solution to the problem that might be equally good for different reasons? Other people revising this text certainly did. This revision reflects this writer's plan for what he thought the text should do. Although we don't see it here, his comments show that he had already done some thinking about the goals of the handout, and we can imagine him reading to get a sense of the gist. He then uses those goals and that gist to revise the paragraph. That is, he tries to make it sound like a recruiting document and to focus on the real topic, rather than just fix the errors. A second thing that makes him an expert is his ability to connect his general diagnosis (such as "negative" and "wordy") to specific parts of the sentence. This kind of concrete and operational diagnosis of how these words are working lets him zero in on the words and sentence patterns he wants to change. (In Chapters 12 and 13 we will look at some of these techniques for testing and modifying your language itself.)

Experts like this one see global problems, but they also connect that diagnosis to actual parts of the text.

This three-step Detect, Diagnose, and Revise strategy helps you approach your text like a problem solver *when you need to*. Using this strategy lets you do each of these three quite distinct parts of the process better.

Working with a Collaborator/Imagining a Reader

Because only you know your own goals, you are the best detector for some problems. But if you know a topic too well or are new to the conventions of some discourse, it can be hard to read like your reader. For these and some other problems a collaborator is the best detector. And a collaborator may come up with a surprising diagnosis because he or she is bringing a different but valuable set of goals to the reading of your text. In addition, after working with a collaborator you begin to anticipate how other readers respond and become able to simulate a reader's response on your own when you need to.

Although you can always simply give your paper to a friend for response and advice, some times all people can say is how *they* would have written it. But their goals may not be yours. There are a number of ways to work with a collaborator that can be more informative. Here is the simplest: Ask your collaborator to go through your draft in the same way you did as a detector, marking places that cause confusion, break the flow, or seem somehow problematic as well as places with local problems and errors. Then ask your reader to say what he was responding to (but tell your friend that he doesn't have to say how it *should* be written or how to fix it!). Asking friends to work as detectors, not revisors, makes them willing to see you come back again.

However, if you are part of a writing group where everyone is working together, there are even more helpful ways to collaborate. Remember, you are managing this revision process to meet your own goals. So diagnose your own problems first and ask your collaborator to read with your goals and problem in mind. Some of the best collaboration comes when people put their minds to a common problem.

If you are feeling experimental, let your reader see only one paragraph at a time and ask her to tell you the gist of the paragraph and to predict what will come next. Are your signals to the reader clear enough that she gets it right? For an even more surprising test, feed the introduction out sentence by sentence asking your reader what she thinks the problem or issue or thesis is—at this point. Has she already come to a wrong conclusion before you get to your point?

Now consider the whole paper. Ask a friend to jot down two things: first, a nutshell or capsule statement of what he thinks you are trying to do or say (in his own words, not yours) and second, an outline or diagram of your major points and how they are related. If you are even more daring, have him try this some time after he has read the paper to see what really stands out in his memory.

Then, of course, you compare this reader's version against your own. To keep everything honest, you should jot down your own nutshell and outline *before* you read his. Bear in mind that there is always the chance your reader will misread or forget, but consider this as a signal that you need to increase your cues or redesign some part of your presentation. It also helps to know where your reader felt bored, because that is usually a signal that you have confused him or that your point is unclear.

If you don't have a live reader, you can simulate a reader's response in a number of ways. The simplest is to role-play, as was discussed in Chapter 6. Think yourself into the role of your reader responding to individual sentences in your text. What is she looking for, what does she need to do after reading this, and how would she react to what you just said? If you would like a more elaborate response, simulate a scenario in which you have a dialogue with the reader. Have her ask you questions such as "What do you mean?" "How do you know?" "Such as?" and "Why?" whenever your intuition tells you a real reader might do the same.

Many people find it very helpful to read their own writing out loud. Try it if you have some privacy. Listening to yourself out loud sometimes cuts out that private voice in your mind that fills in all the gaps between ideas and makes everything sound smooth and coherent. Reading out loud also helps you hear how your style sounds and see if your prose "flows" or doesn't.

Finally, if you are fresh out of friends, imagination, or privacy, there is a fourth technique called a highlighter test. You can simulate the comprehension process of a typical busy reader by going over your paper with a highlighter pen in hand and marking off all the titles, headings, and sentences to which convention or position in the paper give special significance. Assume that these are the major elements your reader will see and perhaps remember. Now check to see whether these highlighted parts contain the major information you want the reader to focus on and retain. Ideally the highlighted items will identify the goals of your paper and the top-level elements of your issue tree. If they don't, what have you given the reader instead?

The Revision Process in Action

Here is an example of a student writer's Review, Detect, Diagnose, and Revise process in action. As a reader, try to detect problems you see and make your own diagnosis before you read what the writer, another reader, and her instructor had to say. You may find yourself diagnosing some global problems differently than these readers. If so, ask yourself "why?" Take a look at your own assumptions or criteria for what this paper *should* do. Notice how a diagnosis is often based on the particular goals and criteria a person brings to reading. If you remember our earlier discussion of task representation in Chapter 5, you will see we have come full circle. The goals writers give themselves at the beginning define the task they are trying to do—the problem they try to solve. And those same goals will later dictate how they review their own text, what they even detect as a problem, and how they diagnose and revise the difficulties they do see.

> Draft #1. A problem analysis: Black Students in the College
> *[Points at which readers detected a problem are numbered.]*
>
> More minority students need to be admitted[1] into the College for many reasons. One reason might be to get funds from the government which would benefit the school.[2] Another reason, this gives[3] minorities a chance to learn in one of the best programs in the country. A final reason is to create a diverse social environment for everyone in the College. But right now this isn't happening.
>
> One solution to the problem might be to create an environment more appealing to minorities socially and educationally[4] . . .

Review Goals and Gist

By the time she completed this first draft the writer, Desiree, was sure that the problem she really cared about was recruiting—not just why it should be done, but why it was so difficult to do at her predominantly white school. Notice how this affects what she detects.

Detect

1. "Admitted" is the wrong word.
2. This sentence seems inappropriate. Her reader also put a mark there and simply said, "this feels out of place here."
3. At this spot both Desiree and her readers had to stop and reread the sentence to get it to make sense.
4. The sentence sounds awkward at the end.

Diagnose

1. Desiree chose to write this paper because she wanted to say that the College should admit more blacks. But as she wrote, she discovered that the interesting topic—and the real problem—was recruiting. This early focus on "admitted" no longer fit her master plan. Her detection at #1 was a local, word-level problem in one sense, but she detected it because it jarred with her global plan. And

its prominent location in the first paragraph meant it might mislead the reader, too.

2. People diagnosed the problem with this sentence in different ways. One reader said this idea seemed trivial compared to the other large social reasons, and the potential income was so small, it didn't even seem like a good argument. Another said it set up the wrong set of expectations at the beginning—it made the paper sound like the beginning of a financial analysis written from a company's point of view. These readers saw a relatively local problem with the sentence itself. But Desiree, as the writer, saw a more global problem and an opportunity because she had the big picture of her own goals in mind. Desiree's own diagnosis triggered a whole new plan for revision: the funding sentence was "out of place" because what she really wanted the paper to do was to look at recruiting from a student's point of view and show what the problem was. By describing the problem (rather than giving "reasons") she wanted to show that the College needed a stronger social network for black students on campus first if it wanted to convince students even to apply. Trying to diagnose the feeling of a "misfit" created by this sentence helped her see her real purpose.

3. The instructor diagnosed the first phrase as a sentence fragment ("Another reason *[is that]*") spliced onto another sentence ("This gives . . ."). But the real problem to correct, she said, was faulty parallelism. Since the sentence is logically parallel with the other two sentences that give "reasons," it should be grammatically parallel; for example, "Another reason is to give . . ."

Desiree's diagnosis didn't use technical terms, but it also described the problem. "I started out making this sentence like the one before. But after, the 'another reason' I just started a new sentence. You can make it all make sense if you read it out loud with pauses and emphasis, but it won't work in writing."

4. This local problem was one Desiree didn't detect herself. But when a reader found it awkward she easily diagnosed the trouble. She knew that the words "educationally and socially" were supposed to modify the idea of "appealing," and she had placed them at the end of the sentence for emphasis. But that position made her adverbs appear to modify "minorities," the word to which they were closest. From a reader's point of view these two words were misplaced modifiers.

Revise

1. Although the word "admitted" appeared to be a local problem, Desiree's diagnosis called for a more global action than simply changing the word to "recruited." She wanted to show that there was, in fact, a problem with recruiting. As you will see below, she decided to replace her simple assertion ("minority students need to

be admitted") with an introduction that *showed* why recruiting needed to be done and why the social environment made it difficult.

2. Diagnosing the global problems in sentences 1 and 2 actually helped Desiree form a new plan. She wanted her text to show how recruiting affected students. She considered simply asserting that it caused a problem, but she knew it would be much stronger if she could show the problem directly. So she decided to use her own experience to let the reader see the problem, too. She knew she had two good "reasons" for recruiting blacks, but most readers would already agree with those. What she wanted to write about was her own sense of why ordinary recruiting wasn't working. So as you will see, she reorganized the paper around this new purpose.

3 and 4. Diagnosing these two awkward sentences made Desiree more conscious of some of the options for sentence structure: she could solve the problem by giving all three sentences about reasons a parallel form (for example, "one reason might be to get . . . ," "another reason is to give . . . ," and "a final reason is to create . . ."), and by placing her misplaced modifiers in front of "appealing." But she was smart not to spend time actually working on these two local problems because in her more global plans for revision both of these sentences disappeared, even though the ideas were used later in the paper.

Here is the revision that came out of her diagnosis and plan.

Draft #2 A Black Need

"When the fall comes, we won't be around each other all the time to help work things out. Sometimes we're just going to have to survive on our own." As I walked into Freshman Writing on the first day of classes, these words from a fellow student in our Pre-College Program echoed in my mind. I was suddenly hit with reality; not only was I in a room full of people that I had never seen before, but what was worse, I was the only black. This strong feeling of uneasiness was one of the many reasons that made me feel that more black students needed to be recruited for the College.

Even with increasing recruitment, the total number of black students who apply to the College is low. Last year, for instance, the number of black students admitted nearly doubled. But still only a small number (about 11%) of the applications come from black students.

Review, Detect, and Diagnose

In reading this new problem statement, how would you define the particular issue this text is presenting? To review her new draft, Desiree tried to play the role of reader and imagine your response, by asking herself, "what would I think at the end of this paragraph? How would I state the gist?" She predicted that most readers would see her first point—new black students face a real problem. But she realized that readers might *not* infer her second point—that in order to recruit minorities, the College needed a social community of black students first.

Detecting that something is missing in the text, when it is clear in your own mind, is one of the hardest problems to spot. Her reader helped by asking why she leaped into discussing applications in the second paragraph; it confused him. His diagnosis was, "This needs a transition." But Desiree diagnosed the real problem by comparing the gist she had in mind with what her text really said. Here is the sentence she added at the end of the paragraph. Does it change your picture of the problem?

> The College is a great school academically, but its predominantly white environment discourages many black students from even applying. It needs a stronger black social community already here as the first step in recruiting.

As a reader I find Desiree's revised paper far more significant and interesting; I learned something by reading it. But the important thing about her revising process is that it let her reach and actually discover *her own goals*. Desiree went at this problem like the experienced writers described at the beginning of this chapter. She didn't spend all her time perfecting a first draft nor correcting local, sentence-level problems when she detected them. She wrote a thoughtful first draft but used it as a springboard to revision which began when she reviewed her own goals and tried to state her gist to herself. This writer used a number of techniques to detect problems, including listening to real readers and simulating a reader's response in her own mind. But notice how important her own diagnosis was. As the writer she kept testing the text against her own goals, so she was able to see opportunities for global revision. And because she hadn't spent all her time writing sentences and perfecting the first version, she was happy to throw away her prose but keep her good ideas for the second draft.

Seeing Desiree's process as four different steps—Review, Detect, Diagnose, and Revise—makes her thinking look like a slow and formal process when in reality many of these decisions happened within minutes or even seconds of each other. But breaking up the revision process this way lets you see that there really are separate actions that you can choose to take or to skip. You obviously have to make a conscious choice to use the strategies of reviewing your goals and diagnosing, since these may require a few minutes of focused thinking. But bear in mind, experienced writers regularly use those strategies because a little extra thinking can often make a large difference in writing.

In the rest of this chapter, we will look at some other problem-solving strategies you can apply to more local problems of structure and style.

GOAL 8

TEST and EDIT Your Writing

No matter how well they speak on their feet, few people can write their most vigorous, direct, or logical prose on a first draft. In fact, if you are working in an organization or attending an institution such as college, it may even seem natural to write in the padded style of organizational prose. If you are working with technical material, it may come naturally to write with a great deal of jargon or technical language. Or, if you are trying to juggle a number of facts and ideas, it may be easiest to write out a paragraph that looks more like a list than a well-balanced tree. When writing this way comes most naturally to you but you know it won't work for your reader, the most efficient procedure is to *write* it—however it comes—and then *edit*.

Some writers will ask, "Why not make each sentence and paragraph perfect the first time so you won't have to look at them again?" The answer is that if you separate the two operations of generating and editing, it is easier for you and you can get better results. The ultimate goal is always polished, reader-based prose. What changes are the immediate subgoals on which you choose to concentrate. Certain things, including organization and style, are sometimes better handled by an editor than an idea generator. *Editing can come at any point in the composing process*—after you have written a phrase, a sentence, a paragraph, or an entire draft. Sometimes editing is simply a final stage for fixing up details. But it is always a powerful strategy for writing.

The method is essentially the same one used in generating ideas and designing them for a reader. A writer-based prose style or unedited draft may be a reasonable and natural way to say what you have to say at that particular moment. Once your thoughts are out of short-term memory and down on paper, you can come back as an editor with a much clearer sense of where you are going and what you want those words to do.

The editing techniques you will learn in this chapter are not concerned with frills or with adding commas and dotting "i's." For an experienced writer, editing is a major tool for making meaning. A writer may in fact spend more time editing and restructuring a first draft than he or she did generating it. Once you know a few basic editing techniques, you will be able to transform sentences, paragraphs, and even entire discussions into far more effective statements of your meaning.

Knowing how to edit a first draft doesn't guarantee that you will produce elegant writing. But it does mean that you will be able to cope with three major problems professional writers have, and that you will be better able to write:

Economical prose that says exactly what you mean.

Forceful prose that holds your reader's attention.

Logical prose that expresses the hierarchical structure of your ideas.

 ## STRATEGY 1   EDIT FOR ECONOMY

The goal of this editing strategy is to help you write clear, direct statements that come quickly to the point and say exactly what you mean. Probably the most frequent complaint made about college and professional writing is that it is stuffy and inflated or overly technical and full of jargon. And yet, it is often written by dynamic people who can think clearly and speak forcefully when they are face to face. These people often use inflated or "institutional" language because they hope it will sound more impressive.

The problem with institutional language is that it handicaps the writer who really has something to say, burying his or her point beneath a load of excess language. Think of all the college catalogues, final reports, or political statements you never finished reading. As readers of such institutional prose, we all know how readers respond to an inflated style. It makes us mentally rewrite sentences to find the point and we soon begin to skip, skim, and read with diminishing attention. If you really have something to say and want to keep a reader alert and reading, you need to write economical prose that comes to the point.

INSTITUTIONAL PROSE AND THE ABSTRACTION LADDER

A direct prose style is much like the style people use when they speak. One of the chief differences between an institutional style and a personal speaking style is the level of abstraction. In fact, one decision you make every time you speak or write is how abstract or concrete you want to be.

Say someone asks you, "What do you expect to be doing tomorrow afternoon?" There are a number of ways you could convey your situation, ranging from abstract at the top to concrete at the bottom.

Abstraction Ladder

Expect to still be living and breathing, if all goes well.
  Will be busy.
    Will be busy part of the afternoon.
      Have a previous appointment at 4:30.
        Have my Friday afternoon tennis match at 4:30 with
        Joyce at the Stanton Avenue courts.

The level of abstraction you choose in replying will depend on who asked you and why. For example, on the phone you might choose to tell Ms. Howard, the chairperson of a committee to which you belong, that you "will be unable to make the meeting because of a previous appointment at 4:30." However, ten minutes later when talking to a friend, you might translate that highly abstract "previous appointment" into: "Oh, I have my usual tennis match with Joyce at the Stanton courts." One difference between the two statements is their level of abstraction.

When you write you likewise have a range of options, going from general, abstract terminology at the top to specific, concrete information at the bottom. In choosing your abstraction level, each choice carries an advantage and a price. By going to the top of the ladder and using nice, fuzzy abstractions you gain the advantage of breadth—and if you are high enough it's hard to be wrong. Weather forecasters do this when they say, "Unfavorable weather patterns may materialize in the near future." However, the problem with abstractions is that they are likely to be misinterpreted or just plain ignored. If you say, "It's going to rain like hell between now and 3 A.M.," you've put yourself on the line, but you can be sure your listeners will pay attention. In writing, you'll usually get much better results with concrete language.

Likewise, a vivid, direct prose style works because it cuts out unnecessary padding and puts powerful words in powerful places. This lets the main words and major ideas stand out prominently and, because the prose is direct and to the point, encourages the reader to listen.

KEY-WORD EDITING

One method that can help you achieve such a style is key-word editing. The method has five steps:

1. Divide the sentence into meaningful units.
2. Identify the key words or phrases in each unit.
3. Cut out unnecessary words, and build your statement around the key terms.
4. Pack in more concrete words when possible.
5. Let the actors act.

Consider this verbose sentence from a student paper:

The condition of excessive redundancy that exists in such a great degree in the academic paper assignments produced by members of the student body should be eliminated by grading policy and the example-setting capabilities that lie at the disposal of those who instruct such students.

The editor's first step is to divide the sentence into its natural, meaningful units. The next step is to pick out the key words and phrases in each unit—in other words, look for words that seem to be carrying the weight of the sentence's meaning. Thus:

> The condition of excessive *redundancy* / that exists in such a great degree in the academic *paper* assignments / produced by members of the *student* body / should be eliminated by *grading* policy and the *example*-setting capabilities / that lie at the disposal of those who *instruct* such students.

The third step is to cut out as much of the nonfunctional padding as possible and try to write a sentence around the key words.

> Redundancy in student papers should be eliminated by grades and the example set by the instructor.

The fourth step is to try to pack the sentence with concrete information where possible, replacing abstractions with more specific words. For example, since "redundancy" could mean wordiness or repetition or both, the writer needed to ask himself: "What exactly am I trying to say?" He decided he meant:

> *Wordiness and repetition* in student papers should be eliminated by grades and the example set by the instructor.

The final step is to let the actor act. Usually the person or thing that carries out the action of the sentence should also be the grammatical subject.

> *Instructors* should use grades and their own example to eliminate wordiness and repetition in student papers.

Here is another example. Try the key-word editing technique on this sentence, then compare your result to the revision that follows.

> In the event of your participation in a charter flight, the thing that should be noticed is the fact that there is a possibility of a change in fare necessitated by a last-minute change in fuel prices.

Writer's Stages of Revision

Steps 1 and 2: Divide into meaningful units; identify key words

> In the event of your *participation* in a *charter flight* / the thing that should be *noticed* is the fact that / there is a *possibility* of a *change in fare* / necessitated by a *last-minute change in fuel prices.*

Step 3: Cut out unnecessary words; build around key terms

> In participation in a charter flight, the possibility of a change in fare necessitated by a last-minute change in fuel prices should be noted.

Steps 4 and 5:
Pack in more
concrete words;
let the actor act

When you sign up for a charter flight, remember that a last-minute change in fuel prices can increase your fare.

Note that in the final revision the writer realized that the real actor was "you," the passenger, and translated the vague "change in fare" into the concrete "increase your fare."

The primary goal of key-word editing is to *put powerful words in powerful places.* As you could see in the first-draft sentences, the words that carried the writers' meaning were buried in verbiage. The subject and verb are the two most powerful parts of a sentence, and as readers we rely on those parts to contain the writer's essential information. The object position is also a strong one. In the first draft of the airline paragraph, the words in the powerful subject, verb, and object positions only told us: "the *thing is* the *fact.*"

Key-word editing, therefore, helps you say what you want to say by putting powerful words in these grammatically powerful places. Naturally you won't always want to use such a spare, economical style, but it is important to know how to write direct, concise sentences when you need them. When you try to write economical prose, think of yourself as giving a brief, well-prepared oral presentation. Imagine yourself in your reader's office: You have three minutes to tell him or her the gist of what you have to say. Concentrate on the essential points you want that person to remember. Think about the structure and emphasis of what you have to say, rather than making your phrases flow. You may well find that your key words are emerging, your excess words are dropping away, and you have become more direct and concrete.

STRATEGY 2   EDIT FOR A FORCEFUL STYLE

If you still feel your writing sounds heavy-handed, indirect, or verbose, other trouble-shooting techniques may help. Try some of these editing approaches.

1. LOWER THE NOUN/VERB RATIO

Test the following sentence for vigor by counting the ratio of nouns to verbs: Nouns/Verbs = _____ / _____ . Then rewrite the sentence using more verbs and fewer nouns.

The effect of the overuse of nouns in writing is the placing of excessive strain upon the inadequate number of verbs and the resultant prevention of the flow of thought.

Note that the original sentence contained one verb and eleven nouns, few of which were serving any useful purpose. Here is a revised version with a ratio of two verbs to seven nouns:

Using too many nouns in writing places strain on verbs and prevents the flow of thought.

Note that in some sentences you simply have to use many nouns—for example, you have a compound subject involving four or more essential nouns. But if you improve the ratio of verbs to nouns as much as possible, your prose will be more forceful.

2. TRANSFORM HEAVY NOUNS BACK INTO VERBS

Many of the heavy, polysyllabic nouns that make prose hard to read were made in the first place by adding a Latin ending to a verb. Often, your sentences will improve if you transform these nouns back into their original form. The five Latin endings below are the most common ones to watch for.

Remove this Latinate *ending*	from a *noun*	to produce a *verb*
-tion	resumption	resume
-ment	announcement	announce
-ing	dealing	deal
-ion	decision	decide
-ance	performance	perform

3. AVOID WEAK LINKING VERBS

The verb "to be" can be used as a linking verb ("The water is hot") or as an auxiliary or helping verb ("The water is boiling furiously"). The verb can take these forms:

be	is	was	been
am	are	were	being

When used as linking (or state-of-being) verbs, these words are simply saying that "something = something else." They can't act. If you want to state a definition, linking verbs are often very powerful ("To be or not to be, that is the question"). If, however, you are discussing an action, whether it is physical, mental, or metaphoric, linking verbs can weaken your sentence.

For example, you might write: "Galileo's telescope was helpful in the explosion of the myth of an earth-centered universe." But by

using a form of "to be" you waste some of the potential of the powerful verb slot in your sentence. To make the sentence more forceful,
transform the words "helpful" and "explosion" into verbs: "Galileo's
telescope helped explode the myth of an earth-centered universe."
Look for ways to change linking verbs into action verbs.

4. TRANSFORM NEGATIVE EXPRESSIONS

Sentences containing several negative expressions ("No, I didn't
know that the book was not on the shelf") are more difficult to
comprehend than positive expressions ("I thought the book was on
the shelf"). Negatives require increased mental processing time, and
they decrease the chance that a person will correctly remember
what he or she has read. Studies have even shown that implicit negatives such as "forgot" (didn't remember), "absent" (not present),
and "hardly," "scarcely," and "few" have a similar effect.

Obviously, negative expressions are necessary at times. But remember that they can dilute the forcefulness of your statements and
make your writing difficult to read. Test the following paragraph. Is
the meaning clear on a first reading? How many negatives does the
passage contain? Revise the paragraph and see how many negatives
it is really necessary to use.

> To avoid assuming the rapid decrease in temperature implied by the
> weather charts described above, other factors, used to make a prediction
> from past data, were not ignored. We feel the method can scarcely fail
> to predict the direction of temperature change for the not-so-distant
> future.

According to the writer, who hoped that all these extra qualifica-
tions would make her prose sound more scientific, what she really
meant was:

> In order to make a prediction from our past data and not simply assume
> a rapid decrease in temperature that the weather charts imply, we used
> a variety of factors in the calculation. We feel this method will effec-
> tively predict the direction of temperature change for the near future.

5. TRANSFORM PASSIVE CONSTRUCTIONS INTO ACTIVE ONES

Passive expressions, like negative ones, are harder to understand and
harder to remember. The difference between an active and a passive
construction is a simple one. In an active construction, the subject *acts:*

s   v
Moe made a decision.

In a passive construction, the subject is *acted upon:*

S ⌐—V—⌐
A decision was made by Moe.

While this example was a simple one, complex passive constructions create problems. Often readers must mentally transfer such
constructions into active ones as they are reading in order to comprehend them. If you see a number of passives, your reader may not
be willing to put in that extra effort; furthermore, you are forcing
him to waste energy on processing your prose when he should be
concentrating on what you have to say. Passive constructions may
also twist your meaning, because they push the actor, which should
be the subject of the sentence, into a less significant grammatical
position.

To transform a passive construction into an active one, try these
techniques:

1. Find the hidden actor in the sentence and let him (or it) act.
2. Convert an important noun in the sentence into a verb.

Usually, going from passive to active means switching from an impersonal to a personal style.

Passive
Negotiation of a contract with the Downtown Jazz Club was conducted
by our agent after an initial booking was used to establish contact. Performances are planned to start in two weeks.

Active:
Our agent negotiated a contract with the Downtown Jazz Club after establishing contact through an initial booking. We plan to begin performing in two weeks.

There are, of course, many times when a Latinate noun, a passive
verb, or a negative expression is exactly what you want to say. For
example, passives let you put emphasis on the result of an action
when the actor is not important, as in: "My telephone has finally
been repaired." The important thing is to know how to make your
prose direct and vigorous when you need to, and to recognize the effect your choice will have on a reader. A thank-you note that says,
"The assistance received from the members of your department was
appreciated," doesn't convey the warmth and sincerity of a more direct statement such as "I sincerely appreciated the help everyone in
your department gave me."

If you believe in an idea and want to stand up for it—but still be
serious and formal—you can do it in active, direct language. Which
of these conclusions to a planning report would you be more likely
to act on?

The conclusions drawn from the Co-op Board's study indicate that it seems advisable under present circumstances to initiate the adoption of the new work-sharing plan. If a presentation of all the facts of the plan is duly made to the co-op members, our opinion is that their approval will be forthcoming.

or

As a result of our study, we believe the Co-op Board should adopt the work-sharing plan. Once the members fully understand the plan, we think they will favor it.

PROJECTS AND ASSIGNMENTS

1   Give a 3-minute oral review of *your plan* for your paper based on reviewing your first draft. Ask your listeners what they want to know and what they expect to hear based on the plan you have in mind.

2   *Checklist: Using the Detect, Diagnose, Revise Strategy with a Collaborator.* Here is a systematic way to use this strategy.

   ☐ a.   Review your goals and review each major section of your paper for its gist in order to prime your detector.

   ☐ b.   Read your paper to detect and mark global then local problems.

   ☐ c.   Diagnose your global problems (writing down your analysis of the 2 or 3 most important ones) and try to diagnose or identify your local ones (here your handbook can help you figure out some diagnoses; you might wish to start a personal checklist of your most common problems).

   ☐ d.   Make a plan for revising that will solve your global problems (write your plan down for the 2 or 3 major ones) and make a note on how to fix your local ones.

   ☐ e.   Now you are ready to meet with a collaborator. Ask your reader to detect (anything) and to diagnose (1 or 2 global problems). Compare your reader's response with your own diagnosis and revision plan.

   ☐ f.   Then update your plan and revise.

3   Try the Detect, Diagnose, Revise strategy in a more informal way. Mark detections and jot only brief notes to yourself about your diagnoses and revision plans. (Is diagnosis more or less useful on different kinds of problems?) As you Detect, Diagnose, and Revise, test out two or three of the various techniques mentioned in the text, such as using a highlighter or a collaborator. Keep notes on how well those particular strategies worked for you *on this particular paper* and *why*. Write a brief (1–2 page) commentary on your decisions and on what you observed about your revision process to hand in with your revised paper.

4   Do you see different things in a text depending on your own role or your goals? Use the detect and diagnose steps as described in Assignment 2 (on a paper provided by your instructor) to respond *as a student who wants to learn* *something.* Now shift roles: you are an instructor whose main role at the moment is *to help the writer learn more about being effective.* Use the detect and diagnose steps. Write a paper on what you observed from this comparison, using your revision notes as examples.

5 Revise these sentences using the key-word editing technique.

☐ a. The thing that tended to bring about the manager's decision to stop hiring was the crisis caused by the sudden departure with company funds of the accountant.

☐ b. The key factor in the inflation of the cost of health care in the United States at this time would appear to be the unnecessary duplication of medical services.

☐ c. There has been an increase in the number of publications of pornography that sell at newsstands from zero in 1953 to a number well over thirty in the last five years.

☐ d. Although a great many of our citizens do not have any wish to see pornography that is of a soft-core nature in our public drugstores, the dictates of the "high percentage" rule allow the storeowner to be paid extra sums of money by the distributor to enable the display of magazines of this nature.

6 For each passage below, figure the noun/verb ratio, note the heavy nouns and negative expression, and locate any linking or passive verbs. Then rewrite each paragraph to make it as forceful as you can. Score your results and compare them to the original paragraph.

☐ a. Wanda Stevens, secretary, called public attention Friday to the organization of a demonstration to be held by the Walton Community Council. The demonstration is planned as a protest against the slowness of the city's clearance effort in a vacant lot in the Walton area. Usage of the lot as a playground by local children is not unusual, although it is filled with trash and garbage, and rats and other vermin are often reported there. A clean-up of the vacant lot is expected to be triggered by the demonstration.

☐ b. An announcement was made by Rhoda Brown, secretary, of the resumption of operations by the Consumer's Lobby. The decision of the lobby to increase concentration on local issues was noted in the announcement. Enrollment of members is expected to be encouraged through the elimination of previous office locations at some distance from local neighborhoods. In dealing with future legislation, legal recognition of neighborhood rights will be the intention of the lobby, Ms. Brown asserted.

IF YOU WOULD LIKE TO READ MORE

If you would like to know more about editing for style and editing with a reader in mind, see:

Farb, Peter. *World Play: What Happens When People Talk.* New York: Knopf, 1974. / This book provides a fascinating discussion of how people use language.

Gibson, Walker. *Tough, Sweet and Stuffy: An Essay on Modern Prose Styles.* Bloomington: Indiana University Press, 1966. / This book shows the connection between a person's writing style and personal style: whether he or she appears tough, sweet, or stuffy.

chapter twelve

Editing for a Clear Organization

GOAL 9
EDIT for connections and coherence

Edit your paper to ensure that the relationships between ideas are clear and that the logic of your structure is evident to the reader.

> *STRATEGY 1*   **TRANSFORM LISTLIKE SENTENCES**
> *STRATEGY 2*   **REVEAL THE INNER LOGIC OF YOUR PARAGRAPHS**

Everyone wants his or her writing to be well organized, to have a clear, logical structure. But what makes a structure clear to a reader, and how can you tell if yours will indeed be clear? In this section we will focus on one of the most important things you can do to organize and structure your writing: Make connections between ideas explicit in the text.

GOAL 9

EDIT for Connections and Coherence

One goal of a writer is to present his or her message so clearly that readers can build in their minds the same (or nearly the same) structure of ideas that the writer had in his or hers. However, writers often have important relationships in mind that they simply don't express in their words. Take, for example, this passage on how to take care of old pocket watches:

>   (1)   (2)
> Old pocket watches are delicate instruments. It's fun to look at the
>   (3)
> mechanism working, but don't open the case very often.

For the writer the connection between the ideas I've numbered (1), (2), and (3) is absolutely clear. Is it to you? Could you explain it? In the writer's mind there were meaningful connections between all of these ideas, but in her message there is only one important hook, the word "but." Here is how she revised it to clarify:

(1)   (2)
Old pocket watches are delicate instruments. *Although* it's fun to *un-*
                                                    (3)
screw the back and watch the mechanism working, don't open the case

very often *because even fine dirt can damage or stop the moving parts.*

Notice how the revisions work. In the first draft there was indeed a connection between idea 2, "it's fun to look at the mechanism working," and idea 3, "don't open the case." However, the focus of the sentence was on the idea of "fun," whereas the passage was intended to be about watch care. By adding the word "although," the writer indicated that idea 2, having fun, was subordinate to her main point, the warning about not opening the case. Then by adding the "because . . ." clause at the end, she spelled out why that connection or recommendation was reasonable, since opening the case can damage the watch. Here she had to add information that was missing from the first draft.

Finally, the writer added the phrase "unscrew the back" when she realized that some readers might not make the connection between having a pocket watch and watching the mechanism unless they knew the back could be opened. So the revision made that information, which previously could only be inferred, explicit in the text.

Editing for clarity means making the hidden relationships in your own thinking clear in your prose. Major points should stand out as important or inclusive; subordinate ideas should be put in their place. When you don't make these relationships clear, you leave part of the work of writing up to your reader. He may find your material hard to follow and end up feeling confused (or, more likely, assume that it is you who are confused). Perhaps even worse, he may fail to see your point and build a very different structure from the one you had mind. In either case you are asking the *reader* to draw inferences and make the right connections between your ideas. As can be seen from the pocket-watch revision, clear writing not only is more informative but is more persuasive because it often tells the reader the "hows" and "whys" behind your assertions.

Let us look now at techniques for testing your prose and making relationships explicit in both sentences and paragraphs.

 ### *STRATEGY 1*   **TRANSFORM LISTLIKE SENTENCES**

In editing sentences for clarity, look for two things. Does the sentence itself emphasize its main point? (Are powerful words in powerful places?) And are the underlying connections between sentences made explicit in the text?

One common irritant to readers is a sentence that reads like a list. For example: "The thing about a sentence with a listlike form is that there are a number of tiny points with independent bits of meaning that are set out in the sentence in a line so that the series of words and phrases read like so many pieces of popcorn strung out on a string." (Compare this to: "A listlike sentence, with its many independent points, lines up words and phrases like popcorn on a string.") Although easy to write, listlike sentences tend to be wordy and boring to read. Furthermore, like a list, they reduce all details to the same level of importance and make it hard for the writer to highlight what is significant.

TESTING FOR A LISTLIKE STYLE

To test your draft for a listlike style, look for an abundance of connective words (*that, which, and, plus,* etc.) and prepositions (*in, of, from, for, by, over, with,* etc.). Consider this sentence:

The demand (on the part) (of students) (for a greater number of films), (in addition) (to increases) (in film rental fees) (of most) (of the companies), has led us to request an increase (in the Film Society's allocation) (from the Funding Committee).

This sentence is weakened by two things. First, the grammatical subject of the sentence, "demand," is not the real actor (see Chapter 11). Second, the strings of prepositional phrases bog down the sentence. When you write a phrase such as "on the part," you create an independent little unit of meaning. A string of such independent units makes a weak sentence because it doesn't distinguish between major ideas and mere subordinate details, nor does it show their connections. A complex logical relationship is blurred into a simple list.

To transform listlike sentences, do three things:

1. Mark the prepositions (as was done in the preceding example), then promote key words to grammatically powerful places.

   We request that the Funding Committee increase . . .

2. Put subordinate information into a subordinate clause.

   Because students want more films . . .

3. Transform less important nouns into modifying words, and eliminate unnecessary prepositional phrases.

   . . . in addition to *increases* in *film rental fees* of *most* of the *companies* becomes

. . . and most companies' film rental fees have increased

Revised sentence:

Because students want more films and most companies' film rental fees have increased, we request that the Funding Committee increase the Film Society's allocation.

Here is another way to combine elements of a sentence. Many sentences contain more than one "simple sentence," that is, more than one subject-and-verb unit. When you review your writing, ask yourself two questions: (1) Have I made the connections between my simple sentences or ideas explicit? (2) If not, how else can I combine them?

In English there are three major ways people combine simple sentences or ideas: by making them parallel or coordinate to one another, by making one subordinate to another, or by adding one to another as a modifier. Each way of combining simple sentences asserts a specific logical relationship between ideas. Furthermore, our language offers a number of devices (grammar, punctuation, and signal words) for indicating this relationship and making it more explicit. Here are some familiar patterns for combining simple sentences.

Coordinate Pattern

This pattern sets up two equal simple sentences in parallel or in contrast with one another. Like all sentence patterns, it has signals that tell you to look for a coordinate structure.

> EXAMPLE: Mac is our accounts manager, *but* he works out of London.
> SOME SIGNALS: *and, but, or, :, ;*

Subordinate Pattern

This pattern lets you show a subordinate relationship between two ideas by making one grammatically subordinate to the other.

> EXAMPLE: *Although* he works out of London, Mac keeps a flat in Paris. *Since* Mac does keep the books, he will know the answer—*if*, of course, anyone can find him.
> SOME SIGNALS: *if, although, because, since, when, where, after*

Modifying Pattern

This pattern lets you pack additional information into a sentence by turning one simple sentence into a modifying phrase or clause.

EXAMPLES: Mac, *who never did pass math methods,* manages our accounts.

(Simple sentence: Mac never did pass math methods.)

Managing our accounts from London. Mac drinks dark ale at the Stewed Horse.

(Simple sentence: Mac manages our accounts from London.)

Our accounts, *ineptly managed by Mac in London,* are going to pot.

(Simple sentence: Mac manages our London accounts ineptly.)

SOME SIGNALS: Relative pronouns *(who, which)*

Verb phrases that tie the expression to the main part of the sentence (in this example, *managing, managed by)*

PLACEMENT OF SUBORDINATE OR MODIFYING MATERIAL

As we have seen, an independent simple sentence can be reduced to a clause or phrase and inserted somewhere in another sentence. The next question is, how do you decide where to place it? For example, say you have the sentence "Doggy Odor-Eater powder is now on the market," and you want to add the idea, "It was developed in the last ten years." You have three major alternatives:

Left-branching sentence   *Developed in the last ten years,* Doggy Odor-Eater powder is now on the market.

Mid-branching sentence   Doggy Odor-Eater Powder—*developed in the last ten years*—is now on the market.

Right-branching sentence   Doggy Odor-Eater powder is now on the market, *after being developed for ten years.*

Here are comments on the different types of placement.

Left-Branching Sentence

This pattern places the modifying clause at the beginning. Setting up a reader's anticipation with background or qualifying information placed first, left-branching sentences rely on the strong clarifying effect the subject has when it comes. But the longer the reader has to wait without knowing your subject, the more he is likely to become confused. Reread the second sentence in this paragraph, which was a left-branching one. Did you become impatient waiting for the subject, "left-branching sentences"?

Mid-Branching Sentence

This pattern—inserting modifying material between the subject and the verb—tends to create suspense, even to the point of taxing the reader with perverse demands on his attention. (The sentence you just read was a mid-branching one.) If the interruption is too long, the reader is forced to hold major ideas in suspension until the sentence is completed. Used more discreetly, the mid-branching sentence begins with a grammatically powerful element, shepherds modification into the middle—often isolating it with dashes—then makes the mind accelerate toward a tie-up idea and closure. For example: "Clearly, multinational corporations—the giant conglomerates that have covered the globe and permeated many foreign economies—are often the source of a country's economic stability."

Right-Branching Sentence

This type of sentence is developed by adding material: creating a structure that follows a natural pattern of the human mind just as this sentence does, with a series of qualifying phrases added one after another. Right-branching sentences are easy to write and easy to read—to a point. Their weakness is that the writer may tend to ramble on and create listlike sentences without sufficient force or emphasis.

THE SIMPLE-SENTENCE TEST

In editing for connections, watch out for paragraphs made up of a list of simple sentences. Here is an easy diagnostic test you can use to see if your paragraph reads like a list of ideas and if you need to add more cues to help the reader see connections between your phrases and sentences. Consider the paragraph below:

> Rescue dogs are often specially trained. They work in areas where a bomb or earthquake has buried people in debris. Their job is to locate where the persons are buried. Rescuers can dig them out before they suffocate or die from other injuries. The dog must guide rescuers to the spot and be willing to sit and bark until help comes. Some dogs can be easily trained for rescue. Collies, shepherds, Airdales—in fact, most working breeds—will happily bark. Spaniels, setters, pointers, and some hounds refuse to bark once they have found their person. They will bark at home if someone comes to the door, but not while they are working. These breeds have been selectively bred not to bark while working and not to scare the game.

To test this first draft of the paragraph, we can look for three things:

1. How many sentences *begin* with the main subject and verb (such as "dogs are," "they work") rather than with a signal word or a

subordinate or modifying clause? If all of your sentences start right out with the main subject and verb, your paragraph probably will read like a list of unrelated assertions. In Figure 12–1, the main subjects and verbs are shown in boldface; 10 out of 10 sentences have the initial pattern of main subject plus main verb. This helps explain why each sentence reads like one more item on a grocery list.

2. Next, count up all the additional simple sentences that are embedded within each sentence and that function as modifying or subordinate material. In Figure 12–1, all of the subordinate subject and verb combinations (or embedded simple sentences) are underscored. Add this number to the number of combinations you found in Step 1.

Now compare this total to the total number of sentences. How many simple sentences (including embedded simple sentences) did

FIGURE 12–1
An Application of the Simple-Sentence Test

1 main S/V	Rescue **dogs are** often specially **trained**.
1 main S/V, 1 subordinate S/V	**They work** in areas (where) a bomb or earthquake has buried people in debris.
1 main S/V, 1 subordinate S/V	Their **job is** to locate (where) the persons are buried.
1 main S/V, 1 subordinate S/V	**Rescuers can dig** them out (before) they suffocate or die from other injuries.
1 main S/V, 1 subordinate S/V	The **dog must guide** rescuers to the spot and **be** willing to sit and bark (until) help comes.
1 main S/V	Some **dogs can be** easily **trained** for rescue.
1 main S/V	**Collies, shepherds, Airedales**—in fact, most working breeds—**will** happily **bark**.
1 main S/V, 1 subordinate S/V	**Spaniels, setters, pointers**, and some **hounds refuse** to bark (once) they have found their person.
1 main S/V, 2 subordinate S/V's	**They will bark** at home (if) someone comes to the door, (but) not (while) they are working.
1 main S/V	These **breeds have been** selectively **bred** not to bark (while) working and not to scare the game.

you average per sentence? The example has a ratio of 17:10—almost two simple sentences per sentence. This is not bad, but could be improved given the closely related ideas in the paragraph. As discussed before, combining simple sentences into more complex sentences is an effective way to make more explicit connections.

3. Finally, count the number of signal words (they are circled in Figure 12–1) that tell the reader you are using a coordinate, subordinate, or modifying pattern. The example has 9 word or phrase signals and no punctuation signals.

In the following revision, the writer tried to vary the simple-sentence beginnings, combine more ideas per sentence, and increase the number of signals to the reader. In the revised paragraph, only 3 of the 6 sentences have simple, main-subject-plus-verb beginnings. The ratio of simple sentences (including embedded sentences) to total sentences is now 17 to 6, or nearly three simple sentences per sentence. And the passage now contains 14 signals to the reader.

Rescue **dogs are** often specially **trained** to work in areas (where) a bomb or earthquake has buried people in debris. Their **job is** to locate (where) the persons are buried (so that) rescuers can dig them out (before) they suffocate or die of other injuries. (Since) the dog must guide rescuers to the spot, **he must be** willing to sit and bark (until) help comes. (As a result) some **dogs,** (including) collies, shepherds, Airedales, and, in fact, most working breeds, **can be trained** for rescue; **others can't. Spaniels, setters,** and some **hounds,** (for example,) refuse to bark once they have found their person. (Although) they would bark at home (if) someone came to the door, these hunting **breeds have been** selectively **bred** not to bark (while) working (because) it would scare the game.

Remember that there are no set rules for how many sentences you should embed; simple sentences can be very effective. Nor will you always want to go to the trouble of counting up subjects and verbs. But this simple diagnostic test can help you focus attention on three common writing problems. It encourages you to make as many connections and give as many signals as seem reasonable in view of what you have to say. The final self-test in editing is always: Does my style fit my purpose and reflect my underlying meaning?

STRATEGY 2   REVEAL THE INNER LOGIC OF YOUR PARAGRAPHS

A paragraph is a working unit or functional part of a paper designed to accomplish something for you and the reader. Before editing a paragraph, you need to know two things: What is the point you want this paragraph to make, and how are your ideas actually connected? Then, when actually editing the material, you apply the test: "Have I indeed been able to make my point and connections clear in the text?"

Many people, however, rely on a weak editing test. They simply read the prose to see if it seems to "flow" or "sounds right." But what does that really mean, and how can a writer test effectively for these qualities?

Because "flow" is such a subjective concept, it is hard to test your own writing for flow as a reader would. What seems clear to you may not seem clear to a reader. The problem is that in rereading your own prose, it is easy to unconsciously supply the missing verbal and logical connections and happily conclude that the paragraph is indeed clearly organized. Flow, it seems, is a quality that rests in the eye of the beholder. Your organization may be logical to you as a writer, but it is only clear if the reader sees the connections that lead from one idea to the next. As editors, then, we need a more practical, operational definition of "flow" in order to test our writing from a reader's perspective, not our own.

BASIC PATTERNS READERS EXPECT

One of the simplest ways to test your paragraph organization is to see if it matches one of the basic patterns readers expect, such as topic sentence-revision-illustration, problem-solution, cause-effect, or chronological order. Patterns such as these have a special claim to fame because they are general patterns readers have learned to expect in expository writing. They are not necessarily the best patterns for every purpose, or ones you *should* use, but they are patterns your readers will expect and therefore can easily follow.

The TRI Pattern

Probably the most familiar way of developing a paragraph is to present the topic in the first sentence, refine or restrict it in some way in the next sentence, and use the rest of the paragraph to develop or illustrate the point. A shorthand name for this pattern is the TRI pattern (topic-restrict-illustration). If the paragraph is long or complicated, writers will often return to the topic at the end with a concluding statement that sums up the discussion. The pattern becomes a TRIT.

The paragraph above that began with "Because 'flow' is such . . ." is a good example of a TRIT pattern. The first sentence sets up the topic, "flow is hard to test," and the next sentence refines or restricts the meaning of "flow" as clarity. The rest of the paragraph illustrates why the assertion in the topic sentence is true. Finally, the last sentence makes some restatement of the topic, while also reaching a new conclusion based on points made in the paragraph.

This pattern requires a topic sentence at the beginning. However, for dramatic effect, writers occasionally want to save their point and lead up to it at the end of a paragraph. Sometimes this can be done with great impact, especially in literary or dramatic writing where readers expect to be pleasurably surprised. However, whenever your paragraph begins without a topic sentence or a preview of your point, ask yourself these two questions. First, will my discussion be so interesting or dramatic that I can risk keeping the reader in the dark—violating the reader's topic sentence expectation—and still have him with me when I do make my point? Secondly, will the paragraph be so clearly developed that the reader will be building the same idea tree I am, even though I haven't given him the top-level idea at the beginning? Topic sentences are only a convention, it is true, but they are powerful ones with sound, practical reasons for their existence.

The Problem-Solution Pattern

A second familiar paragraph pattern has only two parts, a problem and a solution. Paragraphs that start with rhetorical questions such as "How did earlier societies build such monuments as the pyramids?" often take the problem-solution pattern.

The Cause-and-Effect Pattern

This pattern is equally familiar. When a paragraph starts out "If the university chose to raise tuition by 10 percent . . . ," the reader automatically expects a discussion of the possible effects.

Chronological Order

If a paragraph starts out, "The first step in training a horse is . . . ," the reader is immediately primed for a chronological organization. He may expect a series of detailed steps for what to do first, second, and third, or he may anticipate a more general organization based on importance (for example, the first thing is to gain the horse's confidence, then worry about breaking it to lead).

The advantage of using one of these patterns is very simple: Readers know and expect them. By building on your reader's expectations, you increase comprehension and make your prose easier to follow. By the same token, when you use another pattern because it would better fit your purpose, you should increase the cues that tell the reader how ideas are related. Phrases such as "for example," "on the other hand," and "a final point" let the reader see your plan.

THE UNDERLYING LOGICAL STRUCTURE

This second test is both more rigorous and more helpful since it lets you see if the paragraph is logically developed around its main point. The test itself is merely an extension of the issue tree that can be used to organize ideas. In a hierarchically organized paragraph, there will be one top-level idea, which we can label level 1. (Generally speaking, this will be the first or topic sentence of the paragraph.) In the rest of the paragraph every sentence should be *related to* this level-1 sentence. It should also be either *parallel or subordinate to* the sentence above it.

There are two ways you could test your paragraph. One is to pull a key word or phrase out of each sentence and sketch an issue tree. The second, which we will discuss here, is the Francis Christensen method, indenting each part of a sentence or paragraph to show its relationship to the elements around it. This can be demonstrated with the following paragraph on creativity. Notice how the level-2 sentences expand or develop the ideas in level-1, the level-3 sentences develop level 2, and so on.

1 The stage of preparation must be taken seriously if one expects to be creative.

  2 Having relevant knowledge does not guarantee creativity, but it is certainly one very important condition.

    3 Van Gogh, while a revolutionary artist, had extensive knowledge and appreciation of traditional artists.

      4 Further, he spent years practicing technical skills, especially drawing, which he regarded as fundamental.

  2 Acquiring the knowledge needed for creativity may require a great deal of work.

    3 Indeed, the only trait Anne Rose found that was common to the leading artists and scientists she studied was the willingness to work extremely hard.

  1 and 4 Those who plan to relax until their creative inspiration seizes them are likely to have a long, uninterrupted rest.*

---

*John R. Hayes, *Cognitive Psychology: Thinking and Creating* (Homewood, IL: Dorsey Press, 1978).

Note that each idea in this paragraph is clearly and logically related to the ideas that went before it: It is either parallel or subordinate to the ideas above. For the reader this paragraph would "flow" because there are no gaps in the logic and no unrelated ideas to sidetrack the discussion.

A second thing to notice is that this paragraph follows the TRIT (topic-restrict-illustration-topic) pattern. And yet the final sentence is really serving two functions. From one perspective it is a level-4 idea that seems to develop the idea above it, that leading artists and scientists work hard. At the same time the final sentence offers us a more detailed statement of the topic introduced on level 1. It serves to recapitulate the main idea and tie the entire paragraph together.

Checking the structure of a paragraph can often help you detect any sentences that break the logical flow or depart for the paragraph's central focus. Such breaks in logic or focus are often very hard to identify by just reading, because the "unconnected" idea may be clearly connected to something in your own mind even if it does not fit into what you wrote on paper.

The paragraph below has just such a problem. The writer had let the topic and its train of associated ideas dictate what she said in the paragraph. Notice how the two italicized sentences are indeed *related* to the topic she is thinking about but are not clearly connected to the main *focus* of this paragraph, which is to describe, from the tenant's point of view, the possible results of protesting a rent hike. In the act of composing, the writer had simply been sidetracked from the point of the paragraph by her own knowledge.

(a) The primary objective of a rent-hike protest is to have the increase reduced or, ideally, eliminated. In practice there is little chance of either of these occurring. Realtors tend to be unresponsive to tenants' complaints about rent increases. *Some of the most frequent and unannounced rent hikes are found in the tight rental situations around urban universities.* But a protest can have positive results for tenants if it serves to limit future increases or influences the landlord to improve the building's upkeep. Ironically these benefits accrue only to those who remain in their apartments. For tenants who find the rent hike truly prohibitive, the only hope is to inform the realtor that they are moving out

(b) solely because of rent. *Sometimes entire groups of tenants get angry enough to leave in protest.*

Clearly this is a time for the writer to turn editor and evaluate this paragraph as a functional unit. Is each sentence here pulling its weight and contributing to the purpose the writer had in mind? One of the quickest ways to test the fit of each idea is to sketch a small issue tree of the paragraph, using the key words from each sentence. As you will see in Figure 12–2, the top idea of this tree is not an exact phrase found in the first sentence but a key word "results," that captures the point of the paragraph.

FIGURE 12–2
Testing the Logical Structure of a Paragraph

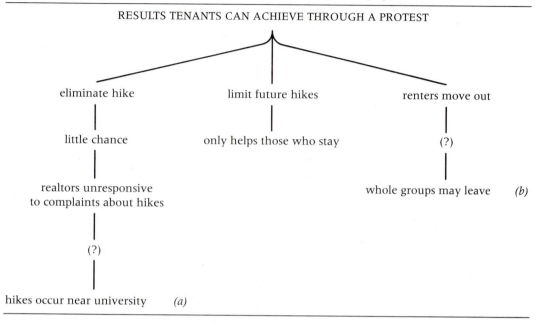

RESULTS TENANTS CAN ACHIEVE THROUGH A PROTEST

eliminate hike   limit future hikes   renters move out

little chance   only helps those who stay   (?)

realtors unresponsive
to complaints about hikes   whole groups may leave   *(b)*

(?)

hikes occur near university   *(a)*

One of the first things this tree tells us is that sentence (a) concerning rent hikes around universities does not develop the key idea above it (realtors are unresponsive) or the top-level idea (results of a protest). It is really connected only to the term "rent hikes." At the time of writing, the sentence had probably seemed to follow, since it does relate to the last words in the preceding sentence. But to the eye of an editor it is clearly irrelevant to the larger purpose of the paragraph and should be deleted.

Sentence (b) presents a slightly different problem. Although it does seem related to the main point of the paragraph, that connection is not explicit enough. The sentence is focused on what groups do, not on the results that such a protest can bring. By seeing this on her tree, the writer realized that she had shifted focus. Sentence (b) is indeed developing a part of the sentence above it, but it is not connected to the top-level idea of "results tenants can achieve." So she rewrote the last sentence to make it fit her real focus on results: "If an entire group of tenants can decide to leave in a group, this last-ditch effort will sometimes get results."

To sum up, then, checking the hierarchical structure of a paragraph by using either the Christensen indentation method or an issue tree lets you test the logical flow of a paragraph in two ways. It helps you see if each idea is logically related (parallel or subordinate) to other ideas and if all the ideas are logically connected to the main focus of the paragraph.

CUES FOR THE READER

Issue trees and the Christensen method let you see if the underlying organization, or skeleton, of your paragraph is logically constructed. But notice how both of these methods rely on your turning the paragraph into a *visual* pattern with numbers and levels in order to see its structure clearly. Unfortunately, as writers we are usually confined to writing lines of words on a page, which the reader must mentally construct into a hierarchy of ideas as he or she reads. This problem is a real one for the writer, because in the process of reading, people often misunderstand complex discussions and restructure the writer's ideas.

Fortunately, our language also provides us with a large repertory of cues, hooks, and signals that let us make our structure and connections explicit. Some of these devices have been touched on previously. They range form grammatical signals such as conjunctions, to punctuation signals such as colons, to visual cues such as paragraph indentation, to verbal cues such as pronouns and repeated words. Look at the paragraph in Figure 12–3 and notice how many hooking devices the author has used to tie the paragraph together.

Here are some types of devices used:

1. *Pronouns.* The "we" in sentence 4 hooks back not only to "higher animals" but to the readers themselves, referred to in the first sentence with "our."
2. *Summary nouns and pronouns.* The "this" in sentence 6 pulls together the entire paragraph by referring to "experiment" and "play" in sentence 5 and to the "process of learning" in sentence 1. Sometimes a summary noun will do this job. For example, sentence 6 might have read: "Perhaps the nature of a *trial run* is what gives. . . ."
3. *Repeated words.* "Scientist," "learning," and "errors" reappear.
4. *Repeated stems.* Bronowski used "an experiment" (the noun) followed by "experiments" (the verb).
5. *Rewording of the same idea.* A "harmless trial run" is later redefined as a "setting in which errors are not fatal."
6. *Punctuation.* Colons usually tell us that an example or a list follows. Semicolons connect two main clauses that generally are closely related.
7. *Parallel construction.* The grammatically parallel construction of "the scientist experiments and the cub plays" (sentence 5) emphasizes the parallel connection Bronowski wishes to make.

Figure 12–3
A Passage with Many Word and Phrase Cues

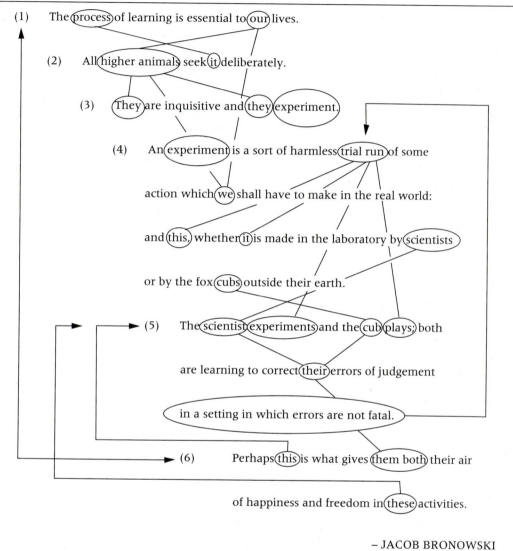

(1) The process of learning is essential to our lives.

(2) All higher animals seek it deliberately.

(3) They are inquisitive and they experiment.

(4) An experiment is a sort of harmless trial run of some action which we shall have to make in the real world: and this, whether it is made in the laboratory by scientists or by the fox cubs outside their earth.

(5) The scientist experiments and the cub plays; both are learning to correct their errors of judgement in a setting in which errors are not fatal.

(6) Perhaps this is what gives them both their air of happiness and freedom in these activities.

– JACOB BRONOWSKI

Source: Jacob Bronowski, *The Common Sense of Science* (Cambridge: Harvard University Press, 1953).

The writer's judicious use of repetition is effective because it meets an important expectation readers bring to prose. Normally, readers expect sentences to begin with something they already know about or with a word or topic that was previously mentioned. We might call this the sentence's *old information*. Readers then expect the sentence to add something new, the sentence's *new information*. Notice how this pattern of old information leading to new information works in the following series of sentences.

Shopping for a Turkey

The old information was stated in the title

Old . . .   New . . .
In buying a turkey, you get more meat for your money from a whole bird than from a boned, rolled turkey roast.

The reference to "the whole bird" is old information from the preceding sentence

   Old . . .   New . . .
And the bigger that whole bird is, the more meat you will have in proportion to bone.

The reference to a turkey's weight is old information, but the fact of one-half waste is new

Old . . .   New . . .
A turkey weighing less than 12 pounds is one-half waste.

"As a result" is old information, referring to the points made previously in the paragraph

Old . . .   New . . .
As a result, it is more economical to buy half of a large, 20 pounder than to buy a small, 10-pound turkey.

At times this pattern of moving from old information to new information is broken. For example:

Old . . .   New . . .
And the bigger that whole bird is, the more meat you will have in
          New . . .   Old . . .
proportion to bone. One-half waste is what you'll get with a turkey

weighing less than 12 pounds.

Sometimes the sentence with new information at the beginning is confusing and needs rereading. However, by violating expectations, you can also create surprise and emphasis, as the sentence above did by surprising us with the phrase, "One-half waste . . ." To sum up, then, you can use various kinds of repetition, including the old information/new information pattern, to make clear connections between sentences.

In addition, you can make explicit connections by using some of the common words and phrases listed in Figure 12–4. These not only

FIGURE 12–4
Common Cues for the Reader

CUES THAT LEAD THE READER FORWARD

To show addition:

		To show time:	
Again,	Moreover,	At length	Later,
And	Nor,	Immediately thereafter,	Previously,
And then,	Too,	Soon,	Formerly,
Besides	Next,	After a few hours,	First, second, etc.
Equally important,	First, second, etc.	Afterwards,	Next, etc.
Finally	Lastly,	Finally,	And then
Further,	What's more,	Then	
Furthermore,			

CUES THAT MAKE THE READER STOP AND COMPARE

But	Notwithstanding,	Although
Yet,	On the other hand,	Although this is true,
And yet,	On the contrary,	While this is true,
However,	After all,	Conversely,
Still	For all that,	Simultaneously,
Nevertheless,	In contrast,	Meanwhile
Nonetheless,	At the same time,	In the meantime,

CUES THAT DEVELOP AND SUMMARIZE

To give examples:	*To emphasize:*	*To repeat:*
For instance,	Obviously,	In brief,
For example,	In fact,	In short,
To demonstrate,	As a matter of fact,	As I have said,
To illustrate,	Indeed,	As I have noted,
As an illustration,	In any case,	In other words,
	In any event,	
	That is,	

To introduce conclusions:	*To summarize:*
Hence,	In brief,
Therefore,	On the whole,
Accordingly,	Summing up,
Consequently,	To conclude,
Thus,	In conclusion,
As a result,	

highlight the logical connection between your ideas, but often give the reader a preview of what is coming.

PROJECTS AND ASSIGNMENTS

1   *Checklist: Signals for Diagnosis.* This chapter has presented a number of editing techniques you can use to test your prose.

These techniques help you see whether you have made the connections between your ideas as explicit to your reader as they may be to you. The problem with such tests, of course, is knowing when to use which test. When you first detect a problem, you may know only that "this doesn't sound right." Here are some procedures that can help you decide which test to use and diagnose problems that are really there.

☐ a. Learn to listen for any faint sense that the text doesn't flow. Notice, for instance, when you have to rescan a sentence. Like an amplifier that boosts a weak radio signal, try to cultivate your awareness of those signals that say you have "detected" a problem.

☐ b. When you have detected a possible problem spot (for example, an unclear connection, a confusing phrase), spend 15 seconds trying to diagnose the problem instead of immediately rewriting.

☐ c. If your text sounds long and **wordy** or **unfocused,** then test for a **listlike** style and try other sentence patterns.

☐ d. If the text sounds too simple and **choppy,** then try the **simple-sentence** test.

☐ e. If a paragraph seems hard to remember or if you cannot see the **gist** of it once you have read it, then you might test for (1) does it have a **topic sentence** and (2) could it fit one of the basic **paragraph patterns?**

☐ f. If the text seems to **jump, not flow,** or if you need to **reread,** then test for the **cues** you have given the reader.

☐ g. Finally, bear in mind that sometimes the logic of a paragraph or discussion is not explicit in the text because it is not really clear in your own mind yet. Your text is simply telling you to think a little more. When that happens, concentrate on making the connections for yourself first, and on fixing the text itself second.

IF YOU WOULD LIKE TO READ MORE

If you would like to know more about editing with a reader in mind, see:

Becker, A. L. A tagmemic approach to paragraph analysis. *College Composition and Communication,* 16 (October 1965) 237–42. / This study includes a discussion of basic paragraph patterns.

Christensen, Francis. A generative rhetoric of the paragraph. *College Composition and Communication,* 16 (October 1965) 144–56. / This article gives a detailed discussion of hierarchical paragraph organization.

Larson, Richard. Toward a linear rhetoric of the essay. *College Composition and Communication*, 22 (May 1971) 140–46. / The author studies the function of paragraphs in a developing argument.

O'Hare, Frank. *Sentence-Combining: Improving Student Writing Without Formal Grammar Instruction*. Urbana, IL: National Council of Teachers of English Bulletin, 1973. / This book gives a detailed discussion of ways of combining simple sentences, or kernels, into complex sentences.

chapter thirteen

Two Case Studies: Research Writing

In the case study of Joan (Chapter 3) we watched a writer trying to generate ideas and make meaning out of her own experience. The two writers we will look at here face a different part of the writing problem. They have done a lot of research and have a great deal to say, but they must transform what they know to meet the needs of their readers. For Kate this will mean meeting the expectations of a professor and responding to an assignment; for Ben this means collecting his own data to explore a hypothesis and presenting his interpretation of both the data and his sources. For his paper to succeed it must be both persuasive and well supported. In watching Kate and Ben's papers develop we will see how both writers have to actually rethink and reorganize their ideas in order to design their papers for a reader.

 ## CASE STUDY OF KATE: DEFINING A RESEARCH QUESTION

Kate, a sophomore, is writing her first college research paper and facing that great unknown: "What does the teacher want?" or, more accurately, "What is it academic readers in general expect?" Kate is still making the transition from high school writing to college writing and is trying to figure out how to write a serious academic paper that does more than just display what she knows. This case study describes some of the processes she went through in trying to get an answer.

Kate's assignment, from a course in cognitive psychology, was a relatively open-ended one: "Write a paper on creativity based either on your own experimental project or on a biographical study of some 'creative person.' In doing so, treat some of the theories and principles covered in this course." Papers by other students ranged from studies of Einstein and Shakespeare to one on "Walt Disney: An American Original." Kate had enjoyed her own research on Charles Darwin, and the writing problem really began when she sat down to do a draft of the paper. At this point, Kate had done her homework well, although she felt the research would have been easier if she'd

had an idea of exactly what to look for in the first place. Nevertheless, she had accumulated a great deal of information and it even fell
into a rather tidy outline.

Kate's plan was to start with a catchy beginning, something like,
"Creativity is a thing envied by those who feel they are noncreative.
Quite often a noncreative person will marvel at other people's abilities and talents and exclaim on their impossibility and unbelievabil-
ity. . . ." Then she planned to work through her outline, which is
shown below, filling in the material she had found in the library.

   I. Definition of creativity
  II. Darwin's theory of evolution
      A. Social effects—controversy at the time
      B. Main points of the theory
 III. Darwin's biographical background
  IV. Four theories of creativity
      A. Romantic
      B. Freudian
      C. Wallas' stages
      D. Problem-solving

Everything seemed ready to go, but the minute she began to write
she knew this was going to be a second-rate paper—boring to write
and dull to read. Although it looked well organized, there was nothing holding it together, no reason to write. Kate felt she would simply be plodding through each topic on the outline and writing it up.
This method—outline the topic and fill in the blanks—had worked
well enough in high school, but she feared it wouldn't produce an effective academic paper. It was hard to imagine a good reason for anyone to read it—or write it.

Here was the dilemma: Kate had worked hard on the course and
on Darwin, and had learned a lot, but her paper wouldn't show that
she could *do* something with her information. Perhaps a "flash of inspiration" could have saved the paper, but the more frustrated and
helpless she felt, the less likely she was to become inspired. Kate felt
stuck.

It's hard to say whether frustration, common sense, or the lateness
of the hour was responsible, but the next step in Kate's writing process was a return to the basics. She and three friends sat down one
night to figure out what the reader's expectations really were, or, as
they put it, "If I were the professor, what would I want?"

JAY: Well, I can tell you what I *wouldn't* want. I wouldn't want someone to recite the textbook back at me and feed me another summary of
creativity theory. There are 25 papers to read from this class. I'd climb
the walls if everyone just repeated the ideas back to me.

ANN: I don't think I'd be so keen on reading large chunks of straight
biography either. I'd keep asking myself, "What's the point?"

KATE: OK, I agree, but you've just demolished two-thirds of my paper. What did I do all that research for if I can't use it? And the assignment says to treat some of the principles of the course. You have to work that stuff in to show you've learned something.

CHEN: Well, if *I* were assigning this paper, here's what I'd want. Naturally I'd want you to show me you know the course material, but what I'd really want to see is if you can *use* those theories—not just repeat them. I'd expect you to *apply* the theory to some new problem like explaining what made Darwin or Shakespeare creative. The exam will show if you've read the text; I think a paper like this should show you can *think*.

ANN: I agree with that. I'm working as a grader for a freshman history class, and we were told to look for two things: if the person can discuss the readings well, that's a "B" paper; but in order to get an "A," they have to come up with their own ideas and be able to support them. That's what a real historian has to do, of course. So we're supposed to treat these papers as if they were going to be submitted to a magazine or journal. I think what Professor Howard wants is for everyone to learn the material and then be able to think like a historian and really *use* it.

KATE: All right, but how do I use creativity theory? What is there to analyze about Darwin? He made a huge splash—though, of course, come to think of it, he wasn't the first person to talk about evolution; Lamarck was. Would you still call him creative? . . . You know, what I could do is use the theory to test Darwin—was he truly a "creative" thinker—and at the same time test the various creativity theories. Do they really account for a person as important as Darwin?

JAY: Now I think you're getting somewhere. Chen was right about applying the theories, not just repeating them. It sounds as if you've come up with a real problem or issue to analyze here. The paper is even starting to sound interesting. I think it would meet the professor's expectations because you'd be using the material in the course to support your own thinking.

Actually, talking this over may help me with my own paper I'm doing for the course, on Thoreau. I was working up sort of a straight-forward informal outline, but maybe I should pursue a thought that kept occurring to me when I was doing my research. One of the most perplexing things about Thoreau is that today everyone thinks he's a genius, but in the 1860s no one thought he was creative at all. The botanists thought he was incompetent, and the poets thought he was just imitating Emerson. I think I could tie this contradiction into some of the creativity theories we've been studying.

According to Kate the discussion went on for another hour, but the main ideas that emerged were relatively simple ones:

1. Professors who read academic papers have two very clear expectations. Naturally they want to see that you are learning, but they also expect you to show your ability to think: to use your knowledge to *create* and *support* your own ideas.

2. One important way of coming up with new ideas is to identify a problem, conflict, issue, or contradiction associated with your topic. Papers that merely "cover" a topic are often only school-room exercises. But once you define a real problem or issue within that topic, you have created a real-world writing problem: You have a reason to write and your reader has a reason to listen to you.

Example 1 shows the new plan and introduction that Kate developed. Compare it to her old outline and notice these two differences: First, Kate's paper is no longer a survey of information. Instead, it is organized around a problem or question that the reader (and Kate) will find compelling. Darwin's biography and theory no longer sit in a section of their own. Instead Kate *uses* the information she found in the library to support her own ideas about Darwin's creativity.

Secondly, the paper now has a hierarchical structure. Kate's old plan was a list of topics. Now she states her two top-level ideas in the first paragraph and organizes the paper around them. Notice too that Kate isn't using a traditional topic outline. Her new outline is more a plan for what she wants to accomplish in each section and a reminder of what information she should use to do that. What follow are the first draft of her problem/purpose statement, which sets up the issue she intends to address, and a plan for what she wants to do in the rest of the paper.

KEY FEATURES OF RESEARCH WRITING

Essays are often based on the writer's own experience and thinking; memos and short reports are often written when the author has special knowledge to pass on. Research papers, however, are a form of investigative reporting. The writer not only tracks down new information but tries to test and support these new ideas in the paper itself.

Example 1
Kate's Goal-Directed Plan

The Creativity of Charles Darwin

Introduction

In 1859 Charles Darwin, a British naturalist, published The Origin of Species, and its impact on the world was tremendous. Indeed, Origin is probably the most influential biology book ever written, and some historians even go so far as to claim that this book ranks second only to the Holy Bible. And yet, Darwin's ideas were not strictly new; he did not actually "create" the notion of evolution. Was he just a controversial thinker rather than a creative one?

In this paper I will look at the creativity of Charles Darwin by asking two questions. Does Darwin's work support or contradict current psychological definitions of creativity? And secondly, what is the best way to account for Darwin's own kind of creativity? Which of the major theories best fits the facts of Darwin's life and work?

Discuss point 1: Is Darwin "creative"?

Define creativity. (Use Hayes, p. 215: "a novel, surprising, and potentially useful act.")

Does Darwin fit? Yes, because

1. He contradicted the theory of the special creation of man held by the church and the general public.

2. His notion of natural selection raised a controversy in the scientific community as well.

3. While Lamarck proposed the idea of evolution before Darwin, Darwin was the first to make the theory scientifically plausible. (Use quote from Farish, p. 333: "No one had ever presented evolutionary theory so forcefully and so well documented.") Back this up with a description of Darwin's biological knowledge and research methods.

Sum up answer to point 1

Discuss point 2: Which theory fits Darwin?

1. Romantic inspiration. No.
    Discuss the 20-year development of Darwin's theory and cover his four key principles here.

2. Freudian sexual energy theory. Possible.
    Mention limited biographical evidence from Darwin's 5-year voyage on the *Beagle*.

3. Four-stage theory—Wallas. Partially true.
    Discuss the biographical information that fits this pattern, but note the misfit with the third stage.

4. Problem-solving theory. Best fit.
    Show how Darwin spent years of study and slowly pieced his ideas together, trying to fill in gaps in order to form an integrated theory.

Sum up answer to point 2

Many of us are familiar with a watered-down version of a research paper done in grade school—the library paper that was mostly a string of quotations and paraphrases, lightly glued together with transition sentences. My memory is that the goals of such papers were usually to collect a lot of note cards, say ten pages or more on some **topic,** and get the footnotes right. I didn't enjoy them.

A *bona fide* research paper, however, is genuinely exciting to do. To begin with, it is based on a problem or question in which you are already interested, not on a **topic** picked out of the blue. People choose to write research papers because they have a vested interest in knowing the answer. (Most of the books and articles cited in the bibliography of this book were written by just such people.) The "research" behind a researched paper can be done in many ways—in a library reading original manuscripts or reviews and criticism, in a medical laboratory running experiments, on the computer calculating alternative effects, in the field collecting notes and taped interviews, or in experimental conditions as you watch people trying to solve a problem.

Researched writing is a kind of detective work that rests on two premises:

1. A number of good heads are better than one (so that's why you consult other sources, run experiments, or base your own conclusions on a collection of ideas and results from varied sources).
2. People are more likely to read and believe good ideas if your analysis is supported by evidence you can document and/or by data you can show.

But the excitement of research is that investigative urge to answer a question worth answering or to solve a problem—even if your question starts out as wide open as:

What really happens when . . . (people argue, learn to run 20 miles, and so on)?

Why is it that . . . (some tennis rackets are better than others, this novel is called a "romance," and so on)?

How did this strange thing come about . . . (the Texas cattle drives, the changes in computer software, and so on)?

Investigative drive is probably the key to good research writing in most fields. This goal-directed use of research is part of what it means to "think like" a historian, a physicist, a psychologist, or a critic. Here is how a historian once described it to me. He said, "When I write a paper, I start already knowing a lot about my subject, the Korean War. And I have a hunch, a sense that I have something new to say. So I go after the data to find out what *did* happen—to prove or disprove my hunch—and I write to argue and prove my point. By contrast, it seems that some of my students use what I call the "grocery cart" approach to history papers. First they pick a topic, go to the card catalogue, find there is nothing on it, and then begin to wander down the appropriate library shelves, picking out the new-looking books—like dropping oranges in a grocery cart—looking for "good quotes."

Although the grocery-cart process has a certain appealing simplicity, it is unlikely to produce a good paper; it won't give you any experience in thinking like a researcher; and it certainly isn't a very exciting way to spend time. If you are interested in doing research—not just doing a "research paper" with footnotes—the first step is to put yourself in the place of that historian, or as close to it as you can get. Start with an area you know something about or care enough to find out about. I often set aside some time simply to read, refresh my memory, get the big picture, and just think. But most of all, try to locate a question, a problem, or an issue that will reward your effort and guide your research. Be flexible, because your notion of the problem itself is likely to change. But Minsky's Maxim applies: Any plan is better than no plan.

Finding Information

Doing research-based writing presents you with two tasks: (1) finding information (which we shall consider now) and (2) arguing with evidence (which we shall consider later). Rather than try to outline a single procedure for finding information, let me offer you some rules of thumb experienced researchers use.

1. Go to "expert" sources. One of the best-known techniques for doing good research is to ask another expert. If you have good questions, you will usually find that people are quite willing to share their knowledge. Some good sources are (a) a teacher in the subject area who can often send you to the major books and sources first, (b) a practitioner who may have practical knowledge not found in books, (c) a research librarian who is a professional whose job is to help you find the best sources, including indexes and guides you may not know about. Don't wander aimlessly in a library when an expert can point a better way. The bibliography in the major books you consult is another expert source—the author has already done some of the searching for you.

   "Expert" sources can also be defined as those best adapted to the job. If you are trying to decide what to read, look for an annotated bibliography that comments on sources. If you are investigating an established area, look for books that give an overview and synthesis. But if you are working on a recent development or a current question, consult up-to-date periodicals and scholarly journals.

Finally, a full-size standard handbook like the *Harbrace College Handbook* will give you detailed information on standard library sources and on standard procedures for documentation. You should probably own a handbook for other reasons, but they are also available in the reference section of libraries.

2. Good questions get good answers. Like any detective, you need a good cover story when you begin a search for information. Try to write this script for yourself:

   a. The question/problem on my mind is _____ .
   b. I want to review the scholarly debate on _____ . Who are the major sources?
   c. Or, I am interested in applying ___(this theory)___ to (my question). How could I learn more about it?
   d. Or, I have a hypothesis that _____ is relevant to (my problem). How could I test that idea?
   e. The key words associated with my topic (which might appear in library guides and in book indexes) are _____ . Where can I learn more?

   Use these "loaded questions" when you consult your expert sources and when you review books.

3. Be pragmatic. Define a problem or question you have the time and space to handle. A fifteen-page paper is only about 30 minutes of talk (less than half a class session). If the question is too large, you will be left making broad, airy generalizations (discussing the nature and history of "romance," for example) when you could be saying and supporting something specific (showing how one kind of romance tradition works in this novel). The problem is that readers quickly begin to skim these grand but unsupported statements—even if they agree—because they are looking for evidence in the text. So give yourself the kind of focused problem that will let you do solid, intelligent work that can stand on its own, even with a reader who doesn't agree.

4. Leave a clear trail as you work. There are certain tricks of the trade researchers use, because the extra minutes they take in the beginning often save hours in the long run.

   a. Write down basic bibliographic information on each book or source you consult when you use it: call number, author, title, publication date and source for books, and the beginning and ending page numbers for quotations.
   b. Keep separate ideas and topics on separate pieces of paper or cards. The order in which you find ideas and take notes

will not match the logical order you will want to impose. It helps to be able to physically sort and shuffle all of the information.

c. Keep track of the sources of any information—whether it is a quote, a paraphrase, or an idea—on the note. Don't count on finding that place again if you don't. And take any quotation down exactly as you find it, including underlining and punctuation.

d. Think before you take a note. Where it is possible, make your notes show a gist, or main idea, from your point of view; annotate as you go along. Most important, don't just collect information and plan to figure it all out later. It is a lot faster in the long run to do your thinking and planning as you search.

e. Finally, as you read, look for the facts, data, or arguments that support any ideas you find. Remember that the other researchers you read, even published ones, are like you; they can be wrong and they certainly could be argued with. If it is an important issue, you are likely to find that your sources disagree with each other. That is normal and healthy, but it means you must read with a critical eye, not only for good ideas but for the evidence that supports them. Your paper will be stronger if you argue from evidence rather than merely cite authorities.

Arguing with Evidence

At heart, a research-based paper is no different from any other analysis—you must define a central problem or issue, think it through, and try to present and defend your conclusions. But because a researched paper also tries to provide evidence in the form of other sources or data, it has some special conventions. If you examine them, they are actually quite sensible ones.

Using Documentation. Accurate documentation, in the form of footnotes and a bibliography, allows other people to use your research by going back to original sources and to evaluate the strength of your argument by seeing its foundation. If you use an idea, a paraphrase, or an exact quotation, document its source. Do this, first of all, because it is honest; give other researchers their due. Secondly, do this because such support is evidence for your own argument. The reader is more likely to believe you if you can show that people already agree about much of the issue and that you are adding knowledge or clarification. Readers are naturally more skeptical of writers who set up weak straw men only to knock them down or who suggest that everything they say is original. Research is, in part, the art of building upon what other good minds have created. Documentation is one way you can convince the reader and build a foundation for yourself.

Using Format.   A researched paper does not have to be a single, flowing argument, the way a short essay does. You can use different sections with headings to do different kinds of work for you. Here are some optional sections found in many research papers:

> *Introduction.* This sets the stage, creates a context, or provides background if the reader needs it.
>
> *Problem/purpose statement.* This section may run from a paragraph to a page or two long. It is the initial statement that defines the problem, presents your question or thesis, and gives the reader a road map for reading the rest of the text.
>
> *Review of research.* Data-based studies sometimes move from a concise problem/purpose statement to a review of the relevant previous research or theories. This then leads into a discussion of the writer's own study.
>
> *Research methods.* For reporting studies based on data you have collected, this is a necessary statement about how you collected that data, what methods or research design you used, and who your subjects were. It should be quite concise but detailed enough to let someone else duplicate your study. Data-based papers may also use separate sections titled "Results" and "Discussion."

Sometimes journal editors and teachers will request specific formats or methods of documentation (such as MLA or APA style). Your handbook will show you the details. But in general you can look on format as a tool. In organizing a paper, use whatever format and headings that will fit your purpose and present your material. Here are two general formats often used:

Argument-Based Papers	*Data-Based Papers*
Problem/Purpose Statement	Problem/Purpose Statement
Discussion	Review of Research
Section Headings based on	Research Methods
the argument	Results and Discussion
Conclusion	Conclusion

CASE STUDY OF BEN: DOING RESEARCH

The following case study of a research paper by Ben Craft gets us a bit closer to the process itself. These excerpts from his process log show some of the decisions, plans, and problems that go into doing a researched paper.

Process Log

In keeping this log of his own composing process, Ben said his goal was to discover something about the kinds of choices and decisions he had made at the major turning points in his writing process—that is, what had he done and why. The design and content of the log reflect his goals.

Ben Craft
Process Log for Research Paper

DAY	ACTIVITY	OBSERVATIONS AND COMMENTS
Oct. 8	Discuss in class	I didn't come away from class with a topic. No ideas leap out. Massive lack of excitement. I don't think I have much to say on anything. Listed topics, photography, logic, argument, sportscasting techniques. All seem enormous.
	Reread assignment	Noticed phrase in assignment, "think about problems noticed in your own experience or reading." That puts me on a different track. Thought of problems like trying to have a reasonable discussion with my roommate. But how do I turn that into a paper?
Oct. 9	Trying on ideas	Keep coming back to a mental image of 2 people in front of library arguing. Want to work on argument somehow I think.
	Checked card cat. after lunch	Discouraging. The topic doesn't hang together. Plato, debate, rhetoric, linguistics, legal, history of, how to win, family arguments . . . Can't turn my mental image into a topic.
Oct. 10	Prof. Enos said something about "power of the printed word"	Chance comment. It kept sticking in my mind. That's the question: are written arguments more powerful just because they are written? *Powerful arguments.* Felt very clever!

(Continued)

DAY	ACTIVITY	OBSERVATIONS AND COMMENTS
Oct. 11	Spent about 20 minutes listing features of arguments	This was one of several not very systematic efforts to get a handle on the question or to get a hypothesis. Kept feeling stuck. Not sure just what I should be doing, because I don't know the answer to my question. And yet how should I know it? Decided to talk to Prof. Stratman who teaches argument.
Oct. 13	Looked at 2 introductory books	Talking to Stratman and reading 2 books he mentioned is a great boost. Realize now I felt blank because I needed to read. Got really hung up for awhile on reading about the oral vs. written language—a big controversy. Was going to come up with a theory about oral vs. written argument. But finally realized it would just end up being another one of those speculation papers.
Oct. 15	Still reading	Breakthrough. Have an image of my problem as people arguing in the dorm, but the argument always seems to go in circles. Yet written ones seem to go forward. Reading to find out why, but no one talks directly about it. Ended up realizing it was the form or structure of the argument itself that seemed different. I remember being excited about this, and instead of scanning the books for answers or just speculating, I started writing down all the examples I could think of, of actual arguments and the moves people made. Then went to the Union to eavesdrop on real arguments and test my ideas, made more notes. Felt I really had something solid.
Oct. 16	Went to the library	Had some ideas now, but realized reluctantly that I needed more info on the form of argument. Yet felt when I went to the library that I was procrastinating and should have stayed at home writing. But reading turned out to be the correct decision. Used to think that that blank feeling was just a block that would

DAY	ACTIVITY	OBSERVATIONS AND COMMENTS
		go away. Why is it so hard to realize it when that blocked feeling really means "go read"? Felt sleepy and overwhelmed by the info while reading. But told myself I would wake up and sketch out a new plan tomorrow from 8–10 A.M.
Oct. 17	I did it! Have a real problem now	Now I am starting to work systematically. Is it supposed to take this long to really know what you are doing? Talked to Stratman again, this time about how to collect some data on my own. I'm psyched.
Oct. 20	Collecting data	
Nov. 2	Doing a draft. Actually putting pieces together	Didn't realize how undisciplined my writing process was! For example: 3:15 fell asleep 3:30 went out for coffee 3:50 got up to take a walk and get a plan 4:15 got coffee and stopped to talk 6–7 went to dinner; talked about argument, got a buzz, and was taking notes on the napkin 7–12 wrote draft; didn't look back In retrospect I realize how much real work got done when I wasn't legally "writing" but was walking around thinking and talking about it.
Nov. 4	Tried to explain my ideas to two other guys	Found out they kept thinking of all arguments as fights. Had to explain the idea of argument as it comes out of logic and rhetoric. That gave me my introduction.
Nov. 7	Doing a second draft	Change I am most pleased with is changing from a sort of boring description in some places to a more persuasive style.

Some of the problems, decisions, and breakthroughs Ben described are unique to him and this paper. But some are common to the process of research writing. Let me note just three.

Ben seemed to be trying two different strategies for finding a research question. One was to fish for a topic and go through the card catalog for subtopics, a version of the grocery-cart tactic. The other way was to think of a problem that interested him and use a combination of reading and mulling it over to define a researchable question—that is, a question or hypothesis he could really test or answer.

Another major decision Ben made was to drop his grand theory in favor of a more limited, solid, supportable idea. Research writers sometimes *do* propose grand theories, but they usually spend some years testing and supporting those theories, and their papers are based on evidence. From your experience, what is the logic behind the grand-theory strategy when students, who don't have the time to support such claims, use it?

In rereading his log Ben said he was surprised to see how many times he had felt blank, confused, or stuck. But he also noted that the breakthroughs came when he took that feeling as a signal to change his strategies—to read more, talk to someone, think of concrete examples, or actually collect some data. This is not an uncommon situation. People often get blocked when they are writing because they really need to do some thinking or reading. The fact that words don't flow is just a symptom. Yet, as Ben says, it is often hard to recognize that feeling as a signal to change strategies or learn more before you write.

Look over Ben's log for evidence of other common problems and breakthroughs you recognize. How would you say Ben handled his problems? What led to his breakthroughs?

The Final Paper

Below is an excerpt from Ben's final paper. I find it particularly interesting to note how his process log entry on November 4 turned into the problem/purpose statement that begins his paper, and to see how he has organized his reading and research around the ideas that begin to emerge on October 15–17. In fact, the paper shows how extensively he has *re*organized the material he read around *his* problem; that is, he *uses* his reading and research to provide background for his question, to present some alternative hypotheses, and to offer various sorts of evidence for his own conclusions. If we could have somehow glimpsed Ben's inner, mental representation of what he knew about the topic "argument" on October 10th or 13th or even 16th, it would have been very different from the structure of ideas we see in the paper. The research writing process that led to Ben's paper is that of a detective rather than a bricklayer. Instead of simply piling up layers of facts—bricks of information from various sources—the research writer turns information into clues and evidence for the case he or she is building. In reading Ben's paper, notice what he has done with the Toulmin theory he read about and with the research he conducted himself. And notice the various ways he tries to signal this idea structure to the reader. Is he successful?

EVERYDAY ARGUMENTS: USING STEPHEN TOULMIN TO UNDERSTAND ORDINARY ARGUMENTS

Students who study logic learn to construct syllogisms such as:

All men are mortal.
Socrates was a man.
Therefore, Socrates was mortal.

They look on these syllogisms as challenging games. However, they usually don't see a strong connection between these logical puzzles and ordinary, everyday arguments that go on in the dorm, at ball games, or even in writing papers. Recently, some people in education, philosophy, and psychology seem to be agreeing with the view that ordinary argument has its own logic.

In both ordinary argument and "critical thinking" people talk to themselves or to someone else. They use this as a way of "checking over or testing ideas as they are presented in everyday encounters."[1] Some philosophers argue that thinking in "natural language" can lead to better, richer inferences than thinking that goes on in "formal languages" or abstract systems of formal logic like the syllogism. Gilbert Ryle is a major critic of these formal systems. He objects to the way they reduce meaning to a "carefully wired marionette of formal logic." He goes on to say:

> Of those to whom this, the formaliser's dream, appears a mere dream (I am one of them), some maintain that the logic of the statements of scientists, lawyers, historians, and bridge-players can not in principle be adequately represented by the formulae of formal logic.[2]

Formal logic attempts to reduce words to mere abstract patterns. However, some philosophers and logicians, siding with Ryle, argue that the meaning of words is in their use. J. L. Austin, in How to Do Things with Words (J.O. Urmson, ed, Cambridge: Harvard University Press, 1962) sees the meaning of words in terms of the use to which they are put—such as making a promise or a request. Stephen Toulmin, in The Uses of Argument, makes a similar point. An argument is not simply a matter of logic and definition, but it is an act people perform in order to support or test a claim.[3] Toulmin says that an argument is made up of three basic elements: the claim you make, the data you have, and the warrant that lets you go from the data to your claim. This system for describing arguments offers a way to analyze real arguments that occur in "natural language" and to evaluate how complete and effective they are as persuasion.

How do people really use argument in discussions of the kind heard in the library or the dorm? Do they always supply the warrants or data when they make claims? In particular, I was interested in why these ordinary arguments often seem so inconclusive. Everyday conversational arguments seem to go in circles, repeat themselves, and often no one is convinced. Written arguments often seem to move forward, to answer questions, and to reach conclusions that seem persuasive, at least at the time. Would an analysis of the elements of the arguments help account for these differences?

This study is based on the hypothesis that Toulmin's analysis of written arguments could help track out an ordinary oral argument and evaluate why and how it succeeded or failed. In the first section of this paper I will discuss Toulmin's system and use it to analyze an argument from a textbook used in a university course. In the second section I will use the system to evaluate an ordinary oral argument that I tape recorded between two college students.

I. Toulmin's Pattern of Argument

Although Toulmin is a logician, he says that when people argue, they do not use formal logic. Instead, they think more like lawyers in a courtroom. They make claims and then try to justify or support them with evidence. Listeners test (and accept or reject) arguments in the same way. They look at the evidence that supports the claim.[4]

According to Toulmin, the layout of an argument includes three major elements (claims, warrants, and data) and two minor ones (backing the warrant and qualification of the claim). The Toulmin layout shows how you go from data to claim with the support of your warrant (or back the other way if you are testing an argument). See Figure 1.

I will illustrate each of these parts of an argument by using them to analyze some of the claims made in a textbook chapter on creativity. The authors, Hayes and Bond, make a global claim that starts by recognizing that women have a lower record of productivity in highly

Figure 1.   Toulmin's Pattern of Argument

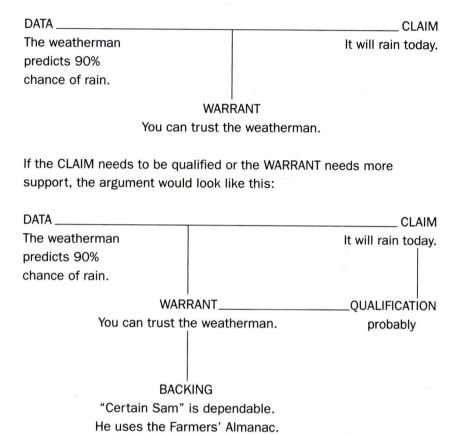

DATA _____ CLAIM
The weatherman   It will rain today.
predicts 90%
chance of rain.

WARRANT
You can trust the weatherman.

If the CLAIM needs to be qualified or the WARRANT needs more
support, the argument would look like this:

DATA _____ CLAIM
The weatherman   It will rain today.
predicts 90%
chance of rain.

WARRANT_____QUALIFICATION
You can trust the weatherman.   probably

BACKING
"Certain Sam" is dependable.
He uses the Farmers' Almanac.

creative achievements (they have only won 5% of the Nobel prizes).
But, they claim, this is because of cultural influences, not nature.[5] To
support this claim they make a number of subclaims and arguments in
the chapter. I will apply Toulmin's system to two of these arguments,
which I will paraphrase from Hayes's book. (See Figure 2.)

CLAIM

Arguments begin when a person I will call the Claimer makes an
assertion or claim about something, and another person I will call the
Tester disagrees or is not immediately convinced.
Claim 1: Creativity demands an investment of an enormous
amount of time. (See Figure 2.)

Figure 2.   The Pattern of a Written Argument

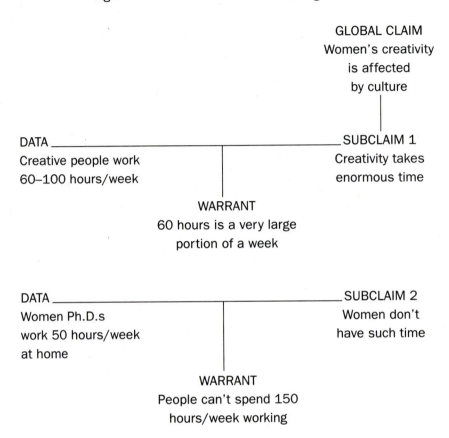

GLOBAL CLAIM
Women's creativity
is affected
by culture

DATA _____ SUBCLAIM 1
Creative people work   Creativity takes
60–100 hours/week   enormous time

WARRANT
60 hours is a very large
portion of a week

DATA _____ SUBCLAIM 2
Women Ph.D.s   Women don't
work 50 hours/week   have such time
at home

WARRANT
People can't spend 150
hours/week working

DATA

   People disagree about the claims in an argument. But one thing
both sides agree about is the data or evidence. This means the
Claimer must be able to refer to some neutral data, facts, or
observations as the evidence for the claim.
   Data for Claim 1: University of California professors average 60
hours/week on teaching and research. Nobel Prize winner Herbert
Simon spent about 100 hours/week in the years he was doing the
work that won the Prize.

WARRANT

   The warrant is the crucial logical step between objective data and
a claim. It is the "since this is so . . ." statement that says, "if you

accept the data, then you should also accept my claim, because . . ."
If you think of a claim as an inference someone makes from data, then
the warrant is the "license" to make that inference. It is like a fishing
license; it shows you have the right to do certain things. Some
warrants or licenses seem to be based on common sense, such as
the assumption that you can believe what the weatherman says. As a
result, they are often not stated by the Claimer. But sometimes they
are really important assumptions that need to be said, since the
Tester might not automatically come up with the same assumptions
about weathermen or might even disagree.

Warrant for Claim 1: Since there are only 168 hours in a week, it is
obvious that intense creative work of this type takes precedence over
everything else—including sleep!

Table 1 summarizes my main points about these three key
elements of an argument.

Sometimes arguers add two other elements to an argument.

QUALIFICATION

Sometimes a Claimer wants to qualify a claim either to soften or to
increase what Toulmin calls its "force." This seems to be what Young,
Becker, and Pike would call showing the "area of validity" or just how
far this claim holds.[6] Words such as perhaps, maybe, probably, we
must believe that, and unless x happens show that a qualification is
being made.

DATA	WARRANT	CLAIM
What does it offer?		
Evidence	Logical link	Assertion
Do people agree?		
Both parties agree	Some or most people agree	Two parties disagree
What are cue words?		
If this is true . . .	Since it is reasonable that . . .	Then . . .
Is it stated?		
Sometimes	Often not	Usually

Table 1.   Features of Data, Claims, and Warrants

Qualification for Claim 1: Even that much time and effort might not be enough for creative achievement.

BACKING

Sometimes the Claimer needs to give some sort of backup or support that makes the warrant itself believable. However, in my example the warrant for Claim 1 is based on such obvious common sense that there is no need for any backing.

The written argument in this chapter is typical of the arguments Toulmin and others describe. It uses more than one subclaim to support its major claim, and the subclaims are themselves linked in clusters and chains.[7] The following example is one of the subarguments in Hayes and Bond that supports their claim.

Claim 2: Our social expectations make it hard for women to invest that amount of time and energy.

DATA: 95 percent of women marry. Married female Ph.D.s typically spend about 50 hours/week doing housework, their male counterparts, 10 percent.

WARRANT: People who spend 100 hours a week on research and 50 more on housework won't survive long, let alone with a Nobel Prize!

BACKING: The authors give no explicit backing, but if someone said to them "Why do you assume your warrant is reasonable?" they could offer a case study or a calculation that showed that 168 hours in a week minus 150 hours of work equals 18 hours, divided by 7 days a week yields 2 hours a day to sleep, eat, and see movies.

II. Predictions About Oral Arguments

Section I outlined the structure of an effective written argument. But what happens when people engage in ordinary oral arguments? What makes these arguments seem incomplete or less persuasive? Based on my reading of textbooks and the research on ordinary argument already cited, I think we can make certain predictions:

1. The data or evidence is likely to be based on informal, personal observation (not the systematic and experimental observation that goes on in science). Or it will be based on someone's testimony (on the fact that "Charlie said so" rather than on facts, statistics, or logical inferences).[8]

2. The arguers will drop the attempt to make logical arguments and will resort to "nonargumentative" forms of persuasion such as insults, yelling, and unfair remarks.

3. Some parts of the argument, especially the warrants, will be missing.

4. The missing warrants will create a problem because the Tester in the argument will not see why or how the data are significant (the Tester won't come up with a warrant on his own) or the Tester won't agree that some implied warrant actually makes the logical step from warrant to claim. In other words, the people don't really agree on the warrant, but they don't know they disagree about that.

RESEARCH METHODS

My research was designed to do three things: (1) to try to apply Toulmin's theory to ordinary oral argument, (2) to see why and where that kind of argument was weak, and (3) to test my predictions. My method was to tape record an argument in the dorm without letting the people know I was doing so. Then immediately afterward, I told them why I had recorded and I asked for their written permission to transcribe the tape. I also told them that names, etc., would be kept anonymous. I then analyzed the transcript, coding it for data, claims, and warrants (so the first claim for speaker A would be coded A-C-1). The coded transcript is found in Appendix 1.

PROBLEM AREAS IN THE ARGUMENT

The argument I chose to analyze is a very common kind of friendly but serious argument—two guys discussing the record of Franco Harris, star running back for the Pittsburgh Steelers. His lifetime rushing record for yards gained had just broken the previous record held by Jim Brown of the Cleveland Browns. From a rhetorical point of view this is a definition problem. Should we define Franco's record as "awesome" or nothing? Is he as good as Jimmy Brown?

In the argument, the major claim is pretty clear: Franco is (is not) as good as Brown. Both A and B stick pretty close to that issue throughout the argument. As seen in the transcript, both A and B offer many pieces of evidence for the major claim, as well as evidence that later changes into claims. Warrants, however, are rare. Both people assume that yardage and game time are considered criteria for judging running backs. But they seem to be drawing different inferences from the same facts.

Their warrants or assumptions about what high game time means are in conflict. This problem keeps coming up in the argument. For example, A feels that because Franco has lasted so long in the league, Franco is a good player. B feels that this only gave him more playing time and explains Franco's high yardage. If A were to explicitly state the warrant for the evidence—"Only a durable, skillful player can last as long as that"—B would have had more difficulty undermining A's argument. Similarly, B could have made it clear why he feels that the duration of Franco in the league is the reason for his high yardage and not his skill.

Unlike some "friendly" discussions of this kind, the data are not simply testimony (such as "everyone says he's great") but include statistics on yardage, games and seasons played, and other players. However, they do resort to some nonargumentative tactics. When B says, "without his line he wouldn't do jack shit and you know it!" we can see two examples of nonargumentative persuasion. First, there is the use of very strong words. Saying "jack shit" instead of "very few yards" or some other substitution shows how B is trying to intimidate A. He is subtly insulting A with the use of such terms as a response. And then the statement "and you know it" is unfair. I see B as saying all of the following with that statement: "You're lying, you're uninformed, you're ignoring the truth, etc." The same thing occurs when he says, "That's not what I mean and you know it."

Another feature of this argument . . .

CONCLUSION

Ordinary arguments can't be reduced to a syllogism. But they do have their own logic and structure. Stephen Toulmin's theory of argument can be used to evaluate the structure of both written and oral arguments. It reveals that . . .

FOOTNOTES

[1] R. R. Allen, Jerry D. Feezel, and Fred J. Kauffeld, A Taxonomy of Concepts and Critical Abilities Related to the Evaluation of Verbal Arguments, (Madison: University of Wisconsin Center for Cognitive Learning, 1967), p. 1.

[2] Gilbert Ryle, "Ordinary Language," in Philosophy and Ordinary Language, ed. Charles E. Caton, (Urbana: University of Illinois Press, 1963, p. 108.

[3] Stephen Toulmin, The Uses of Argument, (Cambridge: Cambridge University Press, 1958).

[4] Toulmin. This analysis will be based on Chapter 3 of the book.

BIBLIOGRAPHY

Allen, R.R., Jerry D. Feezel, and Fred J. Kauffeld. A Taxonomy of Concepts and Critical Abilities Related to the Evaluation of Verbal Arguments. Madison: University of Wisconsin Center for Cognitive Learning, 1967.

Ehninger, Douglas. Influence, Belief, and Argument: An Introduction to Responsible Persuasion. Glenview, IL: Scott, Foresman, 1974.

Hayes, John, R. The Complete Problem-Solver. Philadelphia: The Franklin Institute Press, 1981.

APPENDIX 1: Coded Transcript of Oral Argument

A: Wrong!

B-C-1   B: Franco isn't even in the same class as Jimmy Brown!

A-D-1   A: No, he just has 11,000 yards rushing . . .

B-D-1   B: Yeah, on 10,000 carries!

A-C-1   A: Bullshit. Franco's awesome; look, he is still playing after 12 seasons. Jim Brown only lasted 9, or something like that.

B-W-1   B: Which is why he is so great! Franco has been running for more years but he still has more yards than him.

A: But . . .

B-W-1   B: And do not forget that Jim Brown only played like 9 or 12 games a season. Franco plays 16.

A-W-1   A: But that just proves what a good runner he is! He has durability.

B-W-2   B: That is because he runs out of bounds before he gets hit, or else he falls down.

A: Right! That is why he has lasted so long!

B: Well then how can you say he is better than Jim Brown?

A: Woooo! I did not say that he was better than Brown. I said he was in his class.

B-C-2 B: Still though, no way Franco is in his class even. He stinks!

A: Oh, you do not even know what you are talking about.

(PAUSE)

B-W-2 B: If he is so damn good, then why does he have to carry the ball more than anyone else?

A: Well if you want yards you have to carry the ball, right?

B: What about Walter Payton?

A: What about Walter Payton?

B: He's right up there with Franco and he hasn't been playing nearly as long.

A: He's good; I'm not saying he isn't.

B: But if Franco gets the ball so much more than he does and he only has a few more yards, then how can he be great?

A: Because he . . .

B: And what about his offensive line? Payton doesn't even have one but he still gets the yards.

A: So does Franco!

B: But that's because he has an offensive line. If he played for Chicago he wouldn't get half the yards he does!

A: Oh bullshit. He'd get his yards playing for any other team.

B: But his line . . .

A: Just because he has a line doesn't mean that, well, he gets his yards by himself.

B: Without his line he wouldn't do jack shit and you know it!

A: Oh yeah, Mike Webster carries the ball for him, does he?

B: That's not what I mean and you know it.

A: Everybody has a line. It's the runner that gets the yards.

B: But the offensive line means everything. If there are no holes then the runner isn't going anywhere.

A: But Franco finds his own holes by ducking and stutter-stepping.

B: Yeah, and all that does is give the other team time to catch up with him.

A: Then he turns on the speed and the moves and he's gone!

B: What moves? He never jukes anybody.

A: Which is why he has 11,000 yards!

B: Because he carries the ball so often.

A: Oh, let's not start that again! Regardless of whether he gets the ball . . .

Ben's process log gave us a glimpse into some of the ways he developed and reorganized his ideas during the process of writing. For many writers much of this thinking and restructuring is often done in revision, once they have a first draft in hand. Trying to make a first draft more focused and effective for the reader can often lead the writer to breakthroughs in his or her own thinking. Here is a section of Ben's first draft, which shows how revision affected a short segment of Section II. (The small numbers in circles refer to the comments which follow, and the brackets enclose material Ben added in his second draft.)

Revised Section of the First Draft

~~Hypothesis~~

~~Conversation and Argument~~

Predictions About Oral Arguments①

[Section I outlined the structure of an effective written argument. But]② What happens when people engage in ordinary oral arguments? [What makes these arguments seem incomplete or less persuasive?]③ Based ~~on my reading, I think~~④ on my reading of textbooks and the research on ordinary argument already cited, I think ~~it is possible to~~ we can make certain predictions:

a. The data or evidence is likely to be based ~~on personal statements~~⑤ [on informal, personal observation (not the systematic and experimental observation that goes on in science). Or it will be based on someone's testimony (on the fact that "Charlie said so" rather than on facts, statistics, or logical inferences).8]

b. The arguers [will drop the attempt to make logical arguments and] will resort to ["nonargumentative" forms of persuasion such as] insults, yelling, and unfair remarks. ~~Many political arguments use what are called ad hominum arguments (i.e., against the man) which try to personally discredit the opponent.~~⑥

Ben's changes on this short section are a good example of how you can use a second pass to make a paper more substantial by going back and making clearer connections between your ideas, by elaborating important points for the reader, and by packing in specific information where your first draft was general. Note some of Ben's changes:

1. The headings in his first draft indicate only a fuzzy relationship between his two topics: his own study and Toulmin's theory. Ben didn't write a good heading until he had actually worked out the relationship by writing about it. (People often have this problem writing topic sentences and introductions. It is often best simply to lay the framework in the first draft and return to clarify it in the second.)

2. In the final version of this paper, Ben added an introductory sentence that makes his transition from written to oral arguments more explicit. Getting this top-level structure clear (and clearly expressed) is one of the chief ways revision can make major improvements in a paper.

3. On rereading, Ben realized that this was really the point of the previous sentence. He hadn't stated it originally, because—at the time—it had seemed too obvious to say. On the second day he realized it was obvious only because he had been thinking it.

4. Ben wrote this, thinking about the books and papers lying right there on his desk, then realized that the reader, who didn't have them to look at, might want to know what sources Ben, the writer, had in mind.

5. In writing this sentence Ben said he suddenly drew a blank. It said what he meant and he couldn't think of anything else to say. Yet he knew he hadn't said enough. It was too short for such an important point and it felt incomplete. His solution was probably one of the best ones a research writer can use: He turned around and asked himself, as a slightly skeptical reader might, "What do you mean by that? Can you give me an example, show me some evidence?" This led him back to his data and some concrete examples that not only supported his point but made it a more explicit, two-part idea.

6. This is a sentence that got off the track. It was true; it was interesting; and it was connected to the sentence just before it. But after 10 minutes of trying to fit it in, Ben realized that it simply didn't support the main point he was trying to make. It was leading him down the garden path.

This case study of one student's experience writing a research paper is an appropriate conclusion to this part. For one thing, it illustrates how writing often begins with trying to define and explore a problem in one's own mind. Here that exploration led to a thesis and ended in a paper which tried to support that thesis with an argument and evidence. The formal features of the research paper were used in order to support what really mattered—helping the writer and the reader consider an interesting problem.

Secondly, the process log and the revisions let us glimpse a goal-directed writer who is aware of his own writing process. He uses that awareness to give himself choices and alternative strategies as he works on planning and revising, and, as he does on October 16, to learn from his own experience. In fact, the most interesting thing about this case study may be the way it shows a learning process and a writing process which are inextricably intertwined. The strategies which helped Ben write an insightful paper are the ones which helped him define and understand an interesting problem. And the strategies which helped him structure and revise this paper for the reader are also the ones which helped him develop and organize his own thinking. He has turned his own writing process into a serious and powerful tool for thinking.

PROJECTS AND ASSIGNMENTS

1 Part of the argument transcript from Ben's paper has been left uncoded. From reading his discussion of Toulmin's method, can you now code the rest of the transcript?

2 Based on your analysis of the transcript, what points would you advise Ben to add to his paper, either to support his main point or to add new ones?

3 Given the argument of the paper and your own analysis, write a Conclusion for the paper as you would do it. The Conclusion should show the link between the initial problem, the writer's predictions, and the actual results of the analysis. Use it to sum up what you and the writer have learned through your research and reading.

4 Use Ben's report as research reports are meant to be used. Treat it as a theory you can test and/or a research method you can use to do your own research. Do your own study. Does your analysis of a written and/or an oral argument support Ben's? Remember to cite him as a source.

5 *Checklist: The Overall Evaluation of a Paper—from a Reader's Point of View.* This checklist covers the major features readers look for in any well-written analysis or report. Notice that it includes a number of features we have looked at throughout the book.

☐ *The problem analysis:*
Is there an effective problem/purpose statement? Does the paper define a real problem (instead of just describing a situation or recommending a new program)? And is this problem centered around a shared goal? *(or)* Does the writer state a clear issue or thesis that the research paper will explore?

☐ *The overall structure of ideas:*
Is the paper organized around an issue tree that is focused on the problem or thesis?

Does the paper provide cues, such as headings, that help the reader see this top-level organization?

Is the overall structure reader-based rather than writer-based?

☐ *The structure of sentences and paragraphs:*

Has the writer chunked his or her ideas and provided organizing ideas for the reader? Is the function of each paragraph clear? Has the writer provided *cues* for the reader, such as overviews and transitions, that make the relationship between paragraphs or sentences clear?

Do the paragraphs have a reader-based organization?

☐ *Editing:*

Does the paper use vigorous prose?

Does the writing make the underlying relationships of ideas clear?

Is the writing proofread and free of errors?

☐ *Overall academic or professional quality:*

Does this paper show the overall attention to research, analysis, and presentation that you would expect from a professional researcher, consultant, or academic writer?

Will this report have a real intellectual or functional value for its intended reader?

PART II

COMMUNITY WRITING
Problem Solving in
Civic Discourse

chapter fourteen

Out of the Classroom and into the Community

GOAL 1
PONDER your role

Think through why you are here and what you can contribute and learn.

WHY AM I HERE? IT'S ABOUT COMMUNITY AND RESPONSIBILITY

WHY AM I HERE? IT'S ABOUT LITERACY

WHY AM I HERE? IT'S ABOUT INTERCULTURAL INQUIRY

GOAL 2
ACT and adapt

Plunge in, evaluate the results, then replan and press on.

STRATEGY 1 **ACT BOLDLY**

STRATEGY 2 **EVALUATE AND ADAPT**

We began this book in Chapter 1 by listening to the way two college students interpreted the expectations of academic discourse or, as Carter described it, "learning how to write 'college style.'" Community writing—as it is done in public and nonprofit institutions and by everyday people in grassroots communities—will take us into a very different world of literate practice. Listen to Joan describe what it is like to walk out of the discourse of a classroom into a community—as a writer.

What could Lindsay and I have possibly imagined sitting in a writing classroom on the first day of school? Four weeks later, we took on an investigative assignment for Michigan Literacy, Inc. Instead of agonizing through the sixth draft of a boring essay on Ben Franklin, we were at the state capitol reporting on a raucous senate budget hearing. . . . By actually interacting with senators, we had only seen on television, we found that service-learning provides an exceptional alternative to students otherwise sentenced to serve time in the bondage of a classroom.

From Joan Cripe. (1995). In David D. Cooper and Laura Julier (Eds.), *Writing in the Public Interest: Service-Learning and the Writing Classroom: A Curriculum Development Resource Guide*, p. 23. East Lansing, MI: The Writing Center at Michigan State University.

The big news for Joan is the dramatic change in the rhetorical situation. We will come back to that. But did you also notice how much she and Lindsay have in common with Carter and Jennie? To start with, they have to think like goal-directed problem solvers, trying to understand this new rhetorical situation on the senate floor, adapting old strategies, and learning new ones. They have to collaborate and use their writing to pose and analyze problems for audiences with very different points of view. As readers and writers, they are also *meaning makers*—they are working hard to build not only a complex personal, but also a written, public representation of what "literacy" means, and doing it in the midst of a loud congressional debate, surrounded, as all rhetors are, by a circle of ideas, goals, values, and "voices" past and present. In short, the basic planning, writing, and revising strategies Carter and Jennie will have learned in the first part of this book are just as necessary in this new context as they are in school.

The difference for Joan and Lindsay is that they are immersed in what we will call the discourse of community writing. Like the broad category we call academic writing, it is really a large family of discourses and occasions to write. It can involve writing *about* the community and its issues, writing *for* communities that have invited your help, or writing *with* the members of that community. What

---

What kind of writing could I do about community issues?

Reflections, personal experience essays
Critical inquiries, problem-solving analyses
Arguments for change, feature articles
Performance scripts, videos

What kind of writing could I do for community groups?

Newsletters, profiles, brochures
Reports and fact sheets on policy, legislation, problems
Guides, tip sheets, educational handbooks
Public service announcements and videos

these kinds of community writing have in common is their focus on participating in a democratic society, on the problems and possibilities that go with creating a more inclusive community, and on the desire to be of service in bringing about such a vision.

Community writing is a personal tool for critical thinking and reflecting on what community experience taught you. It is also a social tool for raising issues, naming problems, working with others, and making change.

GIVING AND GETTING

Why do so many college students seek out the chance to do community writing? Like Joan, many are eager to get out of the "ivory tower" and into the world for a broader education. They want to put what they have learned to use. Once in the community, they find that the writing skills learned in school—whether for analysis, argument, or exposition—start to make new sense when they can see real people naming problems, building cases, or explaining ideas in public contexts that matter.

Other students talk about the new roles they get to take on and the skills that come with that role. In community writing, they are no longer just students but may become tutors or mentors, helping someone else to read or write. Or they may take on responsibility as a professional writer, helping a community organization get its work done. Or they may take on a public voice as feature writer, critic, dramatist, problem analyst, or proposal writer joining in a community's effort to get its story out to the public. Each of these roles lets a writer try out distinctive literate practices, ranging from doing observation-based reflection, to teaching, to persuading a public audience.

For many students and faculty, the strongest reasons for leaving campus are a sense of commitment, responsibility, and concern for the larger community. They may want to give something back to those who have supported them. They feel that their education and the resources of elite institutions like colleges and universities should be used for the public good. They are disturbed by the growing gap between the lives of the "haves" and the "have nots" in our country. They want to give social justice a human face and make contact with children who are struggling to grow up and adults who are struggling to get by in our inner cities and poor rural communities. They want to make a difference.

WHERE ARE YOU NEEDED?

As the box suggests, the opportunities for doing community writing take many forms. In our discussion of how you as a student can

Opportunities for Community Writing:
Where Can You Find Them?

Campus Club or Service Group

The service fraternity on your campus has joined the Reclaim the River project, and you are writing tip sheets for volunteers.

Volunteer Clearinghouse

Your school's volunteer bureau lets you look at many opportunities, such as working with big multiproject groups, like the Red Cross. But this time you tracked down a small neighborhood drama troupe on the list and are designing a flyer for their next performance.

Community Service Credit

To earn community service credit at your school, you go off-campus 6 hours a week to read with children and do "as-needed" jobs at a homeless shelter, while other students are volunteering at a hospital, a nature center, and a community center. To earn credit, you keep a journal and write a final reflection on your experience.

Disciplinary Course Project

Some of your college courses offer the option of a community writing project as a way to develop knowledge in that discipline. In a writing course last semester, you combined library research with your volunteer experience at the Women's Crisis Center to write a newsletter article on how children respond to domestic violence and what adults can do. This term, in Urban Economics, one group did a fact sheet on the shrinking job market for inner city youth, which a neighborhood nonprofit called "On the Job" used to lobby local businesses for jobs. Another group in the class wrote a guide to what employers need (called "Gettin' Down and Gettin' The Job") which the nonprofit used in their job readiness training.

A Community-Inquiry, Community-Service Course

Some college courses are built around community-based experiential learning. One course on campus prepares students to tutor in a neighborhood school. Another combines studying the philosophy of citizenship and politics of democracy with working in a nonprofit agency. A third course explores issues in literacy and intercultural communication in the classroom. Meanwhile, at a community center, you help urban teenagers write a newsletter about the problems they face in the inner city, which they publish as calls to community action. All of these courses call for academic reading, for close observation and regular journal writing about your own experience, and for a final paper based on reflection and significant inquiry.

write in and with the larger community, we will be concerned not only with projects done for what are called "elite" civic groups that represent middle-class society, but with projects that link you as a writer to grassroots communities—places where people are struggling with problems of poverty, where race, social class, and lack of jobs create barriers for children and adults. In these communities under stress, people of different races, cultures, and social backgrounds are working together because they see need, they value justice, they feel compassion, and they recognize the larger social fabric that ties us all together.

Having said that, I want you to notice that there are some tensions and contradictions built into the way we talk about community. To begin with, people often make a distinction, just as Joan Cripe did at the beginning of this chapter, between the discourse of the *academy* and classroom and the discourse of *community* or civic institutions. But what is community writing itself? Is it the discourse of the middle-class, mainstream, *civic*, and *professional* establishment (which has a lot in common with the world of colleges and universities)? Or is it what people call the discourse of the "*grassroots* community" and "community folks," the community organizations and everyday people who speak for working class and poor neighborhoods in cities and rural areas, for minority and marginalized groups?

Making these social, economic, and cultural distinctions within the concept of community can help us notice how different communities use power and prestige and how they conduct democratic action. On the other hand, there is a real danger in letting these categories polarize discourses and pigeonhole people. For instance, many of the strategies you learn for academic discourse are powerful tools for community writing. And the problem orientation of community action can improve your academic papers and professional reports. (You may also notice that community service and professional internships have a lot in common. Both can give you an entree into a new discourse, even new cultural groups. The difference may be what you want to learn and in the priorities you set.) In this book, I have chosen to emphasize the work of grassroots communities for two reasons. Here the challenges and the need are greatest, and here the opportunity for shared inquiry and intercultural collaboration—the invitation to understand alternative ways of interpreting the world—is at the heart of the experience.

Many of the examples in this section will come from my own experience at Pittsburgh's Community Literacy Center (CLC). The CLC is an intercultural, community/university collaboration founded on the idea that literacy, especially writing, is a way of taking action. At the CLC, college student mentors and inner city teenagers work together to produce a document and public Community Conversation on issues facing urban teenagers, from issues of risk and respect to curfews and work. (See Chapter 18 for some of their writing.) At the

CLC, college student mentors are collaborative planning partners, supporting the expertise the teenagers have on urban issues.

But community writing takes many forms. You will see other examples from students at colleges across the country who are supporting environmental causes, tutoring young children, working with urban housing agencies, and writing community histories. In different ways, these community outreach experiences plunge students into new discourses and intercultural collaborations. They begin a conversation with people who can offer some startling new perspectives on life in the community around you.

To get that conversation started, the next section offers some background on the history of these community/university relationships. You will see some thought-provoking—and controversial— comments by historians, sociologists, and educators on the role community-based, experiential learning plays in a college education. And you will be asked to consider what role you will play in the community.

COMMUNITIES AND UNIVERSITIES: OUT OF THE IVORY TOWER

In the 1930s, visionary educators like John Dewey argued that education should be rooted in experience and tied to the community. As a result, many schools began to offer practicums and internships. But the strong desire to combine public service and academic learning really belongs to the current generation of students—to your generation. However, this desire has a history, and the relationships between town and gown have not always been smooth. Conflicts between universities and the struggling urban communities at their doorsteps have been particularly problematic. Listen to how the founders of a groundbreaking community service program at the University of Pennsylvania describe that history.

Harkavy and Puckett think universities should be more socially responsible. But as historians, they go on to show that even when people began to act on social commitments, and when in the 1930s elite institutions, such as colleges and universities, started paying attention to communities, the problem wasn't over. The university, with its education and prestige, apparently assumed it should take on the role of the visiting expert, the consultant, and the authority. In this new relationship between town and gown, people from "elite" institutions tried to dispense charity or wisdom to their neighbors, without realizing how much they themselves needed to learn. But, as they eventually discovered, change comes only when both parties are partners in solving the problems. Once universities finally realized their responsibility, they still had to move from an "elitist" position to what the writers below call "participatory action" or how to work *with* communities on the community's own agendas.

Thought Provoker on
Communities and Universities

Why do they focus so strongly on institutions rather than individuals?

It is generally recognized that universities have done precious little to help collapsing urban communities. They have, in general, behaved in a most short-sighted fashion, allowing urban pathologies to deepen and to grow around them. Failing public schools, devastated neighborhoods, high crime, and a fortress mentality do little to create a positive campus ambiance. Moreover, given the condition of our cities, it is appropriate to question whether institutions of higher learning are fulfilling their civic responsibility. It is even reasonable to ask whether colleges and universities can legitimately and effectively foster a civic consciousness among students given their own disregard of their neighbor's plight. At the very heart of genuine civic responsibility and social solidarity is the concept of neighborliness, the caring about and assisting of those living near to us. Exhortations to overcome self-centeredness and to develop an ethic of service will necessarily have little effect if institutional behavior belies those sentiments.

Why study real-world problems?

Universities have also been short-sighted because they have missed an extraordinary opportunity . . . [to] make increasingly significant contributions to both the advancement of knowledge and the improvement of human welfare if they direct their academic resources toward helping to solve the concrete immediate, real-world problems of their local geographic communities. . . .

Dazzling advances have occurred in university-based research in science and technology. New ideas, concepts, technologies, approaches, and techniques are developed with ever increasing rapidity. Although designed to improve human welfare, the application of scientific advances too frequently results in new and more forbidding problems. The wondrous possibilities of new medical technologies, for example, have become distorted, helping to create a health care "system" unresponsive to the "low tech" preventive needs of the vast majority of citizens. . . . If universities creatively applied good systems theory and had an integrated mission—a mission that creatively, dynamically, and systematically integrated research, teaching, and service—intellectual resources would be significantly devoted to developing humane applications of scientific knowledge to help those living in conditions of profound poverty and neglect. . . .

How do you see the mission of your college or university?

What is being called for is, obviously, a radical reorientation of American university to become, once again, a mission-oriented institution devoted to the use of reason to improve the human condition.

From Ira Harkavy and John L. Puckett. (1991). Toward effective university-public school partnerships: An analysis of a contemporary model. *Teachers College Record, 92*(4), 557–59.

> ## Thought Provoker on
> ## Experts Versus Partners
>
> **How do you see
> your role?**
>
> Progressive-period academics [in the 1930s and 1940s] pedestaled the expert and expert knowledge. The expert would change the world by introducing his approach, by improving efficiency and skill in governmental agencies, and by designing institutions that would improve the quality of life for the urban poor and the immigrant. Although appropriate to its time, it had the same defects as all expert models: It was elitist, hierarchical, and unidimensional, founded on the assumption that the expert's role was to study and assist, but not to learn from, the community. Current efforts aim at building a collegial, participatory, cooperative, and democratic partnership of university researchers and community members. . . . A segment of Penn faculty and students has emphasized the necessity of learning from *and* with the community, research with *and not* on people, as well as having research contribute to solving genuine and significant community problems.
>
> From Ira Harkavy and John L. Puckett. (1991). Toward effective university-public school partnerships: An analysis of a contemporary model. *Teachers College Record*, *92*(4), 562.

An Ideal Education

What if your college experience taught you how to be a partner instead of an expert? Would your education be better or worse? Many educators say that real learning happens not only "in the tower" but "on the streets" when knowledge is put to the test and to use. One educational theorist, Ernest Boyer, argues that an ideal college would not confine learning to the classroom, the laboratory, or the library:

> [It] would take pride in its capacity to connect thought to action, theory to practice. This [college] would organize cross-disciplinary institutes around pressing social issues. Undergraduates in the college would participate in field projects, relating ideas to real life. Classrooms and laboratories would be extended to include health clinics, youth centers, schools, and government offices. (From *The Chronicle of Higher Education*, March 9, 1994, p. A48)

While Harkavy and Puckett assert that urban communities need more committed universities, Boyer argues that colleges and universities, in fact, need communities. The vision of community writing that stands behind this book combines these reasons to write in the community: It starts with a personal concern for justice, connection, and contribution to the community. It is guided by a level-headed desire for a more liberal, more engaging, and ultimately more practical education. And it always remembers that both social change and wisdom come from a collaborative experience based on mutual learning. So as the writer of this guide to community writing, I am assuming that you want all these things—the new experience, the new skills, and the opportunity for serious thinking and social action. The rest of this chapter will help you think about what you can contribute and learn and how you can begin.

GOAL 1

PONDER Your Role

Why are you here? Many college courses use community collaborations to explore important intellectual issues such as the nature of participatory democracy and personal responsibility, or the meaning of literacy, or the need for cultural awareness. But the question— Why are *you* here?—is also about your personal goals and contribution. What do you hope to learn or contribute? And what role should you take to do that?

As it turns out, the best answer may not be obvious. In the rest of this chapter, we will look at some Thought Provokers that lay out roles people can take in the community. However, you will notice that nearly every one of the writers is talking back to someone who disagrees with them. Each of these writers is aware that other writers or groups in society hold a different idea of what community means and how to maintain it, or of what literacy means and how to support it, or of what an intercultural relationship can or should be. Where do you stand on these thought-provoking questions? And, even more important, what will you do when you find that in the real world, many of these competing points of view each have something useful or true to contribute? How will you negotiate these voices as you construct your own meaning of community, literacy, and collaboration—in practice? Your response will shape what you choose to do as a community writer.

WHY AM I HERE?
IT'S ABOUT COMMUNITY AND RESPONSIBILITY

Martin Luther King, Jr. wrote the following letter while he was imprisoned in a Birmingham jail for participating in a civil rights demonstration. It is a reply to eight prominent Birmingham clergymen who had published an open letter criticizing his disruptive presence in their community, calling it a case of "outsiders coming in."

King's words suggest that he holds a very different sense of where his community and responsibility lie.

In 1963, Martin Luther King knew what his sense of that "inescapable network of mutuality" called on him to do. But it isn't always easy to know how to turn a desire for mutuality into action. Robert Coles, who was also part of the civil rights movement in the 1960s, thought he could best serve its goals by using his expertise as a psychiatrist and researcher to interview the members of the Student Nonviolent Coordinating Committee (SNCC). He wanted to write about not only the motivations for their youthful idealism but also how "the mind struggled with the threats and dangers and stresses and strains that go with such an idealism." But the group's young leaders, including Stokely Carmichael and James Foreman, already veterans of southern jails, were "vastly uninterested" in his credentials or plans. As they turned him down and started to leave, Coles says he blurted out, "'I'd still like to help—any way you'd want.' Silence—then I said, 'Isn't there something I can do that you need done?' More silence, and then Jim Foreman's response: 'You can help us keep this place clean!' . . . . 'Within minutes I [Coles] was sweeping floors, dusting, scrubbing down the bathroom, washing dishes in the small room that served as a kitchen. . . . Days of sweeping . . . turned into weeks, then months. I had an official

---

Thought Provoker on
Community—How Large Is Mine?

I think I should indicate why I am here in Birmingham since you have been influenced by the view that argues against "outsiders coming in." . . . I was invited. . . . I am here because I have organizational ties here. But more basically, I am in Birmingham because injustice is here. . . .

How far does individual responsibility really extend?

I am cognizant of the interrelatedness of all communities and states. I cannot sit idly by in Atlanta and not be concerned about what happens in Birmingham. Injustice anywhere is a threat to justice everywhere. We are caught in an inescapable network of mutuality, tied in a single garment of destiny. Whatever affects one directly, affects all indirectly. Never again can we afford to live with the narrow, provincial "outside agitator" idea. Anyone who lives inside the United States can never be considered an outsider anywhere within its bounds.

From *Letter from Birmingham Jail*. Martin Luther King, Jr. Heirs of the Estate of Martin Luther King, Jr., c/o Joan Daves Agency as agent for the Proprietor. Copyright 1963 by Dr. Martin Luther King, Jr., Copyright renewed 1991 by Coretta Scott King.

position with SNCC: I was the janitor. I even bought us a vacuum cleaner and did such unexpected extras as cleaning the windows.'"

Coles took on the job, feeling at first that he was being tested, maybe cut down to size a little, but feeling proud of his flexibility as a persistent field worker and researcher. And indeed he could have gradually eased out of his janitoring work and into a social scientist role. But he began to discover that this unexpected role was teaching him a different lesson about participation.

In contrast to Coles' personal participation in the life of civil rights workers, American society has translated much of its sense of community and responsibility into the large bureaucratic institutions of social service. As "the system" replaces the individual and our personal participation in the lives of others grows smaller, our role and our relationships with people change as well. John Mc-Knight argues that "service" (as he defines it) can be a dangerous thing to give and to receive. His analysis of medical and social service

---

Thought Provoker on
Participation—What Role Am I Fulfilling?

How would you describe the role Coles eventually created for himself?

Yet as I mastered my janitorial routine, I felt increasingly secure with the position, and I reminded myself that a good half of the black parents I knew did similar work as a full-time career. [One day, nearly a year later (shortly after King had written his letter) Jim Foreman asked him an abrupt question:] "So what have you learned from all this? . . . the janitorial research?" Surprised, I fell silent. . . . I lowered my head and heard myself grasping for words, fumbling incoherently. Jim finally spoke for me, told me he thought I had come to like the work and not feel demeaned by it, indeed, to take a certain pleasure in it.

I concurred. By accident, at a particular moment in the life of SNCC and in the lives of its members and in my own life, all of us had acted in such a way that I was able to connect with a group of young people bent on connecting with the impoverished, voteless, legally segregated blacks. In doing my everyday tasks, I was able to observe, learn, and come to some understanding of how life went for the SNCC workers and for people in the communities where they were living and "organizing." . . . With my SNCC friends, I slowly learned to abandon my reliance on questionnaires and structured interviews and instead to *do*, to experience service, and thereby learn something about what those young people had in mind as they went about their activist lives.

What is it Coles seems to be learning?

From Robert Coles. (1993). *The Call of Service: A Witness to Idealism*, pp. 10–13. Boston: Houghton Mifflin.

policy documents the transition from a community ethos based on care, to a social service system based on the professional management of need. When such "service" replaces "care," he says, the technology and the tools of the expert not only tend to dictate the nature of conceivable solutions, they structure the relationships between people. As you read McKnight, think of any experience you or your family has had with social services: unemployment, public health-care clinics, child assistance, food and clothing supplements, police. What roles were the "service providers" and the "recipients" asked to play in these situations? Could you imagine structuring that relationship or defining the problems of the "recipient" any differently?

Thought Provoker on Care—Where Does It Come From?

Is there another message a community could send?

[The institution of social service sends a message that says:] As *you* are the problem, the assumption is that *I*, the professional servicer, *am the answer.* You are not the answer. *Your peers* are not the answer. *The political, social, and economic environment* is not the answer.

[McKnight argues that when professional expertise and "techno-logical" solutions are in control, the citizen is no longer the problem-definer or problem solver, and the power and initiative of the community deteriorates. Service displaces what he calls "care."] Care is the consenting commitment of citizens to one another. Care can not be produced, provided, managed, organized, administered, or commodified. . . . Care is, indeed, the manifestation of a community. The community is the site for the relationship of citizens. . . . If that site is invaded, co-opted, overwhelmed, and dominated by service-producing institutions, then the work of the community will fail. . . .

Can college students play any role in creating a community of care?

A study of children who became state wards exemplifies the [disabling process of professional service]. The children were legally separated from their families because the parents were judged to be unable to provide adequate care for the children. [Officials] agreed that a common reason for removal was the economic poverty of the family. Obviously, they had no resources to deal with poverty. But there were many resources for professionalized institutional service. . . . The negative side effect was that the poverty of the families was intensified by the resources consumed by the "caring" professional services. In counterproductive terms, the servicing system "produced" broken families.

From John McKnight. (1995). *The Careless Society: Community and Its Counterfeits*, pp. x, 43–47. New York: Basic Books.

❧ WHY AM I HERE?
IT'S ABOUT LITERACY

Why is it that community outreach often focuses on literacy? The writers of the following Thought Provokers all see language and literacy as a powerful (even dangerous?) force. But notice how in the contexts they discuss, literacy gets described and defined in different ways—as a tool for understanding concepts and relationships, as an "identity kit," as a source of conflict, as a form of social action. (Note too some of the unstated alternative views of literacy each writer seems to be working against.) As you read, ask yourself: If you thought of literacy in the way this writer does or focused on this aspect of literacy in your community work, what role would you be playing? How would you answer the question: Why am I here?

Michael Johnson gives one answer: Language liberates. Writing educates the writer. Johnson is the driving force behind a new alternative school—the Science Skills Center High School in Brooklyn—which is drawing minority students into his passion for science.

When we say someone is "literate" (in reading, writing, math, or computing) we mean that they have learned to use a language (of words, numbers, symbols) in some particular way. It means they have learned how to use or control some set of conventions that other people happen to value. In the 18th century, you were literate if you could sign your name. More recently, people talked about literacy as the particular knowledge you needed to read and to write school-like prose in Standard Written English. But there are, in fact, many kinds of literacy. It depends on who is deciding which conventions are the important ones. As we discussed in Chapter 1, all of us—who may be quite "literate" in some contexts, such as school writing—are also quite illiterate in the use of language in other contexts. Do you remember the first time you walked into a strange social situation, a conversation about wine, the stock market, or rap, or joined a new course and quickly realized you were an "outsider": you couldn't follow what was going on, much less contribute? James Gee describes this kind of literacy as the knowledge you have of a given Discourse.

What happens when people acquire different Discourses or learn to use and value different literate or social practices, and then have to work together? Thomas Kochman describes a class of inner-city black and white students he first taught in Chicago in the 1960s. Although neither group was prepared for the discourse of college, the real surprise for both groups of students was the conflict between what Kochman calls "black and white styles of argument." Notice how each of these styles of argument has certain advantages and disadvantages. For instance, as Kochman points out, the discourse strategies the White students use rely on repeating what published "authorities" say to present an idea. That might make it a good fit to

Thought Provoker on
Education—Why Focus on Language?

Does Johnson's view of literacy change the teacher's role?

You ask me why I'm here—it has to do with love. Education's about getting a kid to love words, love language, to love to be able to manipulate numbers. . . . I have students write narratives in math because it leads to deeper understanding. I'll ask them to explain to me what a decimal is. They'll say, "I'll show you." And I'll say, "No, don't show me. *Explain* to me what a decimal is, what it does." They know that when a certain thing happens, you move the decimal two places to the right. But they don't know why. Getting students to speak. To talk about concepts. One thing we do here is rely on study groups. Each student is linked to a buddy, and those buddies are linked to study groups. We'll take a concept—let's say, reproduction in humans—and the students in the study groups cannot move on until everyone understands that concept. The students are teaching other students and are responsible for each other. You'll see a lot of talking going on.

How would you describe the sort of "literacy" Johnson teaches?

I want us to be concerned about language. I want an attention to language incorporated into every aspect of the program. How do we speak to each other? What do we call each other? How do males refer to females? Females to males? How do teachers refer to students? How do we talk to parents? All this is important. The interesting thing about our school is that it'll probably be one of the most multicultural schools you'll find. We'll have a large number of Asian students, Russian, White American, African American, Caribbean American. A mix of students. And one of the things we're concerned about is groups learning to live with each other. Education, in a narrow sense, is not our goal. Can you get along with your neighbor? Can you understand that this person has a different life style? This is as important to me as being able to read.

What might Johnson say to you about your community writing?

We don't want to just educate technocrats, "hired guns," people who can only construct computers and do calculations. We want people who have morals, who can say, "No, you don't do that to people."

From Mike Rose. (1996). *Possible Lives: The Promise of Public Education in America*, p. 219. New York: Penguin Books.

Thought Provoker on
Discourse—Are You In or Out?

At any moment we are using language we must say or write the right thing in the right way while playing the right social role and (appearing) to hold the right values, beliefs, and attitudes. Thus, what is important is not language, and surely not grammar, but saying (writing)—doing—being—valuing—believing combinations. These combinations I call "Discourses" with a capital "D." . . . Discourses are ways of being in the world; they are forms of life which integrate words, acts, values, beliefs, attitudes, and social identities as well as gestures, glances, body positions, and clothes.

What Discourses do you feel comfortable using?

A Discourse is a sort of "identity kit" which comes complete with the appropriate costume and instructions on how to act, talk, and often write, so as to take on a particular role that others will recognize. Being "trained" as a linguist meant that I learned to speak, think, and act like a linguist, and to recognize others when they do so. Some other examples of Discourses: (enacting) being an American or a Russian, a man or a woman, a member of a certain socioeconomic class, a factory worker or a boardroom executive, a doctor or a hospital patient, a teacher, an administrator, or a student, a student of physics or a student of literature, a member of a sewing circle, a club, a street gang, a lunchtime social gathering, or a regular local bar. We all have many Discourses. . . .

The various Discourses which constitute each of us as persons are changing and often are not fully consistent with each other; there is often conflict and tension between the values, beliefs, attitudes, interactional styles, uses of language, and ways of being in the world which two or more Discourses represent.

What does it feel like when you "don't have it?"

How does one acquire a Discourse? . . . Discourses are not mastered by overt instruction . . . but by enculturation ("apprenticeship") into social practices through scaffolded and supported interaction with people who have already mastered the Discourse. . . . If you have no access to the social practice, you don't get in the Discourse, you don't have it.

From James P. Gee. (1989). Literacy, discourse, and linguistics: Introduction. *Journal of Education, 171*(1), 5–17.

what some teachers expect. However, the more personal and performative discourse strategies the Black students used might let students focus on questions they really care about. What really mattered, though, was what happened when the two groups tried to use their different strategies together. In his book, Kochman used the expression "black and white" styles, but it is important to realize that the difference he described is not based on race itself. Race does

---

Thought Provoker on
Conflicting Styles of Argument

Have you ever been in a discussion with conflicting Discourses or styles?

[In classroom debate, Kochman describes how the following scenario would unfold.] White students make statements that they believe are authoritative by virtue of who said them and where they were published. Black students cast the statements into the framework of personal argument and challenge the white students directly on one or another point with which they disagree. Because the white students did not intend their statements to be put in the context of an argument, they see the challenge as inappropriate. Consequently they respond with "Don't ask me, ask McLuhan" or "you ought to be arguing with McLuhan; he was the one who said it." But this response is also a convenient escape, because, not having thought about the validity of the idea as an idea, they have no intellectual basis from which to defend it.

How did you handle it?

The black students consider such responses irresponsible and evasive, as a way to say things without allowing oneself to be held accountable for them. Thus, should white students continue to cite authorities in their presentations, blacks will say, "never mind what McLuhan says. What do *you* say?" . . . Because [the black students are seeing arguments as] a contest, attention is also paid to performance, for winning the contest requires that one outperforms one's opponents; outthink, outtalk, and outstyle them. It means being concerned with art as well as argument.

[On turn taking, white students assume they are] entitled to have their say before new points are considered. Because blacks consider turns to consist of fewer turns than whites, they often come in to argue a point before whites have "finished." This whites consider rude. However, blacks believe a turn is over when a point has been made on which others wish to comment. Consequently they consider whites selfish for "hogging the floor" or not allowing the process of argument to be activated.

From Thomas Kochman. (1980). *Black and White Styles in Conflict*, pp. 24–28. Chicago: University of Chicago Press.

not determine how you speak or think. Discourse strategies like these are part of your social/cultural background. You learn them at home, in the schools you go to, and in the groups you belong to (which might be heavily influenced by race). But many people learn to switch among multiple discourses and styles of argument. Kochman's vivid example of conflicting discourse strategies in a 1960s Chicago classroom raises the question: What happens when conflicting styles meet?

How do you handle a discussion like this in which people are using different discourse strategies or styles of argument? How did you deal with the conflict between them? Sometimes people do what is called "code-switching" or discourse switching because they have had experience participating in both. Other times, people try to switch or participate by "faking it"—doing the best they can, knowing that they don't really belong (to what Gee called the Discourse), and fearing they will slip up and get it wrong.

Gee and Kochman suggest that the practice of literacy in the community can bring us face-to-face with different strongly defined Discourses as well as more informal discourses and alternative literate practices. This raises some challenges to traditional, worksheet literacy training focused on teaching the so-called "basics" in reading and writing, because now we have to ask: What (or whose?) Discourse(s) is a literacy tutor helping a tutee acquire? For instance, is the Discourse of school necessarily the only or the most valuable game in town? If it isn't, how do you decide which Discourse is worth working on together?

Now turn the tables: What Discourses *could* you as a tutor, mentor, or collaborator learn by entering a new community? Which Discourses do you *need* to learn to live in a multicultural society? If you think people involved in tutoring, mentoring, or outreach should learn some culturally different Discourses, you may want to consider how they will do it. Gee says that people learn a Discourse not by studying it but by engaging in the world that uses it (in its social practices). But remember, Robert Coles found that participation meant taking on a role he didn't anticipate. What will you do?

Our next Thought Provoker expands the meaning of literacy even further by describing how "community literacy" (as an alternative to school literacy) can walk off the page and into public action.

WHY AM I HERE?
IT'S ABOUT INTERCULTURAL INQUIRY

Are you ready to enter a new Discourse or work with someone who may hold some different culturally-based expectations? Many people are drawn to community service for exactly this opportunity—to become part of an intercultural collaboration and to experience

Thought Provoker on
Community Literacy—An Alternative Discourse

Does community literacy use your school skills?

Community literacy, as we shall define it, is a search for an alternative discourse. . . . First and foremost, community literacy supports *social change.* On the streets, people in urban communities use writing not as an end in itself, but literally to "compose" themselves for action, for example, scribbling notes for arguments they may later present to city council, circulating petitions, documenting disputes to show evidence of a "problem property" on the corner. . . . Problem-solving takes precedence over canonical texts. . . . Community literacy expands the table by bringing into conversation multiple and often unheard perspectives. Thus, a second aim of community literacy is to support genuine, *intercultural conversation.* . . . But community literacy means more than simply representing different views in conversation. It seeks to restructure the conversation itself into a collaboration in which individuals share expertise and experience through the act of planning and writing about problems they jointly define. The goal is not to resolve the myriad differences that arise in a mixed, working group, but to treat diversity as a resource for solving specific problems. Therefore, a third aim of community literacy is to bring a *strategic approach* to this conversation and to support people in developing new strategies for decision making.

If you took on the four goals of community literacy, would it change how you work with or relate to a community contact or mentee?

A fourth aim of community literacy is *inquiry*—to openly acknowledge not only the difficulty of empathy and the history of failed conversations, but to purposefully examine the genuine conflicts, assumptions, and practices we bring to these new partnerships. There is, however, all the difference in the world between acknowledging that your ways are different from mine (which may be read as "inexplicable, unpredictable and maybe not as desirable as mine") and actively exploring the logic of how you and I are using our literate practices to make meaning.

From Wayne Campbell Peck, Linda Flower, and Lorraine Higgins. (1995). Community literacy. *College Composition and Communication, 46*(2), 205–6.

culturally varied ways of interpreting and being in the world. The problem-solving strategies you have already learned for analyzing problems (Chapters 1 and 8) and for reader-based writing (Chapters 5 and 6) will help you stand in different shoes and conduct such an inquiry.

As our schools, workplaces, and communities become more diverse, we need to understand cultural differences. But some argue that an emphasis on "multiculturalism" often creates unnecessary separation and breaks down the "network of mutuality" Martin Luther King described. We saw earlier how making distinctions between communities and focusing on differences can polarize groups and pigeonhole people. It defines them by their "difference" from the person observing, not their capabilities and character.

"Interculturalism," as we use the term here, is about *working together*, in spite of and because of difference. Moreover, an intercultural inquiry is not an attempt to discover and define difference for itself or to create cultural categories in which to fit other people. (Race is an example of a biological *and* a cultural category. Even though your race or mix of races is a biological question, the *meaning* of race in this country [or the meaning of your particular mix] is something our society has constructed and reconstructed throughout its history.) So an intercultural inquiry is not about discovering pigeonholes for other folks; it is about working with them to interpret problems, situations, or events as someone with a different cultural background or point of view might interpret them. It is an intercultural partnership dedicated to collaborative inquiry into things that matter. That said, how do you carry on such an inquiry?

One way is to make a place for everyone's voice in the discussion. Peck, Flower, and Higgins (Thought Provoker) agree with Gee that many academic and professional discourses create barriers that let some people into the conversation and keep some people out. However, they disagree with Gee that Discourses must have rigid boundaries or that your only options are to be a card-carrying, expert member of a Discourse or to "fake it." They argue that community literacy can (and should) reflect the special strengths of different ways of writing and speaking by creating a hybrid discourse—that is, a discourse of distinctive voices or alternative argument styles in which, as in the example that follows, a policy statement can include not only a policy analysis and a set of guidelines but a rap, a commentary on the rap, and a dramatization.

The urban teenagers and college mentors in the Thought Provoker are conducting an intercultural inquiry focused on the issue of respect. They begin by asking not only what do adults and vice principals demand, but what are the signs of respect students expect from their teachers as well. And how do these equally valid needs for respect escalate into conflict and suspension? Intercultural inquiry can begin with everyday activities, like seeing how people respond to language, music, gestures. But it can lead to insights into problems, too. When people from different cultural backgrounds engage in inquiry together, they often discover they are constructing radically different interpretations of people (such as "authorities"), situations (such as those that involve conflict and respect), or issues (such as what constitutes success). They are reading problems differently.

| Thought Provoker on Intercultural, Hybrid Discourses |

Do you think it is possible to create an intercultural, hybrid discourse where you are?

But what if the discourse we envision is one that must be made, not found? . . . . [In this case], instead of trying to enter or join an established discourse, learning to trade in its commonplaces and authorized meanings, the writers of community literacy are engaged in the process of *constructing negotiated meaning.* That is, they are building meanings or interpretations in the awareness of multiple, often conflicting goals, values, ideas and discourses. . . . For instance, in constructing a teen-based document on the volatile issues of risk and respect in schools, it is not enough for writers to rehearse old stories, share experiences in unstructured reflection, or merely express divergent opinions. Taking strategic action calls for more assertive literate practices that help writers do difficult things—to pose and analyze problems, set goals, simulate readers, generate options and test alternatives. . . . [Trying to create a more intercultural, hybrid text on school suspension] the teenagers decided to publish their ideas in an eight-page newsletter which denounced mindless authoritarianism by adults, illustrated feelings of both students and teachers involved in suspension disputes, and gave a series of dramatic scenarios for understanding how suspensions occur. Raps, followed by explanatory commentaries, sat next to statements of alternative goals and actions both students and teachers could pursue. The hybrid policy discourse that emerged went beyond the school's former rule-based approach, which stressed enforcing order, to an approach that concentrated on maintaining respect and sensitivity among all the individuals trying to think through what to do in a sticky situation. Dialogues between teachers and students showed a teenager's view of how specific feelings and behaviors triggered authoritarian responses by adults. Since the scenarios were written by the same teenagers who were getting suspended, the teenagers felt they had a say in shaping the discussion.

From Wayne Campbell Peck, Linda Flower, and Lorraine Higgins. (1995). Community literacy. *College Composition and Communication, 46*(2), 213.

So why are you here, in a community/university project? If the answer is to join in an intercultural inquiry, you have opened up the door to mutual learning. The focus is no longer just on what you can give or what the community may need, but on what you can learn together and on problems you may need to solve together.

How can intercultural inquiry make a difference? Cornel West, professor of Religion and director of the Afro-American Studies

Program at Harvard, has one answer. He talks here about the "politics of difference," that is, the kinds of social action people take to deal with the fact of difference and with the fact that being different has led to the oppression of many people. He argues that one goal of this new kind of action is to build new, more truthful public and personal representations of people. It is to recognize the agency and the ability of people who are typically ignored, dismissed, or marginalized by the status quo in both capitalistic and communistic societies. For West, having a sense of personal "agency" means you feel the right and the power to set your own goals and to act on your own judgments and motivations.

Although West's language is sometimes abstract, notice how he seems to be arguing for an inquiry that doesn't just make sweeping general claims. His inquiry looks closely at individuals and specifics and then uses those specifics to build connections among people. That is a surprising claim. If you observe someone else closely enough to recognize differences, and see them for who *they* are (not in terms of the images you may bring with you), how does that let you construct connections?

West poses a challenge. Can we use our community experience and writing to engage in inquiry—to cross cultural boundaries in a mutual inquiry with people to discover how they are reading the world? Is it possible to then look beyond the stereotypes that surround marginalized people, especially people who are poor, poorly

---

Thought Provoker on
Seeing Agency, Capacity, and Ability

Why should seeing agency in others be a central theme in intercultural relationships?

The most significant theme of the new cultural politics of difference is the agency, capacity and ability of human beings who have been culturally degraded, politically oppressed and economically exploited by bourgeois liberal and communist illiberal status quos. This theme neither romanticizes nor idealizes marginalized peoples. Rather it accents their humanity and tries to attenuate the institutional constraints on their life-chances for surviving and thriving. . . . The new cultural politics of difference affirms the perennial quest for the precious ideals of individuality and democracy by digging deep in the depths of human particularities and social specificities in order to construct new kinds of connections, affinities and communities across empire, nation, region, race, gender, age and sexual orientation.

From Cornel West. (1993). *Keeping Faith: Philosophy and Race in America*, p. 29. London: Routledge.

educated, in trouble, or in real need? Can we see the agency in others, seeing them as people with goals, intentions, values, plans for their lives (that may be quite different from ours)? Can we look deeply enough into other people (especially those labeled disadvantaged or underprepared) to see the abilities, capacities, and powers in them that command our respect and demand our understanding?

Pondering your role—the focus of Goal 1—is indeed a weighty topic. Sometimes the process of pondering, reflection, analysis, and criticism makes a problem seem too big to handle—What could *I* really do in the face of McKnight's criticism of "service" or West's challenge to construct new kinds of connections? Sometimes these theoretical discussions themselves get so engrossing (and feel so safe) that we are tempted to stay in the academic world and just keep talking to each other. That is why Goal 2, to Act and Adapt, is the necessary companion to pondering. Community writing is about taking the plunge—as a writer and learner—into the world.

GOAL 2

ACT and Adapt

> Last week I finally got up enough courage to call the San Marcos Food Bank. I have a lot of anxiety about calling people that I do not know on the phone; I am afraid that I will appear unintelligent or incompetent. . . . A cheerful voice greeted me from the other side. I introduced myself and began to explain our group project.
>
> From Kelly Driscoll. (1996). In Rebecca Bell-Metereau's Group Problem-Solving Publication: *Young Dog Learning New Tricks*. San Marcos, TX: Southwest Texas State University.

 ### STRATEGY 1   ACT BOLDLY

The hardest part of community service can be a first step into the unknown. But don't procrastinate. Step boldly. In community organizations, people learn by doing, and they will allow you to do the same. As a problem solver, your strength will be the ability to plan and act, then reflect and adapt. But you can't *adapt* until you *act*. Here are some tips for getting started.

Looking for a Project?

Some points to consider are:

- Be imaginative about finding options. Brainstorm your interests and ideas. Look back at the insert on "Opportunities for Community Writing" at the beginning of this chapter and the examples in Chapter 16 and 17 for possibilities.

- Take stock of your strengths. What can you contribute? What are your interests and future goals? Can this project also give you on-the-job-experience or community contacts?
- Ask questions. Be prepared to make a series of inquiring phone calls to find out all you can. Some good starting points will be your campus offices for student and community affairs, the Mayor's office or United Way, and the yellow pages for agencies, community, or religious organizations. And if you ask their advice, each person you call can also help you discover where to go next.
- Use personal contacts. Do you know anyone whom you could call for advice or even an introduction? Having an entree or personal contact can open the door when you are trying to build a new relationship.
- Be pragmatic. Take practical considerations such as transportation and college and community schedules into account from the beginning. Finding the "perfect" project may be less important than finding one everyone can easily and fully participate in.

Ready to Make Contact?

Look ahead to Chapter 16, Goal 4, Create a Working Relationship, which suggests steps you can try.

Hitting a Problem?

Whether you are starting out or getting over a hurdle, the advice of community organizers is to plunge in, start an informal conversation with your community, test an idea, try something, and go from there. This is just what Robert Coles described in his Thought Provoker, when his plan for research with SNCC hit a brick wall—he acted on the opportunity to become the janitor instead and learn what service had to teach him. Paulo Freire, a courageous Brazilian educator, calls this *praxis,* which means an ongoing process of action and reflection. Neither works well without the other.

In practice that means acknowledging problems when they occur and recognizing that problems are often opportunities for learning— remember, that is what you came here for. You may hit a practical difficulty with your campus or community group. Interpersonal relations may be more complicated than you expected. You may just feel uncertain or confused. When these things happen, treat them as a part of the normal process.

- Go talk to someone right away—your group, your instructor, your community contact. Shared problems become manageable problems.
- Try to analyze the problem (Remember Chapters 1 and 8?). Hold a collaborative planning session and explore the problem from different points of view (Goal 7, Seek Rival Hypotheses, in Chapter 17 would help here, too).

- Look ahead to the discussion of Options and Outcomes in Example 18–1. Think boldly and broadly about your options.

Looking for Strategies and Examples?

Community projects take many forms from writing *about* the community, to writing *for* the community, to writing collaboratively *with* members of the community. What will your project involve? The chapters of this section are organized around three tasks that play a significant role in community outreach projects:

- Observing and reflecting on your experiences (Chapter 15).
- Producing documents for a community organization (Chapter 16).
- Sharing inquiry and dialogue around an issue (Chapters 17,18).

Thinking about your own project, use Table 14–1 to see which goals and strategies might have top priority for you.

 STRATEGY 2   **EVALUATE AND ADAPT**

Are you surprised to see evaluation at the beginning of this process rather than the end? Or maybe you have already discovered that the

TABLE 14–1
Which Goals and Strategies Would Help You Most?

If you are . . .	*Pay special attention to . . .*
Beginning any community project	Goal 1. Ponder Your Role (Ch. 14) Goal 2. Act and Adapt (Ch. 14)
Using writing to reflect on your experience as a volunteer	Goal 3. Look for the Unexpected (Ch. 15)
Using and developing your writing skills to produce a community document	Goal 4. Create a Working Relationship (Ch. 16) Goal 5. Listen to Other Peoples' Stories (Ch. 16) Goal 6. Try Out a New Genre (Ch. 16) Goal 9. Start a Community Problem-Solving Dialogue (Ch. 18)
Using writing for deeper inquiry into community and cultural issues as you tutor, mentor, or volunteer	Goal 3. Look for the Unexpected (Ch. 15) Goal 7. Seek Rival Hypotheses (Ch. 17) Goal 8. Enter an Intercultural Inquiry (Ch. 17) Goal 9. Start a Community Problem-Solving Dialogue (Ch. 18)

key to a problem-solving approach is thinking hard about your goals and plans, acting on your best current knowledge, and then reflecting on where you actually ended up so that you can revise, replan, and plunge in again. Here are some tools for evaluation that you can use throughout your project as well as at the end. Use the evaluation tool that seems most appropriate for your current situation as the basis for a personal journal entry or a group evaluation in which you compare your responses. Or use it as a reflective memo you append to the paper or report you turn in to your instructor or client.

Constructing a Reality Check

1. What were my expectations?
2. What was the reality I encountered? (Or what were the expectations of other people?)
3. How am I handling the differences?
4. What can I learn from the comparison (or contrast)?

Naming Issues and Ideas Under Construction

1. Community experience not only teaches new things, it lets you extend, question, or qualify your previous understanding, assumptions, or reading. What ideas have you questioned in your thinking so far?
2. Think back to the way writers actually construct knowledge (Chapter 4). What new understandings, images, or ideas have you been able to construct for yourself from this experience? What have you made of it?
3. Finally, what issues feel unresolved for you? What open questions, rival hypotheses, and "good problems" do you want to keep thinking about? How could you create opportunities to continue this exploration?

Reflecting on Accomplishments and Plans

1. Jot down some of the grand and abstract things you intended to achieve. ("Become a more rounded person." "Help others.")
2. Now do a second version to get down to specifics and concrete details. Brainstorm a list of the small (as well as big) things you actually accomplished for yourself, for someone else, or with someone else. Maybe an accomplishment only seemed important to you because you had never done that before. Or maybe it was only evident in someone else's reaction. But it mattered to you as a part of what you accomplished.
3. Now look at the things you hoped to do but haven't accomplished yet. Stay with specifics. Your "hoped for" goal may be as simple (and as difficult) as starting a conversation about

"things that matter" with a community member of a different race, class, or background. Or it may be crafting and using your writing to really make a difference.

4. Look over your lists. Use your accomplishments to try to name and describe what you have done and where you have arrived. Then look at the "hoped for" list to sketch a plan for where you want to go next and how you might get there.

PROJECTS AND ASSIGNMENTS

1 Think about the particular community outreach project you are about to engage in. What if the various authors of the Thought Provokers we have read were sitting around the table with you, offering their perspective on your project—on what is important or on problems they might see? Ask the different people in your class or group to come prepared to role play one of those authors in a discussion. Pose the question: Why am I here? What should I be doing? Then listen as you, your classmates, and those authors respond.

After the discussion, write a reflection on what you heard. What are the most important issues people raised about *your* project?

2 Did one of the Thought Provokers seem especially relevant to you? Can you see a connection between a concept it described or the position it expressed and your own values, experiences, motivations, or concerns with community service? (For instance, how would the difference between "partners" and "experts" shape the role you want to play?) Write a statement of your own about the connections that passage "provoked" you to see and think about.

3 What do you remember about becoming literate (as a reader, writer, speaker within a given discourse)? Write a narrative about an important moment in your development as a literate person. Your job is to do justice to your story by telling it in a way that your peers will enjoy reading. It will be most interesting if you can *show* the significance, rather than preach it, and if you focus on *one moment* in time, rather than on a long period.

4 What do you *learn* when you learn to be literate? Look at how a student, Lacy Helmer, described learning when she responded to Assignment 3 above, for her community service course at Louisiana State University.

Example 14–1
Personal Narrative on Literacy

From "Inspiration Through My Grandmother"

As I reminisce about the many goals she helped me achieve I can recall her telling stories about her past. . . . [One] story she told me was about her first day of school. My great-grandfather only spoke the French language. Therefore, all of his children did the same. So, my grandmother went to school for the first time and was completely illiterate in the English language. She could not even say "cat" or "dog." To make matters worse, none of the teachers spoke French. She recalls that it was the worst feeling to "have no idea what people are saying to you. It's like you are lost somewhere and you have no clue where you are." I would suppose that it was one of the scariest feelings she ever experienced.

These stories of my grandmother's experiences are one of the reasons I am the person I am today. She not only guided me through the many problems of life, but she also helped me in my writing. When I was younger, I was afraid of writing. I did not want people to know what I was thinking. I always thought that people would make fun of me. I cannot recall why I felt this way, maybe it was because I was shy. Through this period in my life my grandmother was there for me. She knew that I had this problem and helped me with it without even realizing it. You see, my grandmother liked to write stories just about as much as she liked to tell them. Her stories always were about young children. They were all fictitious characters in a very fictitious world. She would read parts of the stories and get me really interested in them. Then she would say that she couldn't think of anything else. She would ask for my ideas and I would not give them to her at first. Then one day I just started blurting things out. I could not stop talking. I was like a baby learning to talk for the first time. She had accomplished her goal. The entire time she had been trying to get me over my shyness about writing. After that day, I just didn't care who saw my writing and what they thought about it. She made me realize that everyone has a point of view and that I should not be ashamed of mine.

From Lacy Helmer. (1996, September). Inspiration through my grandmother. Written for Jan Shoemaker's English 1001, Literacy Narrative Assignment. Louisiana State University, Baton Rouge, LA.

Now look at what an educator, Anne Dyson, sees when she observes children learning. Dyson describes 8-year-old Sammy, a new kid in a multicultural classroom who uses writing to figure out his place in the social world of school. He writes his superhero stories so he can win the attention of other powerful Second Graders in the classroom and script recess play. And when the girls call for more female heroes, he actually goes against the conventions of the genre and revises to meet the demands of peers. Dyson argues that learning to write isn't just learning to "make text" or even meaning. It is what she calls a kind of "interactional" and "ideological" work.

Children are not only meaning makers but also meaning negotiators, learning to participate in the social world, to adopt, to resist, to stretch available words . . . [This means learning to] manipulate relationships, to achieve particular responses from others, though the written medium in a breadth of social situations. . . . Learning to write is not only inter-actional work but ideological work as well; that is it involves writing oneself into, or in some way against, taken-for-granted assumptions, in-cluding assumptions about relations of teacher and student, of adult and child, of people of different races, genders, and classes. (Anne H. Dyson. (1995). Writing children: Reinventing the development of childhood lit-eracy. *Written Communication, 12*(1), 37–38.)

Use Dyson's theory as a lens for reading and analyzing Lacy Helmer's text; that is, use Dyson's concepts to look for specific features in Lacy's text. (When terms or ideas are new to you, trying to apply them will often help you understand them better.) For instance, do you think Grandmother's "social interactions" as a young French-speaking girl helped or hindered her growing literacy? What effect could relationships with other people have had on Lacy as a girl afraid of writing? Do you think either of them ran into or chose to work against "taken-for-granted" assumptions (about non-English speakers, girls, writing) as they become more literate? Were they doing any "ideological work" taking on or resisting social assumptions?

5 Where do you stand? One way to explore that question is to write *an inter-actional literacy autobiography* using Anne Dyson's ideas in Assignment 4 to see new things in your own experience. Think back to your experience as a writer. Do certain critical or memorable incidents stand out? Can you re-member situations in which you realized something new about writing and the other people involved in that experience? Use these critical incidents to write part of your own literacy autobiography focused on the *social work we do when we write.*

First, try to imagine what Dyson might say about your "interactional work." In other words, what role did writing play in your interactions with others? Secondly, what do these incidents reveal about your "ideological work?" To elaborate on that phrase: We all grow up surrounded by ideolo-gies or sets of ideas that work as taken-for-granted assumptions about how the world works or what people should do (e.g., how students, versus teachers, should behave or how people achieve status and respect). Some-times these assumptions are ones you come to question as you grow up and look more critically at the everyday ideologies around you. So how did your writing experience fit into or work against some of the ideologies or assumptions around you?

Write an autobiography about your experience as a writer in this social interaction with people and ideologies.

6 Where do you stand? Another way to explore that question is to write a *dis-course/cultural autobiography*. Here is a way to start:

When you walk off campus and into the community, you will not only be leaving academic discourse, but you may be walking out of your "home" discourse, too. Your home discourse is the one you grew up with, that was shaped by your social and economic class, your race, gender, ethnicity, and family, regional background. All of us are able to walk into a number of discourses—you may be at home in the fact-heavy discourse of school, the inspired discourse of your religious community, the in-talk of sports, or the styling of inner-city raps. Participatory democracy calls all of us to cross boundaries of social and economic background, of race and culture to understand each other enough to work together. But it is not always easy.

How would you describe your cultural background and home discourse or the discourses you possess? Are there any ideological or taken-for-granted assumptions in your home discourse about different ways of talking, writing, speaking? Now, think about a time when you had to do some border crossing, when you had to walk into a new discourse without a well-equipped identity kit. What was that like? What did you learn?

Write an autobiography about your experience from a time you were aware of being "in" a discourse and/or encountering a new one.

7   Where do you stand? Yet another way to explore that question is to write a *going-back-to-familiar-ground autobiography*. You may be one of the many people who engage in community service projects because you come from a grassroots urban or rural community, a working class neighborhood, or a minority background. This project is a way to bring some of your college talents to a community you know well or one that has supported you. However, it can sometimes be hard to return as a "college student" to a "home" community (even when it is not your literal neighborhood). Read the suggestions for how to get started in Assignments 4, 5, and 6 above, recall a critical incident, and then write an autobiography about your experience standing with one foot in the discourse of home and one foot in the discourse of college.

8   Observation and autobiography can help you contextualize and conditionalize theoretical claims. For instance, in his Thought Provoker, James Gee argued that a Discourse has some distinguishing features: It is an "identity kit" that dictates ways of writing, doing, and being; since you only acquire Discourses by the long, slow process of acculturation, you are either "in," "out," or a pretender. Dominant Discourses (used by those with social power) use their features as test to keep people out, but individuals also feel tension and conflict among their own, multiple Discourses. Thomas Kochman looked at two Discourses in context to show what can happen when particular features, such as ways of arguing, come into conflict.

What happens when you take a theoretical concept like capital "D" Discourse and contextualize it? That is, when you study what it looks like—how *it* walks, talks, and performs—in a given context. For instance, do the features Gee sets out appear in the following account by Leo Parascondola and help us interpret his experience? Make a note of any feature from Gee's theory that you can see operating in Leo's account and where you see it.

Example 14–2
A Bulletin Board Posting on Discourse and Class

```
From: Leo Parascondola

Re: Dialect and class

I have stopped running away from my working class
roots, but I must confess that I still have
anxiety about which of the many dialects of
```

English that I speak is appropriate for any given
situation. A brief history: I was a working-class
Italian-American scholarship boy with a tremendous
desire to get out of the working class because
life was hard and unforgiving. I went to college
and soon became an enemy of the government. They
replied in kind. Abhorring the corporate world for
which I had worked so hard to qualify, I went to
"work." Drove a cab, delivered laundry and yogurt,
had other ugly, dirty jobs. Settled as a bus
driver in New York City for 21 years. Safe,
secure, "clean" blue collar job. Got bored, went
back to school. Succeeded and went from an MA
program in New Jersey to a Ph.D. program at CUNY.
And now here I am. Wow! Like the Dead said: "What
a long, strange trip it's been."

The point is that I am now in possession of
several registers of several dialects . . . all of
them inflected by my heavy Brooklyn accent. Not
fuh nuttin' but I find this disorienting. I can
speak the Brooklynese of my youth and home culture
where we "berl the erl," drink "cawfee," and say
the word "fuck" or "fuckin" several times a
minute.

I can speak Black English and Spanglish that I
learned from my coworkers over all those years. I
speak the slightly altered more formal Brooklyn
dialect of Standard which is evidence of stability
and some education among working-class people. I
speak, of course, Standard. And, last and most
problematically, I speak and write in Academic
Discourse, the language of my new work world. I
wear all these hats and identities ALL THE TIME.
They are all available to me on unequal terms
depending on particular conditions and social
contexts. The hardest trick is to avoid
patronizing one's working class-class friends and
acquaintances by not seeming to be speaking "down"
to their level. The flip side of this is the urge
to use words and expressions of some dialect other

than AD when among a group of academics; one wants
to avoid seeming awkward in the company of one's
professional peers. I often feel that there is no
more eloquent way to express resignation and
frustration than "It bees that way." But there's a
price to pay for using that dialect among
intellectuals. They look for irony in all the
wrong places.

From Leo Parascondola. (1996). Dialect and class. On Ira Shor's electronic
bulletin board discussion group on working class issues and literacy. New
York: City University of New York.

When you contextualize a concept like Discourse by applying it to a real
situation, you usually understand more of what it can really mean. However, putting an idea like Gee's in context often raises questions and good
challenges to his argument, too. It can lead you to say, "this claim is true
under these conditions, but not these." That is, you can "conditionalize" a
claim. Gee argues that Discourses have rigid boundaries; that you are
either in or out of the Discourse or faking. Does Leo suggest the possibility
of other situations that might conditionalize or qualify that claim?

9 Having written your own discourse autobiography(s), you and your group
have a set of observations that could open up an interesting conversation
with the writers of these Thought Provokers. Let Assignment 8 be your
guide: take an argument you have heard in these Thought Provokers
(about Discourse, conflict, or intercultural, hybrid discourses, for example). Use your own autobiography(s) to contextualize these ideas. That is,
describe how the concept looks in practice, in your situation. How well
does it fit your context? Then see if your account conditionalizes that concept or argument. Does the concept or claim have to be altered to accurately describe new conditions that may be different from those the writer
had in mind?

IF YOU WOULD LIKE TO READ MORE

If you would like to read more about community writing and about the
kinds of learning that can come from community service and collaboration,
see:

Coles, Robert. *The Call of Service: A Witness to Idealism,* pp. 10–13. Boston:
Houghton Mifflin, 1993. / Coles engaging account shows how the practice
of service shaped his professional practice as a psychologist.

Deans, Tom. *Community-Based and Service-Learning College Writing Initiatives
in Relation to Composition Studies and Critical Theory.* Doctoral dissertation.
University of Massachusetts Amherst, Amherst, MA, 1997. / Deans actually
studied literacy programs in action to see how their philosophies and approaches to writing lead to different kinds of teaching and learning.

Goldblatt, Eli. Van rides in the dark: Literacy as involvement in a college literacy practicum. *The Journal for Peace and Justice Studies, 6*(1), 77–94. / This probing account gets at some of the generative conflicts involvement poses for students.

Adler-Kassner, Linda, Robert Crooks, and Ann Watters (Eds.). (1997). *Writing in the Community: Concepts and Models for Service-Learning in Composition.* (American Association of Higher Education Series on Service-Learning in the Disciplines. Edward Zlotkowski, Series Editor.) Washington, DC: American Association for Higher Education. / This is a valuable introduction to the key issues in service learning. Chapters range from civic literacy and intercultural inquiry, to parallels to writing across the curriculum and the role of reflection, combined with practical advice for conducting a service learning course and a fine annotated bibliography.

Williams Minter, Deborah, and Heidi Schweingruber. The instructional challenge of community service learning. *Michigan Journal of Community Service Learning, 3,* 92–102. / The teachers who conducted this inquiry found that students' engagement with the readings increased when it was students— rather than the reading list—who initially defined the problems.

Peck, Wayne, Linda Flower, and Lorraine Higgins. Community literacy. *College Composition and Communication, 46*(2), 199–222. / This paper introduces community literacy as a form of literate action focused on social change, intercultural collaboration, problem solving, and inquiry, with vignettes from the Community Literacy Center experience.

chapter fifteen

Observation, Reflection, and Conversation

GOAL 3
LOOK for the unexpected

Use observation, reflection, and conversation to help you see with fresh eyes and do justice to difference.

> *STRATEGY 1*   **KEEP AN OBSERVATION/REFLECTION JOURNAL**
>
> *STRATEGY 2*   **START A SUPPORTIVE CONVERSATION**
>
> *STRATEGY 3*   **REFLECT TO SEE FOR YOURSELF, TO RECREATE FOR OTHERS**

When you first cross the border from classroom to community, it will seem like merely "being there" is an education in itself. But the real, deeper learning comes when you step back to reflect, to put words on that experience, to describe the surprises, to recognize the dilemmas, to name the conflicts you have felt and the questions you are continuing to struggle with in your own mind. Nicole Brown describes her learning:

> In the past, I have always perceived responsibility on a superficial and individualized level: to clean a room or get up for school. I never viewed responsibility as a *choice*, but rather as something I had to do. Much to my surprise, however, the teens I interviewed at the CLC did not recognize responsibility as such a close-ended, easily defined issue. . . . Elliot, for instance, responded, "School, well that is something you have to decide to do. . . . [And achievement, it makes] you feel more better, and that starts rubbing off on certain people." Elliot clearly identifies his responsibility to himself as a means of affecting society as a whole. Or, to paraphrase Elliot, to feel better about yourself and pass that on to other people. . . . I now wonder . . .
>
> From Nicole Brown. (1996). From Linda Flower, Jennifer Flach, and Wayne Peck's Community Literacy and Intercultural Interpretation course. Carnegie Mellon University, Pittsburgh, PA.

Some people seem to expect a magical revelation to come at the end of a project. But a reflection is, instead, something you construct. Its power to surprise and reveal will often depend on the efforts you make to create new *connections*.

Revealing reflections are built on active observation, just-after notes, texts, and records of events (including tapes of discussions) you can return to. Revealing reflections thrive on discussion, collaboration, and the chance to compare your tentative thoughts with those of others.

This chapter is about how to see beyond what you already know or expect to see and to do justice to the differences.

GOAL 3

LOOK for the Unexpected

How would you go about expanding your picture of "responsibility"—the idea that intrigued Nicole Brown? John Dewey, the American pragmatist philosopher, said that when we want to learn about a new object (and that includes ideas) we try to see the ties that link it to other things we know. Dewey puts it concretely. To grasp an unfamiliar object of the mind, we discover its qualities by uncovering its relationships: "We turn it over, bring it into a better light, rattle and shake it, thump, push and press . . . for the purpose of disclosing relations not apparent otherwise" (*Quest for Certainty*, 1929, p. 70). Nicole's fascination with responsibility ended up weaving a surprising web of relationships among her own memories and assumptions and the responses of urban and later suburban teenagers. Here are three strategies for uncovering relations that might be "not otherwise apparent."

 STRATEGY 1   **KEEP AN OBSERVATION/REFLECTION JOURNAL**

Observation means looking closely at what is out there, at an event, a conversation, a text that may be different from what you expected to see. It focuses on the external world. *Reflection* means stepping back and thinking about what that event or conversation means for you, how you could interpret it, and how it is connected to other events or ideas. It focuses on the internal world. A double-entry journal like the one that follows is useful. Whether you separate observation and reflection on the page or simply choose to separate them in time, what matters is realizing that they are different tasks. Each requires a different kind of concentration. If your observations are casual or vague or you don't write down specifics at the time, here is the problem: your reflections are likely to *repeat* what you already thought or knew rather than *reveal* what you didn't.

The following example illustrates the two sides of observation. Laura's notes are detailed and specific—she has tried to notice what was really happening. At the same time, she has had to select what to notice and what to record; she has given weight to some things Jay does and little importance to others. Careful close observation is always an interpretation. Our interests, biases, pockets of ignorance inevitably shape what we see and what we think it means, even if we think we are being "objective." Nevertheless, even if observation is an interpretive act, it is still also one of our best ways to counteract our expectations and to seek new understanding. Notice how Laura's observations use Jay's reading strategies to reveal his feelings, while her reflections imagine causes and look at the implications.

Example 15–1
An Observation/Reflection Journal

Observations	Reflections
When Jay gets tired of studying, his eyes roll up in his head and he begins trying to guess at words he is reading, going by the first letter of the word and its apparent length instead of trying to sound it out. He can seem very discouraged. You feel he isn't really trying.	I gathered that in second grade Jay had decided that he wasn't bright enough, and that he was too far behind to catch up. So I try to explain to him that he is bright enough, that he already knows a lot of words, and not everybody learns the same way.
. . . Last week I was struggling to keep his attention on his work. I felt how bored he was with it all. And I just laughed out loud at myself pushing hard, and at us, "our push and pull." And I told him I wanted him to be a good reader so he could have a good life. The next time I saw him he ran up to his books without being told and never took a study break. This serious study behavior has continued! When he reverts to guessing I remind him of it without shaming him; I know this guessing behavior served a purpose for him in the past.	. . . I think the real change came when Jay seemed to make that decision for himself just before Easter.

So what did we really accomplish? I think it is motivation. He answers questions with exclamations of surprise that he can do it. He didn't seem to know that he was able to do these things, but he's finding out he can. |

From Laura Begay's Journal, Tutoring 2nd Grade Students. (1996). In Kirk Yenerall's East End Tutoring Program. Carnegie Mellon University, Pittsburgh, PA.

How Do I Make Revealing Observations?

Some people feel uncomfortable with the idea of "observation" or the feeling they are reducing someone else to an "object." Those are reasonable worries. One way to avoid that relationship is to turn your observation into a shared inquiry. Let your community partner know you are taking notes, and share them with the people involved. Ask them if you got it right. If you tape record a tutoring session, for instance, play back some of the tape to let your tutee hear herself talk, or read the part you chose to transcribe, or share the reflection you wrote the next time you visit. Remember, the reason to do accurate observation (rather than just express your own responses after the fact) is to help you do justice to the reality of other people. Observational records and notes that can be shared let you invite others into the inquiry, often let you surprise yourself. Here are some ways to make good observations.

Pay Attention to the Facts.   What just happened? What did others do or say? How did you and they respond? What was the atmosphere; how was time spent? Some things may make sense only later, so focus at first on what ethnographers call a "thick" or detailed description.

Use the Critical Incident Technique to Explore a Problem. Instead of jumping to generalizations about "why" or what caused the problem, focus on a single, *critical* incident. Be specific about the details of exactly what happened: who did what to whom with what result. Try to get different points of view on the incident. Then use your reflection time to think about "why?" and what it means.

Set Aside Time.   Create a ritual of devoting 10 to 15 minutes to making your observation entries right after a community visit or group meeting, or after a provocative reading.

Bring a Tape Recorder.   It is often impossible to be both an active member of a discussion and a reflective or even accurate observer. Moreover, many people will appreciate your effort to represent them faithfully by taping, if you do three things: (1) always ask permission first, (2) do not quote anyone by name in writing unless they agree to it (usually in writing themselves), and (3) quote others in a way that preserves the intent of the speaker and will not violate their trust in you.

Some people worry that taping seems impersonal or intrusive. Wouldn't it be more natural and ethical just to "talk?" The problem is that memory is an unreliable record: it will distort or filter out things you don't fully understand and seize on things you already know, assume, or expect. Interpretation tends to fit new information and ideas into familiar frameworks or schemas. A tape recording of what was really said lets people speak to you again in their own voices (rather than your interpretative recall of them). It gives you a second chance to grasp another person's drift, to hear things that will surprise you. And it allows you to bring the original speaker or other people into the process of reflection. By asking them to listen to the tape with you, you can develop a collaborative interpretation of interesting events and stories. From an ethical point of view, taping can help you do justice to difference.

You can (if you ask permission, of course) use the recorder on your answering machine to record planning conferences on the phone. Take a tape recorder with you to group meetings and briefing sessions. Even more revealing, record some of the sessions with your tutee. You (and they!) may be surprised at all that goes on. Or ask the people you are working with to let you record a discussion or typical session (try audio- or videotape). Bring a transcript or clip of an interesting, perplexing segment back for collaborative interpretation by individuals or the group.

If you tape an interview, bring an interview release form. You may alter the form on the spot as long as you and the interviewee put your initials beside any changes. You may also ask your interviewee to give you a pseudonym they would like you to use. However, be aware that public schools may have many restrictions on taping or publication of student work by anyone outside the school and will typically require the signature of a parent or guardian too. And if you are doing research you intend to publish, check with the Human Subjects Review Board at your institution for the correct procedure for requesting what is called "informed consent" from participants. See Figure 15–1 for a sample of a brief permission form.

How Do I Develop Revealing Reflections?

Try to Name, Conceptualize, or Make a Key Point About the Experience. Laura's last entry in Example 15–1 does just this. To get started thinking about responses you may be feeling but

FIGURE 15–1
Release Form

I agree to be interviewed and/or taped for [describe project]. I understand that my name will be kept confidential. I give my permission for these tapes and transcripts to be quoted and used in educational documents and/or public presentations.

Signature of Interviewer _____ Date _____

Affiliation   _____

Signature of Interviewee _____ Date _____

Address   _____

Phone   _____

haven't yet "said to yourself," try some of the strategies for generating ideas discussed in Chapter 6 (such as freewriting or brainstorming or talking to your peers who haven't had this experience).

Respect Confidentiality, Privacy, Personal Authority. Remember that your Bulletin Board posts and course papers are public documents. Sometimes you will want to use a pseudonym in talking about a tutee or contact. Others deserve and want the respect of being quoted by name. Think how you would like to represented by others.

Welcome *Good Problems*. When you feel a conflict or confusion, talk about it, wrestle with it instead of sweeping it under the rug. Uncertainties and differences of expectation or style can be windows into the broader, intercultural reality you came here to discover in the first place. Use the strategies for problem analysis discussed earlier to find the conflict, name the problem, and see it in context. (See the Checklist for finding a problem, at the end of Chapter 1, and the steps in analyzing a problem in Chapter 8.)

Define the Problem. If you are reflecting on an undesirable situation, try to define it from different points of view. Ask yourself: why is this a problem for me? But don't get caught in a discourse of complaint and blame, trying to decide who is at fault. Spend the next 80 percent of your reflection on what can be done to solve this problem or detour around the next. Problem posing needs to be a step toward action, even if that action can only be a tentative experiment.

Recognize Contradictions. As you think about how to solve problems, you must also accept the fact you will uncover contradictions. You will probably discover that some of your taken-for-granted assumptions or responses to situations seem to contradict other values or attitudes you hold. And you may run into problems and conflicts that you see no way to resolve. It is important to recognize these contradictions, even if they seem uncomfortable to live with or if you like to think of yourself as being more consistent. Acknowledging contradiction and conflict is the first step to dealing with it.

Share Your Thoughts. Ask your collaborative planning partner to read your first pass at a written reflection. Having someone else ask you what you meant, why you focused on that detail, or why you were surprised by that comment, can help you get at your own assumptions and make new connections to that experience.

❦ *STRATEGY 2*   START A SUPPORTIVE CONVERSATION

Entering the new discourse of community writing can be surprising, confusing, even intimidating at times. And it may lead you to rethink some of those taken-for-granted assumptions we all have. It helps to know you are not alone and to see what other people in your group are seeing, wondering about, thinking. There are a number of ways to create a supportive conversation with other people who are involved in community writing and outreach. The references to "posts" and to the "bulletin board" throughout this text assume that you have set up some way to share ideas on a regular basis. Some groups set up a literal bulletin board, other bring enough copies of their posts for everyone in their class or planning group, and others use an electronic bulletin board. Here are some possibilities:

- Bring a selection from your journal to each meeting with your group, and reserve some time to talk about one or two of these posts each time.
- Set up an electronic bulletin board (b-board) to which everyone posts an entry once a week. Some b-boards, like the one below, focus on different topics each week (sometimes on readings, sometimes on observations) and combine academic talk with personal reflections. Remember two things: (1) People may be trying out tentative ideas or, if they are brave, working through old, limited ideas to new understandings. So support them, even as you offer a differing point of view. (2) Remember that when people use electronic mail (rather than hard copy that they give to a person) they are more likely to be abrupt and dash off comments without imagining how they might be received, or even to engage in "flaming" (venting steam, throwing out one-sided opinions). So imagine yourself as a collaborative planning partner to the other people on the b-board, helping them push their ideas and yours.

Example 15–2
Instructions for an Electronic Bulletin Board

Posting on the Electronic Bulletin Board

Make a post by the end of every week (Sunday night) so we can check in to respond. Suggested length 100–500 words. Use some posts to respond to the questions noted in the syllabus; use others to build connections between your experience, your readings, and your own ongoing inquiry. Think about your posts as serving two purposes:

- Furthering your own inquiry (once a week): Post observations and inferences from your experiences as a mentor or writer; make connections between the course readings and your experiences and inquiry.

(Continued)

> - Continuing the Discussion (when the spirit moves you):
>   Many people find it helpful to use the b-board to talk about
>   what's going on in their community organization. These
>   kinds of discussions are a wonderful forum for sharing
>   ideas and insights with, responding to other writers.
>
>   Since you may wish to review your entries later, build your
>   b-board portfolio by creating a computer folder for your weekly
>   entries. Each week, compose your post in a word-processing
>   program; save the entry in your portfolio folder, and then copy
>   the post to the b-board.

Example 15–3
Excerpt from a B-Board Post

Dan, a college mentor, is writing about the day six police officers came for a dialogue on "Teen /Police Relations" with the teen writers at the Community Literacy Center.

```
Date:  Sat, 8 Oct 17:17:31

From:  Dan Zabell <dz12+@andrew.cmu.edu>

To:  <bb+academic.english.mentoring@andrew.cmu.edu>

Subject:  Amazing (Post #5)


Will [one of the writers] mentioned the
difficulties of going to different areas in the
city where you might get jumped if you are from
the wrong neighborhood or wearing the wrong
colors. One officer (an expert on gangs) said
something to the effect of—it's you own fault if
you get your ass kicked, because you shouldn't
have been anywhere near a situation where you
could get jumped. I don't know where he was coming
from, but what he said seemed to reflect a lack of
understanding. And what about the teens who aren't
involved in gangs, but still get hassled?
   HEY! BEFORE YOU START SKIMMING, IT'S ESSENTIAL
YOU READ THIS NEXT PART. Simply because it's so
```

awesome. Milt [the writer Dan is mentoring] has a
lot to say about expertise, in regards to this
officer. How can you be an expert on an
experience/life style, if you've never actually
had or been involved in it? This could be a
problem the police are having with gangs. Milt's
solution—they needed to get people who were
involved with gangs to help police stop the
violence, to go back with the police into the
neighborhoods.

Here's the thing with Milt. He has had a lot of
bad experiences with police. Though he maintains a
tough guy image, he is a lot smarter than he lets
on, and is also a good writer. If he should decide
to write these stories, perhaps he could read them
at the Community Conversation. If he does write
them he will be writing them for himself.

My thought of the week—how does Milt's theory
of expertise reflect back on us as mentors? We're
acting as editors on subjects some of us may not
have experienced before. How effective are we
going to be? I guess that's why we do readings
like Hero[A Hero Ain't Nothin But a Sandwich].
Still, building that bridge between discourses is
difficult. How does one begin? If one adheres to
Milt's idea of expertise, you can't exchange
experience, but you can get understanding. I want
to work this idea through further for my final
paper.

Here's what I want to go over next week with
Milt.

* Point of view of the officers who have to deal
with this leviathan of a problem. They might say,
"Why not just stay away?"

* To rival Milt's idea, wouldn't former gang
members have the same reluctance Milt would in
dealing with police? How could this be
overcome. . . .

When Mandy replies, she lets Dan know what interested her and responds to some of his ideas. She also uses his post as a way to think

about her own experience and figure out some strategies she wants to use as a mentor. (Note that Dan and Mandy refer to "rivaling," a strategy for imagining rival hypotheses, that is introduced in Chapter 17.)

```
Date:  Mon, 10 Oct 12:00:07

From:  Mandy Kinne <mk53+@andrew.cmu.edu>

To:  <bb+academic.english.mentoring@andrew.cmu.edu>

Subject:  Re: Amazing (Post #5)
```

Wow. I got to the end of your post Dan. You have a LOT in there. It sounds like you've got it together as far as your goals as a mentor (we need them as much as the writers I'm realizing). You have me thinking about my relationship with Monique. I don't think I've been helping her very much. I haven't been particularly good at rivaling. I keep thinking of points of view she needs to consider, but because I can't think of a diplomatic way to say it, I don't say anything, or a watered down version that isn't helpful. So Mandy's homework for tonite will be to set some mentoring goals like: 1) lose the rest of my uncomfortableness, 2) stop worrying about whether Monique thinks I'm cool, and 3) come up with some relevant, appropriate rivals to her text.

From Dan Zabell and Mandy Kinne. (1994). From Linda Flower, Wayne Peck, and Elenore Long's Community Literacy and Intercultural Interpretation course. Carnegie Mellon University, Pittsburgh, PA.

STRATEGY 3   REFLECT TO SEE FOR YOURSELF, TO RECREATE FOR OTHERS

Reflection is a way to get a grip on an experience; to explore its possible meanings; to follow out those hints, thoughts, and feelings that connect it to the rest of your life. In short, reflection is not just looking back, it is actually a way of building a bigger, richer meaning, like the planning process we discussed in Chapter 4. It should be no surprise to you that when you try to capture those meanings and connections in writing—when you try to spell out some of those invisible links—you end up discovering a whole lot more than you realized before you tried to put it in words.

Reflection is also a place to deal with those revealing moments of conflict or uncertainty in your own thinking and experience. When you can say, "On reflection, I think . . . " you are saying you have listened to the different voices in your own mind and their alternative interpretations of this experience. Are they competing or complementary? Reflection lets you sort it out and come to a more inclusive, negotiated meaning.

Now here is the ironic part of this strategy. One of the best ways to discover more for yourself, is to write a reflection that also captures your understanding for someone else. Using drama, images, details, and well-chosen words that bring the reader into a vivid experience let the writer capture even more of his or her own perceptions, feelings, and realizations.

To develop a revealing reflection, start by asking yourself:

- How is this event connected to my experience or to things I am thinking about? What does it mean to me?
- What kinds of "good problems"—conflicts, uncertainties, questions—does it raise for me? How can I weave those different voices in my own mind into the interpretation I have reached now, "on reflection"? (I realize that my understanding may change and grow with further action and reflection.)
- How can I bring a reader into this experience, too, to recreate the experience, the questioning, and the realizations I am coming to?

The texts that follow are carefully crafted reflections. Example 15–4 is the introduction to a paper that explores the challenging issue of individual responsibility for social justice. Is social justice an individual responsibility? The assignment asked writers to weave information from their class readings in with their field experience as support and foils for their own ideas. Notice how this writer uses some techniques from fiction to create a vivid, even dramatic scene. And she uses a metaphor, "just one push" to explain her sense of how individual responsibility works.

Example 15–4
A Reflection on Responsibility

From "Just One Push"

The lighting is poor, just one lamp on the corner of the old wooden table. My fingers trace the scratches and chips on the surface of the table as I watch the two kids stand the dominoes on their ends—each little piece carefully placed so that nothing will fall early. As I watch their determination, I see the smiles in their eyes and listen to the pride in their voices as they announce that it is ready. Sitting on the edge of the chairs, their bodies filled with anticipation, they stare at the small black and white pieces waiting for it to happen. I reach over and gently touch one piece; they clap and cheer as the display folds piece by piece and lays on the table. The two look at each other in pure amazement of what was accomplished because of just one push.

We have all at one point in our lives stood like that character from "It's a Wonderful Life" and questioned whether we have made a difference. Each one of us has wondered what we can do to heal such a hurting world, and each one of us has imagined what it would be like to live in a world where there is no hunger or homelessness, no pain or abandonment, no poverty or sickness, no sorrow or despair. We have questioned and we have dreamed. It is during these times that I cling to my image of the children watching the dominoes fall. I force myself to remember that no one person will be able to save this world from its problems. Rather it will take a little bit from each one of us. We are all dominoes waiting to be pushed.

From Ilona M. McGuiness. (1995, Fall). Education for participation and democracy: Service learning in the writing classroom. *The Scholarship of Teaching*, *1*(2), 3–8. East Lansing, MI: The Writing Center, Michigan State University.

The writer of "Just One Push" uses her reflection to encourage others to persist. The next set of examples seem written to challenge readers to look squarely at a problem. The first paragraph is written by a student, Carla, who started tutoring adults at the Center for Literacy (CFL) in an inner city Philadelphia neighborhood. She came from an affluent family with strongly conservative political views. What do you think she is trying to understand or explain for herself in this reflection? In the text that follows, her instructor, Eli Goldblatt, reflects on Carla's paper, trying to understand how her experience (as he saw it) was connected to her new understanding. He recognizes how hard it can be to deal with sexual harassment in a formal setting and how important the group discussion was for Carla—and her group. The instructor used these two reflections—Carla's paper and the his thoughts on it—as part of an article written for other instructors teaching community outreach classes. What do you think the instructor wanted his audience to understand? What issue as a teacher was he grappling with?

Example 15–5
Two Interpretations of What Literacy Means

From Carla's Text

I saw that differences are never just differences. They are not neutral. They make us threats to one another—color vs. color, class vs. class, male vs. female (as I especially experienced with my learner), and finally literate vs. illiterate. Knowledge equals power. Not in my opinion. The adults I saw at C.F.L. were extremely knowledgeable. Some were dedicated parents, some were diligent employees, some knew how to speak four languages, some had eloquent opinions on everything from black history to single parenthood, to politics in Philadelphia, to religion, to addiction, to suicide. All had knowledge. None had power. This is because, in my opinion, knowledge without outlet for expression is not valued significantly by our society. It is literacy that equals power. Without it, valuable knowledge remains locked inside the heads, the homes, and the communities of those who can't express themselves through reading and writing. . . .

From the Instructor's Commentary

I think Carla's aside about "male vs. female" threats lies at the heart of her insight about literacy and power. Carla originally was assigned a learner named Dave, a man who was about ten years older than she. They worked very well together on the first tutoring session, but Dave began to make inappropriate sexual comments during the second session. Carla firmly told him to get back on task, but the session simply didn't work. On campus at our next class meeting, we discussed the incident. She was upset and guilty in a classic response to sexual harassment. The group reacted forcefully to support her and affirm that she had not been at fault, but what also emerged from the discussion is the powerlessness many learners may feel if they cannot read or write as they think they should. Carla came to see the incident in something other than personal terms. She suspected that the learner was trying to put their relationship on a footing where he could again feel powerful and in control.

From Eli Goldblatt. (1994). Van rides in the dark: Literacy as involvement in a college literacy practicum. *The Journal for Peace and Justice Studies, 6*(1), 77–94.

Our final example is a set of reflections written by Spanish-speaking immigrants, thinking back about their families, life in Mexico, and immigration to Chicago. Some of the writers come from one of the many small writing groups Hal Adams has started in inner city housing projects and libraries. The publication he edits prints a bold assertion on its masthead: "The Journal of Ordinary Thought publishes reflections people make on their personal histories and everyday experiences. It is founded on the propositions that every person is a philosopher, expressing one's thoughts fosters creativity and change, and taking control of life requires people to think about the world and communicate the thoughts to others." In other Chicago neighborhoods, students from the Center for Literacy at the University of Illinois at Chicago are working in literacy centers helping people learn English as a second language and reflect on their experiences with education.

Although the writers published in these two journals didn't know each other, you can read these texts as a conversation that you have been privileged to join. To enter the discussion with your own reflection, ask yourself: What are my connections to these thoughts? What "good problems" do they raise for me?

Example 15–6
Reflections in Conversation

From "Part of My Life"

I arrived in Chicago on March 28, 1990. I found no work after being in Chicago for one month. A friend, who also moved to Chicago from Mexico, told me about a job picking vegetables in Palatine. We went to Palatine to work and for two weeks we had nothing to eat but water and flour tortillas because we had no money until we got our first paycheck. After all of the vegetables were picked, my friend and I moved back to Chicago. I worked . . . [for two years as a dishwasher] working at night from 11 PM to 7 AM. . . . I did not think I could learn to read and write English when I found out how hard the classes were. [My experience at the literacy center] opened the door for me to learn English. Now I can read the newspaper, read books, I write in English, and I can talk with other people in English at the store.

From Jose Anaya. (1995, Fall). Part of my life. *More Possible Meetings* (Vol. 2, p. 33). Chicago, IL: Student Literacy Corps, Center for Literacy, University of Illinois at Chicago.

From "What Our Parents Had"

When I was growing up, there were six kids. My dad, who barely had a high school education, is very intelligent, but skipped around from job to job, with long hours and hard labor. My mom, who had left school at the age of sixteen because she was pregnant, worked as a waitress, sometimes handling two jobs at one time. . . . I know that the only way I am going to succeed is through education. I am, however, a little disturbed that people are judged as far as their future careers go, by what they know from books rather than from what they know about life. My dad can fix roofs, plumbing, electricity, appliances, machinery, and so much more, but because he has never had any formal education in these areas, he cannot get a job in any of these fields.

From Margaret Gonzales. (1995, Fall). What our parents had. *More Possible Meetings* (Vol. 2, p. 24). Chicago, IL: Student Literacy Corps, Center for Literacy, University of Illinois at Chicago.

From "My Mother Compares It with Paradise"

I was born in the north of Mexico, in the state of Durango, in a mineral near a very beautiful river, just below a very beautiful mountain, which is the Sierra Madre. My mother compares it with paradise. [Coming to Chicago] I have no choice but to remember the warm climate of H. Matamoros and to compare the lifestyle of both cities. I have now become accustomed to the fast pace of living in Chicago, and my activities are governed now by that rhythm.

From Maria Aguilar. (1996, July). My mother compares it with paradise. *Journal of Ordinary Thought, 16,* 8. Chicago, IL: Neighborhood Writing Alliance.

From "Humble Families"

Mexico, D.F. is the most populated city in the world, there is too much traffic, too much pollution. Nevertheless, there is not much violence, people treat you right, and discrimination does not exist. But, there is no guarantee of life, the programs to help single mothers or anyone else do not exist. . . . I like it here because we can obtain a lot of material things. They do not leave you on your own; they help you anyway. But, I think the people are very cold, they walk without looking around them, there is the color difference, the language difference, and the great difference in thought. We come from humble families, from third world countries like El Salvador, and our beliefs are different.

From Sandra Bonilla. (1996, July). Humble families. *Journal of Ordinary Thought, 16,* 10. Chicago, IL: Neighborhood Writing Alliance.

PROJECTS AND ASSIGNMENTS

1   As you begin your observation/reflection journal, make the first entry a plan for a small experiment. Choose a few of the observation techniques described in this chapter, and jot down a plan for how you are going to use them. Then, after you have given each of your techniques a try, do a journal entry which compares what you were able to learn from using each: what are the strengths and weaknesses of each? What would a good combination be?

2   At the midpoint and end of your project, review the portfolio of your journal entries or electronic bulletin board posts. Write a memo that evaluates the substance and quality of your work so far (as it is reflected in your b-board posts) in three areas: in your *reading,* in your *learning,* and in your *contributions* to the discussion and learning of the group as a whole.

3   Hold a collaborative planning session with your partner on one of your upcoming reflections. Write up your observations and note some key points that will be in your reflection before the planning session. Get your partner to help you question and develop your initial responses. Then by comparing your notes and your written reflection, notice what emerges. What did the session produce? Why?

4   Look back at your observations, journal entries, or posts to a bulletin board. What do you see as a dominant question you were asking yourself, a problem you were thinking about, or a realization that emerged over this time? Write a reflection that puts the pieces together for you, that responds to uncertainties and questions, and helps a reader join you in the process.

5   What does "community" mean to you and how do you define "service to others"? Explore the meaning of these ideas in terms of the personal experiences, values, or attitudes that brought you to this outreach project and in terms of what happens in the project itself. (Don't search for a grand, universal definition. Think about John Dewey's argument that the *meaning* of abstract ideas [like "service"] lies in the *consequences* of holding or acting on those ideas.)

    As a basis for your first draft, do some exploratory writing on these issues:

    a. List as many "services" as you can that you and your family (parents, grandparents, partners, significant others) have received. For example, government services (student loans, work study, unemployment, AFDC, Medicare). Or other community services (churches, synagogues, nonprofit agencies, training programs, teams, school programs) that you, your family or friends have either received aid from or supported in some way.

    b. Which communities do you belong to? How do they sustain each other and take care of their members in trouble? Did they offer "service" or the "care" McKnight described in Chapter 14?

    c. Think about a time you received or offered service to another. Describe it. What effect did it have on you? On others?

d. Write a personal story or reflection that helps explain a personal connection you feel to the mission or the concerns of the community group you are working with.

e. Write a personal story or reflection that helps describe what service and community means in the actions of the group you are working with.

6 Write a reflection that lets you enter a conversation with other writers, such as the writers of Examples 15–4, 15–5, or 15–6. Let these three questions help you join the discussion as a writer yourself:

- How is this account connected to my experience or to things I am thinking about? What does it mean to me?

- What kinds of "good problems"—conflicts, uncertainties, questions—does it raise for me? How can I weave those different voices in my own mind into a interpretation I have reached "on reflection"? (I realize that my understanding may change and grow with further action and reflection.)

- How can I bring a reader into this conversation and recreate the experience, the questioning, and the realizations I am coming to?

chapter sixteen

Community Writing Projects

GOAL 4
CREATE a working relationship

Switch from the role of student to the role of writer.

    STRATEGY 1   **HAVE A "CHECK IN" CP SESSION**

    STRATEGY 2   **CUSTOMIZE THE PLANNER'S BLACKBOARD**

GOAL 5
LISTEN to other peoples' stories

Use interviews to tell the community's story.

    STRATEGY 1   **PLAN AHEAD**

    STRATEGY 2   **TURN AN INTERVIEW INTO A TEXT**

GOAL 6
TRY out a new genre

If you are writing in a new genre, figure out the features you can use.

    STRATEGY 1   **REVIEW BACK FILES AND MODELS**

    STRATEGY 2   **GO MINING FOR TEXTUAL TECHNIQUES**

    STRATEGY 3   **DRAW ON STANDARD RHETORICAL PATTERNS**

Community writing projects let you collaborate, *as a writer,* with the members of a community association, nonprofit center, or agency putting your college-level writing skills to use in the real world. Working outside the predictable world of the classroom will give you fun, frustration, real challenges, and real satisfaction.

WHO COULD I WORK WITH?

Nonprofit organizations devoted to youth, elderly, jobs,
    housing, literacy, and environment

Neighborhood community centers

Schools

Churches and synagogues

Recreational centers and playgrounds

Child care centers

Clinics and hospitals

Shelters and group homes

Senior citizen homes

Museums, parks

Prisons and courts

Legal services

Government agencies

GOAL 4

CREATE a Working Relationship

For you, this is a personal and academic learning experience. You expect to be a better writer and more informed citizen when you leave and to get course credit for the work. But when you enter a nonprofit as a writer, you are moving out of the role of student to that of professional consultant who donates his or her time and expertise to a project that the volunteer believes in. In this case, the tie between the two parties is not money, but commitment, mutual learning, or complementary goals—you need experience; they need a document. Some people call community service, "the rent we pay for living," and in a minute we will talk about the "contract" you make with the agency for what is to be done. However, community service is not a "business deal" without the money. There are other ways to think of your role in this community/university collaboration.

Communities work best when people can see they are bound together with one another and recognize that what hurts or helps you also hurts and helps me in a different way. Such communities also recognize and value different skills and contributions we each make to the common good. As a college-educated writer, you may have a lot to learn about other parts of the community, other cultures, other talents, other lives, but you also bring a "professional" skill that can make a contribution—if you can carry off your role well. Are you ready to step out of your role as a "student" and to become a "writer"? Here's a guide to setting up a relationship that will be not only workable and productive, but full of mutual respect and enthusiasm.

1. *Make a professional contact.* When you make contact with your nonprofit or agency, be ready to introduce yourself and state your reason for calling, say what you would like to do, leave clear information on how you can be contacted, and/or ask when you can reach the person you need to talk to. Be prepared: You may have to leave all this in a phone message. And you may have to be persistent about calling back. When you do talk, be ready to schedule a meeting. Ask how you could get any literature on the agency or other information you can read ahead of time.

2. *Agree on a plan.* Before you meet, do your homework and read all you can find on the group or its kind of work. Don't expect an "introductory lecture." Show your resourcefulness and interest by finding the basic facts out first. That way you can use the meeting to talk about:
   a. Your goals and their goals and current needs,
   b. Specific projects you might work on,
   c. The timeline you are working under (remember, nonprofits don't live by the quarter or semester system), and, if possible,
   d. An agreement on what you will do, what they will do, and dates and deliverables. Walk away knowing who your future contact will be and when you will speak again.
   Here is an typical agreement form that helps you think of items that have to be discussed. Make a copy of this completed agreement (Figure 16–1) for everyone involved, once it is signed by all.

3. *Organize your group.* If this is a group project, your whole process will need to start with a planning meeting. People whose professional lives depend on team work have found that the time spent building explicit plans not only saves them hours and days of work down the road, but also boosts the quality of their product or performance. Here are some tips on organizing a group process.
   a. Start your meeting by setting an **agenda:** What do you want to accomplish in the next hour and a half? An agenda, like the one below, lays out who is responsible for what by what date. People also bring personal agendas to any project that can become *hidden* agendas and a source of misunderstanding. So it also helps to spend some time talking about the personal goals or images of this project that each person in the group is starting with. It is fine for teammates to have

FIGURE 16–1
A Project Proposal Agreement

Project Proposal
Date
Organization

	Phone	Fax	Address

Contact Person

Writers

1.

2.

3.

Instructor

1. A brief description of the document to be written that includes the topic, the genre or type, the length (especially maximum words)

2. What is the purpose of this document, who will read it, and how will the organization use it (for public distribution, for internal use)?

3. How will the writers get information that they need? Is it on file or does it require research? If it requires interviews, who will set them up? Who are the people/resources the writers can turn to?

4. When and how often will the writers and contact person confer? And when should the writers get feedback on work in progress? If the writers meet their deadline, what turnaround time can they count on for a response?

5. Deadlines:
Progress Report
Rough Draft
Final Text
Signatures
Writer
Writer
Writer
Organization Representative
Instructor

differing priorities; putting them on the table lets you develop a mutual plan. Appoint a meeting coordinator who keeps track of all your decisions in writing and if possible maps out the discussion or issue tree on a board for everyone to see. (See Chapter 7 for help on issue trees.)

b. Once you have a general sense of your project, plunge in by getting operational. (Remember the power of operational problem definitions from Chapter 8?) Brainstorm a **To Do List** of all the tasks that have to get done. Decide who will be in charge of each job—that is, who will be responsible, not for doing all the work, but for seeing that that part gets done on time. Having it down in writing lets you be clear about responsibility and dates and for seeing that the work is evenly divided.

c. To turn that list into a working plan, decide on your major **Milestones**—on the key things you need to accomplish in order to move forward and when they must be done. Your part of a project will often depend on someone else doing their part first—and leaving you enough time to do yours. So look down the road and map out a series of milestones as places that mark the subgoals you need to achieve. Think of each milestone as a point that will call for a mini-celebration over your accomplishment. Then make sure everyone gets a copy of the "official" group notes.

For example, since Esme came to college, she has heard a lot about the problems of poor communities, but very little about their resources, activism, or the creativity she remembered from her own Latino neighborhood back home. Motivated by a desire to celebrate the strengths of the community around their college, the group brainstormed ideas (such as a videotaped oral history, a photo exhibit, music documentary) until they settled on a project to compile a performance schedule and flyer for all the neighborhood theatre work they could find going on in their area and to make a videotaped Public Service Announcement (PSA) that would feature one or two examples of local companies, street theatre, or youth performance groups. They started by creating a list of tasks they needed to do.

To Do	Responsibility
Get information on performances	Everyone
Call contacts	Everyone
Develop PSA script	Everyone

As their To Do List grew, the group realized that to construct a Performance Schedule, they would first have to use any contacts they knew just to locate local groups. Before scripting the PSA, they should probably want to select and interview their featured groups. So at this point they began to organize their To Do tasks under a set of Milestones. And this let them work backwards from each Milestone and ask: What would I have to do to get there?

As Figure 16–2 shows, working toward goals or milestones lets you get more specific about what needs to be done and when. Notice how Loren, who is working under a printing deadline, has two weeks to design the Performance Schedule— but only if the team has finished their calls by Sept. 27. The decision about which group to interview can be made if *most* of the calls are done, so there is a little extra time in that part of the schedule. But some things, like scheduling the interview and signing up for the camera, may have to be done well in advance or the whole process could grind to a halt. A little foresight can save a lot of panic.

FIGURE 16–2
Milestones and To Do List

MILESTONES AND TO DO	RESPONSIBILITY	(PREP TIME) AND DUE DATE
1. List of groups is compiled and we start calling for performance info Call contacts who know about any performance groups & ask for leads		(1 week) Sept 20
• theatres in phone book & theatre faculty here	Loren	
• high school drama departments	Randy	
• community action groups	Esme	
• public access radio, tv, papers	Demond	
2. Calls are completed (mostly). The group to visit & feature in PSA is selected Compare lists and divide up task of calling groups for performance info	Everyone	(1 week) Sept 27
3. Tentative PSA script; Interviews planned & scheduled Develop PSA video with interviews and performance shots		(1 week) Oct 3
• script and schedule interview	Esme (w/team)	
• sign up for (week in advance) & borrow camera	Loren	
• interview director & actors; get performance footage	Randy & Loren (camera)	
• view footage: choose shots & themes	team	
• draft script and shot sheet	Demond & Esme	
• edit tape	Loren	
4. Calls completed & Production Schedule Flyer and Promo design is done to allow time for printing		(2 weeks) October 10

FIGURE 16–3
Milestones Visualized on a Timeline

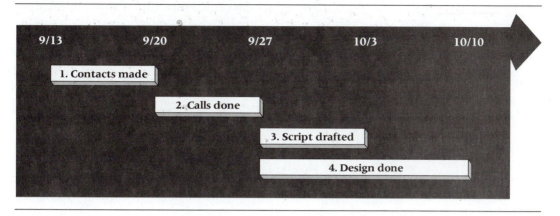

To visualize how each step in the process depends on previous ones, sketch a timeline that marks the date each Milestone
must be reached and shows how long you have to work on it
(Figure 16–3).
4. End your meeting by setting up a **Contact** plan: when and
where can everyone in the group be reached; where can you
drop off information on drafts; when and where is your regular
meeting time? Make a transportation plan for getting to your
organization.

PLANNING AND COLLABORATING

Let's consider some things you will need to know in the context of a
real case. Neighborhood Home Owners, is a nonprofit organization
that has helped low-income families, often single mothers, realize
that they can be homeowners rather than renters. Stan and his staff
of one hold a six-week class that takes people through the process of
financial planning, loan application, and building evaluation. Then
they literally "hold peoples' hands" through the process of buying
and renovating. Neighborhood Homes needs help getting their story
to funders and advice to clients. But, like the people at many nonprofits, Stan and his "staff" are overworked, underpaid, committed,
engaged, and hard to tie down.

That's why the first challenge in any community writing project is
getting a clear plan for your job. Stan rarely has time to be in the office; someone needed him this morning to help negotiate with a con-
tractor who hasn't poured the concrete he promised, and he has six
phone calls waiting, and the new training session starts tonight. He
needs a helping hand, but unlike a teacher with a folder of prepared

"assignments," he is not sure how to delegate a job you can do; and he is afraid he doesn't have the time to teach you all you need to know to write a really usable piece. (In fact, last year after an Intern spent three weeks in their tiny office and lot of his staff's valuable time, the Intern ended up getting his course credit, but all Stan saw was a term paper that wouldn't make sense to his clients, convince his funders, or help him get another person a day closer to a home.) So even though Stan values and needs your effort, this project might not be the top priority on his To Do list for today.

In the journal entry that follows, Kevin is going through the process we discussed in Chapter 5. He is exploring a rhetorical problem (and its social context) and trying to explain to himself what is really at stake here. As you will see, the strategies that help you in academic or professional writing work here too: Kevin needs to figure out not just what *to say*, but a plan *to do* what *needs to be done* for Neighborhood Home Owners. And his intuitions—plus some collaboration just when he needs it—are helping him read the situation and change plans. Kevin's story will also suggest an additional strategy that helps you do community writing, called *Check-In CP Sessions*.

Example 16–1
An Observation/Reflection Journal

This excerpt from Kevin's second draft shows how his text started to pull together a number of goals that he and Stan had suggested.

Observations	Reflections
Sept 10. Met with Stan. Neighborhood Home Owners is in an old house, w loose joints. Papers everywhere; real informal & friendly. People keep calling for advice or meetings.	I think I expected a regular office, like a business or bank. This is like a 3-ring circus run by two people.
My first big idea was to do a trouble shooting guide—for furnace problems, do this; for roofs problems, call. I could get phone numbers etc. so he wouldn't be running around doing all these "house" calls.	Realized later I was doing the "elite institution" thing, wanting to do what "I" had expertise in—writing a technical guidebook—not what NHO actually needed.
Stan just shook his head and looked at me like I didn't get it. He says, "too many different things that come up."	Also maybe these new homeowners don't want someone to hand them a book or information. They want to know that Stan, a person, is going to be there to see them through this.
Then we talked about doing a profile of the new home owners, to show potential funders what NHO was accomplishing. Over the last year they have. . . .	A profile sounds fun, but I have never written anything like this . . .

Observations	Reflections
Sept. 13.	Bank report. WRONG!
Called back for a 5-minute CP session with Stan.	Stan thinks funders listen to stories about real people who are making it. The contrast is that banks give money until people default. But this training (and Stan) shows them how to make it through tough spots and sees them through. So I have to show what NHO does for people, not properties.
Plan A. Do it like a bank or development company report on the past year.	
I would profile the properties and owners in the left column (financing, repairs to house; owner's background etc.) and picture of house + owner on right. Show Stan's point—ownership builds up neighborhoods.	
Plan B. Do a personal profile of a couple of new homeowners, like 30-year-old Darlene, who never thought she would own her own.	
Stan loves Plan B. Said they could set the interviews up for me here at NHO, where people would feel comfortable.	
Later	Looking back at my journal, I realize that I *am* doing the good part of Plan A and showing how NH changes neighborhoods. But I am doing it as part of Darlene's story. Cool.
Met with Ellie for a CP session on my draft. Realized I was working with 2 key points, one about Darlene and one about the neighborhood. Want to make sure that doesn't confuse my story.	

Example 16–2
From Kevin's Draft

> Darlene, a nurse's aid with two teenage children, often sits on the front porch when she gets home from work and talks to people who walk down her inner city street, with its row of old Pittsburgh, two-story row houses. The difference is, this is Darlene's house, not a rental property—its steps have just been repaired and the porch is scheduled for paint with Darlene's next paycheck. And thanks to NHO, Darlene is now someone she never thought she could be—a new home owner. She is also a new kind of neighbor.
>
>   "I sit out and talk cause I'm also keeping an eye on things. I want people to know, 'Listen, this is my house, and on this street we don't want that messin' around.' I talk to my neighbors cause I know, I'm gonna be here."

❧ *STRATEGY 1* **HAVE A "CHECK IN" CP SESSION**

If community writing is new to you, it is doubly important to find a collaborative planning partner at the beginning of the project. Find someone you can call up, run ideas by, show drafts to. It should be someone who knows how to be a CP Supporter (not just a peer reviewer who makes suggestions). And they should know how to use the Planner's Blackboard to ask you the questions about Key Point and Purpose, Audience, and Text Conventions that will help you do the rhetorical planning a real world task requires (see Chapter 5).

But what if your community contact has no experience with collaborative planning or writing? After all, Stan isn't a teacher and is much more comfortable "writing it himself" than having to explain "all he knows" to someone else. However, if you write a whole draft before you get Stan's agreement, it may go down a blind alley and he may ask for major revisions or lose interest in a project he can't use. A good strategy in this situation is to hold a brief "check in" Collaborative Planning session early on, whenever you come to a decision point. Instead of doing a full draft, sketch out your plan in terms of the key point you will try to make and the purposes you see. Imagine how you are expecting the audience to respond (and which readers you have in mind) and then what the text might look like. Like Kevin, you might sketch out two different plans. Then call your contact for a five-minute phone conference: "I've got a plan and want to see if I am on the right track. Can I give you the two-minute version and get your response?" Be prepared to keep it to two minutes and actively solicit feedback not just on the text, but on your image of the rhetorical problem—your purpose, audience, and point.

Stan, it turns out, was very good at responding to a concrete plan, and steered Kevin in a valuable new direction.

❧ *STRATEGY 2* **CUSTOMIZE THE PLANNER'S BLACKBOARD**

The *Planner's Blackboard* in Chapter 5 is a general purpose planning tool. But you and your partner may want to customize it for a specific task such as the task nonprofits often face—writing to win public and foundation support. Since even stories and reports, like the Neighborhood Home Owners profiles, are designed to convince someone of something, rhetorical planning can help you write a more effective text.

To customize the *Blackboard*, write some planning prompts and questions that you could use when talking to your contact, or that your supporter could ask you, when you have a collaborative planning session. Here is an example of a *Blackboard* customized to help you write a persuasive piece about a nonprofit project like Neighborhood Home Owners.

Example 16–3
Planning Questions for a Nonprofit Newsletter

TOPIC INFORMATION

1. What are two or three of the most interesting, typical things that go on at this nonprofit?

2. Tell me about a specific situation that sticks in your mind (see the "critical incident" technique below), that sums up what this place does and stands for.

PURPOSE AND KEY POINT

3. When you were thinking of that critical incident, what did you want to illustrate? What are the key features of this program you want to get across?

4. You have told me some of the big features, like helping people do xyz, but other groups do that, too. What are the surprising, distinctive things about your group?

5. What is the problem you are working on? What are the barriers in this situation that make your presence, your agency really necessary?

AUDIENCE

6. How would you respond (in your text) to a reader who is thinking, "I care. There are a lot of problems in the world, and a lot of worthy causes. And I enjoy reading your account. But as a foundation or individual, I am also wondering why I should support this one. And why now?"

7. What about a reader who thinks, "I am skeptical. I see a lot of wonderful ideas but not as many real accomplishments. What can you show me about the impact of your program? What differences have you made and what is the evidence?"

8. Imagine a reader who responds, "I am a part of this community; I identify with it. So I am looking at how you (the writer) represent 'me' (in your text). Am I treated with

(Continued)

respect? Am I represented as a person with multiple dimensions (not just as a poor person, for instance) and as a person with reasons, intentions, and aspirations, just like the agency that is helping me out right now?"

TEXT CONVENTIONS

9. A standard proposal has some key parts:

  A statement of the problems; of the barriers people and agencies face in dealing with that problem.

  A vision of what could be done.

  Evidence of what has been learned or done so far.

  A plan for the next step.

  Even though you are writing a newsletter article, a profile, or human interest feature, the underlying goal is to persuade. Did you embed any of these elements of a persuasive proposal in your story?

GOAL 5

LISTEN to Other Peoples' Stories

Interviews are wonderful tools for exploring a question or situation in more depth, for getting the "story behind the story," and seeing the human side of an organization or a project. You will be using interviews to get information from your contacts, or you may be publishing your interview as an article (as Judy Harris did, below). But in either case, it is important to realize that as a listener or writer, you are in fact creating a story by the questions you ask, the way you interpret the answers, and the way you remember and present the interview. Interviewing—even when it seems like you are just collecting "the facts"—is a process of creating the story of other people's lives. So use it with sensitivity and rhetorical savvy.

 STRATEGY 1   **PLAN AHEAD**

How do you get a good story? If you want cooperation and enthusiasm from a busy interviewee, you must do two things. First, do your homework. Learn all you can from printed materials or other people, so you can go beyond the standard information. Don't be the wide-eyed and unprepared interviewer who sits down and asks, "So what do you do here?" Secondly, script the basic parts of your interview so you walk in with different kinds of questions—and plenty of them.

Preparing Questions

- Start by preparing standard journalism questions: Who? What? When? Where? Why? You may use these to confirm and elaborate on key facts or terms you turned up in preparation, as when Kevin asks Steve, "Your recent report says that *15 people* just *graduated* from your September Home Owners class. Just who are those *people* and what did they do to *graduate?*"
- Prepare questions that can carry out your purpose. Are you interested in revealing a problem or dramatizing a need, telling a success story, celebrating people, countering misconceptions, showing an organization at a crossroads, calling for action? Are there facts or stories that would help you do that? Your purpose will also develop—and maybe even change directions altogether—as you learn more. But telling your interviewee about what you are trying to learn can sometimes turn the interview into a collaborative effort to figure out what you need to know.
- Prepare both open and closed questions. *Open* questions invite whatever the interviewee has to say on the topic. *Closed* questions call for a yes/no or a specific response. You might also want to try some *scaled* questions as the writers of the "Report Card" did below. *Scaled* questions ask the interviewee to give a value or a rank to his or her response on a scale of 1 to 5. Scaled questions allow you to make clearer comparisons across people.
- Test your questions on your collaborative planning partner: Are some broad enough, others pointed? Are they purposeful, appropriate, understandable? Can you cover the essentials in the time allowed (including time for introductions, chat, and exploring "live issues" that turn up)? Do you have back-up questions if it goes quickly?

In the Interview

- Arrive at least ten minutes before the interview. Use the time to have everything out and prepared. Try to make your interviewee feel at ease with the process by explaining your purpose, saying how you intend to use the information, asking permission to tape the session so you can be sure of accuracy, and by offering to show them your write up for accuracy before it is published.
- Even if you tape, take notes on main points to help you follow the flow of the discussion or refer back to what the interviewee just said. If you can't tape, make sure you record the respondent's own words.

- Open questions let you go fishing for a "live issue" that interests you and/or your interviewee. But following up a live topic also means you can't prepare questions ahead of time. So on your question sheet, jot down the list of general issue tree questions (discussed in Chapter 7): What do you mean? How so? How do you know? Such as? Why? Why not? So what? They can help you explore a "live issue" in conversation or develop it in text.
- How can you keep your interviewee from giving you familiar generalizations or boring abstractions? A strategy called the "critical incident" technique can turn up new insights and interesting specifics. Instead of a general question that asks "Why is this program a success?" or "What is the problem you are trying to solve?" ask your interviewee to tell you about a specific critical incident. Ask them to recall an occasion on which they saw their program "succeeding" or a specific situation in which they "saw a problem" that this program was able to help solve. Ask them to remember exactly what happened, how people responded, how it turned out. Then—after you have discussed a real situation—you might ask them to explain why that was a success or a problem.
- Go over the interview release form (see Chapter 15) before you begin and explain how you will use this material and when you will show it to them for accuracy if it is to be published.

STRATEGY 2   TURN AN INTERVIEW INTO A TEXT

Good, published interviews are not simple transcripts of a conversation, even when they look that way. They are carefully crafted stories and arguments that make the interviewee come to life *and* make a point. What point you make will depend on where the interview is to be published. Here is how one writer presented a community action project to the readers of a faculty and staff newsletter. (Paragraph numbers are added for our discussion.)

Example 16–4
A Published, Purposeful, and Reader-Based Interview

Elaine Atkinson: The Role Models Program

It feels as though the CMU community is beginning to show an increased interest in the quality of its staff life. Slowly, and I hope, steadily, we will help to implement a number of much needed changes in the benefits and policies of our university.

This is the first in a series of interviews with staff members at CMU.

Elaine Atkinson has been a secretary in the Psychology Department for six years. For the past two years, she has been developing the Role Models Program which will be implemented in February.

—Judy Harris

What exactly is the Role Models Program? (¶1)

It's a tutorial program for inner city kids in elementary school, third through fifth grades. The program will serve these children by bringing them into contact with role models/tutors from Carnegie Mellon. The children need role models from CMU because in poor environments there are few people working, or aspiring to careers, or going to college.

This was not always so. Before desegregation inner city communities had a broad representation of lifestyles and role models. Of course, you had your underclass, but you also had the working class in the same community. So when a child looked around he saw people from each group—a working class family, a first generation going to college. Children could look around them and see the possibilities. But after desegregation, people with upward mobility, seeking the American Dream, could finally live wherever they wanted to live. Without knowing it, they drained the inner cities of valuable resources when they moved out.

We're left with communities that provide fewer role models? (¶2)

Yes. Drained communities without exposure to opportunities. Many people in poor neighborhoods can't find work. There's teenage pregnancies, high school drop-outs, and drugs. Poor people are victims of drugs because they can't get a job and they see drugs as a means of employment. That's unfortunate, but if that's all you see, that is reality. Today children from poor communities go to school and go back home in the same environment. They aren't exposed to other realities. . . .

So how will the program work? (¶3)

There will be ten paid role model/tutors who will work with the kids for the semester. . . . I've talked to several professors who will share what they do with the kids. I want the kids to be able to come to the university for a couple of hours after school three days a week—to see the studios, the labs, to watch professors and students in action. . . .

Will the program involve the child's family? (¶4)

Yes, there is a parent's component to the program that will work with parents to help them reinforce the value system and the goals we are trying to establish in these young people. We are working with both the family and the public school system so that the child will receive the same message from the public schools, from their parents, and from us—bombard them with good information. . . .

You told me earlier that children want attention, they need instruction, they need structure, and it is up to adults to give it to them. Isn't this the same for all children, whether they come from a stable community or not? (¶5)

Right. The difference between a child that grows up in a poor community and a child that does not is their perception of what life has in store for them. When children see high unemployment in their neighborhoods, they feel that they will be unemployed, too. But if you ask them what kind of housing, what kind of car do you want, how many children?—then you show them the economic cost of what they want, and the educational background they'll need, then they can start to think for themselves. You can show them how they can have a career through education. So the program should be an education in problem solving, how to advance in society, how to plan to get where you need to be. It's also important to send the

message that poverty is not permanent. That really needs to be said.

You must love children. (¶6)

Yes, I do. I have two children of my own. I was a teenage mother—twice—and when trying to raise these children at first I thought, "Oh my God, they have me! Poor babies!"—which was really a motivating factor for me. What replaced feeling sorry for them was the will that they would not be deprived, regardless of their economic status. They would know that there is no difference in the classes other than what you put into life, what you yourself give.

How did you come up with this program? (¶7)

I think I'm very fortunate. I've experienced life in both worlds. When I was younger, I asked myself why am I suffering so much? Why was I born poor? Why don't we have a car? Why didn't anyone tell me about teenage pregnancy? Why didn't anyone tell me that education would make a difference in my life? It is my intimate experience with being underclass that has enabled me not only to understand the thinking processes of poor people, but to become an independent person, to know the process and the transition that it takes. I'm able to say, what would have helped me in that predicament? And I can answer that it would have helped to have role models, it would have helped to go to college and university campuses and have scientists tell me the joy of being a scientist.

What could've helped me in my housing situation, what could've helped our community? It would've helped if we had workmen and carpenters come in and say, "You all can learn to do this!" I've been able to write the prescriptions for the program because I can go back at each stage of my life and ask myself, what would've helped there?

You liken this experience that you want to share to problem solving? (¶8)

Yes. The foundation of knowledge that I hope to instill in the children and parents of the program is: the way you think is very important to your success. . . . I say this because throughout my life I've been beating the odds. If I had said, because I dropped out of school, I can't pass the GED, I probably wouldn't have taken it. If I had said I've never worked at a university, I cannot work for Herbert Simon, a Nobel Laureate at a university, I would have not come and interviewed for the position. If I had said to myself that I don't have a degree in social work, and that I

am not a school teacher—had I let any of those things handicap me, the Role Models Program would not be in existence today. . . .

So what's the schedule for the Role Models Program? (¶9)

The pilot program will take place at CMU in February 1991; A. Leo Weil School on the Hill will be the pilot school. Anyone who wants more information or who is interested in volunteering time—long-term or a one-day workshop—can contact me at ext. 2801.

From Judy Harris. (1990, November/December). [Interview with Elaine Atkinson, Director, The Role Models Program]. *FOCUS* (Carnegie Mellon University), *20*(3), 7.

Notice in Example 16–4 how Judy Harris anticipates the interests of her readers and makes her points by crafting a reader-based text (see Chapter 10). Here are some techniques she uses.

Highlight What the Reader Wants to Know

Nonprofits typically send their newsletters to people who already support them or their cause. By placing her interview in a more public media (in this case a university newspaper for faculty and staff) Judy Harris would be able to tell a wider audience about the Role Models Program—if the article captured and kept their attention.

Notice how she starts out by tying the story of Elaine Atkinson to the interests and concerns of the readers. Instead of a writer-based description of her topic (see Chapter 10), Judy's reader-based introduction presents Elaine as a staff member (like many of the readers) who is showing initiative and making a difference around her. Judy, who is both a student and a department secretary herself, taped more than an hour of conversation spread across two sessions. How did she turn that into the highly focused "edited" interview you see? One key is in the questions, some of which she actually asked and some of which she created for the *written* interview in order to get her point across. Judy illustrates three kinds of questions that you will find useful.

Use Standard Journalistic Questions

Although this interview is full of answers to the Who, What, When, Where, and Why of journalism, she only uses these questions (which are relatively uninteresting as questions) a few times in the interview when she asks:

What exactly is the Role Models Program? (paragraph 1)
So how will the program work? (paragraph 3)

Use Questions Readers Might Ask

These questions will keep peoples' attention because they raise questions that Judy's imagined readers might be likely to ask, such as:

Will the program involve the child's family? (paragraph 4)
Do you think there is a strong enough desire on this campus to make this program work? (paragraph 5)
So you're confident of CMU's support? (paragraph 6)

Use Key Point Questions

Finally, these questions allow Judy and Elaine to make a key point by turning an idea Elaine wants to emphasize or develop further into a question, such as:

We're left with communities that provide fewer role models? (paragraph 2)
You told me earlier that children want attention, they need instruction, they need structure, and it is up to adults to give it to them. Isn't this the same for all children, whether they come from a stable community or not? (paragraph 7)
You must love children. (paragraph 8)

Some questions serve multiple purposes. How would you say she is using the rest of the questions in the interview? What, for instance, would you say is the real purpose of the final question?

Connect People and Ideas

If you simply want to get the facts across, use an announcement or news story. Use an interview when you want to reveal not only what and who, but why. Let people talk about their intentions, their reasons, their commitments, and their sense of the problems they face and feel. You can also use a human interest story or interview to raise a point, to educate readers, and to encourage them to act. Look at the personal story Elaine tells in response to the rather neutral question, "How did you come up with this program?" Elaine's voice and personality come through here, but she is also using that story to make a point about her credibility and what could or should be done. Do you see other places in this interview that make a point by telling a personal story? As you craft stories and use quotations, always think about the points and the ideas behind the people.

Editing Someone Else's Words

Transcripts of most conversations, and even short quotations, can be amazingly disjointed, full of ums and ahs, unfinished sentences, and padding. If you can, ask permission to write an edited version of your interviewee's words, which you will let them check for accuracy before publication. (Ask for clarification if parts of the transcript are hard to follow.) Then use the editing strategies in Chapter 12 to transform list-like sentences, cut out repetition, and make the connections between ideas and sentence more clear. Most people will appreciate the improvements—as long at they gave you permission to edit their words and if they are allowed to approve the written version for accuracy.

If you are quoting someone without their input, make sure that you quote them verbatim. Do not take sentences out of context. For instance, do not make a statement that referred to a particular situation sound as if it were a sweeping generalization or claim. The ethics of quoting someone dictate that you retain not just the words, but the intended meaning.

GOAL 6

TRY Out a New Genre

One of the thrills of community-based writing is going new places, joining a new discourse, and making a contribution to something worthwhile. Not only will people outside a classroom actually read what you say; you might even affect what they think or do. You could make a difference.

At the same time, trying to work in a new discourse can mean leaving some familiar parts of the academic writing you have been doing for all these years behind. Furthermore, there is good evidence that "writing skill" isn't something you have or don't have. People have skill in the specific kinds of writing they have tried and practiced before, as this student discovered:

I have never written journalism. For three years now, I had been concentrating on technical writing, and I had become very good at technical
writing. I had a very distinct schema for technical writing. When I vol-
unteered to write a news story for a friend of mine, an editor on the Tar-
tan, I thought it would be easy. I am not a bad writer. I had not thought
I would have any problems writing the article—writing is writing. The
truth was very different and very interesting to me. I spent hours agonizing over an eight-paragraph news story, writing and re-writing, and
throwing it out and starting over. When I finally handed in the story, I
was so disappointed in my talents as a journalist that I vowed never to
write for a newspaper again. (7 Mar.)

From Linda Flower. (1994). *The Construction of Negotiated Meaning: A Social Cognitive Theory of Writing,* p. 289. Carbondale, IL: Southern Illinois University
Press.

This student thought "talent" should do it. What she really needed
were better strategies for how to handle a genre that was new to her.
Although this book can't give you a short course in journalism,
brochure design, or oral history, it can offer some good strategies for
scoping out a new discourse or genre and some pointers for what to
look for.

STRATEGY 1   REVIEW BACK FILES AND MODELS

Remember James Gee's claim: a Discourse isn't just vocabulary, but
an identity, a way of talking, writing, and acting. Now you are being
asked to take on the identity and voice of a new community and a
specific organization. Your first step should be to the organization's
back files for examples of the genre your contact has in mind. Once
you have decided on the genre you will be working in—a newsletter
article, an announcement, a profile, or instructions—ask your contact to show you those files and *more than one* example, if possible, of
what they have done before. Or find some models in the literature
of other similar organizations.

In reviewing these models, look for one that has similar rhetorical
goals. For instance, if you are going to describe a new project, do you
want to produce a formal description emphasizing its "news" value,
or a splashy PR version with artwork to convey enthusiasm, or a
personal, signed letter from the director to convey commitment, or a
personal, signed article from you, to convey a newcomer's experience? Notice how you are not just choosing a genre, but a whole attitude and approach to your subject.

How do you make the best choice? Here is where a ten-minute
"check in" collaborative planning session with your contact can
solve problems before they occur. The best rule of thumb for
working as a consultant is: Don't give your client any "surprises."
So to make sure your plan is a *shared* plan, show your contact the
models you are planning to use and get agreement on the genre,

tone, style. If your contact is off campus, you can mail a photo-copy of your choices with a note, and check in with a brief phone call.

 ### *STRATEGY 2*   GO MINING FOR TEXTUAL TECHNIQUES

What if there is no single good model to follow? The next best strat-egy is to look at different examples of your genre—such as multiple newsletter articles—and *mine* these examples for useful textual tech-niques. Look for features you can borrow or adapt to suit your pur-pose as you custom design your own text. When you review these examples, the first thing to hit your eye might be the visual conven-tions or format. These can include the use of type fonts and graphics or organizational tools such as headings, sections, and sidebars (little boxes with quotations or special information). Or you might note distinctive genre features.

But if you really want to mine a text for useful techniques, you need to understand the rhetorical purpose these features serve. Remember how the Planner's Blackboard (Chapter 5) helped you to see the big picture behind your own writing? Ask those same questions about this discourse: "What are the typical rhetorical features (purpose, point, readers, conventions) of this discourse or genre I am examining?" Notice, for instance, how the convention of a journalistic "lead" works to rivet attention and announce the issue.

Now look even closer and remind yourself that there was a real writer behind this text who may have used the very features you are looking at for a purpose. Look at them for a moment not just as features, but as intentional "textual techniques" and ask: "Why did the writer use this (anecdote, quotation, heading, sidebar, picture, factual statement, or narrative) here? What did this textual tech-nique let the writer do at this point?" You can use the questions in Figure 16–4 as a set of "mining tools" as you read the following newsletter articles for features you can add to your personal tool kit. Then when you find yourself working with a community client, use the same process to mine the texts in back files you gain access to.

Examples 16–5 and 16–6 illustrate two genres that seem very different—a press release and a personal essay. But looking closely also shows that they share some of the same goals and techniques: both are success stories that use narrative and personal voices to il-lustrate people overcoming the odds and to encourage readers to support these community programs. Examples 16–7 and 16–9, on the other hand, let us look at two different versions of the same genre—a newsletter article—to show what you can learn by study-ing variations within a genre. We will also take a behind-the-scenes look at the goals and processes that produced these texts.

FIGURE 16–4
Mining a Text for Rhetorical Features You Can Use

Topic Information

- What sort of ideas, facts, or claims get talked about most in this discourse or publication?

Purpose and Key Point

- What matters in this discourse: why are people writing this newsletter? Is the goal to convey information, to raise money, to raise consciousness, to invite action—or all of the above?
- How do writers achieve purposes like these in a newsletter/press release/history? Does that differ from what you would do in academic writing?
- Where do they put their Key Points and how do they get them across? For instance, how do they mix stories and claims?

Audience

- What is this audience expected to care about?
- What does this text assume about their interests?
- How do you anticipate (and speak to) possible readers' responses in a newsletter versus a press release?

Text Conventions (How-to-Do-It-in-Writing)

- What are the striking features of this discourse or genre?
- What are its conventional patterns of organization?
- How does it use visual cues?

MINING A PRESS RELEASE

On the surface, a press release looks like a short, simple statement of a newsworthy event to be reported in the press. But in fact, most press releases issued by nonprofit groups are really arguments, trying to convince (1) the press that their work is in fact "newsworthy" and (2) the public that their work is both valuable and successful. The catch is that the message in a press release will never be seen by the public unless the press release convinces an editor to assign a reporter to cover the story or unless it convinces a freelance reporter that he or she can find a good story here. If so, that reporter may try to "sell the story" or go ahead and write the story "on spec" ("speculating" that a paper or journal might pick it up and print it).

The press release in Example 16–5 is much more than "just the facts." It starts with a problem or conflict and plays up the surprise value of this entrepreneurial success story. It creates human interest through techniques like narrative, quotation, and concrete details. Finally, it ties this success story very directly to the work of the nonprofit and ends encouraging the reader (a member of the press) to contact the author for more information. In a sense, then, the real story here is not just Dorothy's contract, but the work of COPE that is making it possible for people like Dorothy to fulfill their dreams.

Example 16–5
A Press Release Success Story

Standard format/ Contact is a staff person at CRDC

For Immediate Release

May 1, 1996

Contact: Christine Falvey

(415) 775-8880, Ext. 111

Headline to catch attention and put COPE's name in lights

Entrepreneurial Success Story!

Children's Author Dorothy Peterson Makes Her Dream a Reality with a Little Help from CRDC's COPE Program

Location of release Journalistic "lead" moves from problem to success and includes the 5 W's

SAN FRANCISCO, CA—Just over a year ago, Dorothy Peterson hesitantly began a journey down the path where dreams become reality. She is one of the few who made it all the way, but it wasn't luck that got her there: patience, perseverance, hard work, and a helping hand from a supportive nonprofit agency were the ingredients enabling her triumph over the odds. Dorothy, a resident of Hunter's Point, is now a budding author of children's books, complete with a publishing deal, illustrator, and a target printing date for her first edition set for next month.

Facts given human interest through quotes, details, and issues

Dorothy's books are written with a unique contemporary African-American perspective for pre-school to kindergarten-aged children. As Dorothy explains "[t]he stories I saw were written either in an historical setting, meaning slavery, or about African children. I found there was a void in the market [for books written for present-day African-American children], and I decided to fill it." She has already written 38 stories, which she has dubbed, "The Amanda Series." Dorothy hopes that these books—which feature an old-fashioned, all-girl gang patterned after "The Little Rascals," led by the title character, Amanda—will provide a forum to present wholesome family values while at the same time coping with the negative aspects of the high-crime, depressed urban areas where so many African-American children grow up—issues that are usually glossed over or ignored in other children's stories.

Dorothy would like Amanda to become a household name and role model, and her marketing strategy includes producing Amanda accessories, such as collectable dolls. And that's only part of the comprehensive business plan she developed with the assistance of

Shifts spotlight to COPE's success story

the **Community Outreach and Pre-Enterprise (COPE) Program.** COPE is an assessment, planning, and self-employment skills training workshop program geared toward low to moderate income individuals who are interested in starting their own businesses; it is one of many programs administered by **Career Resources Development Center (CRDC),** a private nonprofit organization that has provided education and job training to the community for over 30 years.

Now that the 2 key points have been made (i.e., this individual is succeeding and this non-profit is doing good work), the release can fill in more details, including how the process works and local names and connections

Not knowing what to expect, Dorothy admits to being "a little overwhelmed" at first. "I was surrounded by all these people with such developed plans and ideas," Dorothy exclaimed, "and all I knew is that I just wanted to write." COPE Outreach Assistant, Antoinette Butler, provided the spark that helped bring Dorothy's vision to life. "Dorothy was very eager, and asked lots of questions," said Antoinette. "She worked very hard and did her homework to develop her business plan." The process involved studying textbooks, attending various skills workshops, and doing sample exercises while drafting a real business plan of her own. "It was hard," said Dorothy, "but I kept hearing Antoinette's voice in the back of my head, saying 'you can do it, you can do it,' so I kept plugging away, one page at a time." Antoinette's assistance was instrumental in Dorothy's success. "COPE helped me make my ideas clearer, set goals, and develop a concise business plan," says Dorothy. "I knew I could write . . . but I knew nothing about marketing, business and contingency plans. COPE helped me [establish] that."

Ends with contact information

For more information, contact Christine Falvey at (415) 775-8880

From Kelly Albertson. (1996). From Nora Bacon's Community Service Writing course, San Francisco State University.

MINING A PERSONAL ESSAY

Brian Engle's personal essay appeared in *The Volunteer,* a campus community service newsletter. Like the reflections you may have written in Chapter 15, writing let him talk about puzzles and conflicts in his personal experience—the essay is a way to make sense out of why he spent a year not doing what he was trained to do. But if you look closely, you will see this personal essay is also an argument; it is building a case to other college students reading *The Volunteer* about why service like this is so fulfilling—against all the odds. Like the press release, it starts with a journalistic version of a problem/purpose statement (see Chapter 5), bringing you into

Brian's personal puzzle. Then it promises to show you why the challenge is worth it. Brian could have told the story of his time in Los Angeles, but instead he sets the essay up as set of contrasts, in which each positive detail is one more piece of evidence about why teaching is worth the struggle.

Example 16–6
A Persuasive Personal Essay

Campus Voice: A Year with Teach for America
by Brian Engel

Problem/Purpose Statement names the conflict and sets up contrasts that organize the essay

What has always puzzled me about community service is that, almost without exception, what you receive from the experience is much more than what you put in. Teaching as a member of the Teach for America program has been no exception. That's not to say there haven't been many bumps along the road. Never in my life, have I felt so challenged, but also never in my life have I felt so fulfilled.

Concrete details develop the "down side"— and objections readers might raise

There are the long days—waking up at 4:30 A.M., to get ready and prepare for school at 7:30 A.M.. Finishing school at 3 P.M., only to have a meeting (or meetings) to go to, advise the chess club, supervise my tutoring program, or actually be lucky enough to go home and collapse. Never feeling prepared enough. Never getting enough sleep. Always having grading to do, or lessons to plan. Free time? What's that? School never leaves you, even when you leave school. How about the first day of school when I found out that one of my classes needs to be taught in Spanish? Spanish??!! How about trying to fit 42 kids into 36 seats? Not to mention the kids. There's the days when they get on your nerves, push the wrong buttons, say something they shouldn't, or

Conversational style (even talking to himself!) Big stories told with economical details

do something to disappoint you. Take for instance, Suleyma who, after we had an argument, never showed up to my class again. It's also hard watching the students go through difficult situations that I can't even imagine. Like Yanira who missed 3 weeks of school because her father was murdered in El Salvador. Then try earning the respect of students who are only 4 years younger than you or the veteran teachers who have children older than you. There's the apathetic and often cynical faculty, the bureaucratic obstacles, and so on and so on and so on.

The essay "turns" with a return to the opening claim

But as with volunteering, I'm receiving much more than I'm giving. There's Raul, who said to me at the end of the semester, "Sir, I just wanted to tell you that your Spanish has really improved . . . at the

Uses telling details that keep the conflict in view

beginning of the semester, we had no idea what you were trying to say and now we at least have an idea." Thanks, Raul. There's Ann, who despite her F in my class declared that I'm her favorite teacher. There's Alex who every other week tells me how she's decided to quit smoking. Maria's Christmas present to me of a statuette of the Nativity Scene is proudly displayed in my room (who cares that I'm Jewish?). . . . Having another F student, Chris, run up to me when he sees me to tell me what he's been doing and receive the praise he

Ends with a key point about what those details meant to him— and an argument to the reader Contact information lets the reader consider being a volunteer too and invites a personal call

desperately seeks reminds me why I'm teaching. I love my kids and I love my job. How many people can unequivocally tell you that? Sure, I could be making more money as the engineer I was trained to be, but you can't measure the wealth I receive from teaching.

About the author: Brian Engel graduated last year from Carnegie Mellon with a double major in Civil Engineering and Engineering & Public Policy. He is currently teaching at John Marshall High School in Los Angeles as part of the Teach for America program. The program takes recent college graduates and places them in under-resourced rural and inner city public schools. If you would like more information on Teach for America, Brian can be reached by phone (213) 913-2979 or by e-mail at af394@lafn.org.

From Brian Engel. (1995, April). Campus voice: A year with Teach for America. *The Volunteer,* Carnegie Mellon's Community Service Newsletter, No. 4, pp. 2, 6.

MINING A NEWSLETTER REPORT

The CLC Report Card article in Example 16–7 is from a newsletter introducing the Community Literacy Center to new readers. As you can see, it uses a variety of textual features, including a problem statement, commentary, grouped quotations, lists of features, and a graph. The key to mining this text—to seeing what these features are used for—lies in seeing its purpose. This introductory newsletter was sent to a national mailing list of educators, a local list of community groups, and to funders. For all their differences, all these groups could be expected to ask, "So, what has this program accomplished?" This article responds to that imagined question by saying, "We wanted to see what the teenagers from the last five years would say for themselves." But how do you present such an evaluation: in a letter from the director? in an essay or testimonial by teenagers? This article opted for using a report that combines a rating system (presented in a graph) with key ideas or themes (presented through quotations).

To help put together a piece like this, Lisa, the college writer, had to play a number of roles. To start with, after scripting the interview questions with her contact, she had to be a persistent and engaging telephone interviewer, tracking down teenagers and drawing them into a thoughtful evaluation of their experience. Next she had to be a data analyst, first, tabulating the results of the judgment questions on a 5-point scale, and second, interpreting the open-ended questions. To do that, Lisa and her CLC contact went through Lisa's verbatim notes on all responses to the open-ended questions, sorting them into groups and trying to name the main idea, which became the heading. Finally, Lisa had to be a document designer, using a computer program to turn her data into a graph and figuring out how to display the graph with the "names" of features and the longer description of each feature that would let readers know the question she really asked. In short, she had to "create" a set of text features that would fit her purpose.

Because this newsletter was sent to a diverse audience as an introduction to this program, the text tries to cram a lot of information into the first paragraph. It has to tell people what the *CLC hoped* the teenagers would learn as well as to show what the *teenagers* actually *found* was valuable. Notice how a comparison like this gives the piece a tone of thoughtful inquiry and evaluation. Compare this to the tone of unabashed boosterism and enthusiasm you might expect in a press release or the tone of personal caring or even emotional persuasion you might expect in a human interest feature. Nevertheless, this "report" is still clearly an argument, written to skeptical readers, that tries to make a case for the educational and social value of writing about community issues. (For example, in addition to the survey data reprinted here, a sidebar on the second page compares the CLC's high attendance record to the typical low figures for school.) In short, the Report Card is using its reporting techniques and evaluation to make a point about education.

Example 16–7
A Community Literacy Newsletter: The CLC Report Card

CLC REPORT CARD

The Community Literacy Center has always set its sights high. We want our inner-city teenagers to see themselves as problem solvers, as people who turn literacy into action. At the end of a CLC project they have learned strategies for planning, problem solving, reflection, and collaboration, for rivaling and supporting other voices at the table in an intercultural conversation. They walk out the door as authors of a published document and organizers of a public Community Conversation.

But what do individual teenagers really *take* with them? What do they *remember*? And what *transfers* to their lives after working on a CLC project?

As part of an on-going self-evaluation, we wanted to see what the teenagers from the last five years of the INFORM program would say themselves. We called each writer (some are away at college, some are already parents themselves) to ask open-ended questions: What do you remember most? What happened to you as a result of your experience—did it make a difference at school, in your job, or in your own attitudes? (See quotes.) Then we put our own hopes and expectations on the line, asking writers about 16 features of a typical project, from working with a mentor, to learning to plan or edit, to mixing fun and work: What was valuable to you? Here is what teenagers had to say. (See graph.)

✔ **Most Important Thing Learned**

"What's the most important thing I learned? It's gotta be that it's important to take into account other people's feelings and ideas."—Kathy Lamberson

"My decision-making skills changed big time. Where I live, there's lots of peer pressure. People are always on the streets, doing things that they shouldn't. At the CLC, they always stressed that if you don't want to do it, or you think it's wrong, you just don't do it. All the kids there agreed, and it was cool. I don't take part in the things that happen in my neighborhood on the streets, and I'm proud to say that I don't."—J. R. Robinson

"The biggest influence that the CLC had on me was that I learned how important it is to be yourself and to accept others for who they truly are. There was this girl that I never really knew who went to my high school, and she was very quiet. No one really talked to her, and some people made fun of her . . . so she kept to herself. If I wasn't involved at the CLC, I probably would have been one of the people at school who never talked to her. But, I did get to know her, and she's probably one of the most unique and wonderful people I know. It's important to try to get to know people before you make any kind of judgment." [This friendship crossed racial boundaries.]—Angelene Livingston

✔ **Collaboration**

"Working with mentors helped us learn that we could teach ourselves."—Leanna Lyle

"It was really great to have adults listen to my ideas. That I think was really important."—Tomika Benning

✔ **Unexpected Discoveries**

"When we had the presentation with the Mayor, I felt a lot of pride in my work. I never got recognition like that before, and it was good to see that even important people were interested in what we did."—Rochelle Holloway

---

1. Getting new attitudes and ideas about what you can do.
2. Working hard, yet having fun.
3. Crossing boundaries: Working with people you don't normally "hang out" with.
4. Reflecting back on what you did.
5. Seeing yourself as a writer.
6. Having adults listen to your ideas.
7. Learning to acknowledge the perspectives of other people.
8. Learning to come up with different arguments.
9. Learning to do collaborative planning.
10. Holding a formal presentation where you actually show your work.
11. Having a published document to show for your work.
12. Planning/writing with partner/mentor.
13. Planning/writing with a group.
14. Planning and setting your own goals.
15. Making decision about how to run your document or budget.
16. Proving that teens can do this.

Our interview also asked teens to rate how valuable the following 16 features were for them on a five-point scale from least valuable to most valuable.

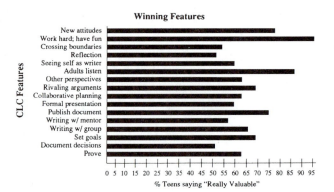

Winning Features

% Teens saying "Really Valuable"

From CLC Report Card (1993, Fall). In *Community Literacy,* p. 6. Newsletter of the Community Literacy Center and The National Center for the Study of Writing and Literacy at Carnegie Mellon University, Pittsburgh, PA.

This article continues with quotations about A Safe Haven, Skills That Carry Over, High Expectations and the Confidence I Could, and Accomplishments—Being a Published Writer plus a sidebar (an insert in a box) showing the high attendance record.

MINING A NEWS FEATURE

Example 16–9, *Streamwalker*, is a different kind of newsletter, written to volunteers, to encourage interest, participation, and political support. Its main textual techniques, including narrative, description, and "news" reporting, differ from those in the Report Card. What was the plan behind this text? In Example 16–8 the two student writers, Dave and Todd, talk about the open-ended instructions and feedback they got on this newsletter assignment.

Example 16–8
Water Watch Project Log (Todd Parker)

Thursday Nov. 2: Meeting at 6 P.M. The newsletter will be something that will explain what the Water Watch program is to the uninitiated and serve to inform the sister Water Watch Programs on other campuses what the Amherst program has done during the Fall semester. The newsletter will consist of four pages (8.5" × 17" page folded in half to make four pages). There will be three or four articles and a small section to thank all organizations that provided assistance to Water Watch this semester. . . . My article will be concerned with the stream mapping projects used to locate nonpoint sources of pollution. Dave will also write another article yet to be determined.

Monday Nov. 6th: Meeting at Worcester DC. Brief discussion on what sort of content the articles should have. Dave also writes for the Collegian and gave me some advice. He commented that many insiders will be reading the newsletter, therefore the language should not be oversimplified. The newsletter will be used for two audiences; so there will have to be some compromises in content.

Monday Nov. 13th: Dinner meeting at Dave's apartment. He showed me how his computer publishing program worked. We formatted the letter so that three of the articles would begin on the 1st page and be continued on the following pages. This would give the reader an idea about the content with a glance at the front page (like a newspaper).

Wednesday Nov. 29th: Met Dave at the dining hall. I showed him my first draft. He suggested that I make my article more objective,

remove some of my personal comments, and streamline the article so
that it is factual—based on quotes and other Water Watch input. I'm
used to putting more of my own material into things I write; so this was
a new twist for me. He gave some pointers on how to write
journalistically.

As you read the two lead articles in *Streamwalker,* do you see the
journalistic features Todd wrote about in his log or not? Are both
pieces trying to answer the journalists' 5Ws (Who? What? Where?
When? Why?) at the beginning, as you would expect in a standard
news article? Do you think Todd followed Dave's advice or does his
"news" article use textual techniques that you might expect to find
in a "feature" article? (Feature articles try to pull you in with
"human interest" material, using anecdotes, vivid images, dialogue,
or a dramatic moment.)

When you read *Streamwalker,* try to "mine" it for techniques you
could use, like the way Todd explains technical terms by describing
the process a sampler goes through. Or the way Dave uses a casual
quotation from Craig Nelson, to point out how big the problem is. To
mine a text like this, stop at the end of each paragraph and ask:
"What was the point and purpose here? And how is the writer trying
to achieve those goals in this place?"

Example 16–9
A Newsletter for Volunteers: Streamwalker

STREAMWALKER

Volume 1 Issue 1   **Fall 1995**

STREAM CLEAN-UPS

Fall Cleanups Take in Over 16 Tons of Garbage

By Dave LaFontana

A group of Five-College students and local citizens braved the cold weather on Saturday, November 4th to clean a section of Cushman Brook in Amherst. Thirty people, led by a team of Water Watch volunteers, removed around 12,000 pounds of glass and debris from an old farmer's dump by Puffer's Pond. Members of the group also worked to remove fallen trees that were restricting the water flow.

The Saturday clean up was the third of its kind in the Amherst/Northampton area, the fourth in western Massachusetts, and was the biggest success to date, according to coordinator Jai Sood. "We collected around two tons each time out before, this time it was close to six," said Sood.

The garbage consisted mostly of broken glass, metal and rubber. The glass was mainly concentrated in one area, with broken shards buried several inches into the top soil.

"When we arrived at the site, the amount of trash didn't appear that bad," said Water Watch member Craig Nelson. "It wasn't until we looked closely in the water

and on the bank, then we saw all the glass."

The group had to rake through the dirt to find all the trash, bag that trash, and haul out bags weighing up to 150 pounds. Most realized early on that the project would not be finished in one day.

"We hope to come back in the spring to finish this job," said member Jeremy Mailloux. The cleaning would be easier after the spring rains expose more of

(see Clean-up *on pg.2)*

MAPPING PROJECT

Walking the Water to Find the Dirt

By Todd Parker

With hip boots and clipboards, Water Watch coordinators Jessyca Harris and Jai Sood have been leading UMass students into the wilds of Amherst in dirty water and its sources. Add a topographic map, a water sampling kit, the willingness to get wet, and you've got the makings of the UMass Water Watch Stream Mapping Project.

The purpose of the project is to locate and record sources of pollution in local rivers and streams. "Once the sources of pollution are found, action can be taken to correct the problem," said Water Watch organizer Catherine Jones.

The primary area being mapped is the Mill River, which runs into Lake Warner. "Lake Warner is a problem because it is

(see Walking *on pg. 2)*

Inside This Issue

2

Clean up (*continued from pg. 1*)

the garbage, according to coordinator Jessyca Harris.

The group removed trees from the water to help the flow of the brook. "The trees in the water were narrowing the brook. This left the potential for erosion on the opposite bank," said Mailloux. The group used a chainsaw and pickaxes to cut through the lumber and dirt that was damming up the water.

The Cushman clean-up is the most recent clean-up for the program. In September, the group worked to clean a section of Amythst Brook in Amherst. The banks of the brook were being damaged by the mountain bikes that rode through the conservation area, and the group, using near-by rocks, rebuilt a section of that bank.

In October, the group did its first clean-up at Cushman Brook and another at the Mill River in Northampton.

Walking (*continued from pg. 1*)

overgrown with weeds and algae to the extent that you can almost walk across it," said Harris.

Jones pointed out that "this is a good indication of eutrophication which may be caused by an overload of nutrients from fertilizers and sewage."

Water sampling kits, provided by the Massachusetts Department of Environmental Management, aided in pinpointing pollution sources. Evidence such as foam on the surface of the water, oily sediments, and sewage odors all suggested that a problem exists.

Samples were taken where tributaries joined together and where there was a change in water quality. Some actively draining pipes were noted on the Mill River.

According to Harris, a considerable amount of the pollution comes from "non-point sources such as roadway runoff and runoff from fields and lawns treated with pesticides and other chemicals."

The Mill River receives runoff from several agricultural fields and a sewage treatment facility at UMass.

When a source of pollution is found, all of the circumstantial information is recorded. "The recorded information includes water temperature, estimated flow and discharge of the stream, types of sediment found, vegetation cover, exact location, and proximity to potential sources of pollution," said Jeremy Mailloux.

All of the information is kept as accurate as possible for potential use by the Department of Environmental Management and by the Water Watch Program.

Jones hopes that in some cases we can work directly with property owners in preventing polluted runoff from reaching rivers and streams.

Jones points out that riparian buffer zones (which are natural vegetation cover) can be planted along water ways to prevent topsoil erosion and to trap pollutants before they enter the water.

In such a case, Water Watch volunteers would provide the labor while property owners, or other sources, would provide the saplings and bushes necessary for the buffer zone.

From Tom Deans' English 113 Class, University of Massachusetts, Amherst.

MINING A LOCAL HISTORY

Examples 16–10 and 16–12 let us compare a traditional, documented history of an organization with a more informal and personal local history. Example 16–10 comes from *Giving Shelter: A History of Volunteers of America, Greater Baton Rouge, Inc., Through 1995*. It is a 20-page booklet produced over two years by Real World Writers—two freshmen classes and an advanced composition class at Louisiana State University. It covers the 80-year history of Volunteers of America (VOA), describing its leaders, changing programs, funding problems, and success stories. The excerpt we will mine comes from the early history section called "In the Beginning," that starts with the first shelter in 1915. One expects a history to contain names, dates, and facts, but even this short excerpt manages to do a lot more. To begin with, it tells the story of people and their sense of mission and places them within the larger economic and cultural history of the time It weaves in the Depression, politics, and social attitudes of the time, which it also links to the present. (As we will see in Example 16–11, it took some research to get this big picture.) *Giving Shelter* uses facts and figures, narratives (about the Flood of 1927 and the Depression), recollections, vignettes, vivid images of a moment in time, quotations, and case studies (see the sidebar on Recycling Lives). These different textual techniques not only maintain interest, but each does a distinctive job. Names, dates, and facts, for instance, can't tell the human history that narrative and quoted voices can. On the other hand, they place these personal stories in a larger, more meaningful historical framework.

Example 16–10
An Archival History of Volunteers: Giving Shelter

Links the facts with the VOA's vision (in a memorable quotation).

In the Beginning

The words of General Ballington Booth inspired [the founders of the Baton Rouge shelter]: "You cannot talk to a man about God when he is hungry and has no clothes and no place to sleep; you have to feed him and clothe him first." With these priorities in mind, Major and Mrs. Belcher established the first mission house as a shelter on Maximillian Street.

Recollection
(placed in a
sidebar) makes
the VOA vision
come to life in an
anecdote

"One cold winter day this man came by. He was freezing, he had been out in the cold, he didn't have any winter clothes. He didn't have any warm underwear. So Papa felt sorry for him and he told him to sit down. He brought him inside and sat him down . . . he went and took the long johns he had on and brought them down and gave them to the man and he put them on . . . Took the clothes off his own back and gave it to him. That's what kind of man he was."

Fred Belcher, about his father, Arthur

The Flood of '27

Places VOA in
local history but
also connects to
the present

In early December 1926, heavy rains bombarded the northern Mississippi River Valley. By May of 1927, the flood waters reached the Baton Rouge area, the most destructive flood in its recorded history. The total damage was close to three million dollars-equivalent to 97.5 million dollars in 1995.

Concrete details
turn facts into
a vignette

While disaster relief was headed by the Red Cross, the local VOA helped by collecting clothes from chapters around the country, transporting them by train to Baton Rouge, and then distributing them from a store front downtown on Third Street. The distribution center, located in Baton Rouge because it was a high point and did not flood, was open for several months.

"Brother, Can You Spare a Dime?"

Places local
poverty and
joblessness in
national history
Uses dates,
numbers, names

As the Baton Rouge area recovered, yet another disaster loomed. Human suffering became a reality for millions of Americans when the Great Depression began in October 1929. "Brother, Can You Spare a Dime?" a popular song of the 1930s, expressed the nationwide despair over the worst and longest period of high unemployment and low business activity in modern times. In 1925, about 3 percent of the nation's workers were out of work. Unemployment reached about 9 percent in 1930 and escalated to 25 percent by 1933. As the Depression continued, thousands lost their homes. Many wandered through the country looking for jobs.

Local details

Before the Depression, no government relief programs were set up for people living in an area less than one year, so the need to help these transients was great. Myron Faulk, a Tulane social work graduate who came to Baton Rouge in 1931 to set up the Transient Bureau, reported that he was soon housing 300 people per night in a converted prison (in 1993, the site of State Police Offices on North Foster).

Puts VOA mission in context of changing cultural attitudes and historical responses to poverty

After his election in 1932, President Franklin Roosevelt put into practice his belief that the federal government had major responsibility for the well being of its citizens. . . . The New Deal provided jobs and money through agencies such as the Civilian Conservation Corps and the Federal Emergency Relief Administration. These agencies helped millions, but not everyone. Some people still fell through the cracks. . . .

More specific examples

Quote by local founder

Most of the families were temporarily stranded in Baton Rouge on the way to or from jobs. Some needed only money for gas to get them on to their destinations, while others needed beds, meals, and respectable clothing. Some were young, single women who in the late 1930s began leaving their homes to find a better life. When they found hardships instead, the Belchers' emergency shelter was a place of refuge until they could reunite with their families. Whatever the need, said Major Belcher, "In each case, we do the best we can to help them get on their feet."

The next excerpt comes from a section near the end of the book describing "Leadership in the 1990s." It is set off as a sidebar with a rule (a border line) and screen (shading over the text).

Title predicts "point" of story

Uses this case study of Cindy to show an aspect of "leadership" different from the history of VOA directors found in the text

> ### Recycling Lives
>
> Cindy spent the 1970s rebelling against her prominent Mississippi family—alcohol, drugs, destructive relationships. She ran away from Sewanee with a drug abuser, divorced, but she was so insecure she kept going back.
>
> In 1986, working for the Tarrant County Child Protection Agency and with two young children dependent on her, Cindy developed medical problems that required surgery. She thought she could go back home to her parents to recover, but she was wrong. There was still too much anger and heartache there.
>
> *(Continued)*

Sidebar sets her story off without other commentary

Christmas 1986 found her living in Hammond with a high school friend who was alcoholic, verbally abusive, and who "hated himself, his wife, and his children." There was no money for Christmas presents for her children. She called the Sheriff's department and told them, "I cannot stay here any longer. I don't know what to do. I don't know where to call. I don't have anybody. I need help! I need to get out of here!" From one parish line to the next, one sheriff's department to the next, she was transported from Hammond to VOA-BR's America House.

But she was still scared. "My first question was whether I was at risk of losing my children. 'Cause the only thing I knew about a shelter was these movies about welfare hotels, and you know, how child protection comes in and the kids are snatched away. I was horrified. They assured me, it's not child abuse to be poor.

Case does double duty by describing not only a new leader (topic of the section), but also the life style of the shelter, and a VOA program

Cindy was still under a doctor's care from surgery and couldn't work. She and her two young children lived in one room at America House for five months. The fourteen other homeless families also living at the shelter provided a sense of family. Her oldest daughter was enrolled in prekindergarten at a neighborhood school. With Bud Snowden, Cindy began speaking for homeless awareness groups. Her life was beginning to come together.

While living at the America House, Cindy wrote a proposal for a preschool program for homeless children. . . . After she moved, Volunteers asked Cindy to work as a case manager and volunteer coordinator at America House. She also speaks to churches, schools, and civic groups on homelessness.

Quotation recalls the mission statement from the first section

Cindy calls the time she and her children lived at the shelter their "cocoon time": "They gave us a roof when we didn't have a roof, gave us food when we didn't have food, gave us a place to sleep."

Recently, as Cindy rose to speak to over 400 people attending a homeless conference she had helped organize for Volunteers of America, there on the front row was Bud Snowden, who had helped her take her steps back to a meaningful life. And sitting next to him was her mother.

From *Giving Shelter. A History of the Volunteers of America, Greater Baton Rouge, Inc. Through 1995.* Real World Writers, Louisiana State University. 1996. Student Editors: Marcelle DeSoto, Julie Paxton, Rose Ricketts. Faculty Editors, Wade Dorman, Susann Dorman.

From Wade Dorman and Susann Dorman's English 2001 and 1002 classes. Louisiana State University.

The writers of *Giving Shelter* decided to write their text as an informal narrative instead of a heavily footnoted history. However, behind this readable story is a well-documented project that draws on previous books, local archives, old newspapers, and oral interviews. The Task List 3 in Example 16–11 shows some of the sources the research group consulted and how they divided up the work.

Example 16–11
Task List for the VOA Archival History

Task List 3
English 2001: VOA History

Record and organize materials on hand [done]
Construct time line [done]
Locate suitable printing facilities: get prices, schedules, format choices [Julie]
Do more follow-up research

More Oral Histories

Dr. Larry Herbert (formerly?) chief of pediatrics at Long Hospital. Spoke at dedication of Makara House temporary shelter for abused adolescents. Member of Child Protection Council? [   ]

John Makara. Still living? Obituary? Husband of late Eunice Makara, for whom House is named. Whoever does this should call Makara house and get date of Eunice's death so as to look for her obituary. [   ]

Cindy McGee. Has lived in a VOA shelter; is now a committed staff member; perspective from both sides. [Sharon]

Follow up interview of Yvonne Teeter, founding member (1959) of Woman's Auxiliary [existing tape is partial, difficult to hear] [   ]

Archives Research

City directories for period 1910–1920 for VOA addresses and men mentioned in the 1915 *Volunteer Gazette* article by Maud Booth. See also *Classified Business Directory.* [Srilatha]

Baton Rouge newspaper for 1927 visit of Maud Booth (this may or may not be related to the great Mississippi flood of 1927). [Rose & Julie]

List members of VOA Advisory Board for as far back as we can find, then use obituaries to build short profiles of their public lives. For ex., John Wolf was the head of Sunbeam Bakery, Robert Petit was the sheriff (and probably father to LSU star athlete Bob Petit). [Stacie]

List the earliest members of the VOA Woman's Auxiliary. Since it began in 1959 some of those women are still alive. Let's see how many we can get an address and telephone number for and then decide how many interviews we can do. [Jennifer and Christy]

Do more Contextual History research

What was happening in: USA [Stacie] & LA [Felicity]
Major social changes: women [Jennifer], families [Lionel],
     prisons/justice system [Diane]
What was happening in social services? (See Falk interview)
     [Sharon]

Histories We Can Start Composing from Materials at Hand

History of the VOA shelter for transient families "Built at turn of the
     century by the Vine family." Occupied since 1932. [Marcelle]
Story of the VOA logo change
History of the VOA Board from merely advisory to true local control

Moving Toward Publication

Apply for grant(s) to support publication
Send press releases on project
Human interest stories from history to try to get into the local paper
Draft history
Edit history; regularize style
Proof final copy
Convey printed histories to Baton Rouge Volunteers of America

From Wade Dorman and Susann Dorman's Advanced Composition—VOA course. Louisiana State University.

MINING AN ORAL HISTORY

History takes many forms. *Pictures in My Mind: An Oral History of South Baton Rouge Community Business and the Business Community* is a vivid record of people and their voices. Unlike the seamless web of history woven in *Giving Shelter,* this document is more like a well-organized scrap book that includes an introduction by the project director, a two-page history of the neighborhood by a resident; short biographical sketches based on 25 interviews with residents, with snapshots of people sitting on the sofa at home, around a table, or at work. The bulk of the text is a series of excerpts (from a single paragraph to two pages in length) taken from the transcribed interviews and organized around themes such as "Getting Started." It ends with a hand-drawn map of Thomas H. Delpit Drive—the historic business corridor of this African-American community.

But even scrapbooks can reflect a strong rhetorical purpose. The secret is in selecting quotations, organizing them, and giving them a revealing title. As you mine Example 16–12, notice first how the writers used interviews in the "Getting Started" sections to sketch a life history of a man and a recollection of a grocery store which was also a history of the times. The local details of these memories help tell the bigger story of a different era, comparing past to present in a way quite different from the archival history techniques we saw in *Giving Shelter,* Example 16–10. Second, look at how the writers grouped interviews in the next section, "Integration Wasn't What a Lot of People Thought." The strong statements and alternative points of view which emerge here let this "scrapbook" raise complex issues about the social and economic impact integration had on this community. In these interviews, people are not only struggling to understand problems and see reasons, but are letting us in on the struggle of the community. Example 16–12 is excerpted from somewhat longer interviews and sections with multiple interviewees.

Example 16–12
An Oral History: Pictures in My Mind

Getting Started

Opening interview shows how business histories are linked to family histories and how both can reveal stories of the times

Joseph A. Delpit: Father was a businessman. [He] came to Baton Rouge when he was about eighteen, worked at LSU in the athletic department with the food services, then he moved. He worked at Dalton's Greenroom which was a department store downtown that had a restaurant in it. At that time, black people couldn't eat in there but we could work in there, and that's where he worked. And in about 1937 he opened his own business which was a sweet shop in South Baton Rouge on East Blvd., and then he changed that to the Chicken Shack. He developed a recipe for fried chicken and he opened up a

Represents the past as a "success story"

business called the Chicken Shack, he and my mother . . . I was born into the business. My daddy died when I was going on eighteen, so I took over the business. I bought my mother and my sisters out. My wife and I, Precious Robertson Delpit, who also attended McKinley, worked hard, were able to expand the business from just one location to as many as five locations at one time. We also started a franchise business . . .

I actually started doing management stuff when I was still in high school. I was about in the tenth grade, so I was fifteen or sixteen, and my mother and father went on their first vacation out of the state of Louisiana and I was able to run the business while they went on a vacation. So I've been in business for many years.

Eats, Treats, and Hangin' Out

Albert Domino: Now down here they had a place in front of Reddy Street they called Fleet's Grocery. Old man used to run it. That's where we used to buy our sandwiches. You know, schools didn't have lunches then. The old lady used to run it. If you didn't have that nickel or that dime she wasn't gonna let you go hungry. Everybody used to love that old lady, she wasn't gonna let you go hungry. And did I tell you about the Dipsey Doodle? That old lady who run that, if you walk in there and just tell her, say, "Well I just ain't got no money, I can't pay for it," she gonna go back there and get you something to eat. [She] always kept that pot back there with them beans or something in it to feed, because boy back then it was hard. You talking 'bout people now having hard times, these people don't know what hard times is.

Section of recollections about places

Anecdote compares then and now; reveals attitudes to poverty

Story retold in dialogue

Returns to comparison

Integration Wasn't What a Lot of People Thought

Joe Delpit: Integration coming—to be frank with you—it had a tremendous impact on our community. A lot of people felt they had the money, they'll go where they want to go, and they forgot about the businesses in their own neighborhood. Therefore people in the neighborhood weren't making any money so they couldn't put money back into their business to keep them up.

Section presents multiple viewpoints on integration and rival hypotheses about its effects

Focus on mobility

Reverend Lionel Lee: African-American businesses in this community didn't necessarily move, then went out of business. Now one of the weaknesses of African-Americans still is that when one generation of business people pass on, the youngsters don't carry on, they close up. That's the weaknesses. I can't think of one right now except for Joe Delpit that followed his father.

Focus on family businesses

Focus on schools through personal story

Peggy Goods: Integration is probably one of the worst things that has ever happened to black people. They farmed us out to schools where we didn't want to be, they closed our schools. That was the end of neighborhood schools which was to me an absolute disaster. . . . [In] nineteen sixty-five they bused us to Lee High and that was a miserable experience. . . . We of course had to go to school with police and it was such a hostile environment. You never understand why people could hate so much people they don't even know. And so I think after the loss of the neighborhood school that did not help the community because then people started moving away, [there was] a flight from the community, and that was a decline.

Focus on social/economic shifts

Alton Ingram: The major changes that I see in the community are that a lot of people who went off to college got degrees and . . . some of the job markets started opening up and hired blacks. . . . And blacks could afford better homes because they had better jobs making more money. So then we had a black flight out the neighborhood. Of course that left people who were low income or no income living in this area and it started to just go down. That is why the businesses suffered because people did not have money to spend in the neighborhood and the people who had the good jobs moved out the neighborhood and they were spending money elsewhere.

Focus on competition

Reverend Charles T. Smith: Once integration came these businesses found themselves competing not just against each other but against better financed white business establishments, and eventually they succumbed to that competition.

Focus on business climate

Fred C. Matthews, Jr.: If black people who were operating restaurants and cafes at that time had expanded and proved their business they had a good chance of being top people in Baton Rouge as far as serving food is concerned, but they let go and they didn't improve. And so these fast-food restaurants like the McDonald's, and Burger King, and Piccadilly, and all those places, they just put us out of business. They didn't necessarily have to put us out of business, but we went to sleep on the job.

From *Pictures in My Mind: An Oral History of South Baton Rouge Community Business and the Business Community.* Collected by Khary Carrell, Nedra Carter, Michael Goods, Rudolph Henry. Sponsored by JTPA. East Baton Rouge School Board and the T. Harry Williams Center for Oral History, LSU. Summer 1996. The T. Harry Williams Center for Oral History, directed by Pamela Dean; project directed by Toby Daspit.

MINING FOR GRAPHIC TECHNIQUES

If your community organization is operating on a shoestring, you may get a chance to work on layout, graphics, and production, as well as text. As we suggested in Strategy 1, review the backfiles. The graphic design of previous work probably has a personality your client may want to maintain. And as you mine new examples, here are some features to look at and some rules of thumb to keep in mind.

Page Layout

Imagine each page as block of visual information. Design it so the eye is led in a meaningful way. But don't forget that any two-page spread (as in pages 2–3 in a newsletter) is also a unit that needs to be balanced. Since you may have to edit your text to fit the space, use your computer to simulate the font size and line length of the final text.

White space (the area where there is no ink) is a critical part of the layout, too. Use it to make the text visually inviting and to break it into readable, meaningful units. Fewer words are often more effective.

Headings

Headings help readers get a quick overview of the organization or argument of your text. As we discussed in Chapter 10, they give the reader valuable cues for how to read the text. Since many community texts are working hard to capture a reader's attention, you may need to put a lot of time into imagining headings that tell the whole story at a glance.

Highlighting

If you want to draw attention to key words or ideas, you can use both white space and various fonts, as well as type features such as boldface, italic, outlining, or underlining. However, it is easy to have so much fun using these techniques that you end up with a cluttered page that actually draws attention away from your text. Evaluate your design in the same way you would your argument—does it support your key point and purpose; is it designed for a reader?

Production

If you are handling the layout and printing of a text, start thinking about the total document from the very beginning and get an agreement with your client on how much money they are willing to spend. Then find out how many copies they want to distribute. Once you have that number (your print order) you can talk to a printer or copy service and find out what your options are, since the costs go up whenever you add a second color, heavier or glossier paper, more pages, or graphics. Find out early so you can weigh the trade offs and work within your budget. And find out ahead of time how long it will take them to print that many copies on that paper. Don't get a surprise just before your deadline.

Then ask your printer to be very explicit with you about what form they expect the text to be in. Are they expecting a formatted computer disk done on a desktop publishing program, camera ready copy "pasted up" for reproduction, or a manuscript they will type-set? Whatever process you use, always make sure you check the final version (sometimes called the blue line) that they create before it is printed. Never assume that your notes or oral instructions were fully understood until you see the final version.

 ### STRATEGY 3   DRAW ON STANDARD RHETORICAL PATTERNS

On the surface, an academic paper, a newsletter article, and an oral history will look very different. In the previous strategies, when you were looking for models to follow and examples to borrow from, we focused on distinctive features and trademark techniques of these genres. By contrast, the patterns that follow are widely used, general purpose patterns that can help you structure many different kinds of texts. They are effective because they are so familiar—readers immediately know what to expect once they see you are using a narrative or a problem-solution plan, and they find your text well-organized and easy to follow because they can predict what is coming next. But when you use these patterns, remember the organizing and preview-ing techniques we discussed in Chapters 9 and 10—give your read-ers plenty of cues about what pattern you are using and what is coming. Figure 16–5 lists some the most general patterns almost

FIGURE 16–5
Standard Rhetorical Patterns

Narration	Not only tells a story in chronological order, but leads the reader on from the beginning (and setting) through a conflict to the end with a climax and resolution.
Description	Gives specifics and details through examples or lists. It shows the parts, features or attributes that make up the whole.
Comparison	Looks at similarities and differences by comparing (or contrasting) object 1 as a whole with 2, or through a feature-by-feature comparison.
Cause and Effect	Looks back at the reasons or causes for the current situation, or looks ahead to the future with an "If/then" argument for what would happen if . . .
Problem Solution	Defines problems by locating conflicts and examines possible solutions.

FIGURE 16-6
Patterns That Pose Motivating Problems

The Unfinished Story	History has lead us to this point. Where is the road leading?
The Crisis	The news is in. The results were disappointing; our plan didn't work out; or we are in trouble. And we must act.
The Opportunity	Circumstances (maybe even bad ones) have just opened a door. Should we walk through it?
The Crossroads	We stand at a decision point, where to not act is to act. We must make a choice.
A Vision	There is a challenge before us, but there is also the vision of a possibility that justifies the effort.

every text uses (in one form or another). Figure 16–6 lists some of the patterns that motivate people to read on.

When Jessie Armstead wrote the following essay, he didn't have to imagine a faceless "general" audience, because as part of the "Meet the Author Program" he knew he would be reading his text in person to the young men at the Dade County Juvenile Justice Center School. Jessie used his credibility as a University of Miami football player and as a someone who had "been there" to write a strong message to these incarcerated teenagers in the form of a personal essay. Do you think Jessie was able to use any of the rhetorical patterns from Figures 16–5 and 16–6 in his essay? For instance, if the point of the essay from his perspective is a personal realization, what is the possible point that motivates the reader? We have used the version of his piece that was reprinted in a magazine for correctional officers. What do you think motivated them to publish it?

Example 16–13
A Letter/Essay: "When You're a Teenager . . . "

They Were Heading the Wrong Way

Editor's note: This is an essay written by Jessie Armstead, a University of Miami student and football player who participates in the Meet the Author Program, followed by a thank-you note from a youth at the Dade County Juvenile Justice Center School.

When you're a teenager, one of the hardest decisions you have to make is "to be your own man." Peer pressure is a powerful force, and not every teenager is strong enough to resist it. One incident in my teen years forced me to make an important decision that has changed the direction of my life.

As I was sitting at the park one late evening, Derric, my best friend asked me to help some players on the high school football team with an armed robbery. First I thought it was a joke: then quickly I realized it wasn't. While I tried to talk them out of it, they didn't believe the things I was telling them. As time went on, I knew they were heading the wrong way.

They committed five or six robberies, and made it through safely, but one afternoon they got caught. On June 11, 1989, they were trying to rob a video store. All the robberies were traced back from Dec. 27, and at the same time, the police department started picking up everyone who was involved. While time passed, everyone was waiting on the judge's decision. Then on Sept. 22, 1989, the judge gave them sentences ranging from 90 days in boot camp to 25 years in prison. Instead of heading off to colleges where they had received football scholarships, they went off to prison.

On Sept. 22, I realized I had made a very important decision. I'm attending the University of Miami and not prison. Every day I realize that if my mind wasn't as strong as it is, I probably wouldn't be here today. As I write this paper, I thank God it wasn't me.

—Jessie Armstead

—————>●<—————

I would like to thank you all for volunteering your time to try to talk some sense into us. When I wasn't in a gang I used to play J.V. football and varsity baseball, so listening to athletes really makes me think about the wrong moves I've made in my life. I see that if I try I can get somewhere.

I'm in here for attempted murder. When I get out I plan on going back to school and continue to play sports and get my diploma and maybe go on to college. I wish you would please consider making another trip over here.

—Shawn

———————————

From Jessie Armstead. (1991, August). They were headed the wrong way. *Corrections Today, 3*(5), 171. From Joyce Speiller-Morris' Meet the Author Program, University of Miami.

PROJECTS AND ASSIGNMENTS

1 The beauty of a plan is that you can change it. Once you have worked two or more weeks on your project, look back at your initial project proposal (Figure 16–1) and your journal. Use Kevin's example (Example 16–1) to write a reflection on the changes that have occurred. How did your plan develop and change? Why? What can you learn from that?

2 After you hold a "check in" collaborative planning session with your community contact, write a memo to your group about how it worked and what you were able to get out of it. Could you redesign your "check in" planning to be more productive?

3 Work with your group to develop a set of customized planning questions (as in Example 16–3) adapted to your task, which you and your partner can use during collaborative planning sessions.

4 Before you go to an interview, develop a plan and script for your interview. Check off how many kinds of questions you have prepared:

- 5 Ws (Who? What? When? Where? Why?).
- Questions shaped by your special purpose.
- Open questions.
- Closed questions.
- Issue tree prompts.
- Critical incident prompts.

Before you go, predict which of your questions will be the most effective. Then in your next reflection compare your prediction to the reality.

5 Judy Harris' interview (Example 16–4) was written for the faculty and staff of a campus community. Write a press release (see Example 16–5) that would convince the editor of another publication to publish a feature article based on this interview. Attach a reflection to your press release that describes the kind of publication you had in mind and how you designed your press release to persuade an editor or reporter to pick up the story. What did you choose to foreground and why?

6 We know that the writers of the *CLC Report Card* (Example 16–7) and *Streamwalker* (Example 16–9) had a number of goals in mind. How do you think the textual techniques they used are working? As you read these three texts, mark each place that feels like a key point, a rhetorical move, or a "turn" in the argument (you may find more than one per paragraph). Then jot a note about how each writer probably expected (or wanted) readers to be responding at that point. Compare your notes with the rest of your class. Did you agree on the writers' intentions and success in carrying them out?

7 Newsletters depend strongly on their headlines and "leads" or opening paragraphs to hook the reader into reading on and to set up the right expectations. Do you think all leads work more or less the same way, or do they reflect the writers' individual purposes? To support your decision, compare the lead paragraphs in the two *Streamwalker* articles (Example 16–9) first to each other and then to the *CLC Report Card* (Example 16–7) in terms of purpose, key point, audience and text conventions. What can you discover about leads?

8   Give your collaborative planning partner an example of the kind of text you may be writing (e.g., a feature story, press release). Working separately at first, use Figure 16–2 to mine the text for rhetorical features you might borrow. Then compare your answers to the questions in Figure 16–2. How many different features did you uncover? Write a memo that shares your joint analysis with your writing group or class, and recommend features you found particularly effective. Don't forget to look for general features such as voice, style, purpose, and relationship to readers, along with the more visible conventions of genre and formatting.

9   Jessie Armstead's personal letter/essay (Example 16–13) uses a number of the standard rhetorical patterns found in Figures 16–5 and 16–6. Which of these patterns do you think creates the strongest effect? Which pattern do you think posed a motivating problem for the different readers of this text: the young men, the editors of the *Corrections Today, 3*(5), and Jessie himself? (A thought teaser: Could these different people read Jessie's text from a point of view different from or in addition to their own?)

10   Looking back over the writing and reflection you have done in your project, write a personal essay about the experience. Attach a memo in which you describe your plan for this essay. Who were you writing to, and where do you think this essay might be published? How did your key point and purpose develop? And what are some of the textual techniques that you think helped you reach your goals?

chapter seventeen

Dialogue and Inquiry

GOAL 7
SEEK rival hypotheses

Actively seek alternative interpretations and competing answers to open questions.

> STRATEGY 1   **IMAGINE GOOD RIVALS TO OPEN QUESTIONS**

GOAL 8
ENTER an intercultural inquiry

Cross the borders of discourse and culture to examine questions together.

> STRATEGY 1   **THE CLUELESS STRATEGY—OR, JUST ASK**
> STRATEGY 2   **SEEK INTERCULTURAL INTERPRETATIONS OF MEANING IN CONTEXT**
> STRATEGY 3   **WRITE A MULTI-VOICED INQUIRY**

When you collaborate with a community group by writing an article, editorial, or proposal, the goal is to support an idea or ideal and to advocate action. But another reason that draws many college students to communities is a desire to learn from and with people from different backgrounds. The goal of such writing is no longer advocacy alone, but inquiry. Instead of presenting or promoting what you *do* know, inquiry starts with open questions, felt conflicts, and good problems to explore what you *don't* know. This chapter is about an inquiry into cross-cultural differences that lets people test and go beyond narrow stereotypes of other groups and, at the same time, discover different sorts of expertise (that aren't based on "academic" skill). It is about inquiry that lets people reflect back on their own taken-for-granted assumptions and cultural habits. And it is about inquiry that lets people go beyond "good will" toward others to a working collaborative relationship with them.

GOAL 7

SEEK Rival Hypotheses

How do you respond to challenging questions such as:

- How can we as a society improve the life chances for children raised in poverty?
- How do you build a sense of community (within a school, an organization, a city) based more on cooperation than competition?
- How do you reduce the cultural biases of standardized testing or what has been called the "savage inequality" of rich and poor public schools?
- Which social and economic policies will encourage free enterprise and self-reliance while at the same time creating compassionate social justice?
- How do you as an individual make a difference? For instance, as a mentor or tutor, how can you best use literacy to support equality, justice, community?

REPORTING, ADVOCACY, AND RIVALING

Questions like these are called **open** questions because there is no single answer. The facts alone won't settle the point; and no simple answer will deal with all the conditions and situations in which any given problem arises. And yet these are insistent questions that we as a society do have to answer in one way or another. Just ignoring the inequalities in schooling, for example, is a decisive answer.

One way to respond to hard questions is to take the stance of a reporter—seek out the facts, see how others have interpreted the situation, and review the conclusions of others. *Reporting* tries to be objective, but that can also be an illusion. Even the most flat-footed, fact-based report has interpreted its evidence by creating an organizing idea and using and linking some "facts" and ignoring others. Reporting can further a discussion, and some writers feel it is safer to just report what others have said. But remember the students we described in Chapter 5, who assumed (wrongly) that their college assignments just asked them to summarize their source texts? The problem with reporting, alone, is that it cannot help you decide how to act (especially when no action is an action).

Another response is to take a strong position, to be for or against something. Stake out a claim about what should be and stand by it, no matter what. This is called *advocacy*. You know it from law courts, and you may have learned how to write arguments, opinion papers, or pro-and-con essays in school, based on the idea of advocacy. The advocacy stance works like this: First, assert a claim; then briefly consider the opposition in order to undercut, discredit, or dismiss it; next, lay out support for your position; and finally, conclude, re-asserting the claim you made in the beginning. Sometimes situations call for strong claims, a clear vision of what should be, and forceful assertion. But advocacy is not the only way to persuade other people. And leaping to conclusions ("knowing" you are right) is certainly not the best way to understand really serious *open* questions. The rival hypothesis stance, or *rivaling*, gives you a third way to enter into a more open dialogue with other ideas and with other people.

The rival hypothesis stance is different from advocacy because it starts with inquiry—with questions rather than claims and with a vigorous and critical search for rival hypotheses. It is different from reporting because it ends in a conclusion or current "best" under-standing—even as it recognizes that the conclusion is always provi-sional and revisable.

 ## STRATEGY 1   IMAGINE GOOD RIVALS TO OPEN QUESTIONS

To take a rival hypothesis stance there are four things you need to do: (1) open the question, (2) seek out rival hypotheses, (3) examine and evaluate the evidence, and (4) construct a conclusion.

Open the Question.   In rival hypothesis thinking, you don't start by asserting a claim, position, or answer (as you might in a tradi-tional argument). You start by naming and describing a real prob-lem—by posing an open question. This isn't a "rhetorical" question that people ask when they actually have an answer up their sleeves. This is a genuine question that reasonable people will answer in dif-ferent ways. It is about a complex problem in which the whole truth will probably include parts of those different, apparently conflicting answers. Moreover, the "best interpretation" in this context, for these people, times, or conditions will not be the best answer for all situations. (Recall our discussion of contextualizing and conditional-izing arguments and claims in Chapter 1, Assignment 8.)

Seek Out Rival Hypotheses.   Once you have opened a question by naming it, you begin an active search for the strongest rival hy-potheses or interpretations you can find. The most direct strategy is to read and ask how other people are interpreting this situation. How do they respond to this problem? And why do they see it that way: What are the values, goals, starting assumptions that shape what they see?

But the rival hypothesis stance isn't just a summary strategy. To rival is to actively generate alternative interpretations, to imagine other positions, to stand in someone else's shoes and envision what some good rivals—to your own ideas—would be.

Examine and Evaluate the Evidence.   To evaluate those rivals, you must look at the evidence. Does any evidence support this position (recall the discussion of data, warrants, and claims in Chapter 13)? There are a number of places to turn for evidence. Sometimes you can turn to facts, data, or other information to test a hypothesis. (Factual information is often good at ruling out some hypotheses; for example, experience has shown that this idea *didn't* work.) Sometimes you can use the word of authorities (but it is important to know what *their* claims are based upon—since "experts" disagree on complex issues all the time). For difficult questions, you may have to evaluate a hypothesis by building an argument or case for it—and deciding how good a case you can build. Start with a claim and walk through the reasons you have in your own mind for supporting (or contesting) it.

Notice that some of your reasons will be *inferences* you draw. An inference is a new idea or conclusion you create—or infer—from what you already know. (See Chapter 9 on inferences readers draw.) Figure 17–1 is a handy inference machine that helps you draw inferences by asking you to explicitly state the connections you see between two events, claims, or concepts. Remember the mentor, Laura in Example 15–1, searching for reasons second-grader Jay would seem to give up during a reading session and begin to guess at words? What was the connection? Was it her tutoring? Jay's ability? Her journal recorded some inferences she drew to help explain these events: "I gathered that in second grade Jay had decided he wasn't bright enough and that he was too far behind to catch up. . . ." And on the basis of these inferences she charted her course: "So I try to explain . . . that he already knows a lot of words . . . ." And it was an inference based on Jay's behavior that led her to conclude she had indeed made a difference: "I think the real change came when . . . ."

We use inferences or connections like this all the time to draw personal conclusions about events. You can also use inferences self-consciously when you need to see connections between ideas or concepts and want to build a case in writing. Often the secret to

FIGURE 17–1
An Inference Machine for Building Reasons

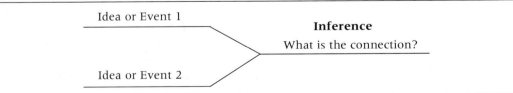

Idea or Event 1

Inference
What is the connection?

Idea or Event 2

being convincing is simply to share this set of your personal reasons or your own chain of reasoning with the reader. For instance, when I wrote the paragraph above, about looking for evidence, I thought for a moment about some of the connections between this need for evidence and "authorities" as a source of evidence. I ended up building a case to persuade you to be a little cautious about arguments based on authority.

Figure 17–2 maps out part of my reasoning, showing some of the inferences I drew as reasonable connections between these ideas. One important connection I saw was that the mere "word" of an authority (or quotation) is often taken as a sort of "evidence" that a statement is true. Furthermore, I inferred, this means that whatever evidence the "authority" used to reach his or her position doesn't have to be revealed—we just know they said so. Given this, don't you think it is also important to notice that authorities disagree? It was this set of inferences, then, that became the basis for my sentence and the reasons I shared with you when I concluded: "Sometimes you can use the word of authorities (but it is important to know what their claims are based on—since "experts" disagree on complex issues all the time)."

Building a case, even when you have good reasons, doesn't "prove" a hypothesis is definitely right or wrong, especially with open questions on which people may have reason to disagree. Sometimes the only way we come to conclusions is through "convincing" each other about what the "best available" hypothesis is. That is why another way to evaluate your rival hypotheses is to put them in conversation with each other. Let one point of view comment on another one. What would they say about each other? What strengths and weaknesses would they turn up?

Construct a Conclusion.   Finally, in taking the rival hypothesis stance you must end by coming to a conclusion. Rivaling is unlike a pro-and-con argument or a high school debate: It doesn't end up by "picking" a side. And it doesn't end by proposing a totally new

FIGURE 17–2
Drawing Inferences as Connections Between Ideas

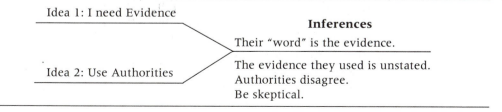

position (that hasn't had its evidence examined, or hasn't been part of the conversation). The goal of rivaling is to build a new, more inclusive, more informed understanding that recognizes the value of rival interpretations. This is called a *negotiated meaning*, because it comes out of the conversation and negotiation of different perspectives.

But what if you can't resolve the conflicts you see? What if there are really deep disagreements over what is the "best" interpretation, what is "right"? Instead of hedging or pretending everyone agrees, a rival hypothesis stance lets you lay out the conflict, take a position, and give your reasons. Remember that your interpretation of this situation is in fact a "hypothesis"—a theory, an informed guess that you made to guide your actions. And you looked for rivals so you could act on the best possible hypothesis.

The real test of any interpretation or any solution is not, "Do I or does some authority think it is 'true'?" but, "What are the consequences of acting on this hypothesis, of acting as if it were true?" As my grandmother used to say, "The proof of the pudding is in the eating." What is the outcome, or what can you imagine the outcome of your conclusion to be? When you face conflicts, then, accept the fact that you must come to the best conclusion you can—not acting is always a form of acting. But at the same time, recognize that your best understanding today is still always a hypothesis that may need to be revised as you learn more or see the consequences that idea has in the real world. At the end of this chapter there is a checklist for conducting a rival hypothesis inquiry *in writing*. It will help you see if your papers have taken a really strong rival hypothesis stance or slipped into the easier task of reporting or advocacy.

The Expert Rivaler

How do you know when you are really good at rivaling? Unlike debate, it isn't when you can demolish all your opponents. And it isn't when you can come up with "an opinion" so strong you think you can defend it against all comers. Both those moves close down inquiry and close down minds. You will know you are a good rivaler when you can come up with genuine rivals to your own ideas, even as you are thinking about them, and when you can recognize the merit of other rivals, even as you make a choice about how to act on the best understanding you have now. The ultimate goal of rivaling is to keep questioning and testing your own thinking.

The following example shows how you can use your bulletin board (whether it is a hard copy or electronic one) to post rival hypotheses about important questions your class is exploring and to connect your experience to the texts you are reading. Which rivals are closest to your initial assumptions or likely to be guiding your actions? Note how each of these rival hypotheses would shape how you go about working in the community.

Example 17–1
Rivaling on Literacy and Social Justice

The Open Question: How Can We Best Use Literacy to Support Equality and Social Justice?

This is a good question, and people have proposed a number of strong rival hypotheses in response to this open question. As a student involved in community outreach, you may have to think this question through for yourself just like these mentors at the Community Literacy Center did as they posted to each other on their electronic bulletin board. As you read the questions and ideas they (and other educators) were wrestling with, notice how they raise some important rival hypotheses about the role of literacy and about their roles as mentors with inner city writers.

Rival Hypothesis 1: We should be teaching grammatical correctness.

In "IQ and Standard English," Farrell (1983) argues, "For people today to develop abstract thinking, they need to know the grammar of a literate language. . . . In this country, that means learning the grammar of Standard English" (pp. 477–78). In her post, Meg takes a similar stance and questions the value other kinds of literacy would have for these teenagers if they are to make it in mainstream society.

```
From:  Meg Anderson <ma+@mellon.cmu.edu>
To:    <bb+academic.english.mentoring_seminar
       @mellon.cmu.edu>


What's the value of community literacy?
Community literacy is nothing like academic
literacy, which means there is no grammar.
Obviously, academic literacy has higher value,
'cause when teens talk in their own discourse,
they come across as less than intelligent.
```

Rival Hypothesis 2: We should be supporting emancipation.

Other mentors bring a very different, Marxist, reading of class struggle to this situation. Or they turn to the literacy pedagogy of Paulo Freire which helps poor and politically oppressed people gain new

power over their own lives. To support emancipation and freedom,
this hypothesis urges us to help learners use literacy as a tool to critically analyze cultural myths, particularly those that position them
in passive roles in which they are consumers of text instead of critical thinkers about it. For example, literacy tutors would help students to separate "education from propaganda" in an advertisement
for cigarettes. As Freire (1988) explains, through such lessons,
learners begin to perceive the deceit in a cigarette advertisement fea-
turing a beautiful woman in a bikini—that is, "The fact that she, her
smile, her beauty, and her bikini have nothing at all to do with cigarettes" (p. 409). Liz describes her goal of getting Chaz to develop this
critical consciousness.

```
From:  Liz Trail <lt+@mellon.cmu.edu>
To:    <bb+academic.english.mentoring_seminar
       @mellon.cmu.edu>


Freire talks about being aware of meaning
and what you're thinking as you're doing it—
getting at a meta-level about . . . culture,
what it means, and what it means to mean and
all that. Chaz has so much to say about
what's going on in his world. That's what I
want to be doing, helping him bring up stuff
that he's never, that he was never conscious
of. Helping him to develop a consciousness
that might not have been there. He wants to
be a professional football player. I
challenge that. He's a little guy, you know.
I ask him to analyze this cultural thing—
football, which I don't think is too much to
ask from someone at this age level [15].
```

Rival Hypothesis 3: We should be inviting free expression.

Advocates of literacy-as-free-expression strive to empower students
in a very different way. This rival perspective would give little attention to teaching grammar or raising consciousness because this position stresses students' "own authority to make meaning as writers,"
not "what they have yet to attain in order to be able to write" (Willinsky, 1990). The ideal literacy project Elizabeth and Marta describe

seems to be based on this hypothesis, which gives top priority to self-expression over the goals of learning a specific genre or writing standard.

From: Elizabeth Kreski <e4+@mellon.cmu.edu>
To: <bb+academic.english.mentoring_seminar
     @mellon.cmu.edu>

It might be better simply to have the teen writers write about whatever they wanted, in whatever genre.

From: Marta Johnson <mj+@mellon.cmu.edu>
To: <bb+academic.english.mentoring_seminar
     @mellon.cmu.edu>

This leads me to question the writing standards of the English language. Apparently these standards don't work. So who's trying to cling to them and why? I'm trying to say that it doesn't matter when you look at it [teens' writing] as communication. This person is trying to say something. Their goal may be just to get something off of their chest. Our goal as a collective is understanding [being] a receptacle of that communication. If meaning reaches any number of us, that person was successful.

Rival Hypothesis 4: We should be encouraging action-oriented problem-solving.

Dewey (1944) argues that effective instruction plunges students into "perplexing situations" and allows them to choose their own courses of action. Literacy can help you learn to ask tough-minded questions and use writing to think through and respond to real problems.

Heath and McLaughlin (1993) argue that schools typically fail inner-city teens, and that community programs often accomplish what schools do not because they can "provide opportunities for youngsters to build a sense of self-efficacy and a series of prevailing narratives of success in different . . . kinds of activities . . . and promote strong pride in . . . specific accomplishments" (p. 24). Keith's mentee, Chanda, is writing about problems she sees in her inner city school, but he is unwilling to let her just "express" her feelings. He keeps asking her tough questions like, "What would you propose as a change? and "How can you get adults to take you seriously?"

```
From:  Keith Harter <kh+@mellon.cmu.edu>
To:  <bb+academic.english.mentoring_seminar
     @mellon.cmu.edu>


Some people probably expect, you know, these
kids to just bring up an idea and then they
would say, "Oh, that's great. Now let's move
on." I don't happen to share that sort of
ideology. Chanda is a good writer, and she
is very articulate. I'm there to push her
thinking. I ask a lot of tough-minded
questions. I know this might sound arrogant.
But I don't mean it to be. I just think that
if she gets the experience or maybe is
expected to push her thinking, then that
might be one of the best things I could do,
just give her something to base her
subsequent thinking on.
```

From Elenore Long. (1994). *The Rhetoric of Literate Social Action: Mentors Negotiating Interculture Images of Literacy.* Dissertation. Pittsburgh, PA: Carnegie Mellon University.

All four of these rivals were raised by mentors during their own inquiries. They are good hypotheses held by reasonable people about how to support social justice through literacy. Like the mentors, the educators quoted here have seen positive outcomes from programs focused on mainstream skills, on emancipation, on self-expression, or on problem solving. The problem is, you can't set all four as a *top* priority; each calls for different actions and commitments. What conclusion or negotiated answer do they help you come to? How will you shape your action as you become a tutor, mentor, or writer in the community?

GOAL 8

ENTER an Intercultural Inquiry

When scientists and philosophers conduct their inquiries, they often use rivaling to help eliminate hypotheses. But when you conduct an intercultural inquiry, your task is to include more possibilities—to capture more of the local truths and local realities that reflect diverse situations, diverse experiences. In practice, this can mean you may need to understand certain ideas, values, or insights that are outside your own experience. Or you may need to enter an unfamiliar discourse, in which people use joking and indirection to put ideas on the table, or one in which arguments are loud and energetic instead of low-key and academic (recall our discussion of discourse in Chapters 1 and 14).

When you enter an *intercultural collaboration* and want to work across differences and boundaries, the rival hypothesis stance gives you a way to recognize and respect perspectives potentially different from your own. An intercultural inquiry is an attempt to explore a problem from different perspectives, and to let each of those visions expand and enrich your vision of the problem. Rivaling is a strong strategy for inquiry, because it is all about actively seeking out alternative interpretations that don't have to come in formal or academic discourse, in Standard English, or from someone with credentials. And it is about trying—with others—to forge a new understanding that embraces diverse kinds of knowledge to build a more accurate and inclusive picture for everyone.

 ### STRATEGY 1   THE CLUELESS STRATEGY—OR, JUST ASK

This comment comes from a tutor's journal entry written after it was too late—on things she wished she had asked her fourth grade student.

> I'd like to spend more time with Dave and figure out where he got his strange surfing-dude accent and why he always procrastinates about doing his work when he seems to enjoy doing it once he gets going. I'd like to ask Ed if he ever returned the calendar he stole from his history teacher's desk (I keep forgetting to ask. . . .) There's so much I wanted to ask these kids and to talk to them about their daily lives . . . Helen

Why didn't Helen ask? How can you avoid waiting until it is too late?

If they had a choice, most people would like to feel like an "insider" or even an expert: knowledgeable, cool, and "with it." So when they walk into a new situation or cross into a new discourse, they try to pretend that they get what's going on, even when they don't. When Eugene, an American-born Chinese student who spoke excellent Chinese, went to Taiwan, he and his group found that they couldn't fake it—they were easily spotted as foreigners no matter how hard they tried to blend in. It wasn't just their accent, it was how they walked and acted. But once they gave up the pretense, they started getting all kinds of help and advice. When Eugene moved into the new discourse of an inner city community house at the CLC, he developed what he called the "clueless" strategy for dealing with difference:

> I saw that I would not benefit from this experience by just "getting by." I realized how much there would be to learn if I asked more questions and accepted my position of no knowledge (instead of just trying to silently extricate myself from situations when I didn't "get it.") As a result, I adopted a "clueless" approach to learning and teaching. I questioned everything that I was uncertain about, and both I and my writer learned more about each other and the task at hand.

To use the clueless strategy, you don't have to appear naive or "totally clueless," just actively interested in things other people know. Use the strategy to ask about:

- Slang (What does it mean when you say _____?)
- Exchanges between people (Why did he say that to her? What was he trying to do?)
- Events (How did you read that event; what was going on there?)
- Texts (Explain this to me; what do you think it means?)

To make this strategy really work, however, you have to be equally willing to share your own thoughts, your reading of situa-

Victor, a community mentor who grew up "in the neighborhood," nevertheless saw a need to "bridge a communication gap between these young men and older black men" like himself and began his own dictionary of current slang. Soon you began expecting to see Vic listening on the edge of conversations, notebook in hand, asking for definitions. And soon teenagers were bringing him good examples for his "collection."

Get ghost = To go	In the cut = Place to hang out
Dope = Good	Shady = Two-faced
Phat = Good	Busted = Lame
All that = Good	G = A friend

From Victor Hogan. (1993, Fall). Mission Possible. In *Street Life: Dealing with Violence and Risk in our Community* (p. 20). Pittsburgh, PA: Community Literacy Center.

tions, and your experience. Inquiry works best when it is an exchange between curious, generous people.

 STRATEGY 2 **SEEK INTERCULTURAL INTERPRETATIONS OF MEANING IN CONTEXT**

In Example 17–1 we looked at rivaling as a way to compare positions on large and abstract issues, such as literacy and social justice. But rivaling can also be a collaborative effort to understand how someone else is reading the world around you. As we saw in Chapter 1, two people can often read the same text, receive the same instructions, or observe the same situation and build significantly different meanings around it. When these differences are shaped by significant social forces tied to race, class, gender, or ethnicity, they can give us insights we might never have for ourselves. These rivals are especially valuable when they introduce a different discourse into the discussion or bring another social history or set of cultural attitudes and practices to the table. They allow you and your partner to build what we will call an *intercultural interpretation,* a collaborative effort to embrace and integrate multiple ways of reading the world.

Notice, this does not suggest that your rival reading partner is limited to a single discourse or to a given racial, gender, or class-based perspective any more than you are. But they may be able to speak out of a discourse or body of experience you cannot. And that is when you may learn the most.

So when you are ready to go beyond casual conversation and want to listen to the alternative stories communities can tell, invite someone to join you in creating "rival readings" of a problem, event, or issue you are concerned about. In a rival reading, the "text" that raises this issue might be an event, photo, transcript of a discussion, or written text; it might come from a newspaper report, a perplexing scene in a book, a claim or proposal advanced by an "authority." When two people look at such a "text" together, they may agree about the surface text—what its words mean, or what the text claims, or what values it promotes. (And of course, they may raise rivals even at the surface level too.) But intercultural interpretation is most revealing when it gets at *meaning in context.*

For example, remember Nicole and Elliott who agreed on the importance of "responsibility" (quoted at the beginning of Chapter 15)? It wasn't until they began to describe "responsibility" to each other as if they were describing a play (where people are doing things, for purposes, in specific contexts) that they discovered they were living in different plays and had very different meanings-in-context attached to the idea of "being responsible."

A rival reading is a useful strategy whenever you have questions such as: What is the meaning of this idea/issue/event in action—as someone else sees that action? How could this idea/issue/event play itself out in the world they know or in their imagination? Who does what to whom in their image of this "text"? What are the consequences of its ideas? In order to do a rival reading that can give you answers—as well as surprises—you will need to ask your partner to give you a sort of blow-by-blow account of the actors and scenes they associate with the text as they read it. When the two of you compare your responses, these rival readings can become a stand-in for how each of you are "reading the world." They can put you on the road to a genuine inquiry.

Here are some tips on how to begin:

1. Always start with your own need to know. Think about a problem or question in your own mind or a text that leaves you puzzled or curious or raises provoking questions. Find some version of it in a "text" you can both look at or listen to. (Remember, a "text" could mean photographs, video clips, a description of a situation, or a tape-recorded conversation.)

   For example, you might be saying to yourself: "I have been thinking about those booklets that promote colleges. When teenagers who've had little exposure to college read them, they may agree with me on lots of things, like the value of education. But what kind of mental images do we each create when we imagine the reality or the story behind these scenes?" Rival readings get at the different ways people's life experience and prior knowledge let them translate the "meaning" of a text into a story of real people (how do they look?) doing something (what?), for (what?) personal reasons? Here are some ways other writers have translated questions they had into a text they could interpret with their partner.

Problem/Question	Text/Image/Event That Invites Interpretation
When a cultural group is affected by a text, do "insiders" and "outsiders" read it the same?	Public policies, ads, media accounts that talk about or talk to a particular group.
What images does the student you mentor have of everyday college life?	Your college or university's promotional video or texts.
A perplexing event or exchange between you and your student or community contact.	A journal account or tape of that event, the dialogue, the setting, the outcome.
How do members of a collaborative group see the roles, goals, or authority of others in the group?	A roster of members, titles or roles, a description of the group.

2. So that you can make clearer comparisons, mark a number of "comment points" at key places. Read the text yourself with a

tape recorder handy, and at each "comment point" think out loud about your own responses. (You may write your response, but taping gives you a more natural and richer record of what you were thinking.) Then ask your partner—someone who can come to it from another discourse or a different cultural perspective—to do the same. Discover what you can learn together.

Three good questions to ask are:

- What does this text, this phrase *mean* (to you, at this point)?
- What is the *story behind the story* at this point? Can you help me see how this (idea/issue/event) would be acted out in real life? What would someone be saying; what would they be doing; what would they be thinking and why? In short, help me turn this idea into an event or action.
- How would you describe either the person talking or being talked about here? What is the *persona* of the speaker, that is, the personality, character, or attitudes that this voice projects?

Tricia, a college mentor, was curious about an ad directed to 20-something African Americans, in which a young man standing beside a Jeep is raising his arms (for joy?) and a young woman in jeans beside him is leaning on the hood, grinning at the camera. The caption on top reads: REAL JUICE WITHOUT THE SQUEEZE. Beneath the picture there is the phrase "FOR UNDER $11,000" in big print, and small print ad copy about some of the jeep's features.

Tricia wondered what this reference to "juice" was all about, and even more, about how urban teenagers respond to the calculated language and images of this ad. Does it manipulate them to want a vehicle they probably can't afford? So she crafted some questions and pulled three teenagers into a dialogue with her. How would you read the ad and answer her questions? Here are some answers she got.

Example 17–2
Rival Readings on an Ad

What does juice mean?

Ray (14): It means the stuff. The real thing.

Nikia (19): It's hard. You know what I'm saying. The power it got.

Vicki (17): I think that when people make ads and they use black people in their ads, they always try to use words they think are slang, that they think are going to attract black people.

Is this ad persuasive?

Ray: No. Because the car is ugly. They hardly tell you anything about the car. The warranty and protection plan might help you out.

Nikia: No. Not really. Someone in their 30's or 40's might buy it, but not me. The ad ain't even all that.

Vicki: Not really. The ad is trying to attract black people with the words it uses, but it doesn't matter because this car is nothing in the streets. If you have some money, this car is nothing. Not unless you have some sounds in there!

What do you think of the man's and woman's expressions?

Ray: He's happy that he got the woman and the truck, and she's happy that she's got the man and get to ride around in the truck.

Nikia: He's thinking, "I'm the man!" And she's happy 'cause he got the jeep and so she stops taking the bus and all that.

Vicki: He's thinking like, "Yeah, I got this car and I got a female on me. You better get on." And she's saying, "I got a man with a car. We're going out tonight."

What do you think of the man's social status?

Ray: He looks like a plumber, because of what he's wearing.

Nikia: I think he's middle class, 'cause he's just so geeked to get the jeep. If he was rich, he wouldn't be so happy.

Vicki: He looks like he's in school and his parents bought it for him.

From Tricia Davis. (1995, May). Strategies for instigating an intercultural conversation. From Linda Flower, Wayne Peck, Elenore Long's Community Literacy and Intercultural Interpretation course. Carnegie Mellon University, Pittsburgh, PA.

How do Ray, Nikia, and Vicki's responses compare to yours? Do they see anything in this situation and this ad that you perhaps didn't see? For instance, Tricia noticed that the teenagers were quite skeptical about advertisers. But they seemed to see the woman in the ad in a lower social and economic position than the man. What was going on?

 ### STRATEGY 3   WRITE A MULTI-VOICED INQUIRY

An inquiry is an open-minded, questioning journey into a problem, issue, or idea. A *multi-voiced* inquiry is one which tries to do justice to multiple ways of perceiving the world and representing knowledge (see Chapter 4) as well as rival hypotheses about the world and events. It starts with strategies you have already used for doing research (Chapter 13), observation and reflection (Chapter 15), trying new genres (Chapter 16) and for intercultural interpretation (this chapter).

But it raises a new problem for you as a writer. In your own mind you hear the voices of many people telling you their stories, sharing their perceptions, letting you participate in their experience. And they raise strong, good rivals that you don't want to sweep under the rug. How do you capture the words, images, and lived reality of your own multi-voiced understanding in a paper or report?

Unlike quotations from a book, such knowledge does not come prepackaged in academic discourse either. It may reflect the language and conventions of community organizing, religious commitment, street talk, oral performance, or local history. It may speak to you in a mix of genres, from statistical analyses, ethnographic studies, or educational research, to history, interviews, and editorials, personal journals, and poetry. Perhaps your community project has made a deliberate attempt to value these different ways of talking and writing in order to create a hybrid discourse. (See the Thought Provokers on Literacy in Chapter 14.) How can you create a hybrid discourse in your own writing?

Here is a three-phase approach you can use to create a more broadly intercultural inquiry and a hybrid discourse that lets more voices, genres, and points of view talk to one another in text.

Phase I. Frame a Question

Inquiry starts in wondering, questioning, feeling perplexed or drawn to understand more. (Notice how this differs from writing an advocacy paper or report in which you begin by finding a thesis to be proven or body of information to convey.) So begin your inquiry by trying to pose a problem or question that is a genuine problem in you own mind or a genuine open question. You might:

- Write a brief narrative that captures your own engagement with this question. Why does this matter to you?
- Write about a conflict you see—in the world, in your own mind.
- Write about what you *don't* know—some questions you would like to explore. If you have very broad questions, try to get operational: what parts of this situation could you actually explore, observe, ask about? How would you start?
- Imagine some rival interpretations of a situation/problem/idea that stimulates your questions. How might it look from different parts of the community? But wait; are your predictions of what others think accurate? What would they really see and say for themselves? How could you find out?

Phase II. Bring Multiple Voices to the Table

Here is where the research skills you have been developing will let you actively seek out different kinds of knowledge and ways of knowing. These might include:

- Outside sources from library and archival research (Chapters 13 and 18).
- Observational data of people "in process": a collaborative planning session, discussion, think-aloud protocol (Chapters 1 and 13).
- Your own observations and reflections (Chapter 14).
- Commentary by participants on tapes, transcripts, or your observations (Chapter 14).
- Dialogues from b-board exchanges (Chapter 4).
- Writing by participants and tools for analyzing it (Chapter 16).
- Interviewing (Chapter 16).
- Intercultural interpretation and rival readings (Chapter 17).
- Community Problem-Solving Dialogues giving you Stories behind the Story, Rivals, and Options and Outcomes (Chapter 18).

Collect interpretations and analyses from at least three different sources/participants and at least three different kinds of data. If, for instance, you are a mentor conducting an inquiry that involves teenage writers, imagine yourself inviting a number of people and/or voices to the table to discuss your question with you. At the table (Figure 17–3) will be voices past and present from books (theorists, researchers, educators, novelists, journalists) as well as your

FIGURE 17–3
Multiple Voices at the Table

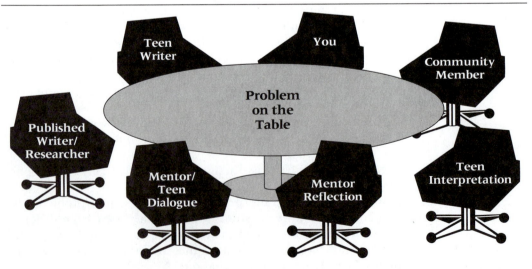

own voice, those of other students, teenagers, and other members of the community. Some will be speaking directly to your question, others offering rival perspectives, and still others letting you draw inferences and achieve insights through their words or behavior. Whether they offer claims, data, observations, or reflections, each can bring a valuable voice to your inquiry.

Phase III. *Reflect Multiple Voices in Your Text*

In writing your own text, you may find that a traditional academic paper—one focused on making and supporting claims or reporting the results of research—would make it difficult to convey some of the tentative, experiential, or unresolved aspects of what you want to express. A multi-voiced inquiry *shapes the text* so that it reflects *the shape of an inquiry*. Like any good analysis, this approach still asks you to be explicit, but invites you to use techniques you know from creative writing and expressive document design to help people visualize this situation and to capture the conflicting voices that are part of a good inquiry. Rather than following a specific outline, try to include the following elements in your paper:

- Name and situate the problem you see or the question that guided your inquiry. (What is the open question? For whom is this problem a problem? What is at stake?)
- Allow the multiple voices you brought to the table to speak and to offer rival interpretations of *what's going on, why,* and *why it matters.* There are many ways to set this up in text. You might follow the path of your own questioning and inquiry if it has interesting turns and points of discovery—beware of a mere writer-based story. Or juxtapose different accounts of the same event or perspectives on an idea. Or create an imaginary script in which the various voices at your table actually talk and respond to one another. However, a juxtaposition or dialogue (which lets us draw our own conclusions) must also be accompanied by a running commentary from you (which tells us how *you* interpret these voices).
- Finally—and this element is crucial—analyze the claims, responses, and dialogues you have created to discuss what you have learned. This can be a challenge—plan on getting feedback on your first draft. You may also feel that your conclusions are tentative—so talk about the rivals that exist in your own mind. But pull your insights, intuitions, and discoveries together into a strong, negotiated interpretation of what this means for you from where you now stand.

In the three inquiries that follow, the writers posed questions that invited intercultural interpretation and experimented with ways using their text to bring the reader into negotiating and integrating some revealing rival readings. The first is from Karen, a college mentor at the Community Literacy Center.

Example 17–3
Posing an Open Question and Rivaling Yourself

Stories-Behind-the-Story of Averageness

My inquiry began as a fervent response to the following passage by Mike Rose:

The paper frames an open question and conflict that is a genuine problem in the writer's own mind

And then there was Ken Harvey. Ken was good-looking in a puffy way and had a full and oily ducktail and was a car enthusiast . . . a hodad. One day in religion class . . . [we] were talking about the parable of the talents, about achievement, working hard, doing the best you can do, blah-blah-blah, when the teacher called on the restive Ken Harvey for an opinion. Ken thought about it, but just for a second, and said (with studied, minimal affect), "I just wanna be average." (Rose 1989, 28)

Ken's behavior as a student angered and frustrated me, clashing with my own persistence in institutionalized education. As early as the fourth grade I recognized the importance of distinguishing myself academically to be considered a successful student in school. I consistently fought my placements in school tracking systems, gaining admittance both to "gifted and talented" and AP programs. Reading Rose's passage made me want to inspire students like Ken Harvey so they might become creative, critical thinkers. I hoped to do for students what past teachers have done for me, what my parents have done for me, and what I have done for myself.

Paper also questions the writer's own assumptions and imagines other possibilities

I was prompted to question my critique of academic averageness, and began to see dangerous glimpses of classist, elitist presumptions in my attitude. Perhaps my notions of averageness as a merely adequate non-exemplary mode of being in the world did not encompass the "stories-behind-the-story" of those who seem average to me. Further, maybe those who seem average to me are seen as greater-than-average in other contexts by other people. Academia is just one setting in which averageness can play a role. Perhaps those who seem academically average are socially outstanding. Or perhaps not. I began to sense the complexities involved in considering averageness and was ready to pursue an investigation of them.

Community experience forms an observation-based rival to the writer's own experience and assumptions

Through my interactions with Delmar at the CLC, I began to get a deeper sense of the contingent realities involved in one student's academic life. Early in our time together, Delmar, explaining street-smart strategies, commented that a good way of staying out of trouble with the police is to seem like everyone else. By stressing the importance of not sticking out or drawing attention to himself on Pittsburgh streets, Delmar illustrated a non-academic facet to just being average. He reasoned the more average he could look on the street, the less threatened he would feel. In this context, then, being average seems a positive reaction to life circumstances.

Reflects on the implications of this rival hypothesis

[This rival interpretation of "averageness" leads Karen to hypothesize why Delmar might also be reluctant to revise his own writing.] As I reflected on the positive notions of social averageness Delmar expressed, I began to think he might value averageness in this more academic context as well. I guessed that average to Delmar represented safety, and it became understandable why Delmar would choose safety over danger. Many students are wary of criticism, especially criticism of personal writing. . . .

Weaves rival readings from library research and dialogues into an exploration of "averageness"

[Karen then builds an expanded intercultural interpretation of "averageness" linking the rival readings of three teenagers to two books on the education of "silenced learners." For example:] Elton offered an additional motivation. He thought students who claim to want to be average and therefore seem to have "no goals in life," are really asking for attention. Ken's "I don't care" attitude seems to constitute for Elton a danger signal to which teachers will pay attention, thereby distinguishing Ken from his peers. *". . . to see how the teacher was using the student's desire for attention in productive ways . . . was significant in this classroom context. (Kutz & Roskelly, 29)*

Ends with a reflection on the writer's own thinking

In reflecting upon the enriched conception of averageness to which the theorists and teens led me, I came to realize the complex and seemingly contradictory ways averageness has played a role in my own life. . . . [in] contradictory desires for social averageness and social distinction. . . .

From Karen Pierce. From Linda Flower, Wayne Peck, Jennifer Flach's Community Literacy and Intercultural Interpretation course. Carnegie Mellon University, Pittsburgh, PA.

When another CLC mentor, Tricia, turned her rival readings on the jeep ad (see Strategy 2) into a written inquiry, she thought about her own methods of inquiry and whether asking the teenagers to help her interpret the ads was the best way to arrive at intercultural understanding. So in her imagination she "asked" a group of other writers, educators, and literacy theorists to "comment" on her project from their perspective. In her paper (see the example below) this became a dialogue in which she imagined what authors she had been reading in the course would have to say to her, about *her* question. Her inferences about how they would respond let her turn her text into a lively "conversation" on a new topic.

Example 17–4
An Imaginary Dialogue Among Writers in an Inquiry Paper

So I begin my inquiry by holding a "discussion" with some of the writers I had read.

A sociolinguist who studied discourse strategies

John Gumperz: This could be an interesting study, but I think it is more important to learn, first, about their cultural assumptions and knowledge.

An English educator who values the literacy skills African-American students already possess

Jay Robinson: That may be, but what you're talking about is an issue of literacy. You're less literate than the teens, when it comes to interpreting these ads. So if you are going to "get at" their literate resources, you'll have to engage them in a conversation in a relaxed setting. [Tricia has Robinson describe how language expresses identity and personality.]

A linguist who documented the sophisticated language skills of ghetto youth

William Labov: When I did my study of language in the inner city, I couldn't really see what the children knew until we replaced our white interviewer with Clarence Thomas, an African American raised in Harlem who knew the child's neighborhood. [Tricia has Labov elaborate on the problems of cross cultural research.]

The student writer responds to their "comments" on her project

Tricia: But, Labov, I don't want to try and find an African-American interviewer to conduct my inquiry. I'm a Jewish-American 20-year old and I want to have the conversation. I want to see what I can learn first hand. I've already been trying different ways to encourage my writers to express themselves to me more. After listening to everyone's advice, I think I can learn a lot by asking the teens to interpret culturally coded advertisements.

From Tricia Davis. (1995, May). Strategies for instigating an intercultural conversation. From Linda Flower, Wayne Peck, and Elenore Long's Community Literacy and Intercultural Interpretation course. Carnegie Mellon University, Pittsburgh, PA.

The writer of this final inquiry raises a personal and public question. In her research proposal, she asked whether the Hmong people, refugees from the Vietnam War, had been assimilated into the American culture in her own community in Eau Claire, Wisconsin, and wondered about the effects of racism on them. "I have seen this racism first hand growing up in the city, but I would like to see it from their side." Example 17–5 excerpts short passages from this multi-genre research paper to illustrate how the writer integrates a variety of genres and distinctive voices in her text. The hybrid discourse Niki creates lets her build a richer conception of what assimilation and racism mean in her town.

Example 17–5
A Hybrid Discourse of Multiple Voices and Mixed Genres

Poem from a refugee biography

Niki's paper begins with a moving narrative poem that captures the experience of being a refugee, quoted from a refugee biography published in Eau Claire:

> The Hmong I See
>
> At night we stayed in schools
> We didn't know who the enemy was
> We didn't know where the enemy was
> One night monks were praying at the school
> In the morning they were Viet Cong soldiers. . . .

Historical and contextual analysis

The next section introduces the refugee problem with discourse of history and political analysis, sketching the story of the Vietnam War— as it shaped the life of Thong, her chief informant for the central section of the paper:

> Thong's parents can't tell him the date of his birth. They know the year and month, but the exact date has been lost in a year of torture for the Hmong in Laos; 1975. That was the year the United States pulled out. . . .

Biographical sketch of Thong based on e-mail interviews

This section turns from the sweep of history to a biographical sketch of an individual. It is based on scripted, e-mail interviews Niki conducted with Thong, who is now at college in another city. (The transcript of these interviews is included at the end of the paper and referenced at the end of the quotations.) Here is a story from Thong's childhood. Thong recounted how many people chose to view the Hmong:

> I was in grade school. I walked home after sliding (winter time) with my cousin at his house; an old lady came out of her house and started yelling at me. She yelled, "go back to your own country!" That was a common sentence I heard growing up. (Thong E-1)

[This section ends with Thong talking about his image of assimilation through achievement, describing himself as overcoming prejudice by showing he was "the only person that could get the job done."] Niki ends the section with her own commentary: "To some he is a 'chink' a 'gook.' To others he is respected. He knows what he wants; he believes in himself."

Reflection based a journal written in high school

Niki brings herself into the story with a passage from her personal high school journal that reflects her own growing awareness of racism:

> *. . . . The next passage is a journal entry from my experience with the Hmong. It takes place after a fight between the Asian and white Supremacist gangs at my school in 1995. . . .*
>
> November 11, 1995
>
> Journal,
>
> Today there was a fight at school. This is pretty exciting news at our high school. . . . They say there is a new Hmong gang in town and they were fighting with a white supremacist gang. I have trouble believing this. . . . Personally, I don't think the fight was between gangs. I think it was more between two racist people. . . .

Letters to the editor

Niki's paper now brings in conflicting voices from the community at large as she turns to another source of data and a different discourse—a series of letters to the editor of Niki's local paper focused on the question, Are the Hmong assimilating? Our excerpted version of Niki's transition and the letters begins: "My view of the Hmong is limited to [being] a classmate of the Hmongs. I can see how the Hmong children are doing socially in the schools, but I cannot see many other views." The next passage is a string of letters to the editor in the local paper which describe the feelings of how other sections of the community thought the Hmong were adapting to America. . . .

> ### The Teacher's View . . .

Letter uses observation to note a continuing problem

> In recent years the students are coming to class with a firm grasp on English [and] . . . getting better grades. . . . [However,] there is also very little interaction between the Hmongs and Caucasians. All the Hmongs congregate in one cafeteria before school, but the other students roam throughout the halls. . . .
>
> James Gilbertson

The Hmongs' View

Letter uses a personal story to raise a policy question on plans to discontinue welfare

Many people do not realize the struggles that the Hmong overcame in coming to America [and today]. . . . We must achieve proficiency at the top level of English instruction before we are prepared to seek full-time employment. . . . Putting ourselves through these classes is no easy task. Many fathers and husbands have two part-time jobs to put themselves through classes, plus they still need to support their families with that money. . . . Many fathers are talking of suicide, because they are ashamed that they can not support their own families. . . .

Yee Bee Xiong

The Numerical View . . .

Letter uses economic statistics to suggest Hmong aren't "trying to adapt"

I've never really interacted with a Hmong, but . . . . 64.5% live in poverty. 90% rent their homes. . . . These statistics don't show an adaptation to our culture; they show a culture that is failing to succeed. . . .

John Doe

Niki ends the paper by attempting to integrate this hybrid discourse with her own commentary which then leads directly into a second poem by the refugee writer quoted at the beginning.

Writer's commentary and poem

. . . . With the attitudes of many citizens in Eau Claire, it might be years before the Hmong feel like they belong and are succeeding in our culture, but it will happen

I never want to forget my homeland,

The culture, the land, the people,

Yet, today I stand before you,

A citizen of the United States . . .

From Niki Burger. (1996). From Amy Goodburn's First-Year Seminar, University of Nebraska, Lincoln.

Writing a multi-voiced inquiry will take you on a journey of exploration sparked by the power of a genuine open question. To do justice to the people, discourses, ideas, and values you encounter on this journey, you must be a prepared observer who listens for what is really there and creates a record open to later reflection. You will

have to actively seek out stories behind the story and rival interpretations. And once you have all these vigorous voices at your
table, you will probably want to mine other texts, including the
examples above, as you invent ways to bring these multiple voices,
discourses and ideas into your own writing. In their different ways
each of the three writers in the examples above is an experi-
menter, seeking ways to express the larger reality. Each is trying to
create a hybrid discourse that lets more people and perspectives
speak to the issue for themselves. And each is working to make this
mix of genres and visions add up to an integrated perspective in
which they as writers are trying to build a new understanding and
a negotiated meaning.

Never forget that the first audience for an inquiry is you. Keep
your eye always on good problems, real questions, and your own desire to understand more. Look back from time to time at Goal 2,
Strategy 2, Evaluate and Adapt (in Chapter 14). Use those assessment strategies to consolidate your learning and reflect on your
progress.

At the same time, remember that when you conduct an inquiry
into community issues, you are also writing to a larger community
of concern on issues that make a difference. Your text could not only
extend the conversation, but your multi-voiced inquiry may allow
those who are often excluded from written forums to speak for
themselves through your text. And as we will consider in the next
chapter, your text could also be the springboard for a live problem-
solving dialogue with your community.

PROJECTS AND ASSIGNMENTS

1   Write a description (for your journal or b-board) of an open question that
    has come up in your work. What is the conflict over? What makes this a
    problem for *you?* And how are reasonable people responding differently to
    this problem?

2   Paulo Freire, the liberatory literacy educator, argues that this process of
    posing, defining, and redefining problems is so important that we are in ef-
    fect not only "naming the world" but in some way "changing it" by the way
    we define the problem. In his words:

    > To exist, humanly, is to *name* the world, to change it. Once named, the
    > world in its turn reappears to the namers as a problem and requires of
    > them a new *naming*. Men are not built in silence, but in word, in work in
    > action-reflection. (From Paulo Freire. (1989). *Pedagogy of the Oppressed*,
    > p. 76. New York, NY: Continuum.)

    Use the various parts of his argument about "naming" to analyze the prob-
    lem you posed in Assignment 1. That is, use his terms and ideas to describe
    as many features of your problem-posing as you can. Then reflect on your
    own analysis: What did you discover about your problem or Freire's notion

of "naming the world" when you contextualized (and maybe conditionalized) it?

3   The Thought Provokers in Chapter 14 raised some controversial topics. Respond to one of those texts by posing an open question and taking a strong
rival hypothesis stance to that problem. Before you write the final version
of your conclusion, hold a group discussion that invites good rivals. Try
then to build a negotiated understanding in your text that takes these genuine rivals into account in one way or another.

4   Give the Clueless Strategy a try. How did it work for you? How would you
modify the strategy and when would you choose to use it or not?

5   The mentors and published writers in Example 17–1 offered some strong
rivals on the question of how to use literacy to support equality and social
justice. Evaluate these rivals by comparing the outcomes they could produce. Read two or more of these rivals as a plan for action and think about
what you would do as a mentor or tutor on the basis of that hypothesis.
What would you emphasize or work toward, and how would that shape
your behavior? Then compare those rivals in terms of the question: If I
acted on this hypothesis, where would it be likely to lead?

6   Use the rival reading strategy to conduct a mini-inquiry. Collect at least one
rival reading and compare it to your own. You and your reader may agree
on the obvious meaning of the text, but try to find out more about the
scene as well as the intentions, thoughts, and values of the people involved
that each of you are silently visualizing as you read.

7   Write a plan for an inquiry. Sketch out the question that is motivating your
need to know. Is this a genuine, open question (not just a claim or belief
you already hold, in sheep's clothing)? Focus on something you really
want/need to learn. Then draft a plan for conducting this inquiry. Describe
what methods (such as taping a mentoring session or doing rival readings)
you are going to use. Then lay out the sequence of dates for when you will
(1) collect your observations, (2) study them and go back to your partners
with questions if you plan to, (3) do a draft of your inquiry, and (4) complete the final paper.

8   *Checklist for Conducting a Rival Hypothesis Inquiry in Writing.* Sometimes writers take a rival hypothesis stance during their inquiry process, but organize
their written text around the conclusion they reached. However, if you
want to bring the reader into an on-going inquiry into the problem you are
writing about, this checklist will help you organize the paper itself around
the process of rival hypothesis exploration. The order of items is up to you;
the question is whether you included each of these thinking moves in the
text.

☐ a.   **Name** the issue or the **open question.** Lay out the unanswered
question or conflict that is at the heart of the problem. (See also
Chapters 1 and 8.)

☐ b.   **Present** two or more genuine **rival hypotheses,** alternative interpretations, competing ways of naming or responding to the problem.
A *genuine* rival (unlike a straw position that you just set up to knock
down) is a hypothesis that calls for serious consideration, one that

you might end having to live with if the evidence ended up supporting it.

☐ c. **Explore** the **evidence** for these hypotheses. Evidence can come
from the written literature on the topic, from discussions and personal experience, or from inferences you draw from what is known.
Sometimes you can find "authorities" to quote, but sometimes the
most persuasive evidence is the series of inferences you draw from
what is known. If you agree or disagree with a claim, you probably
have reasons when you say to yourself, "This is likely or true because
of x, z, y and z." So support your ideas by showing the reader your
own reasoning and inferences.

☐ d. **Evaluate** the **evidence** for these hypotheses. To really compare hypotheses, you may need to evaluate or criticize the evidence people
bring. How strong is it? Where does it come from; What assumptions
is it based upon? Is there any counter evidence in the picture? Or
could you create an alternative explanation based on that evidence?
Don't be afraid to say that some claims and inferences seem to you to
be well supported by the evidence; others you are less certain about,
even though they are worth considering. Your goal is to weigh the
evidence, not to "know" the "answer."

☐ e. **Create** a new or a **qualified conclusion** in response to your initial
problem. First, look back at your initial problem statement. Is this
conclusion strongly tied to the problem you posed? On the basis of
the strong rivals you considered, come to a conclusion that reflects
your current best understanding. Aim for a fuller, more complex position, that recognizes the different sides of the problem. Even if you
end up arguing that one of the original rivals is the best interpretation, show the reader how it deals with or how it is qualified by the
other rivals. Your conclusion may also be a *qualified* or *conditionalized*
position—one that recognizes that some hypotheses are the best answer "under these conditions." Or it may be the best answer if you
qualify or limit the scope of the claim. Remember, the conclusion is
not the place to offer a new, untested position that has not gone
through the same scrutiny of evidence or support that the other rivals
received.

IF YOU WOULD LIKE TO READ MORE

If you would like to know more about the philosophy of dialogue and the
practice of intercultural inquiry, see:

Balester, Valerie M. *Cultural Divide: A Study of African-American College-Level
Writers.* Portsmouth, NH: Boynton/Cook, 1993. / This sensitive study documents the multiple discourse styles African-American students can bring to
college.

Dewey, John. *Democracy and Education.* New York: Free Press, 1944. / One
of the architects of progressive education, Dewey had a vision that joined
learning and community life.

Farrell, Thomas J. IQ and standard English. *College Composition and Communication, 34*, 470–84. / This article, cited in Example 17–1, reflects a familiar bias, now criticized by many linguists, for one's own dialect.

Flower, Linda. Negotiating the meaning of difference. *Written Communication,* 13(1), 44–92, January, 1996. / This is a study not of students, but of the teacher trying to build a fuller representation of others' understandings in the midst of a generative intercultural dilemma.

Flower, Linda. Partners in inquiry: A logic for community outreach. In L. Adler-Kassner, R. Crooks, and A. Watters (Eds.), *Writing the Community: Concepts and Models for Service-Learning in Composition,* pp. 95–117. Washington, DC: American Association of Higher Education, 1997. / After comparing community/university relations built on the logics of cultural mission, technical expertise, compassion, and prophetic pragmatism, this paper argues for the role of mutual inquiry.

Freire, Paulo. The adult literacy process as a cultural action for freedom and education and conscientizacao. In E. R. Kintgen, B. M. Kroll, and M. Rose (Eds.), *Perspectives on Literacy,* pp. 398–409. Carbondale, IL: Southern Illinois University Press, 1988. / This excerpt, cited in Example 17–1, describes Freire's innovative teaching practices.

Freire, Paulo. *Pedagogy of the Oppressed.* New York: Continuum, 1989. / This well-known book is a powerful statement of the philosophy and practice of dialogue that unites theory and action in praxis.

Goldblatt, Eli C. (1995). *'Round My Way: Authority and Double-Consciousness in Three Urban High School Writers.* Pittsburgh, PA: University of Pittsburgh Press, 1995. / This finely detailed and reflective study follows the way writing and talk reflect the emerging identities of three students.

Heath, Shirley Brice, and Milbrey W. Mclaughlin. *Identity & Inner-City Youth: Beyond Ethnicity and Gender.* New York: Teachers College, 1993. / This is a wide-ranging ethnographic project with strong policy implications, that demonstrates the way discourse, dialogue, and community support these young people's powerful drive to construct an identity.

Long, Elenore. *The Rhetoric of Social Action: Mentors Negotiating Intercultural Images of Literacy.* Unpublished doctoral dissertation. Pittsburgh, PA: Carnegie Mellon University, 1994. / The rivals in Example 17–1 come from this fascinating study of the issues and conflicts mentors negotiated in their own minds and writing over the course of a semester.

Willinsky, John. *The New Literacy: Redefining Reading and Writing in the Schools.* New York: Routledge, 1990. / This view of literacy values the creativity and voice of every writer.

chapter eighteen

Community Problem-Solving Dialogues

GOAL 9
START a community problem-solving dialogue

Bring your strategies for writing, dialogue, and inquiry to community problems.

> **STRATEGY 1**   **COME TO THE TABLE ON SHARED PROBLEMS**
>
> **STRATEGY 2**   **WRITE STORIES, SEEK RIVALS, EXAMINE OPTIONS**
>
> **STRATEGY 3**   **DOCUMENT AND EXPAND THE INQUIRY**

Cultural difference means that although you and I are bound in Martin Luther King's "network of mutuality," we may see things quite differently. We are looking at the "same" situation, the "same" problem, but we may be seeing distinctive, sometimes conflicting visions of reality. Maybe that difference exists because our experience has been shaped so differently by race or by gender, or by the class and economic history of our parents. Maybe our cultural backgrounds lead us to work from different starting assumptions, to set different priorities, or to focus on different clues when we read a situation or size up people. Or maybe the discourse that I use to explain things to myself sets up barriers when I talk to you; and your discourse depends on terms, concepts, and attitudes that mystify me. Our styles of argument—the way we use stories, humor, repetition, emotion, evidence, the way we take turns, express disagreement, ask questions—these differences in discourse and style sometimes make it seem like we are talking different languages. (Remember Kochman's description of argument styles in conflict in Chapter 14?)

One way to deal with difference, especially when it is tied to power that gives unearned advantages to one of us and lays unjust burdens on the other, is to focus on that difference. That is, analyze who we are, how we differ and why; to focus on causes and consequences; to examine and critique the power structures, the discourses, and the

433

taken-for-granted ideological assumptions that shape and keep these differences in place. For instance, Tricia in Chapter 17 began to ask why her readers turned a gender difference into a class and status difference.

However, when you and I want to work together, when we want to collaborate on posing and solving some of those problems, we may find it helpful then to shift from the act of critique to the process of dialogue. Instead of analyzing ourselves, our discourses, and our differences, an intercultural dialogue focuses attention on the problem out there, on the situation we are trying to interpret. Difference is no longer the problem under discussion; it is our tool for understanding the problems we face together. The fact that you and I see different dimensions of this situation, that we give priority to different parts of it, and that we can take advantage of different discourses to explain it, lets us build a smarter, more complex intercultural picture of the problem and our options. And it gives both of us a stake in solving it.

GOAL 9

START a Community Problem-Solving Dialogue

Community Problem-Solving Dialogues are a strategy for holding productive collaborative planning discussions with an intercultural group. These dialogues have an informal problem-solving structure that gives more people a way to enter the discussion with their ideas and experience. And they use writing to help people evelop those ideas in a way that will be heard across the wider community.

Working Partners: An Urban Youth Report (Example 18–1) is the product of a series of these community problem-solving dialogues. For three years urban teenagers and college student mentors at the CLC had worked on issues related to risk, stress, and respect. Each nine-week project had ended in a public Community Conversation and a 10–12 page CLC document. *Working Partners* is an example of the insights that can emerge when more people come to the table to pose, analyze, and try to solve problems. Notice how the ideas and voices of urban teenagers work to redefine the problem that is usually described as the issue of "teen violence" when they rename it as problems of "risk, stress, and respect" in their lives.

Working Partners also illustrates the writing, problem-solving, and decision-making strategies used to structure a community problem-solving dialogue. Notice how the document tries to bring the reader into this conversation and see new options. So read it as an example of how a live dialogue could be organized.

WORKING PARTNERS

AN URBAN YOUTH REPORT
ON RISK, STRESS, AND RESPECT

When was the last time you had an open, serious talk with an urban teen? Teenagers like Tony, Shirley, and Mark bring a critical perspective to issues in our community. For these teens and others like them, problems in the news and on the street are not just statistics and stories but reality. Teen pregnancy, drug use, harassment by the police, conflict within schools, racism, gangs, abuse: all create a context of risk and stress which they—like we—long to change.

Tony (13) describes being drawn into a fight in which all of his options looked bad. Analyzing his own choices, he sees how the violence that erupts between neighborhood groups and gangs is often rooted in deep needs for respect—and the absence of productive ways to find it.

Shirley (15) describes the stress of everyday existence in her inner-city neighborhood. The inadequate advice given by adults who "haven't been there" moves her to issue a "wake up call to adults" that pleads for a new sense of community that embraces all its youth.

Mark (15) describes how conflicts between teenagers and adults—including parents, teachers, and police—can arise from the dynamics of risk and respect. And he sketches a decision strategy that can open up better options for police and teens.

Hands On
Community Literacy

THE COMMUNITY LITERACY CENTER
AND
CARNEGIE MELLON UNIVERSITY

Carnegie
Mellon

Hands On
Community Literacy

What do community problems look like from a teenager's perspective?

This report invites you to enter a COMMUNITY PROBLEM-SOLVING DIALOGUE in which urban teenagers join the process of building a better community as *working partners*. And it shows you how to begin a dialogue of your own in your neighborhood, workplace, or school.

Teenagers bring a unique and needed expertise to the analysis of urban problems. At Pittsburgh's Community Literacy Center, they also learn problem-solving and writing skills for shaping and evaluating better solutions.

COMMUNITY PROBLEM-SOLVING DIALOGUES build new working relationships that weave alternative perspectives into a community-constructed plan for action.

Are you ready for a breakthrough?

COMMUNITY PROBLEM-SOLVING DIALOGUES like these are tools for change. They support inter-cultural collaboration that gives respect and voice to the exper-tise of everyone. And they create a platform on which to build workable visions of a more just and compassionate community.

This report draws from the texts, videos, and public com-munity conversations produced by teenagers at Pittsburgh's Community Literacy Center, collaborating with Carnegie Mellon student mentors. It illustrates a process that sup-ports both learning and inquiry through three strategies:

♦ *Getting the Story Behind the Story,*
♦ *Seeking Rival Hypotheses, and*
♦ *Examining Options and Outcomes.*

These research-based strate-gies can help community groups, educators, and policy makers to initiate COMMUNITY PROBLEM-SOLVING DIALOGUES of their own.

WHAT ARE TEENAGERS

THREE STRATEGIES FOR AN

STRATEGY 1: GETTING THE STORY BEHIND THE STORY

Teenagers have expertise—and alternative perspectives—on urban issues that involve youth. They can help us define the problems, describe the hidden logics of youth that adults may not see, and evaluate options. Teenagers in Community Problem-Solving Dialogues use the Story Behind the Story strategy to talk about some critical causes of risk and stress:

♦ Urban teenagers tell how they cope with a constant sense of risk. When the adult community seems to turn its back, teenagers describe the need for alternative groups (including gangs) that can provide three essentials: safety, understanding, and identity.

♦ Urban teenagers tell how they are motivated by deep needs for respect. Respect is hard to find in inner cities. Adults relate through authority—teachers, police, parents rarely ask why, don't seem to care, won't listen. The future holds no solution: old paths to economic adulthood look closed; other roads to achieving respect are hard to find or follow. Finding identity and respect is the problem teenagers want to solve.

STRATEGY 2: SEEKING RIVAL HYPOTHESES: BRINGING MORE VOICES TO THE TABLE AND INTO THE PLAN

Complex questions don't have single answers. So Community Problem-Solving Dialogues use the rival hypothesis strategy (rivaling) to seek out alternative perspectives on risk, stress, respect, and other issues. In their writing and videos, CLC teens document surprising rival perspectives that people often don't expect.

♦ RISK: Stressful and potentially risky situations can be open to rival (alternative) readings by teens <u>and</u> adults. For instance, a group of teenagers standing on the street is often seen as threatening—invested in protecting turf and proving a "hard" identity. A rival reading, however, might argue that, given the options in the inner city, teens are actually seeking a safe and social place to "hang" together. And a third rival reading might see in that group individuals who are struggling with not only social pressure to belong, but practical concerns for safety if they don't join. Adding police to the scene can be read as the arrival of help or of harassment; it can be the imposition of order or the imposition of power without recourse. Rival readings occur every day on the street when women clutch purses at the sight of any young African American male: women see risk; teenagers see racism. And when white adults see black youth dressed in hoodies, cornrows, and baggies, they see signs of antisocial intentions, but urban teens see the mark of "fashion."

CLC URBAN YOUTH REPORT 4

SAYING ABOUT RISK?

Intercultural Dialogue

- **Stress:** In trying to cope with the stress of the street, poverty, racism, and adolescence, teen culture often advises its members to "bury" the stress, to just "hang on," or more proactively, to "be hard." The rival wisdom of adult culture, however, urges teenagers to "just say no," disaffiliate with their peer group, or accept adult counsel. Teenagers, facing everyday risk and stress, bring a deep skepticism to the advice of adults who grew up before the violence started—adults who "haven't been there."

- **Respect:** Is respect the obligatory response one must give to those with age, status, or power? Or, the rival goes, is receiving respect also the right of the young, the powerless, the learner? Authorities often use subordinate "respectful behavior" as a way to judge urban youth (and a prerequisite for even listening). But teenagers (who hold the rival view) often look for signs of mutual respect and zero in on signs of "dissing" (disrespect) from adults—including teachers, police, and business people. They see resistant behavior as part of their demand for dignity. **Adults want to manage behavior; teens are trying to manage stress.**

Strategy 3: Examining Options and Outcomes

It is not enough to listen empathetically. A Community Problem-Solving Dialogue tries to weave rival perspectives into a community-constructed plan for action by, first, generating multiple, competing and complementary options. Secondly it subjects these options to the test of local knowledge—it uses teenage expertise to play out probable outcomes under real conditions. Action plans are then judged, not by good intentions, but by predicted consequences.

- When teenagers talk about options that would make a difference, they start with a direct call for respect, compassion, and serious conversation with adults—a change from the familiar outcome in which adults put out advice, give instruction, and rehearse the situations of their time.
- Teenagers also ask adults to take more committed public action: to create safe opportunities for socializing and athletics in poor neighborhoods, too; to create schools that can motivate, encourage, and educate even the children under stress; to create an economic future for us all. But when policy makers focus on youth, they often end up trying to manage behavior, create constraints, and punish. And the outcome of that policy is polarization.
- Teenagers don't stop at suggesting options and outcomes for adults. As you'll see in later sections of this report, they place equal emphasis on the role this strategy plays in the decisions they make on a daily basis.

A Community Problem-Solving Dialogue follows a strategic path that leads from constructing Stories, to seeking Rivals, to examining Options.

Join the table, and read on to see what this three-step strategic process is revealing.

CLC Urban Youth Report 5

STRATEGY 1: GETTING THE STORY BEHIND THE STORY

In these accounts written by Community Literacy Center teens, Tony gets involved in a fight, while Shirley and Mark encounter neighborhood gangs. Someone might advise, "Just say No. Ignore them." But inviting teenagers to tell the story behind the story—the side adults don't see—reveals more dimensions to the problems of stress and violence. This narrative problem analysis lets teenagers tell us what really happens and why.

WHY FIGHT? A ROUTE TO RESPECT AND POWER

Tony (13) discusses his story of a fight: He and his friends are walking downtown when they encounter a group of 17 and 18-year-old Crips—blue rags hanging out of their pockets. Taunts lead to contact, and he finds himself in a dangerous fight and a situation he can't control. Here Tony describes the "no exit" options he sees for himself and the logic that turns groups into gangs and turns their encounters into violence:

> I am telling this story to let other people know how gangs can take over a neigh-
> borhood or a city without the police able to be there all of the time. I, myself, didn't
> feel comfortable being around when this incident happened. But what else could I do
> but run, and if I ran, then the people I was with would look at me as a traitor. This is a
> tough call to make.
>
> This situation pushes young teenagers into joining gangs for fear of being an
> outcast. I am not for joining gangs, and I wouldn't advise it to anyone else. But why do
> I and others have to sit around and watch the scene being taken over?
>
> People are no longer free to walk around in public (which they have the right to do)
> for fear of having a run-in with a gang. There aren't many options for dealing with the
> situation except running or ignoring the situation. A lot of gangs form in order to
> retaliate against other gangs or out of a need for power and control. If this is the
> reason why people start gangs, shouldn't it also be the solution?
>
> There are other ways to get power and control besides joining gangs, and these
> alternatives are what we need. (From "Gangs Think They Run the Neighborhood")

WHAT IS BEHIND EVERYDAY STRESS?

Shirley describes how her dash for the wrong bus lands her on a corner in the WRONG neighborhood where a group of boys sitting on a car are drinking and smoking weed, asking, "Hey girl, where you from? What school you go to?" The standard adult response to Shirley's story ("just ignore them" or "call a police-man") misses the logic of the situation as Shirley sees it. Like most urban teens, she is personally acquainted with the victims of violence:

> Flashback: The announcement on the news pounds through my head: "Last night a
> young 14-year-old boy was shot 9 times while he was out of his neighborhood. He was
> a freshman student at Oliver." A conversation with a friend runs through my head
> from yesterday: "Hey, Shirley, I'm not staying after school. They might do a drive-by

or shoot someone." These thoughts run through my head, like a tape recorder: "HE WAS SHOT NINE TIMES WHILE OUT OF HIS OWN NEIGHBORHOOD! NINE TIMES! OUT OF HIS NEIGHBORHOOD! SOMEONE'S GOING TO GET SHOT!"

Inner Thoughts: Here I am standing on this corner wondering what's going to happen to me. If I tell him where I'm from, he might have some beef with my neighborhood and make me a victim of his anger just because I was from the wrong part of town. Some people might say, just ignore them. All you have to do is close your eyes and ears. But he's drunk, so if I don't answer him he may come over and start trouble.

On the other hand, the cops drive around here twenty four seven (all the time), but they probably wouldn't stop for me, because the cops around my neighborhood are racist. (Shirley flashes back once again to the park and a hoop game.) The cops were throwing the boys against the fence, hassling them, asking them "Where's your I.D.? You all shouldn't be up here late at night anyway." (They said this even though they had I.D.) But I noticed that they didn't hassle the white kids; they never watched them when they played ball. So should I really call the cops, 'cause it's going to start a whole lot of trouble. All they are going to do is hassle the kids that are asking me questions, throw them against the wall, and frisk them, and make them want to fight back. And when that happens, the kids are going to come back for me. I have to decide soon. . . . (From "A Wake Up Call to Adults")

UNDERSTANDING THE HIDDEN LOGIC

In telling the Story Behind the Story, Shirley, Tony, and Mark are urging adults to get beneath the surface of events and to respond to the hidden logic behind teens' behavior and to the forces that motivate people. They ask us to help manage the problems, not just behavior.

Shirley explains why she called her account: "A Wake Up Call to Adults"

I wrote this to show you that kids go through a lot of stressful things. Some kids get angry at the world because some cops have a bad image of kids and take it out on the kids, but it also works both ways. Kids go through a lot of deaths and have to watch where they are going for their sake too. Some kids may kick and throw things and take their anger out on people like parents, faculty, and staff. Adults, try not to take it personally because that's the only way some kids know how to handle their problems.

In "Maybe the Reason Why . . ." Mark speaks to parents who often ask:

"Why don't you . . . go to the basketball court anymore? All you do is sit around the house all day."

Maybe the reason why... he doesn't go to the basketball court anymore is because a drive-by was done by a rivaling gang there before. But the reason doesn't have to be gang related. Your son could be worried about getting harassed by the police because the basketball court may be considered "hot." The term "hot" means a certain area is known for its heavy drug selling activities.

STRATEGY 2: SEEKING RIVAL HYPOTHESES: BRINGING MORE VOICES TO THE TABLE AND INTO THE PLAN

Inquiry into difficult questions demands a rival hypothesis stance that seeks alternative explanations. Using the "Rivaling" strategy, teens bring multiple perspectives to the table and predict how other people might interpret difficult problems such as those explored in this section: risk, gangs, respect, and work. Using this strategy means listening to others, imagining their thinking, and ultimately rivaling yourself.

RIVAL READINGS OF A RISKY SITUATION

Standing on the corner in the "wrong" neighborhood, Shirley herself read this situation in terms of risk, panic, and helplessness. But teenagers using the Rivaling strategy imagined and dramatized some rival points of view in this example from their video, *Teamwork: Teenagers Working Through Community Problems.*

Christy: You know they're threatening Shirley. It's all gang stuff.

Mia: Wait a minute. Lemme try this one from the guys' point of view, OK? Look again at Shirley boppin' along the sidewalk. She's fresh, she's good looking, she's alone. Get it? I mean, she's like Little Red Riding Hood! They're just having fun scaring her a bit. It's like flirting, you know?

Jake: Flirting! Look again, sister. Look at all that gangsta graffiti stuff all over the old house where those hoods were hanging out. And remember the gang graffiti at the beginning? Man, that stuff's no joke! And that house really looks like a crack house. It all adds up.

Joe: How about if we put ourselves in a cop's shoes?

Joe (speaking as a cop): By the time we get there, the people involved already have ten witnesses saying they're somewhere else. There's just nothing we can do about it.

Jake: Sure. What about a bad cop's shoes?

Jake (speaking as a bad cop): Hold up, kids, y'all need to get away from there—quit messin' with them people. I'm gonna give y'all to "three" to get your punk ass outta there: three

Shaquon: I still want to try standing in the shoes of those three guys.

Shaquon (to himself, as 1st guy): She's kinda cute—I could be tryin' to talk to her, instead of tryin' to get her. I don't even know why I'm doing this. But I guess it's alright; the boys think I'm hard, you know?

Jake: Yeah, we gotta try seeing what was going on in their minds.

Jake (to himself, speaking as 2nd guy): To tell you the truth, I was afraid of not being with those guys.

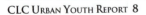

RIVAL Reasons Why Kids Join Gangs

◆ A Teen who associates with a gang says, "I am now 16 years of age and if I was to go to the Hill, Garfield, East Hills, Homewood I would get jumped and possibly shot, because they know where I'm from and assume I am in L.A.W. I am not 'in' the gang, but I stay over at my friends' houses and go places like the movies and the mall with them. . . . So what are my choices? Since everybody thinks I'm in it anyway, and they label me that way, I might as well be in the gang. And I would have someone at my back. I feel that is why 90% of the gang members join."

◆ A Girlfriend who is angry about the gang scene says, "We (the ladies) have nothing to do with what you men are doing, but yet we find ourselves in the middle of it all. If I happen to like a boy from another neighborhood, somehow that makes you angry enough to threaten my relationship."

◆ Another Girlfriend says, "I decided to continue a relationship with Sam because I believe he doesn't do gang things. He just happens to be friends with some of the wrong people, and he's labeled a gang member. But there is a side of me that says. . ."

◆ A Teen whose brother has just been shot, "I joined a gang three years ago. Three years ago there were barely no shootings that were gang related. On the streets, there weren't that many guns. Most of the things we did were positive. My brother and I joined the gang because it was the only way out of getting jumped every day. (We had moved to a new neighborhood.) The guys who are in the gang with me were friends. We played basketball with each other every day, and we would hang together all the time."

◆ A Public Health Administrator says, "When we try to deal with violence, we need to distinguish among the different types of gangs. Some gangs are primarily social groups focused on turf and group identity, while others (that account for the most murders) are organized drug operations." (Deborah Prothrow-Stith)

◆ A member of a Chicago gang talks about the numbing, dead-end work available to adults in his neighborhood, "A job like that is giving up. It just isn't worth it. . . Why do we steal and deal drugs? Because there is no work for us. If we could find work, we wouldn't be doing that stuff." (Deborah Prothrow-Stith)

> **Rivaling gives you views from other mountains:**
> *"One can not climb a number of different mountains simultaneously, but the views had when different mountains are ascended supplement one another; they do not set up incompatible, competing worlds."*
> **John Dewey**

SEEKING MORE RIVAL HYPOTHESES

RIVAL HYPOTHESES ABOUT RESPECT

Rival views of "respect" can turn intercultural contact into confrontation. Urban teenagers lack the things that command respect in the larger society: money, status, education, age, race, and social power. Nevertheless, they feel an acute need for respect, a sensitivity to being "dissed." In the powerlessness of youth and poverty, maintaining respect has a powerful logic.

Adult institutions expect respectful behavior <u>from</u> teenagers and use authority to demand it. But teens may hold a rival hypothesis about the proper balance of authority and respect. Their reading of encounters with authority reveals deep-seated assumptions about mutual respect. Their rival expectations help explain a disappointment and disaffection with the adult community.

CONFLICTING EXPECTATIONS FOR RESPECT: IN SCHOOL

♦ My teacher will tell the class, "You'll never become engineers or math majors." He puts the class down mostly every day.

♦ A student, whose grades aren't so good, doesn't understand the material. The teacher assumes he's slow and ignores the situation. The student gets frustrated, starts to talk in class, falls asleep.

♦ A teacher comments to a student about being late, and she immediately starts to talk back. The teacher says that it doesn't matter, because she is failing anyway. The class laughs at the student.

From a Student's "Checklist for Mutual Respect"

Signs of Mutual Respect

1. My teacher not only cares about individual students, but shows it and makes it known.
2. The teacher knows what is happening in my community and talks with us.
3. Students let others learn by not talking to friends in class. . . .

Danger Signals

1. Teachers humiliate students by talking about grades in class.
2. Teachers assert their authority by shaking fingers in a student's face.
3. Students assert their power by talking, joking, and tripping in class. . . .

CONFLICTING EXPECTATIONS FOR RESPECT: WITH POLICE

Following a problem-solving dialogue with Pittsburgh police, Bessemah concludes:

We all want something. You want us to respect you because you are an adult and it makes your job easier, but we also want respect. . . . I think that we all need to cooperate with each other, but I think police sometimes feel we should just cooperate with you.

Curtis describes the humiliating experience many young black men now go through—an unexplained, aggressive police search:

Seeing my cousin just home from college I give my cuz five (shakes hands) and soon five cop cars surrounded us from different sides. "All three of you — Get up against the wall — NOW!" I was scared ... but if you ask questions that's like getting smart with them.

When the police visited the CLC, Curtis tested his hypothesis: *"One of the police officers stereotyped me. . . . He said, 'I've seen that young man up on Federal Street,' meaning I hang up there. He was assuming I was a drug dealer because I came down in zig-zag braids, black dickies (because of work) and gloves (because of my bike). I wore those things on purpose to see what they would say—their response. What would they take me as? And they fell for it. But if I was a drug dealer, would I be here at the Community Literacy Center? I want to be re-spected and not stereotyped as a drug dealer. I want police to pay attention to the real dealers—to stand up by the bars on upper Federal.*

RIVAL ROADS TO RESPECT — THROUGH WORK

What are the roads to achieving adult status and personal respect in urban Pittsburgh—especially if you are black, your family is poor, your school is inadequate, and the people in your neighborhood can't find decent jobs? How do you find a road into the working community and the economy of Pittsburgh? We need Community Problem-Solving Dialogues to explore these rivals with teens.

JOIN a gang and enter the "street" economy today
- you get quick status, money, and adventure
- you look cool, have power
- you join a community that looks out for you

But the Rivals are:
- you are also likely to get shot or end up in prison
- you can't "leave" when you want to
- what you learn at 13 won't get you work at 25

GET a "McDonald's" job (fast food, grocery store) in the hood
- it offers after-school work for older teenagers
- the "skills" are easy to learn
- you get work experience, minimum wage, and references

But the Rivals are:
- fast food jobs don't open up adequate "roads to work"
- they mean limited skills, low potential
- they fuel fatigue and boredom
- they are an urban symbol of dead ends and giving up—not aspiration

FIND skill-building jobs (from self-employed paper boy & babysitter to clerk, intern, go-fer, trainee)
- these build a wider set of skills
- they offer desperately needed exposure to other worlds, to vocational and professional possibilities
- they lead you into the regular economy

But the Rivals are:
- be realistic: you are competing with adults, college students, and people from better schools
- jobs may exist in the suburbs, but how do you find them, and how would you get home when the bus stops running?

CLC URBAN YOUTH REPORT **11**

Strategy 3: Examining Options and Outcomes

There are no easy solutions to risk, stress, and disrespect. For teenagers, even the "best" options can have bad outcomes one must work around.

Possible Outcomes (From Shirley's account, on page six)

> Some people may say, "why don't you talk to a teacher?" Well that can cause you even more stress. Like when my friend told a teacher (that she trusted) about her problems at home, and then later heard the teacher talking and laughing about it in the teachers' room. Other people may say, "why don't you tell your friends?" I feel when you talk to your friends you just share some of the same anger. It doesn't lead to anything. What you just shared with them may get out and then everyone knows all your business and problems. Some people may say that you're scared of your own race, then make a big joke out of it saying you're just as bad as the cops, you're a racist, too.

This analysis prompted other teens to propose revised options—"Tell teachers just enough so they know you are working through a problem; talk only to friends you really trust"— and other possible outcomes: "You may find you aren't alone after all."

Even when all options have downsides, problem-solving dialogues can transform teenagers' decision-making from a yes/no consideration of one choice, to a process that imagines multiple options and explores possible outcomes. The option and outcome strategy gives many teenagers an expanded sense of possibility and responsibility.

More Options for Teens

Why join a gang? Some teens see a "no exit" decision:

> You can't escape it. Everybody knows that there are gang members almost everywhere. . . . You could stay in the house all the time if you want, but who would want to do that?

However, other writers using the Option & Outcome strategy respond:

> **Option:** Move to the area where your friends are, but watch what you get into. What I mean is if they want to beat up other gang members, I would just stay in the house and play Nintendo. And it does help to tell people you disapprove of beating people up for no good reason—especially when girls disapprove—because most girls don't like dudes that bully. It might get the gang members to think twice about it if people from their own neighborhoods say this. One time I talked my friends out of fighting another group.
>
> **Option:** Don't hang on the corner with known gang members, because you could be the victim of a drive-by. If we see someone from a rival neighborhood, I tell my friends not to say anything. .

Teenagers, it's clear, can use these decision strategies well when they're engaged in Community Problem-Solving Dialogues—in literate action. But even more importantly, perhaps, they also take these strategies into the decision-making in their daily lives. Teens talk about how the problem solving they did as writers transfers to examining life options and imagining their outcomes.

LASTING OUTCOMES

In a recent follow-up study Community Literacy Center teens talk about the impact of these strategy-based Dialogues once the experience is over. When Jason gets challenged he says,

> I try to see why he act like he do. . . . Maybe he think he bad, not want to be thought a punk, low self-esteem. . . . When I'm about to fight, I would now say, he just wants to fight because he's jealous. I look for reasons; before I wouldn't even think about that.

Arlena describes the influence Options and Outcomes had on her decision-making process right after graduation:

> I didn't want to go straight to work out of school; wanted to chill a little. But I knew there were things I wanted and needed and the only way to get them was to work. So I sat down and made a list of "If I don't work (can't get this); if I do work (can get this)."

Arlena went to work and back to school.

For adults and especially for policy makers, a Community Problem-Solving Dialogue with teenagers can not only generate new options, but can also help predict some of the unintended, unpredicted consequences that often make youth policy fail.

OUTCOME-TESTED POLICY OPTIONS

A Dialogue on School Suspension policy at Oliver High School revealed that suspended students were in basic agreement with the policy, but that common practices like out-of-school (rather than in-house) suspension were ineffectual— "you get a vacation" and it puts marginal students even further behind. More importantly, they targeted the source of many suspensions in small conflicts that start with a student disruption, a teacher's desire for authority (and strategies for control, such as not staying to hear reasons, pointing in the student's face), followed by the student's response to being "dissed" and need to save face—events that both parties allow to escalate into confrontations. The document based on their Dialogue with school officials became a tool in teacher training.

How To Create A Community Problem-Solving Dialogue

Preoccupied with other problems, Pittsburgh has left its teenagers to face risky streets, broken schools, declining jobs, and few roads to respect. Gangs offer protection, respect, and identity. Early motherhood confers adulthood and the promise of love. Can we meet this competition—with better options for forging identity, achieving respect? Can Pittsburgh draw its youth into alternative, intercultural communities?

Are you ready for a breakthrough? Urge the groups you know—your neighborhood council, your business, civic, and religious groups, as well as the schools, youth agencies, and policy makers we support—to create working partnerships around the problems on their tables.

1. Invite urban teenagers to the table with you—as partners.

Bring the expertise of those "in the struggle" into the analysis of problems and the evaluation of options for both adults and teens. Don't let the adults become counselors and the teens become advocates. But train your group to work as problem-focused, collaborative planning partners. Creating partners creates an intercultural community.

2. Explore a problem—strategically.

The problem-solving strategies illustrated in this report use writing and discussion (aided by interactive video and computer tools) to scaffold a substantive intercultural dialogue. Working in pairs, teens and adults sketch problem scenarios that uncover the "story behind the story." They come to the table prepared to consider "rival" readings, to generate multiple "options," and to evaluate possible "outcomes."

3. Envision options and outcomes.

A problem-solving dialogue goes beyond the rhetoric of complaint and blame by building options, using the expertise of teenagers to play out probable (and rival) outcomes. It puts these stories, key points, and conclusions down in writing as a springboard for discussion and action.

4. Bring the larger community to the table.

Make your collaborative planning and writing the basis for a wider community conversation, which invites more people to join the table not as advocates or critics, but as collaborative partners in building their own community.

5. Name a place for action.

Turn talk into action by identifying a concrete situation in which alternatives can be tested and revised.

NEED HELP?

A Support System for Community Problem-Solving Dialogues is available at Pittsburgh's Community Literacy Center. The CLC workshops can connect you to a network of community/university advisors, a library of hands-on guides, and a portfolio of interactive videos and computer software that help groups start Dialogues of their own.

VIDEOS

Teamwork: Teenagers Working Through Community Problems. An interactive training video by teens. A lively Community Problem-Solving Team demonstrates strategies for collaborative planning, rivaling, and decision-making as they investigate a problem case of urban stress. A manual and additional video problem cases help viewers transfer strategies to other issues.

COMPUTER PROGRAMS

Rivaling about Risk: A Dialogue Tutorial. An interactive HyperCard program that uses video, writing, reflection, and teen-authored texts to teach critical and rival hypothesis thinking and to give voice to teen perspectives on issues of urban risk.

What's Your Plan? Friendly computer support for a dialogue among young women and health workers, using the strategies in *Teamwork* to make (and print out) one's personal plan for sexual abstinence or contraceptive use.

Struggle: A Dialogue about Life Plans. A personalized computer program that lets teenagers, parents, and caring adults work together to acknowledge struggle, name aspirations, and make committed life plans.

GUIDES

How to Be Heard. A Handbook for Community Literacy. A practical guide to community literacy strategies for teens.

The Community Literacy Primer. An introduction to theory and practice of community literacy in vignettes of literate social action.

Community Literacy Research. A series of reports and reprints of articles on community literacy.

WORKSHOPS

How to Create Problem-Solving Dialogues with Teens. A CLC Training Workshop on designing a Dialogue around your concerns.

THE COMMUNITY LITERACY CENTER IS A COMMUNITY/UNIVERSITY COLLABORATION OF
PITTSBURGH'S COMMUNITY HOUSE AND CARNEGIE MELLON UNIVERSITY

THE URBAN YOUTH REPORT IS SUPPORTED BY THE HOWARD HEINZ ENDOWMENT. IT IS BASED ON
RESEARCH SUPPORTED BY THE CENTER FOR THE STUDY OF WRITING AND LITERACY AT CARNEGIE
MELLON AND THE A.W. MELLON LITERACY IN SCIENCE CENTER AND ON THE ON-GOING WORK OF
THE COMMUNITY LITERACY CENTER SUPPORTED BY THE R. K. MELLON FOUNDATION, THE GRABLE
FOUNDATION, AND THE BINGHAM TRUST.

The Community Literacy Center is a community/university collaborative of Pittsburgh's 80-year-old Community House and the Center for the Study of Writing and Literacy at Carnegie Mellon University. At the CLC, writing lets community members take action, build consensus, and be heard on a broad range of issues. Working together, CMU college mentors and CLC teens develop skills in intercultural collaboration, problem-solving, and writing. CLC projects culminate in public Community Conversations, which bring voices from the neighborhood, city, and university to a common table.

The Community Literacy Center
801 Union Ave
Pittsburgh, PA 15212
(412) 321-3900
Fax: (412) 321-5496
http://eng.hss.cmu.edu/clc/

Dr. Wayne Peck, Community House
email: wp0a@andrew.cmu.edu
Dr. Linda Flower, Carnegie Mellon University
email: lf54@andrew.cmu.edu
(412) 268-2863; Fax: (412) 268-7989

This document represents the work of many people: CLC teens; CMU mentors; and CLC/CMU staff: Wayne Peck, Joyce Baskins, Donald Tucker, Beth Marstiller, Elenore Long, Lorraine Higgins, Linda Flower, Tim Flower, Kathy Meinzer, Jennifer Flach, Susan Lawrence, Julia Deems, Amanda Young, Victor Hogan, Gwen Gorzelsky. Written and edited by Linda Flower and Jennifer Flach; Artwork: Frederick Carlson; Document Design: Amanda Young. © 1996 Community Literacy Center

This work was supported under the Educational Research and Development Center (Grant #R117G10036) administered by the Office of Educational Research and Improvement, U.S. Department of Education. The findings and opinions expressed herein do not reflect the position or policies of O.E.R.I. or the U.S. Dept. of Education.

From Linda Flower and Jennifer Flach (Eds.). (1996). *Working Partners: An Urban Youth Report on Risk, Stress, and Respect*. Pittsburgh, PA: The Community Literacy Center and Carnegie Mellon University.

BRINGING A COMMUNITY PROBLEM-SOLVING DIALOGUE TO COLLEGE

How could you make a Community Problem-Solving Dialogue part of a college class? One way is to build a class around a community project and hold a meeting or a community conversation at the end. But you can also create a space for dialogue within a regular class by inviting members of the community to join you in a discussion. The three strategies described below will help you set up a dialogue and adapt it to your own situation.

 STRATEGY 1   **COME TO THE TABLE ON SHARED PROBLEMS**

A Community Problem-Solving Dialogue is an approach to intercultural collaboration that does three things:

- It puts a shared problem on the table.
- It brings diverse, often marginalized, voices to the table.
- It organizes that discussion into a collaborative, problem-solving inquiry built on learning, on using discourses of both the community and university, and on recognizing diverse kinds of expertise.

Example 18–2 shows the key steps in setting up a Community Problem-Solving Dialogue. (For more on defining a shared problem look back at Chapters 9 and 10.)

Example 18–2
Organizing a Community Problem-Solving Dialogue

Organizing a Community Problem-Solving Dialogue

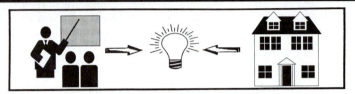

Creating a Space Where Academic Inquiry Meets Community Issues

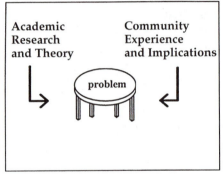

1. Put a Shared Problem on the Table— a problem that can be discussed with community and university knowledge. Name it as a shared problem.

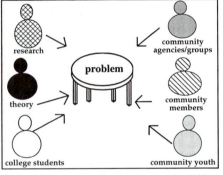

2. Invite Community Perspectives to the Table— in person and in text and media.

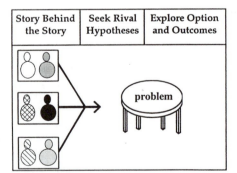

3. Using 3 Problem-Solving Strategies—Getting the Story Behind the Story, Rival Hypotheses, and Exploring Options and Outcomes. Community/University partners alternate between small group planning/drafting and whole table dialogue.

4. Document and Expand the Inquiry by taping and analyzing the dialogue, as a basis for wider discussions.

WHO IS AT THE TABLE?

Think of this table as a real place, where both real and metaphoric voices can be heard. The university contribution to this collaboration will of course include college students and faculty, but you can also bring the "voice" of research and theory into this discussion. When you raise rival hypotheses, let the authors of the books and articles you have read in your course work also "speak" at this table and offer their reading of the problem. (You may even assign people to role-play certain voices from your reading to make sure their rivals are heard.) In many public forums, the "community" is often represented by public and social service agencies, by urban development groups, and by the leaders of various community organizations and agencies. This is a good place to start. But a genuine dialogue has to go beyond making contact solely with the community's professional representatives or bureaucracies. It is essential that your table should include everyday people—folks who live in the neighborhood, who have first-hand experience with problems and situations. If, for instance, you are interested in a problem that involves teenagers or young people, make sure the youth who know the situation are at the table. (And don't expect the honor roll students to have expertise on the problems of those struggling in school.)

❧ STRATEGY 2 WRITE STORIES, SEEK RIVALS, EXAMINE OPTIONS

When you ask "Who is at the table?" you are also asking "Whose discourse is allowed?" as well. A standard academic or classroom discourse—the one you might be most comfortable with—won't do. The three strategies described in Working Partners (Example 18–1) create a *hybrid discourse*. The Story Behind the Story starts with narrative and examples, in which everyone brings their own story and has their own expertise. The second strategy, Rivaling, asks everyone to try to step out of their own shoes for a moment and imagine what the situation looks like from a rival perspective. And the third strategy, Options and Outcomes, tries to ground ideas in and test them against real experience in the community. These problem-solving strategies may seen like more work than just getting together and having a rap session or conversation, but, like collaborative planning, they help create a new discourse in which everyone is a contributor and a learner.

Below is a simple script for a dialogue designed to bring community perspectives to the table. It is organized in three phases around the strategies of getting the Story Behind the Story, uncovering Rival Hypotheses, and exploring Options and Outcomes. If possible, spread the dialogue out over three or more sessions. Once you have posed a shared problem at the table with the whole group, move into "break-out" sessions in which a college and community partner work together to get down in writing a rough version of a Story Behind the Story as the community partner sees it. Bring this rough but written story back to the whole group discussion. Use this same combination of collaborative writing and/or planning and whole-table discussion to bring community-based Rivals and Options to the table. If time is short, you could telescope all three parts strategies into one meeting or combine face-to-face session(s) with computer communications where that is possible. If time is extended, you could give more time to presenting and comparing academic and community interpretations of these problems.

Your Role as a Collaborative Planning Partner

The first step in such a dialogue is to put a problem on the table that is a genuine shared problem. Remembering the history of community/university relationships that we looked at in Chapter 14, be prepared by your actions to convince any skeptical community members that this is a genuine inquiry into an open question—that their expertise is necessary.

To help create this collaborative relationship, your role in these dialogues is to work as a collaborative planning partner. In break-out sessions, you will be the Supporter who helps your community partner/Planner develop his/her ideas (and you may choose to be the person at a computer who writes down the stories, rivals, and options you create). As a Supporter your questions will probably need to focus on ideas, key points and purposes, and audience responses. Here are some prompts:

- On Ideas: "That's interesting. Tell me more about . . . . Tell me why . . . ."
- On Key Point and Purpose: "I hear what you're saying. Now the key point you want to make is . . . ." "Help me understand your purpose in saying that. What are you trying to do here?"
- On Audience: "Tell me how (someone else) might respond to what you just said. So they might be thinking . . . ."

At the table, continue to be a strong collaborative planner by asking Key Point, Purpose, and Audience questions that support and draw out the ideas of the current speaker at the table before you jump in with your own.

You may want to appoint a leader who starts the discussion, keeps track of time, and helps the group work as a collaborative team, supporting each other and focusing on the strategy and goals of each phase.

Having a talking script like the one in Example 18–3 will help you keep focused on the key things you want to accomplish during the dialogue.

Example 18–3
A Talking Script for a Community Problem-Solving Dialogue

Scripting a Community Problem-Solving Dialogue

In a dialogue, college students may work as collaborative planning partners, using breakout sessions with a community partner to draft stories, rivals, and options they bring back to the table as a whole.

Introduction **Whole table**	Leader: Let us introduce ourselves and our connection to the problem. [Overview of collaborative planning process and the 3 strategies that guide Dialogue.]

Getting the Story ***Behind the Story*** **Community/Uni-** **versity partners** **work in pairs** **to sketch** **out problem** **scenarios that** **tell the SBS**	Leader: The media or analysts describe our problem in these terms: _____. But many of you can bring a different perspective. Can we build some problem scenarios that show a fuller picture—grounded in your experience in the community? Let us start by getting the story behind the story. What really happens? And why? Partner: Let's take a typical situation and draft the story behind the story from a community perspective.

Rivaling **Partners return** **to the table** **with problem** **scenarios** **and SBSs**	Leader: *(as partners present problem scenarios)* Standing in different places lets people read or interpret a problem in distinctive ways. Creating alternative readings, or rival hypotheses, gives you a fuller picture. · Who might have a different take on this problem? · How would they read/describe the problem?
The group **generates rival** **hypotheses**	Note: Since a hypothesis is a prediction, rivaling isn't a contest to win, but a strategy for seeing more. Good rivalers rival their own ideas. You can evaluate rivals by asking: where does the support for this rival come from; what is the evidence?

Exploring Options ***and Outcomes*** **Partners break-** **out to plan ideas;** **return to table** **for discussion**	Leader: Given the expanded problem our discussion has created, what are some of the rival options for responding to this situation? Can we go behind the usual options? [Partners may breakout here.] Since none of our options will lead to a complete solution, we have to evaluate them by their outcomes: what is likely to be the outcome of taking Option #1; Option #2?

STRATEGY 3   **DOCUMENT AND EXPAND THE INQUIRY**

Dialogues like these are more than just a one-time learning experience, even if they are limited to a one-time meeting. They can be a source of ideas and exchanges that you can return to, reflect on and mine for insights, just as you mined texts earlier. Here are three ways you can expand the inquiry.

Document the Dialogue

Put tape recorders at two or more locations around the table. Take notes that give you a rough outline of the discussion, its high points, and when they occurred. Relisten to those key points and take notes or transcribe important parts. Keep a copy of all the writing done in the breakout groups. As we discussed in Chapter 16, without good detailed observation (especially tapes that let people speak in their own words, not your memory), you are likely to "remember" what you already knew. Observation lets you do justice to difference.

Use this documented dialogue as a resource, just as you might use any other written document, interview, journal article, or lecture. Read it closely, examine the arguments and evidence. At the same time, notice how it differs from academic discourse. Take advantage of its strengths. Notice, for instance, what you can learn from a story that you can't learn from statistics or theory and visa versa. And notice how the examples and scenarios help you qualify and conditionalize the more sweeping claims found in academic discourse. Under what conditions should those claims be questioned, qualified, or revised? And how?

Use the Dialogue as a Springboard for a Community Conversation

Small groups are a good way to work through issues, to name problems more clearly, to get some strong options and outcomes on the table. Having done that, you may be ready to take a next step and hold a larger Community Conversation in which your group presents its ideas, and engages a larger, more public group in the dialogue. In urban neighborhoods, community centers and churches and synagogues are good places to hold a public discussion. Or you might take your ideas on the road to forums at your college, or to public schools, in ways that let high school students participate in a problem-solving dialogue, too.

Publish a Community/University Report or Video

As a writer you can expand the inquiry by writing a report, not just for a college class. Document the results of this dialogue and give it to the people involved. Or you can take the next step of developing a public document, like the Urban Youth Report, *Working Partners*, included above. Or you might write a feature article which you can submit to your school or city paper, to newsletters, or journals. Through your writing you can not only show *what* you learned, but you can bring other people into the process of an intercultural dialogue as well, and illustrate *how* one can learn in a collaborative dialogue across different perspectives, different discourses.

The text in Example 18–4, *Getting to Know You: A Dialogue for Community Health*, was presented and dramatized at the end of a semester-long project in which neighborhood women at The Rainbow Health Center, an urban health clinic, explored a range of problems that surround health care for women, especially poor women. The clinic saw the extended collaborative process that created this dialogue as itself a new way the clinic could serve its clients. But the booklet's subtitle—*Discussion Points for Women and Their Health Care Providers*—points to another purpose. The booklet is now being used in a medical classroom to train future professionals to see how they are perceived and how they can enter into better dialogue with their patients. This next step lets project organizer Lorraine Higgins "user test" the document with medical students and see how to improve these dialogues. Here is a good example of how writing lets the voices of community people find their way into wider forums of discussion and decision making. The annotations point out ways you can adapt your problem-solving dialogues to the needs of a larger audience and to create hybrid, multi-vocal text.

Example 18–4
Getting to Know You: A Dialogue for Community Health

Title promises a problem/purpose statement (PPS)

Why We Wrote This Book

- Something is wrong. You haven't been feeling too well. Yet, the doctor seems to think it's all in your head. But darn it! It IS your body, and if you know anything, you know your body.

Bullets use events, as seen by patients and health care providers, to dramatize the problem, suggest the purpose

- The patient you are seeing seems so stubborn. Why hasn't she been taking that prescription?

- The doctor is explaining your test results. You can't understand those fancy medical terms that just fly right by you. What's really wrong with you? [. . . .]

Formal PPS defines problem as a medical and community issue

The Importance of Dialogue

[Describes the need for new partnerships between urban residents and health care professionals in health care . . . .]

Purpose is to
show new
strategies

Strategies for Building a Dialogue

[Describes the discussion strategies that produced this
dialogue . . . .]

Note to readers
at end of
introduction
creates a
personal
speaking voice
and us-to-you
relationship as
the writers talk
to other women

Taking Control: A Note to Female Patients

Women often have a hard time talking and relating to doctors and
vice versa. In fact, some of us (admit it) get so frustrated that we
avoid going to a clinic until it is absolutely necessary, and by then it
may be too late. Throughout this booklet, we focus on obstacles to
women's health—issues that have been neglected by the medical
field and its research up until recently. We discuss not only
common diseases and treatments, but the way in which we
communicate about our health with health care workers.

Redefines the
problem in yet
another way, as
also a personal
issue readers/
users face,
and suggests
a personal
Problem/Purpose
Statement for
readers

   The women who have written this book for you are very much
aware of the factors that prevent us from getting good care. For
example, we know that the color of our skin or even sitting in an
emergency room in less than our Sunday finery with our very
active kids can sometimes not generate very much sympathy from
ER nurses. We have been around long enough to know that being
on medical assistance and feeling insecure about ourselves because
we have not gone beyond high school prevents us from speaking up
and being assertive about what is wrong with us and what is best
for our health. This booklet is about taking control of our health.

Will Mom Go to Jail?

One of eight
dialogues written
by community
residents
Each follows a 3-
part format:
• A Problem Case
• What If . . . ?
• Dialogue

By Beth Tull

I was 21-years-old, a single mom
on welfare, when my son began to
have health problems. When Nick
was 4 months old, he developed
a rash. It began at the top of his
head and ran down to his groin. I
had done the usual, rubbing him
down with lotions and oils.
However, this rash continued to
spread. I began to follow some of

the old-fashioned remedies that
were advised by my mother; I
browned flour, switched over to
cloth diapers, but nothing seemed
to be working.

   At this time the rash began to
get infected, and I became
concerned, so I took him to the
hospital. This was the first of
many, many trips. He was seen
through the Dermatology Clinic
and the diagnosis was infantile

eczema. The doctors prescribed several expensive lotions that were not covered on my medical card and antibiotics which were. I was unable to get the lotions, so I just got the antibiotics.

My son would be on antibiotics for 10 days at a time; the infection would clear up and the rash would go away. As soon as it cleared up, it would start all over again, getting worse and worse.

I had my son to three different dermatologists. They were poking at him, and taking skin biopsies and still the diagnosis was eczema. Now because of my own intimidation of doctors, and the fact that I believed they knew what was going on, I didn't question their diagnosis.

This whole ordeal was beginning to take a toll on me. Why could I not make my child well, or comfortable in this situation? I began to feel like a failure as a parent. My guilt was getting the best of me. I also felt responsible for his being sick all the time. Worse than that. I resented that Nick was sick. He was such a beautiful little baby.

At age three he began developing abscesses on his jawbone. They were the size of walnuts, and he always seemed to be running a temperature of 100 degrees or above. The doctors would lance the abscess, prescribe antibiotics and send him on his way.

One day Nick's father came to visit and asked if he could take Nick out. Nick wasn't feeling his best and I was a bit apprehensive about letting him go, but I was also exhausted from dealing with a sick child. So I said yes. So I let him go. When I didn't hear from them at 9:00 I got worried. I wasn't exactly sure where they were. By midnight I was absolutely frantic; where was my baby was all I could think of. Just when I was ready to call the police his father called me from the emergency room. We had just been there a few weeks before. When he called I was furious that he waited so long to contact me; they were at the hospital for hours before I got a phone call. So I'm sure the staff was wondering where the hell is this child's mother. I got to the hospital as fast as I could.

When I got there they were trying to bring down his temperature and arranging the involvement of social services. I was confused, I didn't understand why they were having me investigated for medical neglect. I remember all of the doctors huddled in one corner, and I was sitting in the other. I felt very frightened like I was being tried before I could explain my side. I had no voice in the matter. I had this vision of these powerful men, with long, white beards, and white wigs, and they were discussing my life, my parenting skills as if I weren't even there. Sort of like the Salem witch trials.

Looking back on this now, perhaps they did have reason for concern because Nick had this rash that sort of resembled burns, but why did they not just ask me? At least I would of had the chance to explain. I was put through this grueling process for what seemed like an eternity only for the whole case to be unfounded.

Through this experience I became a little bolder about speaking up. I was so fed up when the abscesses returned, that I demanded to know why my son was constantly sick. They finally admitted him, and called the infectious disease doctors.

My son stayed in the hospital 28 days. They discovered that he did NOT have eczema but chronic granulomatous. He is now on antibiotics for the rest of his life, as a preventative measure, and I have not had any problems with his health outside of colds and chicken pox.

What If . . . ?

What if I had asserted myself by saying to the hospital staff, "I should have been notified earlier? Why didn't you call me?" They might have realized my concern, I didn't because I did not feel I had the right to show my anger to hospital staff.

- What if patients didn't assume that doctors have all the answers and always do the right thing?

- What if I had not been so afraid of his father that I had reminded him to be sure to call me if Nick was not feeling better—to insist he make sure I am involved in emergencies?

- What if patients realized they have the right to insist on more testing?

- What if the doctors were able to see my uncertainty through my lack of questioning and took some extra time to explain? Or what if they told me they weren't exactly sure what the problem was, but they would inform me of all they knew? I might not have beat up on myself so much.

⫸ **Dialogue** ⫸

Different voices see different options

Voice of mother with few resources

A NURSE SAYS . . .

Doctors do need to be aware of costs of medication such as the lotions prescribed here. They or the nurse should ask, "Is someone paying for your prescriptions; can you afford to get this filled? If you find out you are not covered, call back and we'll try to make other arrangements." There is often a generic brand, or the doctor could give free samples or could order a part of a prescription at a time if the insurance will cover it that way instead.

Voice of medical instructor

ER doctors are often rushed, but certainly in this case, this is a very thick file; they should have consolidated or skimmed through it to see the history.

Voice of advisor to patients

Rashes are most difficult to diagnose, and sometimes it is difficult to say, "I really don't know." Some patients imagine the doctor is God, they need to know that diagnoses aren't always 100% clear.

Voice of medical staff, seeing reason for procedure

It is unfortunate that the mom wasn't even asked about abuse, but it is important that they did consider it, because that type of rash can look like burns. Not all physicians pay attention to abuse. It's better to suspect and be wrong. Knowing your doctor and nurse better rather than going to lots of different ERs might have helped avoid the misunderstanding.

From Lorraine Higgins abd Theresa Chalich (Eds.). (1996). *Getting to Know You: A Dialogue for Community Health*, pp. 1–2, 14–15. Pittsburgh, PA: The Community Literacy Center and The Rainbow Health Center.

This book began with a portrait of writing in context—focused as most college textbooks are on the world of academic writing. We looked at the expectations of readers and at strategies for writers. And as we moved from college to community outreach, we saw how writers can adapt the problem-solving strategies learned in one discourse to the needs of another. The challenge lies in using your own knowledge in new ways. This final chapter presents an even greater challenge. It asks us to take our capacity for inquiry and our ability to communicate very seriously, not just as tools for success in the classroom or workplace, but as tools for building a more humane, just, and committed intercultural community around us. Community problem-solving dialogues present us with the challenge and the means to keep on looking at the generative, good problems, to keep on seeking to understand how others are seeing the world we share, and to keep on asking how we can take a collaborative stance with them guided by respect and Martin Luther King's vision of our "inescapable network of mutuality."

PROJECTS AND ASSIGNMENTS

1   To see for yourself how a community problem-solving dialogue can work, hold one with your own class on a problem that affects your college community. Using the steps in Figures 18–2 and 18–3, hold a collaborative planning session with a partner to draft your own collaborative or individual Story Behind the Story in narratives and examples. Returning to the table, discuss these stories as a collaborative group, helping each presenter develop his or her own story. At the same time, work as a group to develop rival interpretations of this same event from the perspective of other people involved. Try to bring as many good rivals to the table as you can—expand and challenge your images and hypotheses. Then return to your pairs or small groups to imagine possible options and outcomes, before bringing these ideas back to the table.

   Tape the discussion or take good notes. Write a reflection on two questions: How did you see the dialogue process working in your class. How could you design it to be more effective? Second, what did you learn from this experience? How did it influence your thinking?

2   Turn a topic being discussed in one of your classes into a "shared problem" that captures not only the way an academic viewpoint would see and "name" it but the way a community might experience and describe it. It might help to think of the community definition in terms of the consequences of a given situation or of holding a given idea.

3   Create an imagined dialogue around the problem you defined in Assignment 1. First, create the invitation list: Who should be at the table? (Since this is in your mind, you can range across space and time to bring people from books and history as well as from your immediate surroundings.) Then let them talk, using either quoted material or your own imagined projection of what they would say if they were asked. Be sure you let them respond to each other. Write a conclusion to this event and add your own reflection on what happened, what was learned.

4   Show your imagined dialogue from Assignment 3 to some of the real people involved. Invite them to your class to respond in their own words and to restage the dialogue. Write about the conclusion of *this* event and add your own reflection on what happened, what was learned.

5   Hold a Community Problem-Solving Dialogue with the community contacts in your current project. Or organize your project itself as a process of convening and documenting a dialogue. You might find it helpful to get experience with holding a dialogue by starting with your own class as suggested in Assignment 1.

6   The Working Partners report in Example 18–1 offers some challenging situations and vivid viewpoints on issues of risk and respect. Select a portion of the report as the basis for a problem-posing video which other groups or classes can use as a springboard for interpretation and discussion. Turn that text into a script which specifies ways to translate words, context, and feelings into visual messages. To pose problems, raise open questions, and stimulate discussion, keep the video short—you can do a lot in two minutes. Design it to suggest or leave open the possibility of rival interpretations.

Use your video as the way to begin a Community Problem-Solving Dialogue in local schools, youth groups, churches, and synagogues.

Acknowledgments

Case Hoyt: Excerpt from *This Is Photography,* by Thomas Miller and Wyatt Brummitt, © 1945. Reprinted by permission.

Center for Literacy: Excerpts from "What Our Parents Had" by Margaret Gonzalez and "Part of My Life" by Jose Anaya, from *More Possible Meetings,* Student Literacy Corps, Fall 1995, Vol. 2, pp. 24 and 33. Reprinted by permission of the Center for Literacy; University of Illinois at Chicago.

Community Literacy Center: Excerpt from "CLC Report Card" in "Community Literacy: A Newsletter of the Community Literacy Center and the National Center for the Study of Writing and Literacy at Carnegie Mellon" by Linda Flower, Fall 1993.

Community Literacy Center: Brochure entitled *Working Partners: An Urban Youth Report on Risk, Stress and Respect,* 1996.

Emily Van Ness: Excerpt from "How to Buy a House on Your Own...with a Little Help from Uncle Sam" by Emily Van Ness, in *Ms.* magazine, March 1979. Reprinted by permission.

Focus: "Interview with Elaine Atkinson: The Role Models Program" by Judy Harris, in *Focus,* November/December 1990, 20(3), p. 7. Reprinted by permission of Carnegie Mellon University.

Golden Books: Excerpt from the Golden Guide® *Birds of North America* by Chandler S. Robbins, Bertel Bruun, and Herbert S. Zim, illustrated by Arthur Singer. Copyright © 1966 Golden Books Publishing Company, Inc. Used by permission.

Harvard University Press: Figure from *The Common Sense of Science* by Jacob Bronowski. Reprinted by permission of Harvard University Press.

Neighborhood Writing Alliance: Excerpts from "My Mother Compares It with Paradise" by Maria Aguilar, and "Humble Families" by Sandra Bonilla, in *Journal of Ordinary Thought,* July 1996, Issue 16, pp. 8 and 10. Reprinted by permission of the authors.

New York Times: "Nutritional Content of Popular Fast Food" in *The New York Times,* September 19, 1979. Copyright © 1979 by The New York Times Company. Reprinted by permission.

Writers House: Excerpt from "Letter from Birmingham Jail" by Martin Luther King, Jr. Reprinted by arrangement with The Heirs to the Estate of Martin Luther King, Jr., c/o Writers House, Inc. as agent for the proprietor. Copyright © 1963 by Martin Luther King, Jr., copyright renewed 1991 by Coretta Scott King.

Index